Bazaar India

Bazaar India

Markets, Society, and the
Colonial State in Gangetic Bihar

Anand A. Yang

UNIVERSITY OF CALIFORNIA PRESS
Berkeley · Los Angeles · London

University of California Press
Berkeley and Los Angeles, California

University of California Press, Ltd.
London, England

© 1998 by
The Regents of the University of California

Library of Congress Cataloging-in-Publication Data

Yang, Anand A.

   Bazaar India: markets, society, and the colonial state
in Gangetic Bihar / Anand A. Yang.
    p. cm.
   Includes bibliographical references and index.
   ISBN 0–520–21099–9 (cloth : alk. paper). —
ISBN 0–520–21100–6 (pbk. : alk. paper)
    1. Markets—Social aspects—India—Bihar (State)—History.
2. Bihar (India : State)—Social conditions.
I. Title. HF5475.I52B54 1998
381'.18'095412—dc21   97–46616

Printed in the United States of America
9 8 7 6 5 4 3 2 1

The paper used in this publication meets the
minimum requirements of American National
Standards for Information Sciences—
Permanence of Paper for Printed Library
Materials, ANSI Z39.48-1984.

Contents

Acknowledgments

A solitary historian forging historical matter out of precious information extracted from dusty archives and out of ideas configured in isolation
is as unlikely a reality as was the much mythologized self-sufficient "Indian village republic" of an earlier generation's imagination. Certainly,
my project could not have come to fruition without the links and networks extended to me by many people and institutions in different parts
of our increasingly connected global village. I hope some of what I have
gained from these ties will come through in the pages that follow.

The first glimmerings of this book date back to my initial research
venture into Bihar in 1973–74. However, I did not begin to actively pur-
sue research on this project until 1983–84. Thanks to Professor Aparna
Basu, my research guide in India, and her colleagues, R. S. Sharma and
D. N. Jha, also of Delhi University, I started on the right footing.
Equally helpful were historians at Patna University, in particular,
Q. Ahmad, S. Gopal, the late V. A. Narain, S. Niyogi, and Y. D. Prasad.
In England, where I have labored seasonally at the India Office Library
and Records in London, I have benefited from ongoing intellectual ex-
changes with scholars from many lands who have also sought out its
outstanding facilities for South Asian studies.

Directors and staff at research centers in India and England have provided another vital link in completing this enterprise. I wish to express
my gratitude to all the folks in Patna who made research possible, at the

Bihar Research Society, the K. P. Jayaswal Institute, and especially the Bihar State Archives, where its director, T. S. Sinha, and his staff kept me well provisioned for almost a year. I also wish to commend a number of Patna families (whose names are scattered across the text that follows) for sharing with me their private records and personal memories about their distinguished ancestors and their commercial and banking activities. Thanks to the professional and caring staff of the India Office Library, I always find myself returning to this research hub. Pat Kattenthorn of that library's Prints and Drawings section deserves a special mention for allowing me to reproduce images taken from its incomparable collection of paintings by the Patna School of painters.

I have been very fortunate over the years to have secured sufficient credit to make my research rounds. A Fulbright-Hays Faculty Research Abroad Grant awarded by the U.S. Department of Education in Washington, D.C., and Dr. Sharada Nayak and the entire staff of USEFI in Delhi greatly facilitated my work in India. Additional research, mostly carried out in England over successive summers, was made possible by grants provided by the National Endowment for the Humanities, ACLS/SSRC Joint Committee on South Asia, the American Historical Association, and the University of Utah.

Over the years I have profited from conversations and arguments with several old and new colleagues: Christopher Bayly, James R. Hagen, Walter Hauser, Christopher Hill, Jim Masselos, Philip F. McEldowney, Gyan Pandey, and Majid Siddiqi. I have also appreciated the feedback I have received from audiences who have heard bits and pieces of this work at meetings and workshops (Indian History Congress, WCAAS, AAS, an SSRC-sponsored gathering in Sussex, Bellagio, and many university campuses) convened at various times dating back to the mid-1980s.

I have nothing but praise for the University of California Press, which has served me well every step of the way, beginning with providing thoughtful critiques of earlier versions of this study to working closely with me in preparing this final version for production. To the Press' referees must go some of the credit for this book; whatever shortcomings remain are entirely of my making. Lynne Withey has been with this book from its earliest version and has steered me through its long journey into production. Thanks also to Suzanne Samuel, Cindy Fulton, and others at the Press who have helped in making this manuscript come to life.

The University of Utah has consistently and steadfastly supported my research and writings efforts relating to this project. I dedicate this book to my sternest and most probing critic, Debz.

Abbreviations

Agric.	Agriculture
AGRPD	Annual General Report of Patna Division
B&O	Bihar and Orissa
BOR	Board of Revenue
C.C.	Champaran Collectorate
CDG 1938	*Bihar and Orissa District Gazetteers, Champaran,* by L. S. S. O'Malley, revised by R. E. Swanzy. Patna: 1938.
CDG 1960	*Bihar District Gazetteers, Champaran,* by P. C. Roy Chaudhury. Patna: 1960.
Colltr.	Collector
Commr.	Commissioner
Consltns.	Consultations
Cr.	Criminal
CSR	*Final Report on the Survey and Settlement Operations (Revision) in the District of Champaran (1913–1919).* Patna: 1922.
CSSH	*Comparative Studies in Society and History*
DDG	*Bengal District Gazetteers, Darbhanga,* by L. S. S. O'Malley. Calcutta: 1907.

GDG 1906	*Bengal District Gazetteers, Gaya,* by L. S. S. O'Malley. Calcutta: 1906.
GDG 1957	*Bihar District Gazetteers, Gaya,* by P. C. Roy Chaudhury. Patna: 1957.
GGIC	Governor General in Council
GOB	Government of Bengal
GOB&O	Government of Bihar and Orissa
GOI	Government of India
GSR	*Final Report on the Survey and Settlement Operations in the District of Gaya (1911–1918),* by E. L. Tanner. Patna: 1919.
IESHR	*Indian Economic and Social History Review*
I.G.	Inspector General
JAHSI	*Journal of Agricultural and Horticultural Society of India*
JAS	*Journal of Asian Studies*
JBORS	*Journal of Bihar and Orissa Research Society*
Jdcl.	Judicial
Magte.	Magistrate
MAS	Modern Asian Studies
M.C.	Muzaffarpur Collectorate
MDG 1907	*Bengal District Gazetteers, Muzaffarpur,* by L. S. S. O'Malley. Calcutta: 1907.
MSR	*Final Report on the Survey and Settlement Operations in the Muzaffarpur District, 1892 to 1899,* by C. J. Stephenson-Moore. Patna: 1922.
Nizt. Adlt.	Nizamat Adalat
Offg.	Officiating
P.C.	Patna Commissioner
PDG 1924	*Bihar and Orissa District Gazetteers, Patna,* by L. S. S. O'Malley, revised by J. F. W. James. Patna: 1924.

PFR	Patna Factory Records
Polit.	Political
Procs.	Proceedings
PSR	*Final Report on the Survey and Settlement Operations in the District of Patna, (1907–1912)*, by J. F. W. James. Patna: 1914.
Pub.	Public
PWD	Public Works Department
Rev.	Revenue
S.C.	Saran Collectorate
SDG 1908	*Bengal District Gazetteers: Saran*, by L. S. S. O'Malley. Calcutta: 1908.
SDG 1930	*Bihar and Orissa District Gazetteers, Saran*, by L. S. S. O'Malley, revised by A. P. Middleton. Patna: 1930.
Secy.	Secretary
Sh.C.	Shahabad Collectorate
ShDG 1906	*Bengal District Gazetteer, Shahabad*, by L. S. S. O'Malley. Calcutta: 1906.
SRR	*Final Report on the Survey and Settlement Operations (Revision) in the District of Saran, 1915 to 1921*, by Phanindra Nath Gupta. Patna: 1923.
Stats.	Statistics
Suptd.	Superintendent
SVN	Saran District Village Notes, 1915–1921
SVN, 1893–1901	Saran District Village Notes, 1893–1901
T.C.	Tirhut Collectorate

The Sonepur Mela.

Scenes from the Bazaar
as Depicted by the Patna School of Painters

Clockwise from left:
Tailor at work, scissors
and needle case behind
him, by Shiva Lal, c.
1850–60.

Grain seller with a
woman customer, by
Sewak Ram, c. 1807–10.

Woman toddy seller
serving two customers,
by Bani Lal, c. 1880.

Cloth merchant measur-
ing cloth, a customer
squatting nearby, by a
Patna artist, c. 1820.

Man driving a pack bul-
lock carrying merchan-
dise, by a Patna artist,
c. 1830.

Market, Village, and Colonial State in South Asia

The *bazaar* in the title of this book resonates on two levels: it identifies the site of investigation and it situates the scene of interrogation.[1] Indeed, the very choice of the bazaar as the site of this study is designed to lead to a distinctive scene of interrogation, a stage for posing fundamental questions regarding Indian society under colonialism and for posing questions about narrative history. Certainly the search for a colonial history through the venue of the bazaar highlights a past less familiar than the ones built around those other sites that have come to embody colonial India. The narrative constructed around the bazaar thus draws us to a different reality because the market itself occupies a different place in the Indian landscape.

Markets have long been a familiar and essential feature of the historical landscape, central places of exchange at which peasants, townspeople, landholders, and rulers have historically converged in South Asia to conduct wholesale and retail trade, to gather news and infor-

---

1. A term of Persian origin that gained currency in Indian and European languages, "bazaar refers to market or marketplace, generally a permanent market or street of shops." Henry Yule and A. C. Burnell, *Hobson-Jobson: A Glossary of Colloquial Anglo-Indian Words and Phrases* (1903; reprint, New Delhi: Munshiram Manoharlal, 1968), pp. 75–76. For a different interpretation of the bazaar, see Rajat Kanta Ray, "The Bazaar: Changing Structural Characteristics of the Indigenous Section of the Indian Economy before and after the Great Depression," *IESHR* 25 (1988): 263–318.

mation, and to engage in various social, cultural, religious, and political activities. Thus, like their counterparts in other societies, markets "can be viewed as microcosms containing a representative array of the elements comprising a regional environment. Markets provide a compressed display of an area's economy, technology, and society—in brief, of the local way of life."[2]

To read markets of the colonial era as historical texts of exchange relations emblematic of the "local way of life," however, requires journeying through the "Oriental market," that exoticized Other place of Western imagination. No mere figment of Orientalism, the discourse relating to the bazaar in colonial India comes wrapped in layers of Orientalism.[3] To represent it therefore requires an act of deconstruction, detaching that place from its Orientalist moorings. Such unpacking, although standard practice for historians who are trained to sift through source materials, now demands the added rigor of sorting out the workings of power and knowledge that Foucault has shown us is implicated in all textual productions: "power produces knowledge . . . [and] there is no power relation without the correlative constitution of a field of knowledge, nor any knowledge that does not presuppose and constitute at the same time power relations."[4] Orientalism, in other words, "is not just a way of thinking. It is a way of conceptualizing the landscape of the colonial world that makes it susceptible to certain kinds of management."[5]

For historians of modern India, so dependent on working through the documentary project of the colonial state, such sifting is even more critical. It requires what Bernard S. Cohn has termed "exegetical and hermeneutical skill,"[6] for the legacy of the elitist historiography that

2. Herbert M. Eder, "Markets as Mirrors," in *Markets in Oaxaca,* ed. Scott Cook and Martin Diskin (Austin: University of Texas Press, 1976), p. 76.

3. Edward Said, *Orientalism* (New York: Vintage, 1979); Ronald Inden, *Imagining India* (Oxford: Basil Blackwell, 1990).

4. Michel Foucault, *Discipline and Punish: The Birth of the Prison,* trans. Alan Sheridan (Middlesex: Penguin Books, 1977), p. 27. See also idem, *Power/Knowledge: Selected Interviews and Other Writings, 1972–1977,* ed. Colin Gordon (New York: Pantheon, 1980); Paul Rabinow, ed., *The Foucault Reader* (New York: Pantheon, 1984).

5. Carol A. Breckenridge and Peter Van der Veer, eds., *Orientalism and the Postcolonial Predicament: Perspectives on South Asia* (Delhi: Oxford University Press, 1994), p. 6.

6. "The Anthropology of a Colonial State and Its Forms of Knowledge," paper presented at the International Symposium on "Tensions of Empire: Colonial Control and Visions of Rule," Mijas, Spain, Nov. 5–13, 1988. See also James C. Scott, *Domination and the Arts of Resistance: Hidden Transcripts* (New Haven: Yale University Press, 1990), for a provocative discussion of the "public transcripts" of domination and suppression and the oppositional "hidden transcripts" of the dominated that are rarely preserved.

hitherto dominated South Asian studies does not ease the task of reconstruction and representation. Nevertheless, neither the biases of the historical record nor those of the historiography have prevented scholars—Ranajit Guha and the Subaltern Studies collective, for example—from pursuing the voices of subjects and subjectivity submerged in but not completely silenced by the historical record and the received historiography.[7]

To begin by problematizing the interrelationship between reading bazaars as historical texts of social, political, economic, and cultural worlds and recovering markets textualized in the historical records is to draw attention to the problems of representation and evocation. For in trying to extract history from such texts, I face several questions—not only how to represent the bazaar in history but also how to construct its narrative history and in what voice to present it.

Such questions turn on the implicit notion that the writing of history involves textual construction, that the act of writing itself, regardless of the discipline, necessarily entails poetics and involves artifice.[8] That is, the rhetorical strategies deployed here to unravel the history of the bazaar in colonial India and the authorial and authoritative conventions used to present this history are problematics of this investigation.

To appreciate the literary or even the aesthetic quality of historical writing does not mean that I accept *all* the premises of postmodernism. Certainly, I do not share in the postmodernist enterprise of aestheticizing history and severing "it from its formerly accepted grounding in

7. For a discussion of the growing emphasis in colonial history on locating the colonial subject and making the subject "speak," see Ranajit Guha and Gayatri Chakravorty Spivak, *Selected Subaltern Studies* (New York: Oxford University Press, 1988); Gayatri Chakravorty Spivak, *In Other Worlds: Essays in Cultural Politics* (New York: Routledge, 1988), esp. pp. 197–221. See also Ranajit Guha, *Elementary Aspects of Peasant Insurgency in Colonial India* (Delhi: Oxford University Press, 1983), pp. 1–17, and the series entitled *Subaltern Studies*.

8. For the debate over the extent to which historical writing is framed by its literary dimensions, see, e.g., Hayden White, *The Content of the Form: Narrative Discourse and Historical Representation* (Baltimore: Johns Hopkins University Press, 1986); Robert F. Berkhofer Jr., "The Challenge of Poetics to (Normal) Historical Practice," in *The Rhetoric of Interpretation and the Interpretation of Rhetoric*, ed. Paul Hernadi (Durham: Duke University Press, 1989), pp. 183–200; Peter Novick, *That Noble Dream: The "Objectivity Question" and the American Historical Profession* (Cambridge: Cambridge University Press, 1988). See also James Clifford and George E. Marcus, *Writing Culture: The Poetics and Politics of Ethnography* (Berkeley and Los Angeles: University of California Press, 1986), on the current postmodern debate and its theoretical foundations and problematics.

4 Market, Village, and Colonial State

conditions of truth and reality."[9] I do not take this as an opportunity to rehearse and demonstrate the predominantly rhetorical character of history. Rather, I seek to write about relations of power in the colonial period from a specific point of view: that of a postcolonial historian writing about the past with a conscious nod to present-day issues—the lived experiences of people in a world increasingly dominated by a market economy, by a capitalist world-system, to use a term and concept coined by Immanuel Wallerstein;[10] the interplay of the market with modes of power and relations of production; the project of the colonial state and its effects on peasant society; and the interrelationship between the projects of the colonial and the postcolonial state.

I therefore do not approach the documentary record as a detached observer, and my reconstruction of the past from this record is not an innocent or neutral recounting of what contemporary texts themselves had to say about their times. I am interested in different textual strategies, ones that break with or at least interrogate the conventional historical technique of writing from an Olympian and omniscient narrative voice in order to approach polyphony. It is not that I am so confident of my ability to reproduce the voices of the past without my own mediations, but I would like to generate a more dialogical history. I would like to build a reconstruction in which I am not the voice over all other voices but rather a voice in conversation with the voices of historical contemporaries as well as of present-day historians. Historical writing, in this conception, is hewn of the fabric of intertextuality, a fabric that weaves together history, historian, and historiography. This intertextuality of past and present is forged by the contamination and complicity generated by the historian's source materials emanating from particular fields of knowledge and power. Such a narrative seeks to privilege different points of view in the reconstruction of history. Not that this necessarily overcomes the problems of trying to recover the past from the subjects' own points of view, but such an emphasis at

9. Perez Zagorin, "Historiography and Postmodernism: Reconsiderations," *History and Theory* 29 (1990): 264; F. R. Ankersmit, "Reply to Professor Zagorin," in the same issue, pp. 275–96; and his "Historiography and Postmodernism," *History and Theory* 28 (1989): 137–53.

10. *The Modern World-System: Capitalist Agriculture and the Origins of the European World-Economy in the Sixteenth Century* (New York: Academic Press, 1974); *The Modern World-System III: The Second Era of Great Expansion of the Capitalist World-Economy, 1730–1840s* (New York: Academic Press, 1989); Ravi Palat et al., "The Incorporation and Peripheralization of South Asia, 1600–1950," *Review* 10 (1986): 171–208.

least represents more of a stretch to capture the inherent multivocality of all texts.[11]

The intention in foregrounding the texts of this historical investigation is not to follow the "Descent into Discourse," to use the title of a spirited attack on the "reification of language" in recent social historical writing.[12] The so-called linguistic turn in history, a direction advocated by the postmodern project, has currency here only insofar as it emphasizes a critical scrutiny of the hegemonic texts produced by colonial power and knowledge (the bulk of our standard historical sources), a scrutiny necessitated further by the recognition that ordinary men and women in history (mostly peasants in this case) occupied ideological and power positions that were subordinated to, but that also resisted, the articulations of this hegemony. Nor does the postmodernist belief in the death of the subject have much play in this work: its central concern is to rescue subjects and their subjectivity from the hegemonic systems of power and knowledge that subordinated them and not to privilege textual attitudes and discursive practices. Postmodernism and the new turn in history figure here in the sense that this study shares the rising interest in the cultural context of relationships between state and society and between the groups comprising indigenous society, as well as in their representations in history.[13]

To investigate the historiographical rupture provided by the bazaar, let us begin by contextualizing, by drawing its spatial and textual coordinates in relation to the more scrutinized sites in the historiographical landscape—those of caste and village. Like caste, the village was isolated by the colonial discourse as one of the major sites at which the "real India" was knowable. And like caste, the village—cast in the role

---

11. A recent attempt to engage such questions is Eugene F. Irschick, *Dialogue and History: Constructing South India, 1795–1895* (Berkeley and Los Angeles: University of California Press, 1994). See also Dipesh Chakrabarty, "Postcoloniality and the Artifice of History: Who Speaks for 'Indian' Pasts?" *Representations* 37 (1992): 1–26; Gyan Prakash, "Writing Post-Orientalist Histories of the Third World: Perspectives from Indian Historiography," *CSSH* 32 (1990): 383–408; Rosalind O'Hanlon and David Washbrook, "After Orientalism: Culture, Criticism, and Politics in the Third World, " *CSSH* 34 (1992): 141–67.

12. Bryan D. Palmer, *Descent into Discourse: The Reification of Language and the Writing of Social History* (Philadelphia: Temple University Press, 1990).

13. For a discussion of the cultural currency and exchange aspects of colonialism, see Nicholas B. Dirks, ed., *Colonialism and Culture* (Ann Arbor: University of Michigan Press, 1992); Edward Said, *Culture and Imperialism* (London: Vintage, 1994); Peter N. Stearns, "Social History Update: Encountering Postmodernism," *Journal of Social History* (1990): 449–52.

of the "Indian village republic"—attained paradigmatic status as a representation of rural society and as a template of the structure and organization of indigenous society and economy.

A classic formulation is the description of village India limned by Sir Charles Metcalfe in 1830:

> Hindoo, Patan, Mogul, Mahratta, Sikh, English, are all masters in turn; but the village community remains the same. . . . The sons will take the places of their fathers; the same site for the village, the same positions for the houses, the same lands will be reoccupied by the descendants of those who were driven out when the village was depopulated. . . . This union of the village communities, each one forming a separate little state in itself, has . . . contributed more than any other cause to the preservation of the people of India through all the revolutions and changes which they have suffered, and is in a high degree conducive to their happiness, and to the enjoyment of a great portion of freedom and independence.[14]

From such stirrings in the pages of early-nineteenth-century administrative reports, where the idea of the "village republic" or "village community" was "primarily [as] a political society," there emerged a second notion of it as "a body of co-owners of the soil." Subsequently, it developed into the "emblem of traditional economy and polity, a watchword of Indian patriotism."[15]

The political version of village India issued from the pens of Sir Henry Maine and Karl Marx who, although "poles apart in other respects . . . came together retrospectively as the two foremost writers who have drawn the Indian Village Community into the circle of world history. In keeping with contemporary—Victorian—evolutionary ideas and preoccupations, both saw in it a remnant or survival from what Maine called 'the infancy of society.' "[16] For both men the village denoted a community of interests forged by collective economic and political interests: economic in that the "organized society" of the village tied together by real or fictive kinship held land and cultivated it jointly, political in that authority was wielded by the village council of five, the *panchayat*.[17]

14. "Minute on the Settlement in the Western Provinces," Nov. 7, 1830, in *Minutes of Evidence Taken before the Select Committee on the Affairs of the East India Company*, III—*Revenue, Parliamentary Papers, 1831–32*, vol. 11, pp. 331–32.

15. Louis Dumont, "The 'Village Community' from Munro to Maine," *Contributions to Indian Sociology* 9 (1966): 67.

16. Ibid., 80.

17. Ibid., 80–89; M. N. Srinivas, "The Indian Village: Myth and Reality," in *Studies in Social Anthropology*, ed. J. H. M. Beattie and R. G. Lienhardt (Oxford: Clarendon

Such a view of village India as self-sufficient economically and politically meshed commodiously with the rising nationalist sentiment of the late nineteenth and early twentieth centuries. Romesh Dutt, for one, deployed these images in attacking the colonial condition whereby such "ancient and self-governing institutions" had passed away "under the too centralised administration of British rulers," their destruction construed as proof that "an alien Government lacks that popular basis, that touch with the people, which Hindu and Mahomedan Governments wisely maintained through centuries."[18]

Periodically transformed but never completely transfigured by shifting intellectual currents, the representations of this imagined village persisted well into the twentieth century, the village's many-layered images accommodating the projections of colonial administrators and scholars (e.g., Metcalf and B. H. Baden Powell), theoreticians (e.g., Marx and Maine), and nationalist leaders and scholars (e.g., Gandhi, Nehru, Dutt). Although scholars since the 1950s have been steadily dismantling the village that the Raj built—some argue that this edifice has by now not only been condemned but also razed—the mythologized village, like caste, has not entirely relinquished the considerable analytical and theoretical domains it annexed and possessed for more than a century and a half. Indeed, it has persisted, although with less vigor than has caste, as one of the "few simple theoretical handles [that have] become metonyms and surrogates for the civilization or society as a whole."[19]

Press, 1975); Clive Dewey, "Images of the Village Community: A Study in Anglo-Indian Ideology," *MAS* 6 (1972): 291–328; J. W. Burrow, "'The Village Community' and the Uses of History in Late Nineteenth-Century England," in *Historical Perspectives: Studies in English Thought and Society*, ed. Neil McKendrick (London: Europa Publications, 1974), pp. 255–84; Daniel Thorner, *The Shaping of Modern India* (New Delhi: Sameeksha Trust, 1980), pp. 257–72, 349–82.

18. *The Economic History of India*, vol. 2, *In the Victorian Age 1837–1900* (1882; reprint, New Delhi: Government of India, 1960), p. 143; Srinivas, "Indian Village," pp. 47–49. See also Breckenridge and Van der Veer, *Orientalism and the Postcolonial*, pp. 12–13, for the now familiar charge about the close linkages between Orientalism and nationalism.

19. Arjun Appadurai, "Theory and Anthropology: Center and Periphery," *CSSH* 28 (1986): 357. Appadurai argues that anthropological studies—by focusing largely on caste and hierarchy—have tended to ignore other institutions (e.g., tribes, cities, families, temples, ascetic groups) and "other ideological problems, such as authority, legitimacy, privacy, and domesticity (rather than just hierarchy and its twin—purity/pollution)" (p. 360). One attempt to overcome this tendency is Nicholas B. Dirks, *The Hollow Crown: Ethnohistory of an Indian Kingdom* (Ann Arbor: University of Michigan Press, 2nd. ed., 1993). See also Bernard S. Cohn, *An Anthropologist among the Historians, and Other Essays* (Delhi: Oxford University Press, 1987), pp. 136–99; C. J. Fuller, "British India or Traditional India? An Anthropological Problem," *Ethnos* 42 (1977): 95–121.

The concept of the village republic has its roots as much in "European ideas" as in "Indian prejudice." "Like the Mughals, the Nizam of Hyderabad, Sultans of Mysore, and Nawabs of Dacca and Arcot worked revenue systems in which ruling elites knew the countryside only as a set of points for revenue collection. At every point, settled agriculture and trade generated state revenue."[20] In other words, the colonial state settled on the village as the core of the Indian social, economic, and political body because of its primary interests in maintaining law and order and in extracting taxes from the subject population. Fiscal concerns demanded that the countryside be conceived of as a fixed set of points.

An instrumental space for the project of the colonial state, *the* Indian village, as constructed in the colonial discourse, did not, however, fit squarely with British revenue arrangements. In north India the unit of revenue management was the *mahal* (estate, parcel of land), which increasingly did not coincide with the *mauza,* the revenue village; most settlements, moreover, were made with specific individuals (landholders, or zamindars) and not the village community. The idea of the village republic also ran counter to the *raiyatwari* settlement of south India, which sought to engage the cultivator (*raiyat*) directly. "For, if the village was the basic unit of agrarian organization," as Burton Stein has noted, the "proposal for revenue [in south India to be] paid by individual cultivators on specific fields appears misconceived."[21] Explaining away this contradiction required a rhetorical incorporation that "altered the idea of 'raiyat,' who is changed from being a part of a corporate village body into an equivalent of 'tenant,' thereby generating the transcultural metaphor or analogy—Indian sovereign or East India Company to landlord, raiyat to individualized tenant. In this way both the corporate village and the individual peasant cultivator were preserved . . . while at the same time maintaining the purportedly-direct historical relationship between cultivator 'tenant' and government 'landlord.' "[22] Contradictions between revenue theory and revenue

20. David Ludden, "Agricultural Expansion, Diversification, and Commodity Production in Early Modern India: Labor Mobility in the Peninsula, 1300–1800," paper presented at the meeting of the Association for Asian Studies, March 1988, San Francisco.

21. "Idiom and Ideology in Early Nineteenth-Century South India," in *Rural India: Land, Power, and Society under British Rule,* ed. Peter Robb (London: Curzon Press, 1983), p. 45.

22. Ibid. Distortions of the colonial era, not surprisingly, are reflected in present-day confusions regarding "village." Polly Hill, *Development Economics on Trial* (Cam-

practice notwithstanding, village India remained at the core of the colonial ideology precisely because it was more valuable as an invented tradition. And in this capacity it serviced colonial power and knowledge, which, to follow the lead of Foucault and others, focused on the manipulation of the body, relying on techniques of discipline and technologies of power to fix people in space by restricting or encouraging their movements and actions and their development and reproduction.

Furthermore, the historically constituted and constructed notion of village India illustrates not only how the technology of colonial power conceptualized one key site—categorizing, classifying, rationalizing, and delimiting in space indigenous society—but also how such ideas expressed the imaginative geography of Orientalism. The village, in other words, comprised one of the many sites or units (others being criminal tribes, urban spaces, forests, women, and communities of one sort or another) appropriated by colonialism. It therefore speaks to us about the workings of colonial power, not only in exercising political, social, and economic control and domination but also in inscribing itself into the domain of culture and consciousness.

A site at which colonial power could produce the "colonized as a fixed reality," the village also qualified as a worthy object of colonial knowledge and power because it was "at once an 'other' and yet entirely knowable and visible."[23] As an Other, it belonged to a different time; it embodied tradition.[24] The village as tradition, moreover, strengthened the colonial ideology because it represented the backwardness of the subject peoples—it legitimated the right of the rule of modernity, of the Raj.

---

bridge: Cambridge University Press, 1986), pp. 45–46, writes of encountering a census-defined village that had little sociological or administrative relevance.

23. Homi K. Bhabha, "The Other Question: Difference, Discrimination and the Discourse of Colonialism," in *Literature, Politics, and Theory*, ed. F. Barker et al. (London: Methuen, 1986), p. 156. Also Foucault, *Power/Knowledge*, pp. 37–77, 134–65; *Foucault Reader*, pp. 141–256; Anthony Giddens, *The Constitution of Society* (Berkeley and Los Angeles: University of California Press, 1984), pp. 110–61.

24. Pervasive in the scholarly literature is the equation of the "traditional village" and its "closed peasant community" with "premodern agrarian societies" and the attribution of its development into an "open peasant community" to economic and political modernization. The former is typically characterized as "corporate, self-sufficient, introverted, particularized, encysted; the latter non-corporate at the community level, relatively dependent on larger economic systems, socially extroverted, culturally open—a type of social system whose bounds are blurred and whose boundary-maintaining mechanisms are weak." See William Skinner, "Chinese Peasants and the Closed Community: An Open and Shut Case," *CSSH* 13 (1971): 271; Eric R. Wolf, "Closed Corporate Peasant Communities in Mesoamerica and Central Java," *Southwestern Journal of Anthropology* 13 (1957): 1–18.

Thus the notion of a conservative rustic population glued to its villages reflected the penchant of disciplinary power for fixing people in space and time, a penchant whose preferred category was naturally a sedentary population. How closely this tied in—as cause or effect or both—with the changes sweeping the subcontinent over the first century of colonial rule remains to be worked out fully. (So do the many applications of this process, whether targeting other sites or units, e.g., caste, or other groups in the population, e.g., women.) But initial findings suggest that changes in ecology (e.g., extensive deforestation, the advance of the plow) and in modes of agricultural production and exchange, and the shifting fortunes of the once prominent nomadic and pastoral sector, all converged on advancing settled agriculture and peasant petty commodity production.[25]

Did such villages ever exist? Stratification within the village community may have occurred as early as the first millennium B.C. The "self-sufficient village," as Romila Thapar states, may have been undermined by the integration of villages via "horizontal links" with "local markets and fairs, networks of religious centres playing an economic role as well[,] and trade in essential items by itinerant herders, artisans and traders."[26] Similarly, Cohn and Marriott note the many connections linking villages to the wider world, ranging from "trading networks" to "networks of marriage ties" to "political networks" consisting "primarily of ties of clan and kinship among rulers and the dominant landlord groups of the countryside."[27] Morris E. Opler's classic 1956 article identified various "extensions" of the Indian village, fashioned by common origin and descent, with a cluster of villages encompassing an area of seventy square miles; village exogamy, which established ties to other villages; ties of caste to people of similar castes residing in other villages; customary work obligations involving artisans or workers from other villages; supravillage religious or political movements; pilgrimages to sacred sites and visits to the village by religious specialists; the pull of the market town, which offered goods

25. C. A. Bayly, *The New Cambridge History of India, II, 1, Indian Society and the Making of the British Empire* (Cambridge: Cambridge University Press, 1988), pp. 96–99. See also Irschick, *Dialogue and History,* pp. 77–78, 193–94, on the "sedentarization process."

26. *From Lineage to State: Social Formations in the Mid-First Millennium B.C. in the Ganga Valley* (Bombay: Oxford University Press, 1984), p. 165.

27. Bernard S. Cohn and McKim Marriott, "Networks and Centres in the Integration of Indian Civilisation," in Cohn, *Anthropologist among Historians,* p. 81.

and services not available in the village; and migration to take advantage of education facilities available elsewhere.[28] "Networks of trade, worship, royal authority, kinship, and caste," as David Ludden has observed recently, "enmeshed a characteristic South Asian village in 1750 within a web of social relations that was essential to agricultural production."[29]

These links, networks, and extensions, however, have yet to be mapped out fully. Because the village was elevated so far above all other sites in significance, much of the rural landscape remains beyond the pale of scholarly investigation. The peripheralization of other sites is especially apparent regarding the "whole subject of agricultural marketing."[30] As Shahid Amin's introduction to the glossary of the colonial ethnographer William Crooke notes, the "prior notion of the changelessness of the physical world of the Indian peasant," led to undue emphasis on the "*production* process" and put "*exchange* relations in parenthesis." Thus, in Crooke's reconstruction, the world of his peasants is "principally inhabited by implements and gadgets, utensils and appliances." "Awkwardly squashed between weights and measures and the rituals of rural life, 'trade and moneylending' are almost pushed out of reckoning."[31]

In part this oversight reflects an historiographical orientation that "has often been peculiarly antagonistic to the rural market; on the basis of rural-romantic or primitive-communistic views of rural self-sufficiency, it has viewed the market as a specifically alien institution. In particular it has often portrayed the denizens of the market as low types who were able to steal the major part of the peasant's produce."[32] In part the historiographical blinders stem from the "obsessive British concern with Indian Land Revenue."[33] In part the bazaar

28. "The Extensions of an Indian Village," *JAS* 16 (1956): 5–10.
29. "Productive Power in Agriculture: A Survey of Work on the Local History of British India," in *Agrarian Power and Agricultural Productivity in South Asia,* ed. Meghnad Desai, Susanne Hoeber Rudolph, and Ashok Rudra (Berkeley and Los Angeles: University of California Press, 1985), pp. 58–59.
30. Hill, *Development Economics,* p. 58.
31. William Crooke, *A Glossary of North Indian Peasant Life,* ed. Shahid Amin (Delhi: Oxford University Press, 1989), pp. xxxiv–xxxv.
32. Christopher Baker, *The Tamilnad Countryside* (Oxford: Clarendon Press, 1984), p. 235. Hill, *Development Economics,* p. 58, erroneously argues that scholarly interest in and official documentation for markets in Africa as compared to South Asia indicate the "greater importance of rural periodic markets in the former region." She also asserts "that large periodic markets in India tended to be urban not a rural phenomenon as in West Africa."
33. Hill, *Development Economics,* p. 58.

has remained largely occulted in a historiographical terrain over which the dominant monuments of village and caste have cast their giant shadows. The biases of the historiography, that is, reflect the biases of the colonial record in which village and caste were tropes of an unchanging India.

Indeed, relatively little scholarly research has been conducted on the crucial role of markets in articulating the economy and society of an area. Nor have they been systematically analyzed as parts of a wider network of markets. Instead, studies of marketing in India, as for other areas of the world (Africa, Asia, and Latin America),[34] are predominantly ethnographies of individual marketplaces and their settings and about certain aspects of market exchange.[35] A few works, primarily by economists, have looked at the efficiency of food grain marketing but only to evaluate their functioning as measured against the models of competitive markets. There are, however, some significant exceptions: Hagen's scrutiny of the system of colonial education in Patna district in the nineteenth and twentieth centuries within the context of the local society's marketing system; Bayly's examination of the roles of "urban, mercantile and service people" in the towns and bazaars of north India in the period from 1770 to 1870; and Wanmali's synchronic analysis of the lowest level of marketing, periodic markets, in Singhbhum district.[36] Notable also—although largely synchronic in their focus—are the recent studies of local and regional markets and fairs by geogra-

34. Carol A. Smith, "Economics of Marketing Systems: Models from Economic Geography," *Annual Review of Anthropology*, ed. Bernard J. Siegel et al., 3 (1974): 167–201; R. J. Bromley and Richard Symanski, "Marketplace Trade in Latin America," *Latin American Research Review* 9 (1974): 3–38.

35. E.g., see Richard G. Fox, *From Zamindar to Ballot Box: Community Change in a North Indian Market Town* (Ithaca: Cornell University Press, 1969); Irawati Karve and Hemalata Acharya, *The Role of Weekly Markets in the Tribal, Rural, and Urban Settings* (Poona: Deccan College, 1970); Leon Swartzberg Jr., *The North Indian Peasant Goes to Market* (Delhi: Motilal Banarsidass, 1979); David L. Curley, "Rulers and Merchants in Late Eighteenth-Century Bengal," Ph.D. diss., University of Chicago, 1980; Michelle Burge McAlpin, "The Effects of Markets on Rural Income Distribution in Nineteenth Century India," *Exploration in Economic History* 12 (1975): 289–302.

36. James R. Hagen, "Indigenous Society, the Political Economy, and Colonial Education in Patna District: A History of Social Change from 1811 to 1951 in Gangetic North India," Ph.D. diss., University of Virginia, 1981; C. A. Bayly, *Rulers, Townsmen, and Bazaars: North Indian Society in the Age of British Expansion, 1770–1870* (Cambridge: Cambridge University Press, 1982); Sudhir Wanmali, *Periodic Markets and Rural Development in India* (Delhi: B. R. Publishing Corporation, 1981). Also Ray, "Bazaar"; Sudipta Sen, "Conquest of Marketplaces: Exchange, Authority and Conflict in Early Colonial North India," Ph.D. diss., University of Chicago, 1994.

phers and anthropologists that concentrate on the spatial, economic, and anthropological dimensions of patterns of exchange.[37]

Studies of markets in India as well as in other parts of the world, while continuing to draw their conceptual sustenance from the central-place theory developed initially in the 1930s by the German economic geographer Walter Christaller, offer a diversity of models of market organization.[38] But they share a common interest in highlighting markets as nodes in a complex pattern of economic and social exchanges organized hierarchically as well as by such factors as economy, geography, transportation, politics, and administration. However, the tendency in the literature—until recently largely the product of geographers and economists—has been to follow the classical idea of central place to see either how markets organize the geography of retailing or how they serve as collection points for the available goods and services of an area. An underlying theoretical construct in this literature is the notion of a central place as "a settlement or an aggregation of economic functions that is the hub of a hierarchical system which includes other settlements or communities relating to it on a regular basis; . . . the hub of a region because goods, people, and information flow primarily between it and its less differentiated hinterland."[39] Increasingly, locational and economic analyses of markets—with their emphasis on such geographical and economic variables as population, ecology, transportation, and a competitive market economy—have been enriched by studies (many by anthropologists) recognizing other factors relating to social, political, and cultural conditions and circumstances also involved in structuring marketing systems. This body of scholarship,

37. E.g., see R. O. Whyte, *The Spatial Geography of Rural Economies* (New Delhi: Oxford University Press, 1982).

38. Leslie J. King, *Central Place Theory* (Beverly Hills, Calif.: Sage Publications, 1984); G. William Skinner, "Marketing and Social Structure in Rural China," *JAS* 24 (1964–65): 3–43, 195–228, 363–99; Ralph L. Beals, *The Peasant Marketing System of Oaxaca, Mexico* (Berkeley and Los Angeles: University of California Press, 1975); Cook and Diskin, eds., *Markets in Oaxaca;* Isaac Ayinde Adalemo, *Marketplaces in a Developing Country: The Case of Western Nigeria* (Ann Arbor: Michigan Geographical Publications no. 26, University of Michigan, 1981).

39. Carol A. Smith, "Introduction: The Regional Approach to Economic Systems," in *Regional Analysis,* vol. 1, *Economic Systems,* ed. idem (New York: Academic Press, 1976), p. 6. See also Avijit Ghosh, "Rural Distribution Systems in Newly Industrializing Societies: A Survey of Its Economics and Geography," *Discussion Paper Series,* Discussion Paper 25, Department of Geography, University of Iowa; Brian J. L. Berry, *Geography of Market Centers and Retail Distribution* (Englewood Cliffs, N.J.: Prentice-Hall, 1967).

much of it largely synchronic in focus,[40] relies on and reinterprets and modifies central-place theory.

Although the central-place theory of the structure and function of marketing systems is critical to this analysis, it is not applied indiscriminately. On the contrary, in seeking to fashion a narrative history around the bazaar, this study takes its inspiration from Karl Polanyi's "substantivist" insistence on recognizing the social parameters of economic action and economizing behavior. Indeed, this study is very much grounded in its local contexts defined by the society and culture of the northeastern Indian region of Bihar. Although I do not seek to revive the well-known substantivist-formalist polemics of the 1960s, I consider the Polanyi contribution valuable for directing "us away from narrow tautological functionalist arguments and from Parsonian conceptualizations of societies as functionally interlinked subsystems, to the significance of institutional control of distributive systems and its consequent effect on production."[41]

The spotlight on bazaars, conceptualized as an empirical counterweight to the imagined village, is therefore designed to emphasize the links, networks, and extensions that enmeshed villages within larger units of rural society organized around the marketing system. At this level of analysis, the investigation examines the structure and functioning of the rural marketing system in north India by focusing on the specific economic and social setting of Gangetic Bihar, that area along the Ganges River in the former province (now state) of Bihar. The data utilized here will draw particularly on information relating to that substantial portion of Gangetic Bihar carved out administratively in the colonial period as Patna Division. (See Map 1)

Much of Gangetic Bihar forms part of the "Middle Gangetic Plain" that extends into present-day Uttar Pradesh (formerly United Provinces and the North-Western Provinces before that) and represents a transitional zone between the drier Upper Gangetic Plain, with less than thirty inches of rainfall annually, and the Lower Plain of Bengal with

40. A discussion of old and new approaches can be gleaned from Smith, *Regional Analysis*.

41. Sutti Ortiz, ed., *Economic Anthropology: Topics and Theories,* Monographs in Economic Anthropology, no. 1, Society for Economic Anthropology (Lanham, Md.: University Press of America, 1983), p. 5. The classic is Karl Polanyi, C. W. Arensberg, and H. W. Pearson, eds., *Trade and Market in the Early Empires* (Glencoe, Ill.: Free Press, 1957). For continuing echoes of this debates, see Richard Hodges, *Primitive and Peasant Markets* (Oxford: Basil Blackwell, 1988); Ortiz, ed., *Economic Anthropology;* Stuart Plattner, ed., *Markets and Marketing,* Monographs in Economic Anthropology, no. 4, Society for Economic Anthropology (Lanham, Md.: University Press of America, 1985).

more than sixty. This transitional area falls between the predominantly wheat culture of the upper plains and the predominantly rice cultivation of the lower plain. Gangetic Bihar is largely a flat alluvial plain, except for the Himalayan foothills in the north occupying 364 square miles of the northernmost extremity of Champaran, the Barabar Hills of Gaya, and the Kaimur plateau of Shahabad in the south. North of the Ganges lie the old districts of Saran, Champaran, Tirhut (divided in 1877 into Darbhanga and Muzaffarpur), and the northern portions of Bhagalpur, Monghyr, and Purnia. The Gangetic plain area of south Bihar is made up of the old districts of Patna, Gaya, Shahabad, and the southern extensions of Bhagalpur and Monghyr.[42] Further to the south is the area known as the Chotangapur plateau, where the land rises one to two thousand feet above sea level, setting that area apart as an ecological region different from the Gangetic plain. Patna, Gaya, and Shahabad south of the Ganges and Saran, Champaran, Muzaffarpur, and Darbhanga north of the Ganges together comprised Patna Division, an area totaling 23,675 square miles and inhabited by more than 15 million people in the late nineteenth century, and almost 17 million in 1931. After 1908 this division was split into two: Patna Division consisting of Patna, Gaya, and Shahabad, and Tirhut Division comprising Saran, Champaran, Muzaffarpur, and Darbhanga.[43]

This study will reconstruct the dynamics of the regional and local (district-level) marketing systems of this area, down to the lowest level, the *haat*, or periodic market. Of interest here are the organization and interrelationships of markets spatially (in terms of the taxonomy of sites as well as their hierarchical relationships) as well as temporally (including their relation to the local agricultural and religious calendar). The structure of the marketing systems will also be considered within the framework of the pattern of horizontal and vertical trade: the movement of local agricultural and craft commodities and of nonlocal products from higher-level markets.

42. Gyan Prakash, *Bonded Histories: Genealogies of Labor Servitude in Colonial India* (Cambridge: Cambridge University Press, 1990), chap. 1, argues that the north/south difference was a colonial construction.

43. Enayat Ahmad, *Bihar: A Physical, Economic, and Regional Geography* (Ranchi: Ranchi University, 1965), pp. 1–26; Jagdish Singh, *Transport Geography of South Bihar* (Varanasi: Banaras Hindu University Press, 1964), pp. 3–17. In 1931 Patna had a population of 1,846,474, Gaya 2,388,462, Shahabad 1,993,489, Saran 2,486,737, Champaran 2,145,687, Muzaffarpur 2,941,025, and Darbhanga 3,166,094. See GOI, *Census of India, 1931*, vol. 7, *Bihar and Orissa, Part II.-Tables* by W. G. Lacey (Patna: Bihar and Orissa, 1932), p. 2.

In contrast to many other studies of marketing, however, the emphasis here is not exclusively on mapping the spatial aspects of the human landscape as patterned by markets or looking at markets as economic phenomena. Rather, the focus is on reconstructing and narrating the lived experiences of people as played out in the arena of, and against the backdrop of, markets. I also look at the role of marketing systems as units of social, cultural, and political organization—units within which power and influence were dispersed and exercised and within which people increasingly developed and acquired notions of identity and community. And throughout I am interested in the evolving relationships between the colonial state and indigenous society as mediated through the local marketing systems. Finally, this book also considers rural society against the template of the local marketing system.

On the one hand, such concerns are intended to reveal the organization and interrelationships of markets spatially and temporally; on the other, they can bring out the fit of the locality and the region in the larger national and world systems. In part, the lens of the market reveals the changing relations of power and dominance between and among the different categories on the land. However, because the emphasis is on viewing local society and culture through the lens of the marketplace, not much attention is directed at highlighting the incorporation of the region into the capitalist world system.[44]

The book is permeated by a sense of the market as the "epitome of a spatial boundary," a "space where local society materially and culturally reproduced itself." Against this vernacular space are featured events and people that foreground the market as a "social nexus," as a "typical site of collective discourse," as a container and crucible of solidarities as well as of antagonisms and contradictions of a particular locality.[45]

Bazaars realign our imaginative geography by insisting on a more dynamic view of agrarian society than has hitherto been emphasized in a historiography that has defined colonial society largely in structural and legal categories. Both as an analytical unit and at a metaphoric level, bazaars speak the language of exchange and negotiation, of

---

44. A recent attempt to incorporate and relate South Asia to world systems theory is Sugata Bose, ed., *South Asia and World Capitalism* (Delhi: Oxford University Press, 1990).

45. Jean-Christophe Agnew, *Worlds Apart: The Market and the Theater in Anglo-American Thought, 1550–1750* (Cambridge: Cambridge University Press, 1986), p. 33. For a different emphasis—on markets as an ethical phenomenon—see B. L. Anderson and A. J. H. Latham, eds., *The Market in History* (London: Croom Helm, 1986).

movement and flow, of circulation and redistribution—in short, of ex-
tracommunity or supracommunity connections and institutions. The
India of *Bazaar* is therefore not confined to a particular site at the expense of wider ties. Such linkages, after all, did exist, and the village
never suffered from that rather artificial quality of isolation that had
been constructed for it in the colonial imagination.

The heart of the book—chapters 2, 3, and 4—centers on the perspective of three different sites in the regional system of marketing.
Framed by two contextual chapters (chapters 1 and 5), each of the
three core chapters attempts to engage the possibility of narrating history from different points of view by looking at the lived experiences of
a specific individual or specific groups; each of these chapters is located
at a different point in time; and finally each of these three frames of
perspective, level, and temporality is organized into episodes.

Chapter 2 starts at the apex of the regional marketing system. Its locale is the central place of Patna, the "City of Discontent" in the late-
eighteenth-century age of "revolution," as seen through the lens crafted
by its contemporary historian, Ghulam Husain. It concentrates on a period that saw the emergence of British colonial power, the incorporation of the subcontinent into an expanding European world-system,
and the beginnings of a process of deindustrialization characterized by
a decline in the nonagricultural sector of the regional economy.[46] While
not entirely accepting the Patna historian's version of the deleterious effects of the "revolution" on the city and the region, it acknowledges—
albeit with modifications—his argument about the reduced salience of
the city and its local and regional aristocracy.

The focus then shifts in chapter 3 to the fairs (*melas*) of Bihar as portrayed from afar and near by pilgrims, particularly Enugula Veeraswamy, in the first half of the nineteenth century, when colonial hegemony was firmly established. By highlighting pilgrimages and fairs, I
have placed the emphasis here on situating markets and the process of
exchange in a larger cultural and religious setting. This chapter also
demonstrates the extent to which the local centers of political gravity in
the consolidated colonial system of power and control had shifted

46. Two sides of this hotly debated topic are represented by Amiya Kumar Bagchi,
"Deindustrialisation in Gangetic Bihar, 1809–1901," in *Essays in Honour of Professor
S. C. Sarkar,* ed. Barun De (New Delhi: People's Publishing House, 1976), pp. 499–522;
Marika Vicziany, "Imperialism, Botany, and Statistics in early Nineteenth-Century India:
The Surveys of Francis Buchanan (1762–1829)," *MAS* 20 (1986): 625–60.

away from cities and towns and their urban elite to the countryside and its local controllers, the landholders, or zamindars. The shift in focus to rural society in the early nineteenth century also fits in well with the rise of deindustrialization and the related growth of a peasant economy, developments that were accompanied by the "collapse of artisanal crafts and domestic urban markets" on the one hand and the rise of "peasant petty commodity production" on the other. "The new world economy of the nineteenth century, into which South Asia was now inserted," to continue in the words of Washbrook, "decreed mass 'peasantization' as the latter's fate."[47]

Chapter 4 then moves out to the hinterland to dramatize the workings of the rural markets by setting them against the backdrop of the early-twentieth-century "Age of Gandhi" and the rise of anticolonial resistance by nationalist and subaltern groups. An era whose economic conditions were shaped by worldwide dislocations resulting from World War I and its aftermath, it was a period in which well-to-do peasants and petty traders played key roles in generating a mass nationalist movement opposing colonial rule and in mounting resistance to continuing landholder dominance. That the Gandhi-led Noncooperation Movement of the early 1920s targeted, among other things, foreign cloth indicates not only the nationalist understanding of the symbolic and practical capital to be realized from challenging the colonial economy but also of reversing the processes of deindustrialization and displacement of indigenous capital. This chapter anticipates the later development of a national market and economy in which indigenous capital and the rise of domestic markets signaled the emergence of business and industry. It also sets the stage for a story that one scholar has narrated as the rise of Indian industrial capitalists from their erstwhile positions as merchants and traders involved in bazaar trade and banking.[48]

By anchoring each of these episodes at a particular site—the urban center of Patna, the fairs, and the rural markets—I intend to privilege the locale itself and its place in the larger networks of sites and boundaries, as well to utilize it as a setting for a "thick description" of local worlds and local knowledge. The shift from the city to the fair to the

47. David Washbrook, "South Asia, the World System and World Capitalism," in *South Asia and Capitalism*, p. 41.

48. Ray, "Bazaar." See also the essays in idem, ed., *Entrepreneurship and Industry in India, 1800–1947* (Delhi: Oxford University Press, 1992).

village market and from the late eighteenth to the twentieth century is by design. Such movement across space and time mirrors the emergence and development of colonialism and capitalism in South Asia. The colonial state was initially anchored in the coastal cities, the port cities of Calcutta, Bombay, and Madras, from which it branched out into the interior. In northeastern India the movement was from Calcutta to the hinterland via the inland port cities of Murshidabad and Patna and then farther into the interior, to Banaras. By the mid-nineteenth century, at the conclusion of the first century of colonial rule, the regime had reached into the countryside, setting up its apparatus of control in towns and larger settlements that were typically also the sites of fairs. And in the late nineteenth century, prior to the rise of large-scale elite and subaltern anticolonial movements, the colonial state sought to tighten its administrative grip over the countryside by forging links particularly to those nodal points that were the settings of small town and periodic village markets. As chapter 4 reveals, it was these markets at the grassroots level that became the locus in the late nineteenth and early twentieth centuries for the great contest between rulers and ruled. The colonial state is a presence throughout the work, but it is not portrayed as a static dominating force from the very outset or an architect of such power that it did not have its own contradictions or did not have to reproduce itself continually to maintain its control.

The movement from city to towns (and fairs) to village is also aimed at foregrounding in situ the principal actors of this historical drama: urban elites, rural magnates, merchants and traders, and peasants. The emphasis is as much on their prominent roles at particular sites in the system of exchange as it is on their interrelationships with one another and to the colonial state.

Each of these settings is further intended to be a period piece evoking a particular milieu: from the city of discontent in the late eighteenth century to the fairs with their *communitas* and carnival dimensions in the nineteenth to the countryside that resounded with the voices of resistance in the twentieth. Each shows the extent to which any system of exchange is shaped by social and cultural forces as it is by economic and political conditions.

The opening chapter is the mise-en-scène, which focuses on the circuits and nodes of Gangetic Bihar as they were reconfigured into a colonial geometry whose points and lines were determined by its own political and economic imperatives. The final chapter details, over the course of the *longue durée* of colonial rule, the changing experiences of the principal actors in the system of exchange. At the village and local marketing level the winners were rich peasants and petty traders (*beoparis*) who carved out positions of dominance through their access to land, either as its owners or tenants and through their involvement in petty moneylending and agricultural trade. In the city and in the towns of the region, this chapter traces the rise of traders and merchants (*mahajans*) who occupied the "sphere of bazaar bankers and merchants working at inland exchanges.... Operating through an older indigenous financial nexus of commission agencies (*arhat*) and bills of exchange (*hundi*), they enabled inland produce and credit transactions before and after the war [World War I] to take place increasingly on an all-India basis."[49]

The conclusion—in part an epilogue because it has less of the limiting and restricting quality that the very word *conclusion* connotes on the one hand and the finality of outcome that it implies on the other hand—reaches its own end by connecting the multiple stories in *Bazaar India*. Thus, the bazaar as a site and scene of colonial history is the setting for a narrative history of the lived experiences of subjects whose lives and livelihood were played out in the larger contexts defined increasingly by the market and the colonial state in Bihar between the late eighteenth and early twentieth centuries. These stories rest on the reconstructions we as historians build from the textual materials of their experiences.

49. Ray, "Bazaar," p. 263. *Beopar* means trade; *beopari* one who engages in trade.

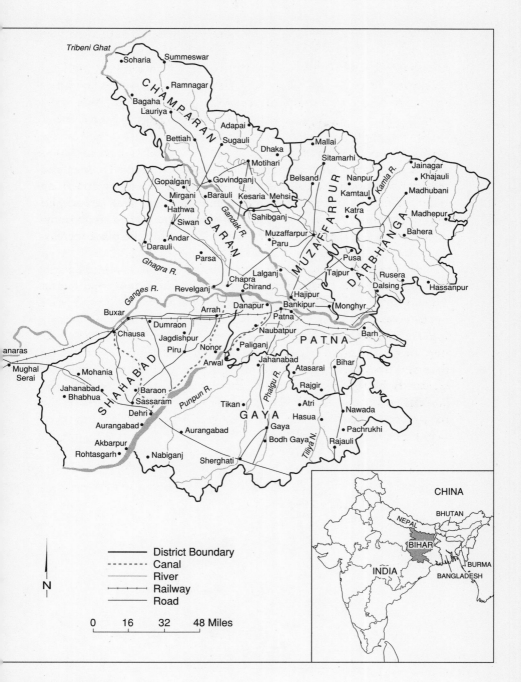

Map 1. Gangetic Bihar

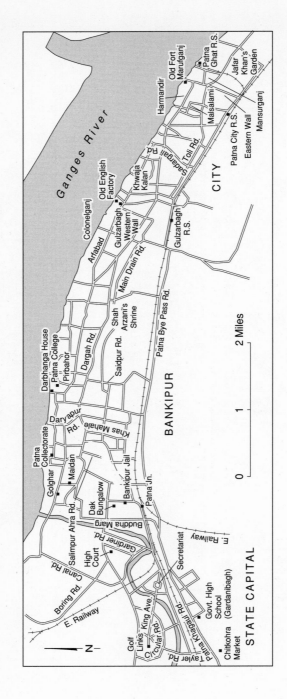

Map 2. The City of Patna

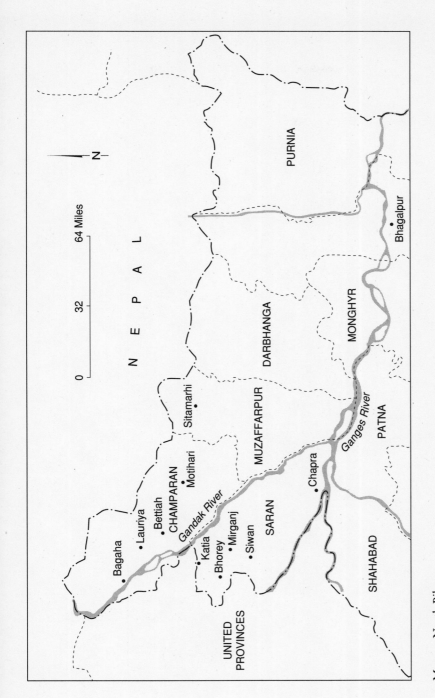

Map 3. North Bihar

CHAPTER I

Gangetic Bihar

Circuits of Exchange and
Modes of Transportation

"Words cannot describe our gratification on seeing the river Ganga [Ganges]." The South Indian pilgrim Enugula Veeraswamy penned this line in 1830, upon seeing this holiest of holy rivers for the first time. It was a sentiment shared by all Hindus, for whom the Ganges is a vital part of religious life and beliefs. Having started his long journey in Madras, he must have been elated at reaching a juncture from which his primary destination of Banaras lay within easy reach. So, too, the other pilgrimage centers (many of which were located on or near the Ganges) he wished to visit were now accessible. For the Ganges opened up north India to him: he could travel on its waters as had generations of people before him, or he could follow the well-worn road that skirted its banks. A seasoned traveler by then, having already been on the road for four months, he recognized from the thriving commercial town of Mirzapur that this river was a major communications artery.[1]

To compare the modes of travel employed by Veeraswamy with those alluded to in the late-eighteenth-century account of the Patna historian Ghulam Husain or those utilized by the early-seventeenth-century Jain

1. *Enugula Veeraswamy's Journal (Kasiyatra Charitra)*, ed. and trans. P. Sitapati and V. Purushottam (Hyderabad: Andhra Pradesh Governmental Oriental Manuscripts Library and Research Institute, 1973), pp. 81–82. See also below, chap. 3, on pilgrimages and their role in the local and regional system of exchange.

merchant named Banarsidas is to confirm the observation made by one commentator that so little change had occurred in the system of transportation in some areas that the mid-nineteenth-century traveler was said to be moving "as slowly and as tediously as in the days of [the third-century B.C.E. Emperor] Asoka."[2] Certainly Veeraswamy's travel experiences reveal that he shared much in common with Banarsidas, who had journeyed across north India conducting business and undertaking pilgrimages on land—by foot, by palanquin, by cart, by carriage, by horseback—and on water, by raft.[3] Indeed, the "tyranny of distance"— Fernand Braudel's evocative metaphor of the constraints imposed by "antiquated means of transportation" on pre-eighteenth-century society and economy[4] aptly characterizes the system of transportation in South Asia in the late eighteenth and early nineteenth centuries.

By the time of Mahatma Gandhi's birth in 1869, however, new means of communication were penetrating extensive areas of the region. This change was primarily ushered in by, to use one traveler's phrase, the "marvel and miracle" of railways.[5] There was moreover the added benefit of construction of new roads to serve as feeders to the rail lines. Thus, by the early twentieth century the triumph over distance appeared to have made its way even into the hinterland. Witness the whistle-stop tours of Gandhi and other leaders in the early 1920s as they crisscrossed Bihar spreading their gospel of Noncooperation, a message disseminated through newspapers and other public media as well.[6]

This chapter examines the effects of these developments in transportation on circuits of exchange—marketing and trade. It shows that "antiquated means of transportation" that relied on waterways and a limited system of roads in the prerailway era hindered the development

2. L. S. S. O'Malley, "Mechanism and Transport," in Modern India and the West, ed. idem (London: Oxford University Press, 1941), p. 235; Jean Deloche, Transport and Communications in India Prior to Steam Locomotion, vol. 1, Land Transport, trans. from the French by James Walker (Delhi: Oxford University Press, 1993), p. 1.

3. [Husain, Ghulam] Seid-Gholam-Hossein-Khan, Seir Mutaqherin, trans. Nota Manus (Calcutta: T. D. Chatterjee, 1902), vol. 4, passim; Veeraswamy, Journal; Banarsidas, Ardhakathanaka, trans. Mukund Lath (Jaipur: Rajasthan Prakrit Bharati Sansthan, 1981), passim.

4. The Structures of Everyday Life, vol. 1, Civilization and Capitalism 15th–18th Century (London: Collins, 1981), pp. 415–30. Also see John Hurd, "Railways," The Cambridge Economic History of India, vol. 2: c. 1757–c. 1970, ed. Dharma Kumar (Cambridge: Cambridge University Press, 1982), pp. 737–39, on the transportation constraints of the prerailway era.

5. Bholanauth Chunder, The Travels of a Hindoo to Various Parts of Bengal and Upper India (London: N. Trubner, 1869), vol. 1, pp. 140–41.

6. See below, chap. 4, regarding Gandhi and the Noncooperation Movement.

of trade across great distances. Inherent temporal limitations played a role, too, as annual disruption caused by the rainy season added to the "tyranny of distance." So did government policies, because the colonial regime opted not to expend the funds necessary to build and maintain a system of roads to overcome these obstacles. What financial commitments it made in this regard were principally directed at forging links between its seat of power, the port city of Calcutta, and the interior.

I will first consider rivers and roads during the prerailway age, essentially the first century of colonial rule, and then turn to the development of railways in the late nineteenth and early twentieth centuries.[7]

The Ganges—navigable throughout the year—was the principal river highway across the vast north Indian Gangetic plain stretching from Delhi to the Bay of Bengal. Vessels capable of accommodating five hundred merchants were known to ply this river in the ancient period; it served as a conduit for overseas trade, as goods were carried from Pataliputra (later Patna) and Champa (later Bhagalpur) out to the seas and on to ports in Sri Lanka and Southeast Asia.[8] During the Mughal period it was used extensively for hauling bulky merchandise, boats of four hundred to five hundred tons regularly sailing on its waters. European merchants in the sixteenth and seventeenth centuries traveled the Ganges in their journeys inland from the Bay of Bengal; so did Europeans coming from Delhi and Agra. For much of the first century of colonial rule, it functioned as the "channel" of the "greatest part of the inland trade of Bengal and Behar, and the whole of the maritime trade both of these and of the [North-]western provinces."[9]

The role of the Ganges as a "channel" for trade was enhanced by its natural links—it embraces all the major rivers and streams in both north and south Bihar. By far the more important channels for trade were the northern tributaries that flow down from the sub-Himalayan

7. See also Yda Saueressig-Screuder, "The Impact of British Colonial Rule on the Urban Hierarchy of Burma," *Review* 10 (1986): 245–77. See also S. N. Mukherjee, *Calcutta: Essays in Urban History* (Calcutta: Subarnarekha, 1993); Sukanta Chaudhuri, *Calcutta: The Living City* (New York: Oxford University Press, 1990); Dilip K. Basu, ed., *The Rise and Growth of the Colonial Port Cities in Asia* (New York: University Press of America, 1985).

8. R. R. Diwakar, *Bihar through the Ages* (Calcutta: Orient Longmans, 1958), pp. 181, 244.

9. Charles E. Trevelyan, *Report upon the Inland Customs and Town Duties of the Bengal Presidency,* ed. Tarasankar Banerjee (1834; reprint, n.p.: Academic Publishers, 1976), p. 128; Henry T. Bernstein, *Steamboats on the Ganges* (Bombay: Orient Longmans, 1960), pp. 13–14; Hameeda Khatoon Naqvi, *Urban Centres and Industries in Upper India, 1556–1803* (London: Asia Publishing House, 1968), pp. 97–98.

ranges in Nepal and proceed in a southeasterly direction toward Calcutta. Of these, the Gandak was the principal river artery for trade. Although navigable throughout the year, particularly the last eighty miles
of its stretch leading into the Ganges, it was a difficult river to negotiate because of its narrow channels during the dry season and its terrific
currents during the rainy season. Boats of up to one thousand maunds
(approximately thirty-six tons) reached Lalganj in the rains, of up to
five hundred maunds reached Bagaha; upstream boats generally carried
half the amount of their downstream loads. Until well into the nineteenth century the Gandak was a major conduit for the trade of Champaran and Muzaffarpur. Grain (especially fine rice), oilseeds, opium,
indigo, and saltpeter were sent down this river and coarse rice, salt,
spices, cotton, piece goods, and other goods brought back in exchange.
Govindganj in Champaran and Lalganj and Hajipur in Muzaffarpur
were the primary centers of trade on this river. Hajipur also benefited
from its proximity to the junction of the Ganges and Gandak.[10]

Two other important northern tributaries were the Gogra (Ghaghra),
which carried much of the traffic across the administrative boundaries
of Saran and the North-Western Provinces, and the Muzaffarpur River
(also known as the Burhi Gandak), which intersects Muzaffarpur and
Darbhanga. Their effectiveness as affluents for trade varied seasonally:
they were best when their waters were swollen with rain. The Burhi
Gandak, for instance, could be plied by boats carrying as much as two
thousand maunds as far as Roshera, and of up to one thousand
maunds as far as Muzaffarpur. Khaguria, located at that river's confluence with the Ganges, and Roshera, Samastipur, and Muzaffarpur,
towns farther upriver, were key sites for "country trade." Much of the
trade on the Gogra was negotiated through Revelganj, which, because
of its advantageous location near the Ganges, emerged as a major trading center in the nineteenth century.[11]

10. A. Wyatt, *Statistics of the District of Sarun consisting of Sircars Sarun and
Chumparun* (Calcutta: Military Orphan Press, 1848?) (Notes on Chumparun), p. 2; A.
Wyatt, *Geographical and Statistical Report of the District of Tirhoot* (Calcutta: Calcutta
Gazette Office, 1854), pp. 4, 15; "Report on a Project for . . . Gunduck," Capt. W. Jef-
freys, Engineer, Dec. 23, 1868, Bengal PWD Procs., Irrigation, Jan.-April 1869, Mar.,
nos. 4–5. Rama Shanker Lal, "Transport and Accessibility in Lower Ghaghara Gandak
Doab," *Deccan Geographer* 7 (1969): 26, estimates that as much as 90 percent of the
trade of the area was formerly conducted by these water routes.
11. "Apprehended Scarcity in North Behar," J. C. Geddes and A. P. MacDonnell, to
GOB, Jan. 24, 1876, Bengal Scarcity and Relief Procs., 1876–77, Feb. 1876 (hereafter
Geddes and MacDonnell report); "Report on the Water Communications . . . of the

The rivers from the south are another story. Short, dependent on rainfall, shallow but rapid when in spate, and tending to branch into many channels in their lower reaches, these tributaries have historically not been significant as lines of communication and transport. Exemplifying these conditions is the Son, which originates in the plateau of central India and forms the administrative frontier of Shahabad with Gaya and Patna. Although the primary river in south Bihar, it never emerged as an important line of transportation because it could not support boats of substantial weight during the long dry season, and its waters turned into rapids in the rains. Large boats utilized the river between July and the end of November; in December it was navigable only by small boats. Therefore, its primary commercial use was in floating bamboos and other timber. Daudnagar and Arwal were the primary trade centers on this river for the movement of "country produce."[12]

Throughout the Gangetic network of rivers and streams, traffic ebbed and flowed in accordance with the rainy season. Traffic on the Ganges was generally heavier upstream in the first half of the year, with the pattern reversed in the latter half of the year when the river, swollen from the rains, carried more traffic flowing downstream. Furthermore, boats were less likely to get mired in sandbanks in the wet weather. Especially in the south the "river-borne export trade . . . [was] brisk only during the months of July, August, September, and October, when the rivers are full of water."[13]

Traffic patterns were also conditioned by the marketing calendar of the staple items of the Ganges-borne trade. Rice, available in the Bengal markets in December and January, was shipped to Bihar and the North-Western Provinces, where demand always exceeded local supply. In the first six months of the year the surplus rice of the great alluvial and deltaic plain between the Himalayas and the Bay of Bengal made up a substantial portion of the up-country traffic. Oilseeds, largely a product of Bihar and the North-Western Provinces, reversed the trade

---

Bhagulpore and Patna Divisions," T. H. Wickes, Executive Engineer, no. 40, Aug. 25, 1874, Bengal Scarcity and Relief Procs., Nov. 1874, no. 42.

12. W. W. Hunter, *Statistical Account of Bengal,* vol. 12, *Districts of Gaya and Shahabad* (London: Trubner and Co., 1877), pp. 20, 163; George A. Grierson, *Notes on the District of Gaya* (Calcutta: Bengal Secretariat Press, 1893), p. 9; Singh, *Transport Geography,* pp. 93–94; J. Macnamara, District Engineer, Shahabad, to Magte., Shahabad, no. 87, Mar. 26, 1867, Bengal PWD Procs., Aug.-Sept. 1867, Aug., no. 4.

13. GOB, *Report on the Internal Trade of Bengal for the Year 1876–77* (Calcutta: Bengal Secretariat Press, 1877), pp. 8–9.

flow in the second half of the year when they were dispatched to the
Calcutta market. First appearing in the markets in April and May,
oilseeds added significantly to the downstream traffic in the second half
of the year because their export to Bengal began in July and continued
through the rainy season. Together rice and oilseeds accounted for
more than half of the traffic on the Ganges.[14] Not all commodities
traveled in that direction, however. Indigo, sugar, hides, wheat, saltpeter, and oilseeds moved with the flow toward Bengal, whereas rice,
opium, and tobacco moved against the current back toward Patna and
the North-Western Provinces.[15]

Overland transportation also followed this rhythm and pattern.
Champaran's exports of largely grain, corn, pulses, oilseeds, sugar, indigo, opium, ghee, and hides were conveyed on the roads in their
largest volumes between November and May. This timing coincided
with Champaran's two major harvests of *bhadai* (autumn) and *rabi*
(spring) crops, which were collected October-November and March-
April, respectively. At the height of the season of overland traffic, in the
five peak months from the beginning of December to the end of April,
as many as eight thousand carts and an equal number of bullocks and
tattoos (ponies) operated by the well-known Banjara pack-bullock
traders passed daily over the roads, many of these destined, either directly or indirectly via intermediate stops, for the major markets along
the Ganges. From there the movement downstream awaited the onset
of the monsoon rains, which typically commenced in June and tapered
off in September. Boats negotiating the swollen river generally moved
twice as fast as those going upstream.[16]

---

14. "The Boat Traffic of Bengal," Resolution, Financial Dept., Stats., Oct. 18, 1875,
P.C. Gen. *Basta* no. 275; *Trade of Bengal 1876–77*, pp. 22, 73. In the lower Gangetic
delta, boat traffic continued virtually year-round. See B. Chaudhuri, "Eastern India," in
The Cambridge Economic History of India, vol. 2, p. 271.

15. Sir R. Temple, Minute "On Railway Projects for North Behar," July 9, 1874, Bengal Scarcity and Relief Procs., Aug. 1874; Jean Deloche, *Transport and Communications
in India Prior to Steam Locomotion, vol. 2: Water Transport*, trans. from the French by
James Walker (Delhi: Oxford University Press, 1993), pp. 18–19. To some extent, the
Ganges served as a dividing line between north and south Bihar, especially during the
colonial period, when it was unbridged.

16. E. McDonell, Secy., Champaran Ferry Fund Committee, to W. Tayler, Offg.
Commr., Patna, no. 16, June 26, 1855, in *Selections from the Records of the Bengal Government*, no. 24, *Correspondence relating to the Ferry Funds in the Lower Provinces*
(Calcutta: Military Orphan Press, 1856), p. 90; Bernstein, *Steamboats on the Ganges*,
pp. 11, 17; *CDG 1938*, pp. 56–60; *MSR*, pp. x–xiii; *SSR*, p. 111. Also below, pp.
131–33, 225, regarding the regional calendar of agricultural harvests and trade.

Limitations notwithstanding, the Ganges and its affluents constituted the most effective and efficient network of transportation. "Nowhere in India," other than in Bihar and Bengal, as one report noted,
"is internal traffic more active ... when the rivers are full of water,
when every river is turned into a highway for the country craft laden
with merchandise, every stream into a pathway, and every creek into a
harbour for boats."[17] Indeed, rivers were the primary highways, a
natural system of internal waterways, because roads were not well developed until the late nineteenth century (at the time when railways
were built). Absent an efficient overland system of transportation, water transportation was not only cheaper but faster. Downstream boats
generally could travel forty miles a day; upstream they managed ten
miles a day. And they were more capacious than overland haulage.

Transportation costs reflected the comparative advantages enjoyed
by water transportation. A mid-nineteenth-century source estimated
that travel by country boats proceeding downriver in the Gangetic area
cost the least; slightly more expensive were country boats moving upriver; and steamers ferried goods more expensively than even country
boats carrying loads upriver. Introduced to the Ganges in the 1830s,
steamboats greatly speeded up transportation but acquired "little of the
ordinary traffic. . . . They get twice as much cargo on their up-stream as
on their down-stream trips. They carry very little of the great staples,
such as oil-seeds, rice, and salt; but carry much of the metals and machinery and much of the miscellaneous European goods which are sent
up-country by river."[18] The costliest way to transport goods was overland: almost double that of country boats heading upriver.[19]

Local investigations bear out these figures. Rates in north Bihar were
as follows: 8 pies or three-quarters of an anna (12 pies equals one
anna) per ton per mile upstream by country boat, as opposed to 2 annas per ton per mile by country cart; downstream the price by river fell
to 5 pies per ton per mile. In other words, the cost of transportation by
boats ranged from approximately one-third to one-fifth the cost of

17. *Trade of Bengal 1876–77*, pp. 8–9
18. C. Bernard, Offg. Secy., GOB, to Secy., GOI, Nov. 1, 1873, P. C. Basta 228, alphabet T and W, nos. 65–76. Seeds and cotton accounted for more than three-quarters
of the downward steam freight and salt and metals for three-quarters of the upward
steamer traffic. See "Resolution," Bernard, Offg. Secy., Nov. 18, 1872, P. C. Basta no.
227, Important Bundles, Rev. Dept., alphabet S, nos. 58–64.
19. Bernstein, *Steamboats on the Ganges,* p. 100; I. D. Derbyshire, "Economic
Change and the Railways in North India, 1860–1914," *MAS* 21 (1987): 526.

overland freight by carts, depending on whether they were moving upstream or downstream. The "miserable nature of the carts, which will
not convey more than five or five and half maunds [less than five hundred pounds] at a time," as one local administrator explained, added
to the costs, making "land carriage . . . the dearest mode of transport,
returning no profit, and mostly inflicting loss, and . . . therefore avoided
to the utmost."[20] Land traffic therefore tended to seek out river outlets.

Traffic, furthermore, converged on the river outlets—especially the
Ganges—because the principal highways paralleled the course of this
great river until the early nineteenth century. Historically, an east-west
highway alongside the Ganges has a long genealogy. A king's road
from Pataliputra to the northwest of India via Banaras existed as early
as the pre-Christian era.[21] Under Sher Shah, and later under the
Mughals, this route followed the Ganges, making a detour at Patna,
where it turned southward along the Son, intersecting Arwal and
Daudnagar before crossing over that river to head for Banaras via
Sasaram and Jahanabad and then across the Karamnasa. A second
route followed the line of the Ganges, intersecting Buxar at the westernmost point of Bihar, and then advanced on to Bhojpur and Arrah
before entering Patna district, where it proceeded through Maner,
Danapur, Patna, and Barh before heading east toward Murshidabad
via Monghyr and Bhagalpur.[22]

The historic road along the Ganges faded in importance, however,
during the colonial period because the new focal point was Calcutta,
which lay south of the major Mughal settlements in Bengal. Looking
outward from Calcutta to its expanding frontier of interests in the
north and northwest, the emerging colonial state recognized, as did its

20. F. M. Bird, Magte., Gorakhpur, to Offg. Commr., no. 135, July 12, 1860, Bengal
PWD Procs., Oct. 1860, no. 182; "Report on Gunduck," Bengal PWD Procs., Irrigation,
Mar. 1869, nos. 4–5.

21. M. M. Singh, "Social and Economic Conditions (600 B.C.–325 B.C.)," and H. K.
Prasad, "Economic Condition of Bihar (c. 187 B.C.–319 A.D.)," in Comprehensive His-
tory of Bihar, vol. 1, part 1, ed. Bindeshwari Prasad Sinha (Patna: Kashi Prasad Jayaswal
Research Institute, 1974), pp. 403, 815

22. Irfan Habib, An Atlas of the Mughal Empire (Delhi: Oxford University Press,
1982), 8B, 10B and pp. 31, 41; Khan Mohammad Mohsin, A Bengal District in Transi-
tion: Murshidabad, 1765–1793 (Dacca: Asiatic Society of Bangladesh, 1973), pp. 12–13;
Abul Khair Muhammad Farooque, Roads and Communications in Mughal India (Delhi:
Idarah-I Adabiyat-I Delli, 1977), chap. 2; Deloche, Transport in India, vol. 1, pp. 37–39.
William Charles Macpherson, Soldiering in India, 1764–1787 (Edinburgh: William
Blackwood and Sons, 1928), p. 97, suggests that the "southern" Mughal route across the
Son and through Arwal was still in good condition in the 1770s.

Mughal predecessors, the urgency of building a highway across north India. Consequently, the routes that received the most government attention in Bihar were thoroughfares connecting Bengal to the North-Western Provinces, from which the highways continued on to Delhi.

From the outset, British policy regarding the construction and maintenance of roads was guided by *"political* and *military* objects."[23] As early as the 1760s British engineers began mapping out a "New Road" (also called the "New Military Road"), which was completed in 1785. From Calcutta, the most expedient and direct connection through Bihar was to follow a more southerly course, a route that veered away from Hughli toward Burdwan and then across Hazaribagh, not paralleling the course of the Mughal main route until it crossed over the Son; from there it proceeded to Banaras along much the same trajectory as the Mughal route. In part, the new trajectory was also designed to extend British control into Chotanagpur, a region that had remained beyond the ken of the Mughals; in part, the southerly direction was aimed at enabling the new regime to meet and contain Maratha incursions that came through central India.

But this new east-west highway—it remained the primary road for some fifty years—never became a major thoroughfare because it was not kept in good repair and was prone to flooding. Writing in 1855 (almost prophetically because the subsequent events of the 1857 Mutiny/Rebellion in Bihar had their epicenter in Shahabad), the Patna commissioner expressed "surprise" at its "imperfect and ill-managed . . . condition. The first fall of rain renders it in parts quite impassable for wheeled conveyances, and nearly so for any other mode of transit, and if any emergency should require the presence of troops at Arrah during the rains, they would have great difficulty in reaching the station from Dinapore."[24]

---

23. Henry St. George Tucker, "Roads in Bengal," (1832) in *Memorial of Indian Government; Being a Selection from the Papers of Henry St. George Tucker,* ed. John William Kaye (London: Richard Bentley, 1853), p. 424. See also Robert Gabriel Varady, "Rail and Road Transport in Nineteenth Century Awadh: Competition in a North Indian Province," Ph.D. diss., University of Arizona, 1981, pp. 28–29, on the relationship between road building and government policy in Awadh.

24. Tayler, Offg. Commr., to W. Grey, Secy., GOB, July 10, 1855, in *Correspondence to Ferry Funds,* p. 68; A. Welland, Colltr., Shahabad, to John Rawlins, Secy., BOR, Oct. 3, 1794, Sh. C., vol. 22, 1794–95; Kalikinkar Datta, *Studies in the History of the Bengal Subah, 1740–70,* vol. 1: *Social and Economic* (Calcutta: University of Calcutta, 1936), p. 395; C. E. A. W. Oldham, "Routes, Old and New, from Lower Bengal 'Up the Country,'" *Bengal Past and Present* 28 (1924): 30–31.

Nor did the Grand Trunk Road, which superseded the more southerly "New Road" by the 1840s, emerge as a major highway for conveyance of goods.[25] But it fulfilled its "paramount importance" as a road that tied Calcutta to government's "most important provinces and political interest together with the great proportion of its military force."[26] Indeed, control of the Grand Trunk Road in the Mutiny/Rebellion of 1857 enabled the British to keep open the lines of communication and supplies between Calcutta and the areas of contention in north and central India. "British military formations moved along it with the sureness of destroyers passing over a dark and turbulent ocean." Access to this highway enabled the beleaguered colonial regime in 1857 to persist as "a fragile form of military occupation." To continue in the words of Eric Stokes, "It was not the last time a colonial power would find that so long as it could secure the key towns and connecting highways leading to the main military concentration of rebellion, it could afford from a narrow military viewpoint to ignore its own loss of control over the intermediate countryside."[27]

Its strategic importance notwithstanding, the Grand Trunk Road was not in much better condition than the "New Road." [28] In fact, its eastern segment acquired little of the majesty that Kipling saw in its northwestern portion in the late nineteenth century. Its "imperfect and ill-managed . . . condition" made it especially unsuited for supporting

25. The Bihar segment, 244 miles in length, crossed over the thinly populated districts of Hazaribagh and Dhanbad before intersecting Shahabad and Gaya. Principal settlements on this route were Sherghati, Aurangabad, Sasaram, Jahanabad, and Dehri-on-Sone. Francis Buchanan, *Journal of Francis Buchanan Kept during the Survey of the District of Bhagalpur in 1810–1811*, ed. C. E. A. W. Oldham (Patna: Govt. Printing, 1930), p. 2; "Letters from Court," no. 9, Dec. 22, 1786, *Fort William-India House Correspondence* (Public Series), vol. 10:1786–88, ed. Raghubir Sinh (Delhi: Government of India, 1972), p. 705; C. E. A. W. Oldham, "Routes, Old and New, From Lower Bengal 'Up the Country,'" *Bengal Past and Present* 30 (1926): 27–30; Sir John Houlton, *Bihar: The Heart of India* (Bombay: Orient Longmans, 1949), pp. 174–80; *PDG 1924*, p. 130; *ShDG 1906*, pp. 98–99; Hunter, *Account of Shahabad*, pp. 112–13.
26. "Minute of the Governor General," Mar. 25, 1831, Bengal Cr. Jdcl. Consltns., Apr. 26 to June 7, 1831, May 3, no. 100.
27. *The Peasant Armed: The Indian Revolt of 1857*, ed. C. A. Bayly (Oxford: Clarendon Press, 1986), p. 25; *GDG 1957*, pp. 235–36.
28. Nevertheless, it received a lion's share of the provincial funds for roads (sixteen thousand to twenty thousand rupees per annum on the Bengal portion alone). By contrast, the Mughal trunk road received little attention and maintenance and faded "into comparative insignificance." T. Sandys, Offg. Local Agent, Shahabad Local Agency, to E. C. Ravenshaw, Commr., no. 6, Feb. 27, 1841, Bengal Cr. Jdcl. Consltns., Oct. 3 to 24, 1842, Oct. 10, no. 49; "Minute of GG," Bengal Cr. Jdcl. Consltns., May 3, 1831, no. 100; *ShDG 1906*, p. 99; O'Malley, "Mechanism and Transport," p. 235; Tucker, *Memorials*, p. 425.

heavy traffic. Take the leg between Calcutta and the Karamnasa River, for instance. Level for the first 110 miles, then rising into hilly country for the next 165 miles before becoming "dead level" again, this stretch of 391 miles was the first road to be metaled—a process started in earnest after 1839. The quality of its metaling, however, varied from place to place, not only because of the different materials used but also because of the different techniques employed to harden the surface. In its hilly portion the tendency was to metal the road by lining it with stones or granite but without packing them down with a roller. Instead the expectation was that the traffic along the road would firm up this bedrock. The result, however, was not as anticipated, because carts and carriages left a rut that other wheeled traffic attempted to follow or that traffic sought to avoid by skirting the sides of the roads.

Rains, furthermore, wreaked havoc, narrowing a road that was only fourteen to fifteen feet wide under the best of conditions and washing away "large parts." Not until it was completely metaled in the late nineteenth century was this road finally usable year-round for all kinds of transport.

Unbridged rivers posed another hazard, as one traveler recounted on reaching the Son, noting that the river

> is three miles across; a volume of water for four months in the year—a waste of sand with only one stream of any consequence for the remainder of the year. At present it takes three good hours to cross it and heavy bullock carts take nearly a day. A good sized carriage such as the one used by all passengers on the line is dragged by six bullocks over the waste of sand which reaches from the right bank of the river to the main stream running along the left bank. Two or three smaller streams are crossed about half way; but they do not compel passengers to embark their vehicles on boats. At the beginning of November the water in these minor streams was scarcely higher than the axles and by the commencement of February it will be quite dried up. The boats used for crossing the main stream are[,] however, of the most faulty and insecure description.[29]

Familiar with these problems was the Inland Transit Company, whose "palanquin carriages," drawn by a horse or sometimes two horses, or "parcel [goods] carts" set off daily from Calcutta on the Grand Trunk Road. Only under optimum conditions could passenger carriages reach Banaras in three days and goods carts in forty hours. During the rainy

---

29. "Note on the GTR," by W. Seton Karr, Jan. 5, 1854, Bengal Pub. Consltns., Mar. 9–23, 1854, Mar. 16, no. 56.

season, the company manager dissuaded passengers from traveling. The "difficulties and annoyances are so great," he explained, "owing to the obstacles . . . that we would rather lose the passengers than run the risk of being blamed for their disappointments." Included in his list of hazards were the "low level of the road between Hooghly and Burdwan which renders it always liable to inundation in the rains. [There is a] want of bridges over some of the principal streams and [a] general want of supervision along the whole line . . . [, and] proper means are not taken to keep it in repair."[30]

Far worse off were the secondary roads, which were so critical to the effective functioning of the principal water or land highways. Like the tributaries from the north and the south that flowed into the Ganges, the most important secondary roads were needed as confluents linking up the countryside with the principal highways. Especially indispensable were north-south roads that could serve as feeder roads for the east-west water and overland highways. Few and far between were crossroads that cut laterally across localities along an east-west direction. As late as the 1870s, many areas reported, as did Shahabad, that not a single "cross-road" existed.[31]

Moreover, secondary roads received little attention until the advent of the railway era because they were not considered to possess political or military significance.[32] Essentially fair-weather tracks, these local roads were largely unpaved, as in the Mughal period, and mostly carved out of dirt surfaces and constructed without much benefit of en-

30. "Statement of the Manager of the Inland Transit Company . . . ," Aug. 3, 1850, Bengal Pub. Consltns., 1850, Nov. 27, no. 148.
31. "Report on the Agricultural Statistics of Shahabad . . . ," M. S. D. H. Ahamed, Deputy Colltr., Shahabad, Bengal Stats. Procs., June 1874–Dec. 1875, May 1875, app. B, nos. 19–20. Patna Division, however, had more roads than Bengal: one mile of road for every six square miles as opposed to one mile for every twenty square miles. H. Leonard, Offg Secy., PWD, to Offg Secy., GOB, no. 1494, Mar. 3, 1868, Bengal Gen. Procs., 1868, June, no. 37.
32. At the local level, most efforts were aimed at connecting settlements of administrative and commercial salience, generally the district headquarters and the stations, if any, occupied by garrisons and battalions. The only other roads that were consistently maintained in the initial century of colonial rule were the short strips in the vicinity of the district headquarters. E.g., the highway from Bhagalpur to Calcutta was in poor condition but the roads around the towns of Bhagalpur and Monghyr were well maintained, apparently "to give the European ladies an opportunity of taking an evening ride." Montgomery Martin, Eastern India, vol. 2, Bhagalpur, Gorakhpur (reprint, Delhi: Cosmo Publications, 1976), pp. 286–87; J. Sanford, 3rd Judge, Patna Court of Circuit, to W. Dorin, Registrar, Nizt. Adt., Nov. 6, 1820, Bengal Cr. Jdcl. Consltns., Apr. 6 to 13, 1821, Apr. 13, no. 27.

gineering principles. As a result, they were beset by problems of drainage and design. They were, for one, prone to flooding in the level plains either because of rains or overflowing streams and rivulets. Furthermore, in the absence of metaling, during the dry season even the best of roads was easily damaged by wheeled traffic. Lacking bridges over the many streams and rivulets that formed barriers particularly during the rainy season, many were also not easily passable. Therefore in the wet months wheeled traffic came almost to a standstill. No wonder roads in this era could be maintained only at inordinate expense, costs that government was not willing to incur.[33]

Their maintenance, moreover, depended on the initiative and interest of local administrators and on funds collected from local landholders. Such contingencies typically meant that most roads were in poor condition. For example, the principal road along the Ganges was difficult to negotiate because bridges on this road were not kept up. Zamindars and administrators were equally to blame, reported the local judge, because they considered the responsibility of maintaining roads "attended with considerable labour and trouble and . . . a subject of temporary or local expedient by the government, [and therefore] the Magistrates are [not] inclined nor encouraged to undertake the duty."[34]

An assessment of the Patna-Gaya road, perhaps the most important north-south route in Bihar, is indicative of the low priority accorded, and the poor condition of, even the most significant of secondary roads in the prerailway era.[35] Patna had long been connected to Gaya, the second most important town in Bihar and a major pilgrimage center; Bodh Gaya, six miles south of Gaya, known historically as the place where Buddha gained enlightenment, was another magnet for pilgrims. The Patna-Gaya road grew in importance during the colonial period

33. A. Cotton, *Public Works in India: Their Importance* (London: W. H. Allen, 1854), pp. 5–7; Farooque, *Communications in Mughal India,* esp. chap. 2; Varady, "Rail and Road in Awadh," p. 23; O'Malley, "Mechanism and Transport," pp. 234–35.

34. A. Welland, Senior Judge, Patna Court of Circuit, to M. H. Turnbull, Registrar, Nizt. Adlt., June 24, 1815, Bengal Cr. Jdcl. Consltns., Jan. 5 to 19, 1816, Jan. 5, no. 21; Francis Buchanan, *An Account of the Districts of Bihar and Patna in 1811–1812* (Patna: Bihar and Orissa Research Society, 1928), pp. 442–43.

35. During the colonial era the Patna-Gaya road followed a more westerly direction because the focal point was the western suburb of Bankipur, also the political center and residence of the British. The precolonial route intersected Islampur, Tilhara, and Hilsa before continuing to Patna. Welland to Turnbull, June 24, 1815, Bengal Cr. Jdcl. Consltns., Jan. 5, 1816, no. 21. By 1821 most travelers resorted to the road through Jahanabad rather than the route through Hilsa. See C. W. Smith, Magte., Behar, to H. Shakespeare, Suptd., Police, Dec. 22, 1821, Bengal Cr. Jdcl. Consltns., Jan. 2 to 25, 1822, Jan. 11, no. 36.

because it served as the link between Patna and the entire country
south of the Ganges. It also tied together the two principal east-west
highways, the Ganges and the Grand Trunk Road. And its extension
beyond Gaya enabled the British to maintain a colonial presence far
into the interior, into the Chotanagpur plateau.[36]

The Patna-Gaya road was also an important trading route. Registra-
tion of traffic along this road in the late nineteenth century shows that
rice, wheat, and other cereals were transported on it, going both ways,
but mostly from Gaya to Patna; oilseeds from Gaya in substantial
quantities and salt and tobacco in large amounts from Patna also traveled this road. In addition, Patna was the source of European cotton
manufactures. During the pilgrimage season the road turned into "one
of the most crowded thoroughfares" in the region as thousands of people converged on it to reach Gaya.[37]

Although the Patna-Gaya road was the best maintained of the
north-south roads in the region, its condition was not much better than
that of most local roads. The first concerted efforts to ensure its upkeep
as a principal road, or high road, were not made until 1811; by 1814 it
was widened to twenty feet and raised throughout its length. By 1832,
however, the road was reported to be in the "worst possible state," the
result of poor maintenance, bad drainage, and unbridged rivers that
eroded its course. Five years later in 1837, "all traces of the road were
in many places completely washed away, while the drain bridges were
so much injured as to be rendered unsafe, and impracticable." By then
it was said to be "impassable even to foot travellers." At the prodding
of postal authorities, orders were issued in 1850 to build up the road as
a first-class imperial road: to broaden, raise, metal, and bridge it. But
when cost estimates topped eleven lakhs of rupees for this road of 77.5
miles, authorization was not forthcoming. Consequently, an alternative
plan to construct a more modest road was put forth.[38]

36. Capt. H. C. Dickens, late Suptd., Behar Irrigation to Chief Engineer, GOB, no.
226, Jan. 13, 1860, Bengal PWD Procs., Jan.-Feb. 1860, Jan., no. 288; Tucker, "Roads in
Bengal," in Memorials, p. 425; Grierson, Notes on Gaya, pp. 15–16.
    37. S. C. Bayley, Commr., Patna, to Secy., GOB, no. 601F, Jan. 27, 1875, Bengal PWD
Procs., 1873–75, Nov. 1875, no. 13; "Road Traffic from Gya to Patna," Bengal Stats.
Procs., 1876–77, Nov. 1875, no. 20; May 1876, no. 116; Singh, Transport Geography,
pp. 53–54.
    38. Lt.-Col. C. B. Young, Secy., GOB, PWD, to GOI, PWD, no. 396, Jan. 28, 1860,
Bengal PWD Procs., Jan.-Feb. 1860, Jan., no. 289; H. D. H. Fergusson, Commr., Patna,
to Secy., GOB, no. 213, Aug. 16, 1859, Bengal Public Works and Railway Procs., Nov.-
Dec. 1859, Dec., no. 16.

Details regarding other secondary roads add to this picture of their limited utility, selective range, and defective condition. In Patna and Gaya the Patna-Daudnagar road (formerly part of the Mughal highway and subsequently extended to the Grand Trunk Road) and the Patna-Bihar road were the other local roads of importance in the late eighteenth century. (Daudnagar was then a commercial center, a place where the East India Company had both cloth and opium interests.) In the early nineteenth century a crossroad was constructed from Daudnagar to Gaya, and from there east to Nawada. Spanning a distance of more than seventy miles, this road too was used to carry goods between the towns on the Ganges and the south, and it became "much frequented by pilgrims from all parts of India."[39] Additional roads linked Bihar to Gaya, although this route was in poor condition in the early nineteenth century, and Bihar to Nawada, from which the road continued on to Chotanagpur.[40]

In Shahabad the primary local road was the north-south link between the two great military highways. Commenced in the 1780s, it was completed in 1793 with Arrah and Sasaram constituting the nodal points at the two ends of this road. Also completed in 1793 was the road linking Arrah to Nasriganj, an important manufacturing and trading center on the banks of the Son and across the river from Daudnagar. Additional north-south lines were formed in the early nineteenth century: Nasriganj was also the terminus of a road running north from Bhojpur to Dumraon, a road that cut through the heart of Shahabad and proceeded on to Gaya via Daudnagar. As a result, it supported "a large traffic for the transport of goods and grains of various kinds . . . and . . . during the greater part of the year [was filled] with travellers and pilgrims."[41]

Other than these few links, however, most roads, as elsewhere in the region, were little better than common footpaths. And, as elsewhere, good roads were a result of the initiative of enterprising local administrators, or zamindars; similarly, neglect could quickly make the best of roads impassable. Familiar also is this list of problems responsible for

39. A. E. Wilson, Offg. Secy., Behar Ferry Fund Committee, to Offg. Commr., Patna, July 14, 1855, *Correspondence to Ferry Funds*, pp. 103–4; Buchanan, *Bihar and Patna*, pp. 705–6; *GDG 1957*, pp. 312–13.

40. Singh, *Transport Geography*, p. 53; Smith to Shakespeare, Dec. 22, 1821, Bengal Cr. Jdcl. Consltns., Jan. 11, 1822, no. 36.

41. Tayler to Grey, July 10, 1855, *Correspondence to Ferry Funds*, p. 70; Welland to Rawlins, Oct. 3, 1794, Sh. C., vol. 22, 1794–95; Buchanan, *Shahabad*, p. 443.

the poor condition of roads: their location on "low ground [that] flooded during the rains, the badness of the soil at such places, . . . the total want of roads sufficiently raised and bridges adequate to meet every contingency of inundation, and last [but] not least, the poverty of the funds."[42] Small wonder then that, as late as the 1840s, Shahabad was said to lack a "durable internal communication as centrically situated as possible, between the great southern Trunk Road . . . and the river transit . . . [and] a general communication to all the marts and stations in the centre of the District."[43]

In contrast to south Bihar, north Bihar had no major thoroughfares spanning its entire breadth. But by the mid-nineteenth century it boasted a much more extensive and better network of roads than did the south. Its major roads headed toward the Ganges highway, to connect either with Patna or other trade and marketing settlements along the banks of the river. The neighboring areas were yet another focus: the North-Western Provinces, Bengal, and Nepal.

Typifying this pattern were the lines of communication in Saran. Its best road at the turn of the nineteenth century skirted its southeastern edge, a line defined by the Ganges and the headquarters town of Chapra. From Chapra the road continued toward the southeastern tip of the district, from which the city of Patna could be reached by crossing the river. Because Champaran was administered as part of Saran until 1866, its better roads also converged on this area. Of the three main arteries in the late eighteenth century, the high road linked Chapra with the commercial center of Revelganj and the old town of Chirand, from which a ferry crossed the Ganges to link up with the military road to Danapur and Patna and to Arrah. Heading northwest from Chapra, this road continued to Manjhi, from which a road crossed the Gogra into Ghazipur. Chapra was also a key locale along a second road that proceeded north through Mashrak and across the Gandak; from there it continued to Motihari, the principal town in Champaran. A third road linked Chapra to Muzaffarpur. But as in south Bihar in the prerailway era, these roads were little better than fair-weather tracks because they were impassable in the rains, with wa-

42. Sandys to Ravenshaw, no. 6, Feb. 27, 1841, Bengal Cr. Jdcl. Consltns., Oct. 10, 1842, no. 49. Buchanan, *Shahabad,* p. 443, states that Shahabad roads were not as good as those of Patna and Gaya.
43. Sandys to Ravenshaw, no. 6, Feb. 27, 1841, Bengal Cr. Jdcl. Consltns., Oct. 10, 1842, no. 49.

ter waist high in some areas; nor were they adequately bridged over streams. Of these only the Chirand-Chapra-Manjhi road—repaired partly by zamindars and partly by convict labor—was said to be "well calculated for carriages of any description."[44]

This high road through Chapra received the most administrative attention in the early nineteenth century. By 1830 it extended beyond Manjhi to Darauli and then across the Gogra. And from Chirand it extended to Sonepur—the site of the region's most important fair—from which it passed on over the Gandak to Hajipur. Apparently because most traffic—people and goods—from Chapra headed in the direction of Patna and Danapur, on the one hand, and Sonepur and Hajipur, on the other, the thirty-mile stretch between Chapra and Sonepur was kept "in excellent repair—and passable for wheeled carriages, nearly the whole year." The Chapra-Darauli stretch, however, was "wretchedly bad."[45] In addition, crossroads, which began with Chapra at one end of the line and headed into Champaran and Muzaffarpur, were also built. One important connection was between Chapra and Siwan, the second largest town of Saran, from which the road continued through the military cantonment of Baragaon before branching out in opposite directions—toward Gorakhpur and Bettiah, the latter being Champaran's second most important settlement and the home of that district's premier landholder. Another road headed directly north from Chapra to Govindganj in Champaran; still other roads headed northeast and east into Muzaffarpur.[46]

Whereas the Chapra high road provided Saran at least one good road in the late eighteenth century, Champaran had not a single effective road, according to its district collector. Within the first decades of the nineteenth century, however, this district developed many good lines of communication. Much of the impetus for road building in the area came from "military and political objects," specifically the outbreaks of war with Nepal. Thus, roads in the early nineteenth century were built to connect Chapra, Muzaffarpur, and Patna, as well as mili-

44. N. Sturt, Colltr., Saran, to Wm. Cowper, President and Members, BOR, July 4, 1800, S.C., Letters sent 1799–1801, vol. 74; W. W. Hunter, *A Statistical Account of Bengal*, vol. 11, *Districts of Patna and Saran* (London: Trubner and Co., 1877), p. 317; Robert Rankine, *Notes on the Medical Topography of the District of Saran* (Calcutta: Military Orphan Press, 1839), pp. 7–9.

45. Rankine, *Topography of Sarun*, pp. 8–9.

46. W. A. Pringle, Magte., to R. H. Tulloh, Offg. Commr., Feb. 2, 1830, S.C., Letters issued from Saran Magte., 1-4-1828 to 14-3-1830, vol. 138 (also numbered vol. 19).

tary outposts, the cantonment of Mallai in Muzaffarpur, and the cantonments along the Nepal boundary. The growing presence of European indigo planters in the area also proved to be a boon, as planters took an active role in local road-building projects.[47]

By the mid-nineteenth century a number of roads traversed a north-south axis, from Champaran's border with Nepal to its boundary on the Gandak: one road to Chapra intersected Motihari; the Chapra-Govindganj route headed into two directions, one to Motihari, and the other to Sugauli, a village halfway between Motihari and Bettiah, and the site of a military cantonment during the Nepalese war. Roads also branched out from Bettiah to Gorakhpur, to Bagaha, in the sparsely inhabited northwest, to Banjaria and to Sugauli. From there the road continued on through Motihari and became the link to Muzaffapur via Mehsi. The Mehsi-Motihari-Bettiah road, a stretch of almost fifty miles across the southeastern half of the district, was said to be in particularly good condition because of the large number of indigo plantations in the area. Planters apparently kept this road and a few others in this area in "excellent, and . . . in good and substantial repair . . . at their private expense."[48]

The condition of roads in late-eighteenth-century Tirhut, which then comprised Muzaffarpur and Darbhanga, resembled that of Saran. As its district collector noted, they were "in very bad state." Even the basic road connecting Muzaffarpur to Patna—a route that would have passed through the important town of Hajipur—was not easily negotiable. The conditions existing on the road between Muzaffapur and Chapra—a route over which rice from the *terai* (jungly and marshy lands in the foothills of the Himalayas) traveled toward Chapra, along with tobacco, hides, horns, and saltpeter from Darbhanga—exemplify the difficulties faced in this era in using roads for conveying goods. Whereas the Saran portion of this road was kept in relatively good condition, the segment from the Gandak to Muzaffarpur required negotiating swollen streams during the rainy season. Over this twenty-three-mile stretch, a hackery (bullock cart) unloaded and reloaded five times, a process that added two days to the journey.

The impulse for developing a network of roads in Tirhut, as in the case of Champaran, came during the Nepalese war and was supported

47. *CDG 1938*, pp. 102–3.
48. Rankine, *Notes on Saran*, p. 9; Wyatt, *Statistics of Sarun and Chumparun*, pp. 3, 2 (Chumparun).

by the indigo planters. Small wonder then that one road that attracted considerable official attention was the connection between Muzaffarpur and the cantonment of Mallai, located almost at the Nepal border. En route it intersected Sitamarhi, and from Mallai this road continued on to Kathmandu. By the mid-nineteenth century Muzaffarpur was also linked to Patna via Hajipur, a route that required crossing the Ganges at its confluence with the Gandak. Other roads connected Muzaffarpur to Chapra, to Motihari and Sugauli, to Darbhanga (a road that continued on to Purnia), and to Monghyr. Branch roads had also been built from these main roads to other important towns and villages and also to indigo factories.[49]

According to one estimate, the roads in north Bihar were as good as, if not better than, those found anywhere else in Bengal.[50] Better they may have been but they still were not good enough to function as major arteries of trade. Even the east-west highways were not consistently usable in this respect because they could not always support the two- or four-wheeled carts pulled by oxen and buffalo that were the primary vehicles of transport for goods and people on the subcontinent, or they were virtually impassable at least during the rainy season. Few loaded carts traveled on even the major east-west highways during the rainy season. The use of such vehicles was therefore restricted to the main east-west highways or to the short strips connecting the major towns, also generally the roads next best to the principal highways. Especially during the rainy season, when most roads were impassable, people and goods therefore resorted to the rivers because of their "facility and cheapness of transit." The absence or poor condition of connecting crossroads further curtailed the volume of cart traffic.

In the absence of cartable roads, goods were carried as "back loads" on oxen or as baggage conveyed by pack bullocks. Indeed, this was the situation in the early nineteenth century in *pargana* Bihar in Patna (*pargana* is a Mughal unit of revenue administration) and the adjoining *pargana* of Samai in Gaya. Surplus grain from this area was transported by pack bullocks because the local roads could not support

---

49. Wyatt, *Statistical Report of Tirhoot,* pp. 2, 5; Capt. W. Sage, Executive Officer, to Col. R. Tickell, Superintending Engineer, no. 112, June 17, 1835, Bengal Cr. Jdcl. Consltns., Mar. 21 to Apr. 11, 1837, Apr. 4, no. 50; G. P. Ricketts, Colltr., Tirhut, to C. Buller, Secy., BOR, Apr. 20, 1801, and Ricketts to G. Dowdeswell, Secy., Jdcl., Feb. 12, 1802, T.C., Nov. 16, 1796 to Apr. 14, 1812, vol. 195 and Aug. 1800 to Feb. 13, 1802, vol. 197A.

50. Geddes and MacDonnell report.

wheeled traffic.[51] But this form of transportation reduced the cost efficiency of overland transportation: pack bullocks were capable of carrying only one-fourth or one-fifth of the load that a cart could handle
and were capable of traveling only about half the distance covered by a
cart. Conveyance by pack bullocks was, according to one estimate,
twice as expensive as transportation by carts.[52]

Human labor—whether one's own or that of coolies—was also
widely used to carry goods to neighboring markets in the initial century of colonial rule. But this mode of transportation had obvious limitations. As one contemporary observer noted, "20 seers [about 44 lbs]
is the utmost a man can carry, for any distance . . . not to mention the
expenses they are put to, in disposing of the produce."[53]

Thus, in the first century of British rule, the Ganges persisted as the
primary highway of transportation because roads were uneven and
largely in poor condition. No wonder the data for the traffic between
Calcutta and Banaras show that the Ganges accounted for almost ten
times as much tonnage of the trade between those two cities as did the
Grand Trunk Road.[54]

A different statistic shows up, however, if the count is of pedestrian
traffic. An early nineteenth-century estimate indicates that the number
of passengers on boats between Calcutta and Banaras totaled 58,378,
whereas the number of "foot passengers" on the Grand Trunk Road

51. *Notes on the District of Behar* (Calcutta: Military Orphan Press, 184?), p. 2;
Buchanan, *Shahabad*, pp. 441–43. Asses and mules were also used in some areas.
Horses, generally not employed for conveying goods, were utilized by well-to-do Indian
travelers; ponies were available for hire in some areas.

52. Pack bullocks provided special opportunities to small traders who were willing to
pursue this line of transportation. See below, chap. 5. GSR, p. 125; Buchanan, *Bihar and
Patna*, pp. 706–7. According to Buchanan, the carrying capacity of a back load was 250
lbs; the load cost five annas per day and could travel twelve miles. A cart, on the other
hand, could take a load of 984 to 1,230 lbs; a cart with two oxen cost four to eight annas
a day, with three to four oxen twelve annas a day. See also Amalendu Guha, "Raw Cotton of Western India, 1750–1850," *IESHR* 9 (1972): 20–21, for comparable estimates.

53. Rankine, *Topography of Saran*, p. 10. Human muscle was also used to carry passenger loads. Ramgopal Singh Chowdhari, *Rambles in Bihar* (Bankipur: Express Press,
1917), p. 37, writes of porters of Kahar caste lifting his *dholi* (litter) onto their heads as
they waded through waist-deep water. European travelers generally preferred the river
highway; some took to the Grand Trunk Road on carriages; and a few resorted to travel
on horseback. Indians "travelers of some rank" often resorted to *ekkas* (carriages generally drawn by horse or pony or sometimes by two oxen). Grierson, *Notes on Behar*, p. 7;
William Buyers, *Recollections of Northern India* (London: John Snow, 1848), pp. 176, 85.

54. This amounted to 181,000 tons annually, compared to only 19–22,000 tons along
the "military road." By land the cost of freight was three to four pence per ton per mile, by
water the cost was two pence per ton per mile. Sandys to Ravenshaw, no. 6, Feb. 27,
1841, Bengal Cr. Jdcl. Consltns., Oct. 10, 1842, no. 49; Andrew, *Indian Railway*, p. 34.

between those two towns added up to 435,000, or almost eight times
as many. Another 30–40,000 passengers traveled by "conveyances of
various kinds."[55]

In other words, roads, their imperfections notwithstanding, were far
better suited to accommodate foot traffic. And one group who relied
on them—in particular, the Grand Trunk Road and the "New Road"
before it—was the military. Generations of soldiers tramped these highways in the late eighteenth and early nineteenth centuries en route "to
the great military stations . . . principally situated in the north-western
provinces, and especially towards the frontier."[56]

Pilgrims were another conspicuous presence on these roads. Veeraswamy was one of many pilgrims in the prerailway age who stopped
off in Patna en route to the holy city of Gaya. And for those traveling
by the Grand Trunk Road, access to Gaya from either Banaras or Calcutta was via Sherghati, a town intersected by the highway twenty-one
miles south of Gaya. Not surprisingly, Bholanauth Chunder encountered enterprising Gaya "scouts" at Sherghati whose purpose was to direct and entice pilgrim traffic. Beggars of every description also flocked
there in order to take advantage of a "place through which there is not
a day that some men or other have not occasion to pass on to Gaya,
distributing alms in their progress, and moralizing to the world that the
path to heaven lies through the gateway of charity."[57]

Well into the late nineteenth century people from all walks of life
joined soldiers and pilgrims on the roads. Ordinary people, especially
the less well-off, were known to walk for days, even weeks, if necessary, to reach distant destinations. Pedestrians generally covered eight
to ten miles a day, much less than the twenty or thirty miles a litter carried by a team of coolies could manage in a day.[58] In fact, so many peo-

55. An Old Indian Postmaster [Sir William Patrick Andrew], *Indian Railways and Their
Probable Results* (London: T. G. Newby, 1848), p. 35. An 1845 estimate of traffic on the
Grand Trunk Road enumerated 663,644 foot passengers, 20,682 passengers on horseback,
14,106 cart *ekkas*, 177,770 pilgrims, 3,244 *daks* (mail carriers), 988 *palkis* (palanquins)
348 box wallahs, and 130 buggies. It also enumerated: 48,062 laden bullocks; 42,050 unladen bullocks, 3,194 laden camels, 75,682 laden hackeries, 3,420 unladen hackeries,
15,454 laden coolies, 182 elephants, 5,220 laden horses, 1,262 unladen horses, 3,982
banghis (bearers), and 164 empty buggies. W. Dampier, Suptd., to J. P. Grant, Secy., GOB
Apr. 23, 1851, Bengal Jdcl. Consltns., Jan. 2–Mar. 27, 1852, Jan. 9, no. 5.

56. Buyers, *Recollections of India*, p. 84.

57. Chunder, *Travels of a Hindoo*, vol. 1, pp. 224–25; *The Travels of Peter Mundy*,
vol. 2, *Travels in Asia, 1628–1634* (London: Hakluyt Society, 1914), pp. 182–83.

58. Hagen, "Indigenous Society in Patna," pp. 71–72; Varady, "Rail and Road in
Awadh," p. 26; Buchanan, *Bihar and Patna*, p. 706; Buchanan, *Shahabad*, pp. 440–43. See

ple walked to their destinations—the cheapest means of transportation—that British administrators often considered a better class of roads to be unnecessary. For "natives . . . any thing in the shape of a pathway beaten smooth by their naked feet suits them just as well, as a more costly one."[59]

The development of railways changed both the modes of transportation and the circuits along which trade flowed. Introduced to the region in the late nineteenth century, railways rapidly became the most efficient and economical means of transportation. The highest priority in railroad construction, as in road building, was to develop a line of communication linking Calcutta to the rest of north India. The Grand Trunk Road of the railways, the East Indian Railway, was started in 1855, interrupted by the events of 1857, and finally completed in 1862. A second line was added in 1870.

Political and military considerations weighed heavily, as they did in the case of the Grand Trunk Road, in determining the location of the East Indian Railway. So did commercial factors, particularly in forming its Bihar segment. Although the shortest route would have been to follow a direct line between Calcutta and Banaras, a course roughly paralleling the path of the Grand Trunk Road, the initial alignment followed the course of the Ganges, that is, roughly the line of the old Mughal trunk route. From Banaras the East India Railway proceeded along the north of Shahabad and Patna, then continued on to Monghyr and Bhagalpur en route to Calcutta. And like the Banaras-Patna-Calcutta road along the Ganges its major stops were, from west to east, Buxar, Arrah, Danapur, Patna-Bankipur, Fatwa, Bakhtiyarpur, Barh, and Mokameh, before entering Monghyr.

This line conformed well with the pattern of settlements that had emerged to capitalize on the political and economic vitality of the Ganges. The rise of Pataliputra in the distant past was no doubt related to its location on the Ganges. The river also provided a link to the major

---

also my "Peasants on the Move: A Study of Internal Migration in Colonial India," *Journal of Interdisciplinary History* 10 (1979): 53, on peasant migrants who walked from Bihar to Bengal in search of seasonal employment. Charitable establishments offered board and lodgings on well-traveled pilgrim roads. For instance, six miles south of Gaya, a monastery provided free food and a place to stay for weary and poor travelers for three consecutive days; its expenses were supported by its holdings in several villages. Grierson, *Notes on Behar*, p. 7; Buyers, *Recollections of India*, pp. 176, 85.

59. Sandys to Ravenshaw, no. 6, Feb. 27, 1841, Bengal Cr. Jdcl. Consltns., Oct. 10, 1842, no. 49.

settlement of Banaras to the west and the prominent town of Champa to the east. Both Banaras and Patna grew to commercial salience because of their strategic location on the river and because of their roles as out- lets for maritime trade; so did the centers of trade and commerce in Ben- gal that stood on the Ganges or its riverine connections: Murshidabad, Hughli, Calcutta, Dacca, and Satgaon.[60]

The administrative headquarters of virtually every district in the re- gion also lay along the riverbanks or within easy access of the river. Patna, Monghyr, and Bhagalpur are cases in point. So too are the head- quarters of Shahabad and Saran—Arrah and Chapra, respectively. (Ar- rah, although at a distance from the river in recent centuries, formerly overlooked the river when it followed a different course.) Before the rise of Patna, Hajipur, near the confluence of the Gandak and Ganges, was the political and commercial hub of the area as well as the seat of the governors of Bihar in the early Muslim period. The town of Muzaf- fapur, the administrative capital of Tirhut, stands on the banks of a Ganges tributary, the little Gandak. So does Darbhanga, the head- quarters of the district of the same name, which was carved out of Tirhut in 1875.

The Ganges also endowed sites with commercial significance. A prime example is Revelganj (or Godna), which rivaled Patna in the nineteenth century and was a major commercial center in north Bihar in the late eighteenth and the nineteenth centuries. From its command- ing location at the junction of the Gogra and the Ganges, it became the focal point of much of the trade in the north until the late nineteenth century, when the confluence of these two rivers shifted eastward. Buxar in Shahabad was another nodal point on the river, the site of the 1764 battle whereby British victory over the nawabs of Awadh and Bengal secured them the control of Bengal. It stood on the frontier of the East India Company's territories in the late eighteenth century. Un- til the early nineteenth century, a garrison of several hundred men was stationed there, the Buxar fort occupying a high bluff overlooking the river. In Patna district, other than the city of Patna the secondary cen- ters along the river were Danapur, also the site of a military canton-

60. Diwakar, *Bihar through the Ages,* pp. 181, 244; Bernstein, *Steamboats on the Ganges,* pp. 13–14; Naqvi, *Urban Centres in India,* pp. 97–98. See also below, chap. 2, regarding Patna's role as the central place of the region.

ment; Fatwa, a place known for its weaving industry; Barh, a center of country trade; and Mokameh.[61]

Political and military interests, paramount in developing this "more northerly course" aimed at tying together the primary towns of south Bihar as well as providing ready access to north Bihar, therefore fitted in well with the commercial advantages so vital for the financial viability of the East Indian Railway: "[T]he first object of the railway from a commercial point of view, was to secure traffic, [and therefore] it was most desirable that these towns should be served. They were the marts for the disposal of the produce of the adjoining districts, including the trans-Ganges districts, which were then, of course, without railroads of any kind. It was more necessary to open out this part of the country."[62] A second thoroughfare across south Bihar was developed in 1900, when the Grand Chord line between Mughalsarai (near Banaras) and Calcutta was inaugurated. Taking a more southerly route—almost paralleling the course of the Grand Trunk Road—it intersected Gaya, then proceeded over the Son to Dehri-on-Sone, and from there crossed the Karamnasa to connect with Mughalsarai.[63]

Rail lines were also laid along a north-south axis. The Patna-Gaya Railway, completed in 1876, followed the pattern of road building in linking Patna to Gaya. Another such connection was forged between Arrah and Sasaram in the early twentieth century. In both instances these north-south lines were important, not only because they linked major towns but also because they tied together towns that were junctions on the primary rail highways, the East Indian Railway and the Grand Chord line. Another feature of the development of railways that paralleled the pattern of road building was their focus on Chotanagpur. In contrast to the earlier objectives of conquest and consolidation of control, however, the late-nineteenth-century convergence on the southern plateau was aimed at tapping the mineral wealth of the area.[64]

61. Havaladara Tripathi, *Bihar ki Nadiyam* (Patna: Bihar Hindi Granth Academy, 1977), pp. 1–118; *SDG 1930*, pp. 131–34, 149–51; *PDG 1924*, pp. 199–200, 207–9, 217; *ShDG 1906*, pp. 126–31; 133–35; GOBi, *Bihar District Gazetteers, Purnea* by P. C. Roy Chaudhury (Patna: Secretariat Press, 1963), pp. 754–59.

62. G. Huddleston, *History of the East Indian Railway* (Calcutta: Thacker, Spink, and Co., 1906), p. 50; Nalinaksha Sanyal, *Development of Indian Railways* (Calcutta: University of Calcutta, 1930), p. 31. Hurd, "Railways," p. 742, refers to "humanitarian" considerations in the placement of railway lines.

63. *GDG 1957*, pp. 244–45; *ShDG 1906*, pp. 100–1; Huddleston, *East India Railway*, pp. 142–43; Andrew, *Indian Railways*.

64. Singh, *Transport Geography*, pp. 55–75.

Railway links were also developed to tie major junctions on the rail highways to important settlements in the interior or to junctions on other rail lines. A branch line between Mokameh junction and Mokameh ghat fulfilled the latter function because it connected up with the Bengal and North-Western Railway running across north Bihar, as did the Bankipur-to-Digha-ghat branch line. The latter, however, required taking a ferry steamer to cross the Ganges and then linking up with the same railway. Branch lines in Patna tied Fatwa to Islampur, twenty-seven miles away, and Bakhtiyarpur to Bihar and Rajgir. The South Bihar Railway, completed in 1895, connected Gaya to Nawada, and the latter to Lakhisarai in Monghyr. Another line was constructed in 1909 between Barun, on the Son River, and Daltongaj in Palamau district; and yet another in 1906 between Gaya and Dhanbad. The Dehri-Rohtas Light Railway, a short line of twenty-four miles in Shahabad, ran between Dehri-on-Sone and Akbarpur.[65]

Railways followed the routes established by roads in another respect as well: the lines spanning the breadth of the region came first. And because the great rail thoroughfares received priority—and their routes traversed south Bihar—railways, except for the Darbhanga State Railway, were not introduced to north Bihar until the 1880s. The line between Darbhanga and Bajitpur on the banks of the Ganges opposite Barh was built in 1874 at the prompting of the great estate of Darbhanga. Subsequently, under the sponsorship of the Bengal and North-Western Railway several additional lines were built linking all the north Bihar districts. One line, completed in 1883, connected Semaria Ghat on the Ganges with Bettiah. In between it cut across the southeastern part of Muzaffapur, intersecting the town of Muzaffapur before proceeding on to Mehsi, Motihari, Sugauli, Bettiah, and points farther north. Another line, which constituted the main line of the Bengal and North-Western Railway in Saran, entered from Gorakhpur into Mairwa, from which it continued to Siwan and Chapra and then on to Sonepur. From there it crossed the Gandak by bridge and continued to Haijipur, and from there to Katihar in Purnia. Tracks laid between Hajipur and Muzaffapur connected these two branches of the railway. Another line proceeded due north from Samastipur in Darbhanga and passed through Darbhanga on the way to Kamtaul and Sitamarhi, with the terminus in Bairagnia. In the early twentieth century this line was extended

65. PDG 1924, pp. 131; GDG 1957, pp. 244–45; ShDG 1924, pp. 116–17.

from Bairagnia into Champaran, where it passed through Raxaul and Bagaha into Gorakhpur, a route that cut across the entire northern rim of that district. A short line between Sugauli to Raxaul linked two railway lines in Champaran; Raxaul, on the frontier of Nepal, became the junction for the railway coming down from that country.[66]

Railroad construction had the effect of sparking a boom in road building. The impetus to improve the existing system was generated, as in the initial century, by the dynamo of "political and military objects," now stoked by the events of the Mutiny/Rebellion of 1857. And with railways regarded as the major mode of transportation, the late-nineteenth-century policy of constructing roads was driven by the urgency to lay feeder roads directing overland traffic to the stations of the rail lines.[67]

The famines of 1874–75 and 1896–97 were critical moments in road building too: roads were constructed as a major project of famine relief activity. Also of significance was the Road Cess (tax) Act of 1875, which established a fund for the construction of roads, especially their metaling and bridging. A clear picture of these developments can be gained by comparing the 1861 roads with later descriptions. In 1861 Saran had 895 miles of roads, Champaran 477, Tirhut 1,078, Shahabad 495, Gaya 436, and Patna 316. Many lacked bridges, and almost all of them were unmetaled, except for the stretch of 54 miles of the Grand Trunk Road through Gaya, a short strip of 7 miles between Revelganj and Chapra, and two brief portions of 10 and 6 miles connecting Maner to the military station of Danapur and Patna to Fatwa, respectively.[68]

Beginning slowly in the 1870s, when the better roads in Saran were still primarily confined to the vicinity of towns, the district gradually accumulated 1,150 miles of district roads and 1,419 miles of village roads by 1928–29. Of these, 234 miles were metaled. A similar spurt undertaken during the famines of the late nineteenth century eventuated in a total of 1,081 miles for Champaran by 1906, and more than 2,300 miles by the 1930s; 91.5 miles of these roads were metaled.

Equally impressive gains can be documented for other areas. By 1875 Muzaffapur, benefiting from the road building of 1874, already held 719 miles of roads. By the turn of the twentieth century its roads extended

66. W. W. Hunter, *A Statistical Account of Bengal*, vol. 13, *Tirhut and Champaran* (London: Trubner and Co., 1877), pp. 121–24; *CDG 1938*, pp. 103–4; *SDG 1930*, p. 95; *MDG 1907*, pp. 108–9.

67. Varady, "Rail and Road in Awadh," pp. 41–42.

68. Suptd., Roads to Fergusson, Commr., Apr. 15, 1861, P. C. Basta 237, Important Bundles Jdcl. Dept., Alphabet S-Z; Lal, "Transport in Ghaghara Gandak," 14–34.

more than 1,769 miles, of which 82 were metaled, and 543 comprised
village roads. Darbhanga's road building followed a similar trend. The
648 miles counted at its formation in 1875 increased more than threefold
by 1905–6, when it had a total of 1,953 miles of unmetaled road,
52 miles of metaled road, and another 766 miles of village roads.[69]

Statistics paint a comparable picture for south Bihar. By the first
decade of the twentieth century Shahabad boasted 181 miles of metaled, 253 miles of unmetaled, and 882 miles of village roads. In addition to the Grand Trunk Road, which had been metaled in 1861–62, the
other metaled roads included the Buxar-Arrah portion of the Banaras-
Patna military road and the 61-mile-long Arrah-Sasaram road. By the
1920s the total mileage of the district's roads exceeded 2,000.

From a total length of 469 miles in the 1870s, Patna's roads in the
early 1920s increased to 157 miles of metaled and 455 miles of unmetaled roads; another 756 miles were village roads. But, as in the
eighteenth and early nineteenth centuries, these lines of communication
focused on the city of Patna. Therefore the western part of the district
had a far better network of roads than the center or the eastern part.[70]

Great strides in road building were also made in Gaya, particularly
during the famine of 1874. By 1906 the district had acquired 30 metaled
roads, 69 unmetaled roads, and 193 village roads, comprising 163, 715,
and 628 miles, respectively. Another 67 miles of metaled and 168 miles
of unmetaled roads were administered by the Public Works Department.
Not only had the district acquired the most mileage in terms of metaled
roads—much of this representing its 68-mile leg of the Grand Trunk
Road—but it had also developed links between the major settlements in
the interior. In addition to the roads extending from Gaya to the Grand
Trunk Road, to Daudnagar, and to Sherghati, new lines of communication had been established both in the north and the south, between Jahanabad and Arwal, and between Rajauli and Nawada, respectively.[71]

In the course of overcoming the long-reigning "tyranny of distance"
in the region, the rise of railways, tied to a growing network of roads,
also precipitated the decline of water transportation. Their speed and reliability, as well as their competitive prices, increasingly made them the
prime mode of transportation. By the early 1870s they had already

69. *MDG 1907*, p. 107; *CDG 1938*, p. 103; *SDG 1930*, pp. 96–97; *DDG*,
pp. 109–11.

70. *PDG 1924*, pp. 130–31; *ShDG 1906*, pp. 99–100; GOBi, *Bihar District
Gazetteers, Shahabad* by P. C. Roy Chaudhury (Patna: Secretariat Press, 1966), p. 365.

71. *GDG 1957*, p. 237.

sharply curtailed the flow of goods along the roads, a trend that was evident in the rapidly declining traffic on the Grand Trunk Road.[72] And
by the end of that decade, railways accounted for 54 percent of the import and export trade of the region; river transportation, in comparison,
carried 39 percent and roads the remaining 7 percent. Information gathered from traders themselves confirm this growing dependence on railroads. According to the wholesale dealers of Arrah a substantial portion
of their trade in grains and piece goods was transacted by rail in
1883–84. Even those goods that were sent along the canals were destined for the railways. Similarly, spring wheat, grown in north Shahabad
for export and formerly transported by boats, was increasingly shipped
to Patna or other stations from which it was carried away by rail. Thus,
by the early 1880s, the district's "exports and imports by road" were
described as "not large" to "inappreciable. Some trade passes by the
Grand Trunk Road . . . mainly in ghee and other supplies for the city
[Banaras], and some between Sasseram and Chota Nagpore."[73]

By the turn of the twentieth century, railways virtually monopolized
the trade of the region. In the five years between 1900 and 1905, 99.9
percent of the imports and 99.5 percent of the exports of Gangetic Bihar
were carried by rail; water transportation made up the remaining fraction. With the development of railways, Bihar was bypassed, a situation
mirrored by the experiences of the city of Patna, which also owed its
primacy to its strategic location on the river highway.[74] The extent to
which this city served as the central place of the region from the late-
eighteenth-century age of "revolution" onward and maintained that position in the colonial period is the focus of the opening episode of the
next section, which constitutes the heart of this bazaar narrative. Let us
turn first to the Patna historian Sayyid Ghulam Husain Khan Tabatabai.

72. Col. F. P. Layard, Superintending Engineer, Bihar, to Offg. Chief Engineer, Bengal,
no. 354, Jan. 31, 1872, Bengal PWD Procs., 1873–75, Jan. 1873, no. 63.
      73. AGRPD 1883–84, p. 45; Report on the Internal Trade of Bengal for the Year
1877–78, pp. 72–91. By the mid-1880s, in the neighboring North-Western Provinces,
"the last vestiges of competition from traditional transporters in long-distance commerce
has [sic] been overcome and railway freight rates had fallen to low levels." By this date
railways were exerting a considerable influence over economic changes in the province.
Derbyshire, "Economic Change and Railways," p. 528. Contrast with Awadh, where a
better system of roads existed and where railways apparently were not as successful in
competing with roads. The evidence, however, is more compelling for the initial decades
of the late nineteenth century and more persuasive regarding passengers than goods. See
Varady, "Rail and Road in Awadh," chap. 4.
      74. AGRPD 1892–93, p. 22; AGRPD 1882–83, pp. 32–33; Sunil Kumar Munsi,
Geography of Transportation in Eastern India under the British Raj (Calcutta: K. P.
Bagchi and Co., 1980), pp. 108–11.

CHAPTER 2

The "City of Discontent"

Patna in the Age of "Revolution"

The city of Patna: what better way to begin this bazaar narrative than
with the central place of the region, and what better way to recount its
initial colonial career beginning in the eighteenth-century age of "revolution" than to turn to a map drawn by Sayyid Ghulam Husain Khan
Tabatabai (1727–28 to 1797–98), who lived in that era as both observer and participant. His magnificent, multivolume chronicle—familiar to subsequent generations as *The Seir Mutaqherin, or View of Modern Times*—has much to say about the *inqilab,* or revolution, of the
eighteenth century, which led to the decline of the Mughal Empire, the
rise and fall of the successor state of the nawabs of Bengal, and the triumph of the East India Company in north India.[1] Many other contemporary voices, Indian and British, also represent the tumultuous events
of the times as a revolution or an upheaval, not in the sense of a social
revolution but as "a change in rulers, a change of dynasties, a reversal

---

1. E.g., see *Seir,* vol. 3, p. 161. The four-volume history—written in Persian in the
early 1780s and translated into English as early as 1789—covers the period from 1707 to
1782. See M. A. Rahim, "Historian Ghulam Husain Tabatabai," *Journal of the Asiatic
Society of Pakistan* 8 (1963): 117–29. The date of Ghulam Husain's death is a matter of
some controversy. I have used 1798–99, the date given in R. M. Tilghman, Secy., BOR,
to Holt Mackenzie, Secy., May 2, 1823, Bengal Rev. Consltns., June 12–19, 1823, June
19, no. 23.

of luck or fate" resulting in "a destruction of the old economic order, a distortion of the old social order."[2]

To add context to these voices and to fill in their silences, I have also drawn on colonial records. As the historian of *Modern Times* was aware—the "English" themselves referred to him as "the historian" (an appellation intended to distinguish him from his namesake who was the landholder of Sherghati)[3]—his "English" followed "some practices" that were novel for his countrymen, such as their "custom" of gathering information: "counting the inhabitants of every town and city, and examining how much they may have earned, and how much spent; how many are dead, and how many are their children and how many their old men."[4] Such data collection about the Other, a critical imperative in the development of the colonial state, centered on a series of "investigative modalities" relating to "the observational, the historiographic and the museological" as well as the "survey," "enumerative," "surveillance," and "sanitary" modalities. Each of these was vital to the collection "of a body of information, needed in a governing project."[5]

By locating contemporary local voices in the socioeconomic setting that can be sketched from the colonial documentation project, this chapter intends to look both at the poetics and politics of the revolution as articulated in contemporary written texts and at its effects on the human and physical landscape as represented in the lived text that was the city of Patna.[6] The initial focus here is on the experiences of the elite inhabitants of Patna, whose downfall was lamented and proclaimed by many voices. Indeed, to follow the leads furnished by Ghulam Husain and his contemporaries is to converge on three major developments defining the "modern times" of the city: the diminution in power and influence of its elite, the rise in power of zamindars, or land-

---

2. Frederick Louis Lehmann, "The Eighteenth Century Transition in India: Responses of Some Bihar Intellectuals," Ph.D. diss., University of Wisconsin, 1967, pp. 18–19, 170; P. J. Marshall, *New Cambridge History of India, II, 2, Bengal: The British Bridgehead, Eastern India 1740–1828* (Cambridge: Cambridge University Press, 1987), p. 1.

3. Thomas Law, Colltr., Gaya, to S. Charters, Pres. and Members, Calcutta Committee, Sept. 3, 1785, Bengal Rev. Consltns., Feb. 2–23, 1786, Feb. 2, no. 146

4. *Seir,* vol. 3, p. 162. To rephrase this in Said's terms, Orientalism is predisposed to "engage in the particularizing and dividing of things Oriental into manageable parts." *Orientalism,* p. 22. Also see Arjun Appadurai, "Number in the Colonial Imagination," in *Postcolonial Predicament,* chap. 10, for a discussion of the uniquely colonial character of "enumerative strategies."

5. Cohn, "Anthropology of a Colonial State."

6. Useful here and in other sections are the ideas of Peter Stallybrass and Allon White, *The Politics and Poetics of Transgression* (Ithaca: Cornell University Press, 1986).

holders, and the economic decline of the city and the region as a result of changes—termed deindustrialization by some scholars—that had dire consequences for the livelihood of large numbers of ordinary men and women as well. A scrutiny of these developments highlights the current historiographical debate about the kind of rupture colonial rule generated in the fabric of South Asian society, culture, and economy.[7]

To what extent these developments can be discerned by tracing the career of the city of Patna as the central place of the region forms another focus of this chapter. In part this requires surveying its changing relationship with its hinterland, as the region and subcontinent became incorporated into an expanding world system, and in part it entails focusing on the city itself—its built environment. To locate this historically, I will contextualize Ghulam Husain's view of his "modern times" by extending his history backward and forward in time, to the precolonial era as well as to the colonial period that he did not live to witness.

The ostensible purpose of Ghulam Husain's *Modern Times* was to provide "an insight into the phenomena of the Almighty Artist's full powers, and a glimpse into the most glorious part of the Creator's performance"; it also aimed at offering the "public at some distant time hereafter, an idea of the preceding reigns; and to prevent his being stopped short, as by a chasm, on discovering that links are wanting from the chain of past events."[8]

Revelation and genealogy—in other words, history—were the underlying principles of this work. Apprenticed to the same master narrative, both principles served to outline an identical political plot, tracing the fall of the old order of the historian's countrymen and coreligionists and the rise of the lineage of the Company, or British Raj. And as a historian who preferred to retell events that he had personally witnessed or heard about, Ghulam Husain constructed his "chain of past events" along a narrow "idea of preceding reigns." His history opens with high drama: the death in 1707 of the last great Mughal emperor, Aurangzeb, which engendered a war of succession over the throne in Delhi, and the emergence of a host of regional contenders in the provinces.[9]

Lacking a *longue durée* perspective, Ghulam Husain's *Modern Times* ignores earlier "revolutions," thus leaving in the dark the many up-

---

7. For a discussion of this debate, see Bayly, *Indian Society,* pp. 1–6.

8. *Seir,* vol. 1, pp. 24–25.

9. Ibid., p. 1. The geographical focus of his work is also restricted, essentially confined to his home province of Bengal, which then included Bihar.

heavals that the region had experienced during "preceding reigns," as well as the long career of Patna.[10] Nevertheless, its past as the ancient capital, Pataliputra, formed part of the historical consciousness of the eighteenth and early nineteenth centuries: a site of remembrance although not as yet a site of archaeology. Buried under layers of history, the Pataliputra of ancient greatness had to await the archaeologist's spade in the late nineteenth and early twentieth centuries. Only with the coming of the "museological modality" could it surface as a physical site; and even then it was excavated at the outskirts of the "modern" city, an appropriately distant, ghostly reminder of an almost irrecoverable past.[11]

Like eighteenth-century Patna, Pataliputra was a riverine city. However, unlike Ghulam Husain's Patna, it was situated not only on the Ganges and the Son, but near the confluence of the Gogra and Gandak as well. Its centrality was also sustained by a hinterland that had long enjoyed agricultural prosperity and a high population density. From the sixth century B.C.E. until the beginning of the Christian era, the kingdom of Magadh (roughly Patna and Gaya districts) constituted the major center of power in north India: five successive dynasties based in this area formed in these centuries supraregional or pan-Indian empires. A more productive resource base enabled the Gangetic plain generally and the Magadh area specifically to exercise hegemony over the rest of the subcontinent in the ancient period.[12]

From the very outset the rise of Patna as a central place was tied to a political act: the establishment by a Magadh ruler of a fort in the village of Patali in the fifth century B.C.E. Pataliputra emerged from this site to become the capital of the Mauryan dynasty in the fourth century B.C.E. and the core of the first centralized empire under King Ashoka, who transformed the dynasty into an all-India empire.[13] Although still

10. The *longue durée* approach favored by the Annales school of historians looks at structures over the long term in order to highlight "the continuities, the immobilities, the structures." Fernand Braudel, *On History*, trans. Sarah Matthews (Chicago: University of Chicago Press, 1980), p. 122; E. LeRoy Ladurie, *The Territory of the Historian*, trans. Ben and Sian Reynolds (Chicago: University of Chicago Press, 1979).

11. B. P. Sinha and Lala Aditya Narain, *Pataliputra Excavation, 1955–56* (Patna Directorate of Archaeology and Museums, 1970), pp. 6–7; Manoranjan Ghosh, *The Pataliputra* (Patna: Patna Law Press, 1919). The first concerted attempts to locate the city were made by Major Rennell in the 1780s.

12. Joseph E. Schwartzberg, ed., *A Historical Atlas of South Asia* (Chicago: University of Chicago Press, 1978), pp. 254–59; Ahmad, *Bihar Geography*, p. 210.

13. Diwakar, *Bihar through the Ages*, pp. 186–89; B. P. Sinha, "Social and Economic Conditions (Mauryan Period)," in *Comprehensive History of Bihar*, vol. 1, 1, pp. 692–93. See also Gideon Sjoberg, *The Preindustrial City: Past and Present* (New York: Free Press,

at the heart of an empire under the Guptas (ca. 320–647 C.E.), it diminished in importance during this era because the center of gravity of north Indian power shifted westward toward Banaras. The breakup of the empire into many kingdoms, each with its own strategic central place, added to this growing peripheralization of Magadh. Pataliputra's star, tied as it was to the careers of its political masters, faded after almost a millennium of brilliance. The locus of power continued to migrate westward, eventually coming to rest in the Delhi-Agra region, where it has remained for almost the last five centuries, except for much of the colonial period discussed here, during which Calcutta was the capital of the empire.[14]

Ghulam Husain's history is also silent on the fate of Pataliputra from the time of the Guptas to the initial Muslim presence in the region, a historical "chasm" that has remained largely unfilled because of a paucity of information. Muhammad Bakhtiyar Khalji's successful conquest of the region at the end of the twelfth century extended Turkish rule into the area, but the new rulers shifted their base from the town of Bihar (also known as Biharsharif) to Lakhnauti (Malda district) in Bengal. In the thirteenth and fourteenth centuries the region was a contested frontier area, the object of political and military jockeying between the sultans of Delhi and the independent kings of Lakhnauti. The rise of the kingdom of Jaunpur (North-Western Provinces) in the fifteenth century added another player to the conflict. Throughout much of this period (1206–1526) Patna was a secondary settlement, subordinated to the town of Bihar, whose primacy was acknowledged by the fact that the entire province was named after it.[15]

Nor does the historian of *Modern Times* identify the "preceding reigns" that led to the rebirth of Pataliputra as Patna, an omission that is all the more glaring because the monuments of his age were conspicuous relics of the remembered and quotidian landscape of the eighteenth century. Although the rise of the Mughals in the early sixteenth century led to the formation of a subcontinent-wide empire centered in

---

1960), p. 68, on the close relationship between growth in preindustrial cities and the "consolidation or extension of a political apparatus, be the result a kingdom or an empire."

14. Schwartzberg, *Historical Atlas*, pp. 258–59.

15. Qeyamuddin Ahmad, "Aspects of the Historical Geography of Medieval Bihar," and Jagdish Narayan Sarkar, "Economic Life in Early Medieval Bihar, 1206–1526," in *Comprehensive History of Bihar*, vol. 2, part 1, ed. Syed Hasan Askari and Qeyamuddin Ahmad (Patna: Kashi Prasad Jayaswal Research Institute, 1983), pp. 1–11, 445.

north India, Bihar was initially only nominally under their government. Different groups of Afghans carved out regional kingdoms in eastern India that effectively resisted the direct control of Delhi. By 1540 the most notable of these kingdoms, under the leadership of Sher Shah, had managed to wrest control of much of north India from the Delhi rulers. During his short-lived Sur dynasty, Pataliputra emerged as "Pattana"—meaning a place of commercial importance, a mart—and gained ascendancy over the town of Bihar. Sher Shah built a fort to encompass the city; its extant eastern and western gates stand a mile and half apart. Mughal victories over his heirs eventually led to the imposition of direct Mughal rule over Bihar by the 1570s: this new political reality was reflected in the organization of the region as one of the provinces (*subahs*) of the empire in 1580.[16]

With Delhi wearing the crown during the Mughal period, Patna became the seat of the region. Abdul Latif compared it favorably in 1608 with his prosperous hometown of Ahmedabad in western India. Noting that it had supplanted the town of Bihar and become the capital and residence of the Mughal governor, he termed it the "best [city] of the province.... All kinds of articles needed ... for food and clothing are twice or thrice as cheap and abundant here as in other places. In truth, it is a place fit to live in; hence many traders and comfort-loving men have chosen it for their homes. In no other city of India can be seen so many men of Iraq and Khurasan, as have taken up their residence here."[17]

In the seventeenth and eighteenth centuries Persians, Central Asians, and Armenian traders were active in the city, as were members of several business communities, including Khatris from the north and Jains from the west. The well-known eighteenth-century banking house of Jagat Seth had its beginnings in Patna in the seventeenth century. Banarsidas, the early-seventeenth-century Jaunpur merchant, made both Patna and Banaras major stops on his business circuit.[18]

Missing from Ghulam Husain's "chain of past events" is also a "link" about his so-called English who appear suddenly in the 1756–57

---

16. Jagadish Narayan Sarkar, "Patna and Its Environs in the Seventeenth Century—a Study in Economic History," *JBRS* 33 (1947): 126; Lehman, "Eighteenth Century Bihar," p. 22; Qeyamuddin Ahmad, *Corpus of Arabic and Persian Inscriptions of Bihar (A.H. 640–1200)* (Patna: K. P. Jayaswal Research Institute, 1973).

17. Cited in Jadunath Sarkar, "Travels in Bihar, 1608 A.D.," *JBORS* 5 (1919): 598–99.

18. Banarsidas, *Ardhakathana*, p. 67; Surendra Gopal, *Patna in 19th Century* (Calcutta: Naya Prokash, 1982), p. 2; Naqvi, *Urban Centres in India*, pp. 92–94.

phase of his history and who are already powerful enough to intrude dramatically onto the Bengal stage to play a critical role in the overthrow of its nawab, Siraj-ud-daula. Yet long before this Plassey Revolution—made possible by the British victory over the nawab at the famous Battle of Plassey in 1757—established the British as a major political force in the region, Europeans had been making inroads into the regional economy. In fact, a considerable portion of the Bengal economy was in European hands in the early eighteenth century. Rather than view this development as indicating the beginning of deindustrialization, some scholars have proposed that direct European intervention and involvement in textile production "was part of a process, later transferred to agriculture, which led to the incorporation of South Asia within the world economy and the establishment of British colonialism."[19]

Europeans had been knocking on Patna's commercial doors as early as the late sixteenth century. By 1620 the English East India Company had set up a factory to purchase calicoes and to process raw silk obtained from Bengal. Although the factory was closed within a year, the Company returned in 1632, when Peter Mundy, accompanied by an Indian broker, sought a market for quicksilver and vermilion in Patna, with the goal of investing the returns in the purchase of articles of trade. Notwithstanding this second failed attempt, the Company organized a branch factory at Patna in 1657, which became its outlet for local trade. Increasingly, the Company's main focus was saltpeter, an essential ingredient in the manufacture of gunpowder, which was collected in Patna from the entire region and which was of interest to several European powers; it also sold broadcloth, lead, and quicksilver.[20]

Patna also enjoyed a reputation in the seventeenth century as a center of trade in cotton and silk goods; the hinterland within a fifty-mile radius of the city was engaged in cotton production. It was particularly well-known for two types of cotton cloth: "emmerties" and "calicoes." Manucci found many merchants in Patna's "bazaars" in 1683 trading in fine white cloth and other products. Silk was produced locally at

19. Jim Matson, "Deindustrialization or Peripheralization?: The Case of Cotton Textiles in India, 1750–1950," in *South Asia and World Capitalism*, p. 215; Marshall, *Bengal*, p. 80.

20. N. N. Raye, *The Annals of the Early English Settlement in Bihar* (Calcutta: Kamala Book Depot, 1927), pp. 65–90; Narayan Prasad Singh, *The East India Company's Monopoly Industries in Bihar* (Muzaffarpur: Sarvodaya Vangmaya, 1980); Sarkar, "Patna in the Seventeenth Century," p. 126.

Baikunthpur, as well as imported from Bengal. Two other valuable products were rice and opium.[21]

Ghulam Husain's Patna had therefore been a rising political and economic center for almost a century and a half before the revolution. Furthermore—although not the focus of his history either—the city had received a considerable fillip in the beginning of the eighteenth century, when Prince Azim-us-Shah, the grandson of Emperor Aurangzeb and the governor of Bengal (including Bihar) in 1703–7, decided to settle in Patna. While his plans to transform it into another Delhi never got off the ground, Patna, now renamed Azimabad after him, prospered, as his courtiers and nobles flocked to the city to live in the presence of their prince. Azimabad, moreover, persisted as the name of the city until the turn of the nineteenth century; it was the name used by Ghulam Husain.

Nor did the declining power of the Mughals put an immediate brake on this pace. On the contrary, with Delhi's hold over the region weakening, Bihar, although subordinated to and "not as wealthy an area" as Bengal, attracted in-migration. Lehmann explains that "a regular flow of nobles, poets, soldiers, Sufi saints, and other people came in from Delhi and other parts.... The result was that the city of Patna blossomed forth as a major center of Mughal culture in the eighteenth century."[22]

Patna became home to one of the so-called regional "bazaar schools" of painting that developed as art patronage in Delhi faded with the decline of the Mughal Empire. According to the family tradition of the Patna *kalam* (school of painters), their roots in the city date to about 1760. They apparently settled in Patna not because it was in the throes of a revolution but because it was a prosperous city offering them the patronage they needed in order to survive as painters. Their paintings, featured in this study, focus particularly on bazaar scenes and festivals, vivid historical vistas that can be only partly evoked from textual

---

21. Raye, *The English in Bihar,* pp. 43–46; A. K. Sinha, *Transition in Textile Industry* (Delhi: Capital Publishing House, 1984), pp. 9–12; A. Sami, "Evolution of Commercial Centres in Patna," *JBRS, L. N. Mishra Commemoration Volume* 63–64 (1977–78): 640–41; Shafaat Ahmad Khan, ed., *John Marshall in India: Notes and Observations in Bengal, 1668–1672* (London: Humphrey Milford, 1927), pp. 23–24.

22. Lehmann, "Eighteenth Century Bihar," pp. 22–23; G. P S., "Patna, during the Last Days of the Mahomedans," *Calcutta Review* 147 (1882): 115. A separate province (*subah*) in the Mughal period, Bihar was absorbed into Bengal in the early eighteenth century.

sources. Supported by both Indian and colonial patrons, this school continued to thrive well into the late nineteenth century[23]—further evidence of the economic vibrancy that characterized the city long after the age of revolution.

Thus the perspective of *Modern Times,* with its focus on the decline of the city, was a backward look at a century that began with Patna reaching new heights of prosperity and prominence as Azimabad, and one that closed with a city seemingly reeling from the shock of the revolution. The retrospective gaze of this historian was therefore circumscribed (as it is for any historian), in part by his "genealogy" as a historian representing a specific moment in time, and in part by his specific personal outlook. As an elite member of "Hindostan"—-the north Indian heartland—and as a Muslim, his concept of revelation and genealogy was shaped by the extraordinary events that had led to the demise of an Indo-Islamic empire and a regional kingdom and the birth of a new power. This turn of events necessarily foregrounded the contradictions stemming from Ghulam Husain's own faith as a Muslim—sometimes specifically as a Shiite Muslim—and from the other religions of the historical actors of his *Modern Times.*[24] To this set of contradictions were added the further complications of his multiple personal and family attachments to, at one time or another, the Mughal Empire, the successor state of Bengal, and, for him personally, the East India Company. Critical of the old order, particularly that of the nawabs of Bengal with whom he had had the most direct contact, he nevertheless lamented its passing because it led to the triumph of the "nation of Hat-wearers." To him, the British were "alien to this country," in his words, "both in customs and manners; and quite strangers to the methods of raising tribute as well as to the maxims of estimating the revenues, or of comprehending the ways of tax-gathering."[25]

23. It is a dying art form now. See my "Visualizing Patna: History and the Patna School of Painting," paper presented at the meeting of the Association for Asian Studies, Los Angeles, Mar. 25–28, 1993.

24. These categories are used here to indicate the multiple layers of identity that defined any person or group in this era, and are not meant to be equated with the communal identities that emerged a century later. See Gyanendra Pandey, *The Construction of Communalism in Colonial North India* (Delhi: Oxford University Press, 1990), pp. 1–22, on the "historical character of 'communalism.'"

25. At the time he wrote his history—early 1780s—he was already a believer in the "permanence" of British rule. *Seir,* vol. 3, p. 162; vol. 2, pp. 155, 231. Rahim, "Ghulam Husain," pp. 125–26, emphasizes his pro-British sympathies; Lehmann, "Eighteenth Century Bihar," pp. 66–91, recognizes the multivocality of his history.

Ghulam Husain was not alone in ruing the social structural ruptures caused by the upheavals of the eighteenth century. Consider the *Shahr-i-Ashob,* or "a poem on a ruined city" or the "city of discontent" written in the 1750s or 1760s by Shah Ayatullah Jauhari (1714?–96) in the style of a narrative poem (*mathnavi*). Its most striking note concerns the fact that "the times are changing, everything is contrary, bearing the impression of changing fortune." "Worthy men, good fortune, prosperity" in the new epoch, he intones, "all are gone from this world. Friendship and love have dwindled, and beastly avarice has increased."[26]

A similar lament was penned by Ghulam Ali Rasikh (c. 1749–1823) in his narrative poem entitled "Description of the Times of Upheaval [*Inqilab*] and Lamentation to Heaven, and a Summary Statement of the Circumstances of the Inhabitants of the Town of Azimabad." His evocation of a "ruined city" describes a time when "the inhabitants... have become men of bad conduct." So rampant was corruption that the "city [had] been visited with [the] cholera epidemic."[27]

Azimabad, in Rasikh's metaphor, formerly a "rose-bed," had been transformed into "a garden of thorns," "a garden...[with] a shockingly different color" where "spring" had "turned into autumn." The poet laments,

Now this garden is leafless, a place of warning; nothing remains of those wonderful days.
There is no opulent man in this garden, no man of wealth to perfume it like a flower.
Everyone is crushed by poverty; everyone is imprisoned in that condition.
Oh, where is the life of luxury and where the strolls in the garden?
Who can think of such pleasures now, and who has the leisure?
All hope for silver and gold is gone; but now the people have yellowish faces and silvery tears.
The formerly wealthy are now all searching for the evening meal; gentlemen of means have become beggars.
Emperor and Ministers have now become paupers; those who were once wealthy do not even get alms today.

26. See Lehmann, "Eighteenth Century Bihar," pp. 154, 140; and pp. 152–54, for a complete translation of all twenty-seven couplets of this poem.
27. Ibid., pp. 173–83; Khan Bahadur Saiyid Zamir-ud-din Ahmad, "Ghulam 'Ali Rasikh,'" *JBRS* 4 (1918): 44–61. Lehmann has rightly attributed this poem to the last years of Rasikh's life. The cholera epidemic referred to in the poem occurred in 1818. See James Jameson, *Report on the Epidemick Cholera Morbus* (Calcutta: A. G. Balfour, 1820), pp. 5–10.

Now it is the dust of the road on the foreheads of people who were once
    covered with jewels from head to toe.
Fine ermine carpets were once theirs to have and hold, who now cannot
    afford even a palm-leaf mat for a bed.
Those who once were gentlemen, with a hundred slave-girls and slave-boys,
    are now selling themselves for life.
Those who enjoyed good fortunes in palaces and mansions now have
    cobwebs for their home.[28]

A "different color" also characterized the condition of agriculture and
commerce. To turn once again to Rasikh's words:

The profession of agriculture also is without lustre, its goals are now
    unattainable.
When does this profession enrich anyone?
It is impossible to flourish in it.
There is the constant danger of drought in it, and where there is flooding,
    it is a destructive typhoon.
Where is there any commercial capital?
There is nothing remaining, except the ready money of life itself.
Now there is a good business only in poverty, and this business proceeds
    only with sighs of despair.
The platform for a commercial shop is gone, for there are neither sellers
    nor buyers.[29]

But was the sense of "ruin" and "discontent" overdetermined by the
fact that the historian and poets had their fingers on the pulse of the
aristocracy but not on that of the rest of their society? And being all
Muslims, were their voices attuned only to the Muslim segment of the
elite? Not that these "facts" necessarily vitiate the "facticity" of their
observations, but surely they heightened the tone of urgency and despair. For the pall that set in toward the close of the eighteenth century
was largely cast over their predominantly Indo-Islamic "garden" of Azimabad.

Small wonder that Jauhari and Rasikh equated the passing of the
aristocracy with a moral and religious breakdown in society. For
Jauhari especially, "ruin" and "discontent" stemmed from the declining position of Islam in the city as a political power but also as a religious faith. And along with displacement came replacement, Islam giving way to a resurgent Hinduism. As Rasikh saw it,

28. Lehmann, "Eighteenth Century Bihar," pp. 174–75; 169.
29. Ibid., pp. 178–79.

God's house is dark. . . .
Look where you will, and in every temple the gongs are sounding;
Few hear the call to prayer and go to the mosque.
The Brahmans, wearing their sect-marks, are respected in these times.
The use of the (Hindu) rosary is common, instead of recitation of the name
    of God.
The cavalry of Lalahs and Babus goes with such a tumult,
That the Subahdar is a Hindu, and a Hindu holds the Diwani.[30]

In Jauhari's estimation, Hindus occupied the center stage and the British were poised in the wings. "Christians are their protectors," he believed, "and they are the protectors of the Christians; The life of Musulmans has fallen into the hands of their two great enemies."[31]

The disparate religious hues in the pictures of "ruin" and "discontent" painted by Jauhari and Rasikh may in part reflect their different moments in time. As the reference to a Hindu *subahdar* (governor) and a Hindu *diwan* (chief officer) suggests, the former's perspective dated back to the mid-eighteenth century, when Janaki Ram and Ram Narayan held high offices in Bihar, the centralized Mughal Empire and its successor state in Bengal appeared to be on the wane, and British power was on the rise. However, by the time of Rasikh's composition—probably sometime between 1818 and his death in 1823—the British were the supreme political power in the subcontinent. Nevertheless, Rasikh, although ever the "opportunist"—he was known to have dedicated some of his verses to the new regime, at one point describing himself as "a great well-wisher of the Company"[32]—is clearly implicitly if not explicitly indicting the existing regime for having transformed his city and his society into a "garden" of "a shockingly different color."

Although both poets took exception to what they perceived as a displacement of the aristocracy, Jauhari's *Shahr-i-Ashob* was decidedly more religious in its lament. Lehmann attributes this distinction to their different personal experiences and background. "Both . . . had their origins in Sufism but Jauhari remained in a Sufi religious establishment in the small town of Phulwari Sharif, while Rasikh joined in the social and literary circles in the big cities."[33]

30. Ibid., p. 154. See below, chap. 3, regarding pilgrimages and *melas* as manifestations of this resurgent Hinduism.

31. Lehmann, "Eighteenth Century Bihar," p. 153.

32. Ibid., p. 163; Muzaffar Alam, "Eastern India in the Early Eighteenth Century 'Crisis': Some Evidence from Bihar," *IESHR* 28 (1991): 70–71.

33. Lehmann, "Eighteenth Century Bihar," p. 169.

The "shockingly different color" apparently affected everyone and everything in the "garden" because of the multiple roles the aristocracy of Azimabad played in the local and regional society and economy by virtue of their power, prestige, and patronage. The decline in aristocratic fortunes cut a wide swath: "Everyone is unemployed. . . . Masters of learning and skill are wandering from door to door with begging bowls. People with skills are heart-sick, there is no business to help them now." Rasikh's catalog of "everyone" included "saints . . . fearfully enduring misfortune," calligraphers "constantly shedding tears upon the writing of their own fate," teachers "fed up with life," poets "cowardly, greedy . . . shameless," advocates no longer "in a flourishing state," physicians "fatigued," and soldiers without even "a toy clay horse" to command; peasants and traders, too, suffered. Poets were especially affected because their livelihood, as Rasikh avers, depended on the patronage of such elites who "controlled government and patronized the arts and trades of the professional and middle classes."[34]

The poetic language of despair thus issued from a specific "discontent": the passing of an ancien régime that supported a natural hierarchy (naturally) headed by an aristocracy. For when "kings" were turned into "beggars," according to Rasikh, the garden was turned "upside down."[35]

But not all "kings" turned into "beggars." Because the imagined revolution of Ghulam Husain and of Jauhari and Rasikh was fundamentally about the passing of a system of rule, specifically an Indo-Islamic order, the change it produced was by no means a social revolution. Rather, its major consequence was a turnover in personnel; a change that targeted in particular a generation of elites—many of whom were Muslims—whose lives spanned the transitional decades of the late eighteenth and early nineteenth centuries. As Kumkum Chatterjee's recent work shows, the "aristocracy" of the region, comprising the highest level of bureaucrats, merchants, and banking magnates, was adversely affected by the upheavals of the eighteenth century. In Azimabad this "aristocracy" consisted of the elite, with its shared status, wealth, respect, and lifestyle, which set it apart from the rest of society.[36]

34. Ibid., pp. 170, 174–79.
35. Ibid., p. 162.
36. "Intimations of Crisis: The Elite of Azimabad-Patna," paper presented at the meeting of the Association for Asian Studies, Boston, Mar. 24–27, 1994; and her forthcoming book on "Merchants, Politics and Society: Eastern India, 1733–1820." Bayly, *Indian*

Contrast this downward trend of the Patna elite with the rise of a "new" aristocracy that Ghulam Husain bore testimony to, both as a historian and as a historical actor caught up in the latter process. His account of this "new" aristocracy also serves as a contrast to Rasikh's dire pronouncement on the decline of the "profession of agriculture":

> Under the English Government the principal Zemindars being now their own masters, and the hinges of all business in their own lands; and having been so lucky as to carry [sic] some favour with their masters; and all this in contrariety to former institutes, which held it as an invariable maxim, to keep them low; these people do now just as they please, and in what manner they please; nor do they make any thing of fighting amongst themselves, and killing and slaughtering their subjects; whilst the Fojdar [head police officer] dares not to quarrel with them, and is even afraid to give them an order, or to revenge the oppressed ones upon those tyrants, or even to reclaim from their hands the property of those travellers whom they have despoiled.[37]

The "overgrowing power of the Zemindars, and . . . their being trusted too much" was a source of great vexation to Ghulam Husain— he considered them an "incorrigible" and "malevolent race" who were "to a man, a refractory, short-sighted, faithless set of people, that mind nothing but present interest, and require always a strict hand." Notwithstanding "rules of old standing . . . [and] the most approved opinions held equally by eminent merchants, as well as by knowing Princes," "English rulers," he believed, treated them indulgently, even equating them with "Zemindars and land-holders of their own."[38]

Personal experience involving the family's holding in *pargana* Japla, no doubt, exacerbated this negative outlook. (Japla, an earlier designation for Hussainabad, was developed by his father (Hedayat Ali Khan), served as the family's place of residence, and was held as an *altamgha,* or rent-free grant.) But by the early 1790s this claim was disputed by the government—as were many other revenue-free grants and estates. The family's grant was eventually revoked because the deed entitling them to the grant was considered a forgery. Their stake in the south-

---

Society, p. 72, attributes the decline of Muslim influence to the "dismantling of Mughal administrative forms . . . [and] the failure of Muslims to participate in the new commercial opportunities which the Company and European private trade had opened up."

37. *Seir,* vol. 3, pp. 181, 182. By *zamindar* he meant, as he explained to Company officials, a "possessor or proprietor of land . . . who pays rent to the . . . ruler, and is equally applicable to every landholder whether possessing a greater or less number of villages or only a portion of a village." "Questions to [and answers by] Golam Hossein Khan . . . ," translated Feb. 29, 1788, Home Miscellaneous, H/Misc/381.

38. *Seir,* vol. 2, pp. 204–5.

western Gaya *parganas* of Siris and Kutumba, which, according to Ghulam Husain, "had been leased out to our family from a great number of years,"[39] also slipped out of their hands and devolved entirely into the possession of the area's long-standing zamindar, Narain Singh. A brief stint in 1774 as *sazawal* (land steward) for the latter's lands set him back financially because the zamindar's "bad conduct" prevented him from managing the estate profitably. Narain Singh, moreover, continued to enjoy his estate (*zamindari*) even though he repeatedly took up arms against the British (for example, by joining the Banaras rebellion of Raja Chait Singh in 1781) and was remiss and recalcitrant in meeting his revenue payments. Jailed by the authorities, he was restored to his "forfeited" *zamindari* upon his release in 1790. As for Ghulam Husain, he was left with only a small portion of the lands that he had formerly leased, worth Rs. 30,381, compensation for a debt owed him by Narain Singh.[40] Small wonder that Ghulam Husain compared the English unfavorably with earlier rulers who granted rent-free lands to "Noblemen, whether Musulmen or Hindoos, and indeed upon any others indifferently, according to their stations and merits, with the hope of further preferment, in proportion to their abilities and exertions in the service."[41]

Ghulam Husain's *Modern Times* ends its history in 1782 but presaged later developments. It foresaw what has now become a familiar theme in South Asian historiography, a story often related as unfolding around the notion of "land-is-to-rule," the idea that ownership or holding of land enabled its owner or titleholder to control land *and* the people occupying and working on the land. Holding of land, in other words, increasingly defined an economic and political as well as a social and cultural relationship. And in its insistent observations on the "overgrowing power of the Zemindars," the Patna historian anticipated the long-term consequences of the Permanent Settlement of 1793

---

39. Ibid., vol. 1, pp. 423–24, vol. 4, pp. 88–89; W. Money, Colltr., to BOR, Apr. 30, 1822, P.C. Records, From Colltr., Bihar, vol. 10, 1822–23; Lehmann, "Eighteenth Century Bihar," pp. 64–70, 92; GOBi, *Bihar District Gazetteers, Palamau* by P. C. Roy Chaudhury (Patna: Secretariat Press, 1961), p. 497. Japla was transferred from Gaya to Palamau in 1871.

40. The revenue assessment of Siris and Kutumba was Rs. 160,450. See A. Seton, Magte., Bihar, to Earl Cornwallis, GGIC, May 31, 1791, Bengal Rev. Jdcl. Consltns., June 3 to July 29, 1791, June 17, no. 1; *GSR*, pp. 14–15; J. Reginald Hand, *Early English Administration of Bihar, 1781–1785* (Calcutta: Bengal Secretariat Press, 1894), pp. 10–14.

41. *Seir*, vol. 3, p. 202.

that fixed the revenue demand of the state in perpetuity and defined the "legal and administrative framework within which agrarian relations were determined . . . until the zamindari abolition acts of the 1950s."[42]

Legally, this settlement established ownership rights in land, proprietary rights that its framers mistakenly expected would provide the impetus to transform zamindars into "improving" English landlords. Politically and administratively, it led to a policy of "control and collaboration" that generated "a close and mutually beneficial relationship" in which the "new regime held the reins of power and authority . . . but also . . . serve[d] as protector of its allies."[43]

As allies, landholders gained the "overgrowing power" that Ghulam Husain anticipated they would if left unchecked to exercise their "mischiefs."[44] Not that the colonial state was weak. On the contrary, over the course of the nineteenth century, it monopolized coercive power through its military and police forces; it also disarmed its subjects, thereby sharply curtailing local "fighting . . . and killing." But its control was strongest in the cities and towns where its institutions and personnel were aggregated; it became more attenuated with increasing distance from its urban centers.

Endowed with political standing in their localities by virtue of their positions as local allies of the colonial state, landholders thus enhanced their roles as local controllers. They also profited under this new system of control and collaboration because their legal rights were developed and protected by the rule of law. In addition, they benefited from having their revenue payments set in perpetuity while their lands continued to increase in value because of the changing land market. Land gained in value and agricultural prices rose, in part the result of growing numbers of people occupying land that reached its limits in terms of cultivation in the late nineteenth century.[45]

42. Ratnalekha Ray, *Change in Bengal Agrarian Society, c 1760–1850* (New Delhi: Manohar, 1979), p. 1; Walter C. Neale, "Land Is to Rule," in *Land Control and Social Structure in Indian History*, ed. Robert Eric Frykenberg (Madison: University of Wisconsin Press, 1969), pp. 3–15.

43. See my *The Limited Raj: Agrarian Relations in Colonial India, Saran District, 1793–1920* (Berkeley and Los Angeles: University of California Press, 1989), pp. 70–89.

44. *Seir*, vol. 2, p. 394. See also my *Limited Raj*, chaps. 3–5, on the system of collaboration existing between the colonial state and local landed magnates.

45. J. F. Richards, James R. Hagen, and Edward S. Haynes, "Changing Land Use in Bihar, Punjab, and Haryana, 1850–1970," *MAS* 19 (1985): 699–732; Stephen Henningham, *A Great Estate and Its Landlords in Colonial India, Darbhanga, 1860–1942* (Delhi: Oxford University Press, 1990); Jacques Pouchepadass, *Paysans de la Plaine du Gange: Le District de Champaran 1860–1950* (Paris: Ecole Francaise D'Extreme-Orient, 1989).

The primary beneficiaries of these new arrangements were the so-called great zamindars and not the overwhelming majority of zamindars occupying a few acres or shares scattered across villages and of varying status and historical standing with whom the Permanent Settlement was concluded. Although exceptions—but significant exceptions they were—these few "principal Zemindars" were significant "hinges of all business in their own lands." Recognized as rajas and maharajas and treated as the state's most significant and influential local connections, these "great" zamindars possessed estates that extended over vast areas and accounted for revenue payments that represented a sizable portion of the local revenue. Their age-of-revolution story—familiar to Ghulam Husain from his own experiences—often involved an initial phase of resistance or even outright rebellion when faced with the revenue demands of the new regime and with its attempts to curb their growing local autonomy. Most eventually came to terms with the new government, which elected to collaborate with these "old landed proprietors" despite their initial opposition and, in some cases, even vigorous rebellion. The most powerful of these local magnates were Darbhanga in Darbhanga, Bettiah in Champaran, Hathwa in Saran, Dumraon in Shahabad, and Tikari in Gaya. Their stories, which can be pieced together from their estate histories and official records, tell of family upheavals of epic proportions but also speak of the riches and power they acquired over the course of colonial rule. A few numbers will suffice to illustrate the case. Darbhanga, the largest of the great zamindars, possessed an estate ranging more than twenty-four hundred square miles and an annual income of approximately 4 million rupees, a scale on a par with many a princely state. Bettiah's eighteen hundred square miles yielding a rental of almost 2 million rupees made it the second largest *zamindari;* Hathwa's property, although small, nevertheless encompassed 1,365 villages, was inhabited by more than 391,000 people, and produced an annual rental of almost a million rupees.[46]

Notwithstanding the ups and downs in the fortunes of some families, zamindars overall enhanced their roles as both local controllers and political connections of the colonial state over the course of the nineteenth century. Their rising profile in the local configuration of government control paralleled the decline of the "aristocracy" of the region, whose

46. Yang, *Limited Raj,* passim, esp. p. 117; Pouchepadass, *Paysans de Champaran,* pp. 265–92; Henningham, *Great Estate in Darbhanga,* chaps. 1–3.

elite positions in Azimabad were undermined by the upheavals of the
eighteenth century. The relatively stronger government presence in
Patna, as well as in the district headquarters towns, also contributed to
this diminution in power and influence of the urban-based elite.

But the emergence of the new landed "aristocracy" in the wake of
the revolution did not completely eclipse the city's bankers and merchants, certainly not their economic prosperity and well-being. Patna
continued to enjoy its reputation as a place of "enormous wealth" well
into the nineteenth century. "Many of the great men of the city are exceedingly rich," states an early-nineteenth-century source, citing as
proof a *durbar* (audience, court) held by Lord Amherst at which "one
of them offered, and it is said gave, a lac of rupees to have his name inserted at the head of the list of native gentlemen who paid their respects to the governor-general."[47]

Although many more "Lalahs and Babus" joined the roster of the
new aristocracy, Muslims remained prominent among the ranks of the
city's aristocratic families. Throughout the nineteenth and early twentieth centuries, the Guzri, or Nawab Bahadur, family stood out as perhaps the richest family in all of Patna. Like many of the "city's"
wealthy, the Nawab Bahadur's fortunes were tied to banking and trade.
The Guzri family also branched out into the land market, investing
heavily in land through purchases and mortgages to become the largest
zamindar among city residents. As bankers, they acted as the underwriters of many a great *zamindari* family, for example, the Bettiah
raj.[48] However, as was the case with most urban-based nouveaux
riches, this Patna family was not counted among the "old landed proprietors" and therefore was not singled out by government to serve as
its local connection, at least not in the areas where the family held
land. Nor were such absentee landholders generally the salient men of
the locality in which they had acquired rights in land. On the contrary,
actual possession of the land itself often continued to be contested long
after property titles had officially changed hands. As Pouchepadass
notes, "[T]he man who purchased land at a public sale after its 'legitimate' owner had been forced to part with it was not unnaturally

47. "Mofussil Stations. No. IV.—Patna," *Asiatic Journal* 10 (1833): 253.
48. E.g., see Account Book (*Jama Karch*), Guzri family, Feb. 23, 1864–Oct. 12, 1871,
which indicates that loans totaling Rs. 409,000 were given to Bettiah. Account book is in
the possession of Sarwar Ali, former Justice, Patna High Court, and descendant of the
Guzri family.

viewed as an intruder and an usurper, unless he managed to compel recognition by force."[49]

Like many other prominent Patna notables of the colonial era, the rise of the Nawab Bahadur family to the ranks of the local aristocracy is a postrevolution story. The Indian episode of these late-eighteenth-century immigrants begins with Persian ancestors who arrived in the northwest in the train of Nadir Shah's invasion (1730s) and subsequently settled in Awadh. Their Bihar chapter opens with Syed Abdullah, who established himself in Patna at the turn of the nineteenth century. Well-off when he first set foot in Bihar, his riches-to-richer story turns on his success at building up his fortune by engaging in money "transactions," in conducting "trades of different sorts," and by assuming the farms of government estates.

Acknowledged as the "principal banker" of the city by local authorities, he served as the spokesman for Patna's elites. When government sought to resume revenue-free lands, he represented the *lakhirajdars* (revenue- or rent-free holders) of Bihar—many of whom were said to be among "the most influential class of persons in the city," personally lobbying the governor-general in Calcutta and taking the lead in submitting petitions against resumption legislation. Although the *lakhirajdars* were unsuccessful in their efforts—as Ghulam Husain had been four decades earlier—to hold on to the titles that government believed many bankers and moneylenders had obtained from the original owners, this campaign rallied crowds of four to five thousand people at the Patna collector's office and generated all kinds of rumors about the religious motives underlying government intentions and actions.[50]

By the time of Syed Abdullah's death, there was in Patna, in his grandson's words, "no one equal to him in wealth."[51] His annual income was described by one source as nearly amounting to two hundred thousand rupees. His four sons, Mehdi Ali Khan (1793–1850), Mohammad Ali Khan (1797–1826), Kasim Ali Khan (1806–62), and Lutf

49. "Land, Power, and Market: The Rise of the Land Market in Gangetic India," in *Rural India*, p. 84.

50. One rumor that ignited concern was that Patna's mosques were about to be pulled down. It apparently gained currency because many *lakhiraj* grants were dedicated to the support of religious establishments, both mosques and temples. J. B. Elliott, Commr., Patna, to H. Mackenzie, Secy., Territorial Dept., July 6, 1829, Bengal Rev. Consltns., Aug. 4 to Sept. 15, 1829, Aug. 25; "Petitions of certain inhabitants of Bengal, Bihar . . . to Lord Bentinck," Bengal Rev. Consltns., Apr. 22-May 9, 1929, May 19, no. 3.

51. Translation of letter of Wilayet Ali (grandson of Syed Abdullah), n.d., P.C. Double Lock Box no. 5, 190?.

Ali Khan (1812–90), continued to prosper, as did Mehdi Ali Khan's son, Wilayet Ali Khan (1818–99). In the early 1850s the family business was divided up (*batwara*), each of the four branches receiving Rs. 1,840,500. In the wake of the division, separate *kothis* (banking houses) were established by Kasim Ali, Lutf Ali, and Wilayet Ali in partnership with Mohammad Bakur Khan (son of Mohammad Ali). And the family fortunes continued to soar: when Lutf Ali died in 1890, he left Rs. 3.2 million in cash and an annual *zamindari* income of five hundred thousand to be apportioned among his three sons and two daughters.[52] Wilayet Ali also seems to have done well; his inherited properties in Bihar yielded an annual income of fifty-five thousand rupees in addition to the "profits from money transactions." In the 1860s he branched out into the grain business, in partnership with a former commissioner of Patna, William Tayler. According to Nawab Waris Ismail, a descendant of the Wilayet Ali branch, the Nawab Bahadur families had "golden times" in the 1880s and 1890s. With the main *kothis* in Patna and branches elsewhere, and with *zamindari* income bringing in almost a million a year, they did not suffer any reverses until the early twentieth century. In 1915, however, their banking business came to a halt, and in banking, as in other matters, internecine squabbles led the way to the family slipping into "deteriorating conditions."[53]

The most prominent "Lalahs and Babus" were also involved in banking and trading. As in other north Indian cities, in Patna as well, Marwaris and Aggarwals, originally from Rajputana, were especially conspicuous in these activities. Some Marwari families dated back to the Mughal period, others were part of an eighteenth-century migration, and still others constituted part of the now-familiar migration down the Ganges in the nineteenth century. The attraction of Patna was, as a

52. Lutf Ali was suspected of being a rebel in 1857; his father was suspected of being involved in the "Patna Conspiracy" of 1845, which attempted to unite landholders, urban elites, and the rank and file, including prisoners, against government over religious and sociocultural issues. See W. Dampier, Suptd., Police, to F. J. Halliday, Secy., GOB, no. 367, Mar. 16, 1846, Bengal Cr. Jdcl. Consltns., Apr. 1–15, 1846, Apr. 1, no. 42; Anand A. Yang, "Disciplining 'Natives': Prisons and Prisoners in Early Nineteenth Century India," *South Asia* 10 (1987): 29–45.

53. Interview with Nawab Waris Ismail (1909–), descendant of Wilayet Ali, May 19, 1984. Information on this family is also based in part on the Diary of Waris Ismail. See also "Brief History of Syed Badshah Nawab Razvi . . . Gurzi, born 30 July 1858," enclosure to Patna Magte's no. 3326, July 15, 1905, P.C. Double Lock Box, no. 7, 1904–9; F. B. Bradley-Birt, *Twelve Men of Bengal in the Nineteenth Century* (Calcutta: S. K. Lahiri, 1927), chap. on "Nawab Bahadur Syed Walayet Ali Khan, C.I.E., 1818–1899."

present-day descendant of the banking Ramji Ram family put it, the "scope of the business."[54]

The Rohatgi family affords another example of recent immigrants who established themselves in Patna business. In the nineteenth century their Dhawalpura Kothi, or the firm of Kallu Babu Lallu Babu, comprised one of the major banking house: their business included credit note (*hundi*) transactions and some moneylending. They were also involved in the "cloth printing business." By these means they accumulated enough wealth in the nineteenth century to challenge the Nawab Bahadur family, a competition, according to one account, to see which family could—literally—line more of the city streets with gold coins. The winners, the Babus, are said to have bested their rivals by producing a bullock cart filled with three hundred thousand rupees' worth of "Edward coins." Another version of the tale states that the competition was to see how far each of the families would get from the "city" to Bankipur by placing their gold coins alongside one another.[55]

But if the histories of these prominent banking and trading families illustrate the rise of a new generation of aristocrats and the persistence and development of the city as a center of wholesale trade and banking, the chronology of their declining fortunes in the late nineteenth and early twentieth centuries also mirrors the shifts in the city's primacy as a central place. The collective fate of bankers and petty traders in the colonial period further underscores this slump. Their declining condition is an especially revealing index of regional trends because they were instrumental in underwriting the wholesale trade of the area.[56]

At the outset of the nineteenth century the city supported 24 substantial bankers (*kothiwals*) with capital ranging from five thousand to five hundred thousand rupees, 168 moneylenders with capital of one thousand to one hundred thousand rupees, and 30 usurers with small amounts of money. In addition, 321 money changers (*shroff*), some with as much capital as ten thousand to fifty thousand rupees, and 50

54. Interview with Krishna Chandra, Patna City, June 1984. See also below, chap. 5, on traders; and Thomas A. Timberg, *The Marwaris: From Traders to Industrialists* (New Delhi: Vikas, 1978), pp. 41–124. "In colloquial usage, outside of Rajasthan," as Timberg explains, "*Marwaris* used to refer to emigrant businessmen from the vicinity of [Marwar, an area in] Rajasthan" (p. 10). The term is often used loosely to refer to a number of groups from this region, including Aggarwals, Maheshwaris, and Oswals.

55. Interview with C. K. and M. P. Rohatgi, descendant of Kallu and Lallu Babus, Patna City, June 16, 1984. See also below, pp. 236–37.

56. B & O, *Report of the Bihar and Orissa Provincial Banking Enquiry Committee 1929–30* (Patna: Govt. Printing, 1930), p. 186.

money changers with a side business in cotton cloth and cotton and wood also plied their trade in the city. Although the number of bankers totaled 827 by the 1870s, this estimation conceals the fact that the number of large banking houses (*kothis*) had fallen to only ten. The rest were mostly petty moneylenders, except for 43 persons described as principally dealing in the *hundi* trade. By the 1880s, the "few big mahajuns . . . who at one time, by the help of their large capital, ruled over the commercial destinies of the district" were said to be a thing "of the past."[57] Fifty years later the systematic 1929–30 inquiry of banking in the region was hard-pressed to find any large banking houses still operating. According to its report, the few survivors "have . . . ceased to be shroffs . . . as they have lost their deposit business. They have been transformed into zamindars and money-lenders."[58]

Data on *arhatiyas*—commission agents involved in purchasing and selling goods—tell a similar story. In the early nineteenth century when Patna's role as an emporium of trade was still secure, it counted 124 *arathiyas,* some with capitals of up to twenty-five thousand rupees. By the late nineteenth century, however, only 14 were left.[59]

The changing fortunes of Patna bankers and traders as well as the rise of landholders were related to another major development perceived to be a characteristic of the "modern times" of the city and its hinterland: their changing manufacturing and commercial fortunes. This shift, furthermore, affected not only the "aristocracy"—many of whom were involved in the trade of "manufactured" goods or the products of artisanal industries (as the Rohatgi family were)—but also large numbers of ordinary men and women who formed the backbone of this sector of the economy.

Ghulam Husain anticipated this effect of colonial rule when he hinted that the growth of Company trade, backed by special privileges, was overwhelming indigenous competition. As recounted by Amiya Bagchi, this trend resulted in deindustrialization in the nineteenth century, a process of decline in the "industrial" or nonagricultural sector of the economy. His

57. AGRPD 1883–84; Syud Ameer Hossein, "Mahajani Statistics," AGRPD 1876–77, Appendix C; F. Hamilton Ms., "The City and Suburbs of Patna," Mss. Eur. D. 87.

58. *Report of Bihar Banking Committee*, p. 186. A shroff is "able to attract public deposits and draw hundis which are readily accepted or discounted in the market. . . . [T]he money-lender . . . lends only his own money."

59. Hamilton Ms., "Patna"; Hossein, "Mahajani Statistics." Buchanan also mentions 125 *dandidars* (weighmen) and 200 *dalals* (brokers).

argument, based largely on data for Patna, Gaya, Bhagalpur, Purnia, and Shahabad, discerns "a decline in the proportion of the working population engaged in secondary industry to total working population, or a decline in the proportion of the population dependent on secondary industry to total population."[60] By his reckoning, the proportion of people whose livelihood depended on "industry" declined from 18.6 percent in the first decade of the nineteenth century to about 8.5 percent by the end of that century. Patna and Gaya, administered jointly at the outset of the century, added up to 19.5 percent, but only 11.1 and 9.1 percent individually later in that century when the two areas were counted as separate districts. Particularly hard hit was the hand-loom industry, which constituted the largest segment of this secondary industry. As Bagchi's figures show, the population involved in cotton weaving and spinning declined from 62.3 percent to 15.1 percent; Patna and Gaya tallied 58 percent in 1809–13 but only 12.4 and 22.4 percent for Patna and Gaya, respectively, in 1901. In other words, the proportion of the population involved in this artisanal industry dropped by almost four-fifths in the case of Patna over the course of the nineteenth century![61]

Although the question of deindustrialization remains a hotly contested subject in Indian history, there is growing agreement that—although the data is not reliable enough to allow precise quantification of changes and although not all handicraft industries suffered under colonial rule—the hand-loom industry faded in the face of foreign competition. Indeed, whatever the shortcomings are of accepting Buchanan's figures at face value, as Bagchi does to advance his argument, there is a considerable body of evidence supporting the claim that deindustrialization occurred, although later in the nineteenth century than earlier; that is, toward the latter half of the century.[62]

---

60. "Deindustrialization in Bihar," p. 499; *Seir,* II, pp. 468–69. Irfan Habib, "Studying a Colonial Economy—without Perceiving Colonialism," *MAS* 19 (1985): 358, contends that the Patna historian argued that Company trade and policies had harmful effects "on the crafts and internal trade of Bengal."

61. Bagchi, "Deindustrialization in Bihar," pp. 509–14. An intriguing coincidence is the fact that cotton cultivation in the primary cotton-producing area of Patna, *pargana* Ghyaspur, dropped from two thousand maunds in the 1830s to about four hundred by the 1860s, or a decrease of four-fifths! The district never grew much cotton and had to import it from Mirzapur and other western markets in order to meet local demands. H. D. H. Fergusson, Commr., to Secy., BOR, no. 10, May 9, 1861, Bengal Rev. Procs., Apr.-June 1861, June, no. 118.

62. The attack on Bagchi has partly centered on his reliance on Buchanan's data. See, e.g., Marika Vicziany, "The Deindustrialization of India in the Nineteenth Century: A Methodological Critique of Amiya Kumar Bagchi," *IESHR* 16 (1979): 105–46.

Of the 11,000 shops identified in the city by a 1790 report, 153 belonged to Dhunias who prepared cotton for quilts and 50 to people involved in the stamping of cloth; in addition, there were 7 sellers of cotton, 124 sellers of cloth (*bazzaz*), and 71 makers of carpets (*kalin*). Twenty years later, when Buchanan conducted his "survey" and "enumerative" project in the area, he found abundant signs of a vibrant textile industry and as yet no evidence of cloth imported from his own country. His report indicates that Patna district had 175 weaver villages, and weaver quarters (*muhallas*) in virtually every higher-order market. Within a decade, however, "British cloths which pay no duty" were "selling in [the] Patna Bazaar."[63]

Beginning in the 1830s the volume of foreign cloth dumped on India reached significant proportions, so much so that by the 1860s, Patna's inhabitants were said to have become accustomed to "British goods." By then, "the value of English goods disposed off in Patna district" was, in one estimation, "at least four times the value of cloth of native manufacture." Yet another blow to the handicraft industry was delivered by the mills of Kanpur and Bombay, whose products penetrated the local market by the 1870s, also the period in which cheap machine-made thread came into widespread usage.[64]

Increasingly, the only "native manufacture" that survived the invasion of "foreign" products was coarse cloth, known locally as *motia* or *gazi*. Durable and affordable, it persisted as the cloth of choice of the "poorer classes." (It outlasted imported cloth by four or five months, and it was half as expensive.) Yet even the *motia* cloth bore the mark of the new market conditions as it was increasingly woven by combining indigenous thread with machine-made thread![65]

63. Colltr., Govt. Customs, Patna, to Board of Commrs., Bihar and Benares, Bihar and Benares, Board of Commrs., Customs, 1819, Aug. 31, no. 1; G. F. Grand, Magte., Patna, to G. H. Barlow, Subsecy., Dec. 29, 1790, Bengal Rev. Jdcl. Consltns., Mar. 11–25, 1791, Mar. 18, no. 20; Hagen, "Indigenous Society in Patna," pp. 319, 156.

64. Colltr. of Patna, cited in "Abstract of Returns to Circular Order No. 9 of July 1865," Bengal Rev. Procs., July-Dec. 1865, Dec., no. 125; AGRPD 1879–80; J. G. Cumming, *Review of the Industrial Position and Prospects in Bengal in 1908* (Calcutta: Bengal Secretariat Book Depot, 1908), pp. 7–8.

65. T. Inglis, Colltr., Patna, to Secy., no. 541R, June 18, 1897, Bengal Rev. Procs., Apr.-June 1898, Apr., nos. 68–69. The new thread led some weavers to develop new products: a fine muslin made in imitation of Dacca muslins and called Bihar *jamdani* was started up in the 1860s; turban cloth, a plain muslin generally used for turbans; and colored cotton fabrics, manufactured in the 1880s, that resembled the various jute and cotton cloths produced by the mills of Kanpur and other areas.

That imported products sharply curtailed local production is also evidenced by the declining condition of the weavers of Barh subdivision who, based in the market towns of Bakhtiyarpur, Fatwa, and Nawada, once specialized in the making of cotton towels, sheets, and tablecloths as well as coarse country cloth to sell at Danapur and to export to Kanpur. By 1875, machine-made cloth pieces added up to as much as Rs. 3 million of Patna's trade, making machine-made piece goods a more valuable commodity than any other food or nonfood import. "Death by Manchester," as one official report put it concisely.[66]

The decline of the textile industry affected a large sector of the local population involved in different phases of cloth production: Dhunias (cotton carders) who specialized in the cleaning of cotton; spinners, often "women of small means and almost every class [who] used to spin thread out of indigenous cotton"; and weavers, mostly Muslim Jolahas and Hindu Tantwas, who wove the thread into cloth. Buchanan's figures for Patna—278 Dhunias, 23,400 cotton spinners, and 2,010 houses of cotton weavers who together had 2,692 looms—provide one indication of the numbers whose livelihoods were altered by Manchester and later by the development of Indian mills.[67]

Cheap machine-made thread sharply curtailed the role of women in the making of thread out of indigenous cotton. Also hard hit were the weavers, a group much highlighted in the deindustrialization literature because they were generally men of small means whose subsistence depended largely on their earnings from this artisanal industry. Their plight was widely noticed in the 1860s when they were said to be abandoning their traditional occupation in droves. "If all the members of the Jolaha caste had to depend on the produce of their looms, they

66. Deputy Colltr. Mullik, "Notes on the Cotton Fabrics . . . of Gaya," Bengal Rev. Procs., Apr. 1898, nos. 37–38; E. W. Collin, on special duty, Jan. 4, 1890, Bengal Genl. Procs., Jan.-Aug. 1890, July, nos. 12–18 (hereafter Collin report); T. Sandys, Colltr., to G. Gough, Commr., July 19, 1848, P.C.'s records, Letters from Colltr. of Patna, vol. 61, 1848; "Abstract of Returns"; Hagen, "Indigenous Society in Patna," pp. 319, 156. See also Gyan Pandey, "Economic Dislocation in Nineteenth Century Eastern U.P.: Some Implications of the Decline of Artisanal Industry in Colonial India." *Centre for Studies in Social Sciences, Calcutta, Occasional Paper No. 37* (1981).

67. These figures do not include another 126 chintz makers. Typically, after the cotton was cleaned it was spun into thread and then handed over to weavers, who made it into cloth on consignment or who purchased it outright and then sold the finished product in the market. Buchanan, *Bihar and Patna*, pp. 771–74; Inglis to Secy., no. 541R, Bengal Rev. Procs., Apr. 1898, nos. 68–69. Grierson, *Bihar Peasant Life*, pp. 62–76, provides a step-by-step description of how thread was spun and cloth was made locally.

would have disappeared long ago," noted one source. "At present some of them are virtually agriculturists, and ply their trade less for gain than to keep up old traditions. This class has also taken largely to service and trade. Only the poorest of them weave cloth for wages."[68]

Many weavers moved east, migrating to Bengal in search of menial jobs. "Jolahas from south Gangetic Bihar" were especially conspicuous in the stream of seasonal migrants seeking "employment in the jute factories of Hooghly and Howrah, and as coolies and domestics in Calcutta."[69]

Products of a number of other artisanal industries, ranging from carpets, brocades, embroidery, paper, pottery, brass work, toys, fireworks, lac ornaments, gold and silver wire and leaf, glassware, boots and shoes, and cabinets in Patna to linen, furniture, and cabinet ware in the nearby town of Danapur, were also the casualties of deindustrialization. Carpet-making in the city, for instance, which was once centered in the *thanas* (a subdistrict unit of administration) of Sultanganj and Alamganj, was in greatly reduced circumstances by the turn of the twentieth century. So was papermaking, especially in the town of Bihar, which was once the occupation of thirty families. By 1890 this number had been reduced to twenty-five, and the industry was said to be "fast dying out."[70] A similar fate was shared by the area's "most important industry," opium, which increasingly counted for less and less acreage—from 26,314 acres in 1881 to 7,710 in 1911—and was finally abandoned in the early twentieth century.[71]

Much the same narrative about prosperity and decline, even down to the chronological framework of relative prosperity in the eighteenth and early nineteenth centuries followed by decline in the second half of the nineteenth century, characterized the city's overall commercial condition. Its changing condition also reflects its growing subordination to Calcutta and to the larger national and international markets.

68. "Report on the Manufactures and Mines of the Gaya District, compiled by Babu Ram Anugrah Narayan Singh, Deputy Colltr., Gaya . . . ," *in District Census Reports, 1891, Patna Division* (Calcutta: n.p., 1898), Gaya, appendix; R. B. Chapman, Secy., GOB, BOR to Jr. Secy., GOB, Nov. 28, 1864, Bengal Rev. Procs., Oct.-Dec. 1864, Dec., no. 17; Inglis to Secy., no. 541R, Bengal Rev. Procs., Apr. 1898, nos. 68–69.

69. "Report on Gaya"; Yang, "Peasants on the Move." In many areas, weavers who continued to produce cloth did so for their own use or for sale in local markets. See B. Ramapati Chatterjee, Deputy Colltr., "Cotton Fabrics in the District of Champaran . . . ," Bengal Rev. Procs., Apr. 1898, nos. 43–44.

70. Collin report; Buchanan, *Bihar and Patna*, pp. 765, 772.

71. Opium was the most valuable agricultural or nonagricultural item exported from the district. *PDG, 1924*, pp. 122–23; *PSR*, p. 25; Inglis to Secy., no. 541R, Bengal Rev. Procs., Apr. 1898, nos. 68–69.

Patna persisted as the central place of the region in the initial century of colonial rule, Rasikh's pronouncements regarding the absence of "commercial capital" and the advent of "poverty" notwithstanding. Writing in 1790, a group of thirty-three merchants, bankers, and dealers described the trade of the city as consisting of spices, copper, lead, tin, broadcloth, and cotton, and silk goods from the east, mainly from Calcutta and Murshidabad, and such goods as calicoes and cotton from the west. Three-fourths of the trade involved the east, the remaining one-fourth was directed at the North-Western Provinces.[72] At its height, Patna was the "largest of the mercantile centres of Bengal," "an emporium of trade . . . for reconsignment and reshipment . . . [for] through traffic, which is merely sent to Patna on account of the facilities that the city affords for despatching the consignments to their final destination."[73] In other words, it served as the principal entrepôt for the trade flowing between Bengal and the North-Western Provinces, a collection point for the products of its hinterland that were then redistributed locally and regionally, and an important center for the trade with Nepal to the north.

Buchanan's detailed figures from 1811–12 provide one estimate of the extraordinary level of its trading activity, even if his numbers are not precise tallies. According to his "conjecture," exports totaled Rs. 3,259,558, imports almost double that figure at Rs. 6,510,546. Food and nonfood crops constituted almost two-thirds of the value of the exports, with rice and wheat accounting for Rs. 198,100 and 183,200, respectively. Salt, estimated at Rs. 799,200, and sugar, at Rs. 219,100, weighed in as two other significant items. Other major export items were: cotton cloth (Rs. 200,000) and chintz (Rs. 121,500), and metals of one sort or another (copper, zinc, tin, lead, and iron), whose total was reckoned at Rs. 160,750, and shoes (Rs. 100,000). Food and nonfood crops accounted for an even larger share of the imports, constituting almost 82 percent of the overall total. Notable among these were rice (Rs. 521,300), wheat (Rs. 470,000), oilseeds (Rs. 487,900), salt (Rs. 1,778,250), sugar (Rs. 235,850), and betel nuts (Rs. 100,250). Other major import goods were items known as *pasari* (Rs. 163,000), a

72. See "Petition of Joal Dass . . . and Other Merchants, Bankers, and Dealers . . . of Azimbad Gentoos and Musulmen . . . ," Bengal Rev. Consltns., Jan. 6 to 20, 1790, Jan. 6, no. 18; "Extract of Procs. of a Council of Rev., Mar. 23, 1773," Bengal Rev. Board of Commrs., Customs, April 14 to Dec. 15, 1773, Apr. 14.

73. *Trade of Bengal 1876–77*, p. 196.

designation applied to a range of spices and other goods, metals (Rs. 280,650), and cotton wool (Rs. 130,000).[74]

Well into the late nineteenth century Patna remained one of the premier entrepôts of north India. Registered "internal trade" figures, which generally underestimated interdistrict trade, such as that between Gaya and Patna, in fact reveal that Patna had the largest trade of any district in Bengal. In 1876–77, registered exports were valued at Rs. 36,222,400, or 11.1 times the value of goods sent out in the 1810s; total imports were estimated at Rs. 44,651,000, or 6.8 times the 1810s value.[75] This trend accords perfectly with the now well-established pattern of increasing trade in the late nineteenth century, particularly of certain kinds of medium- and low-value agricultural goods.[76]

From nearby districts flowed grains of all sorts, appearing as both exports and imports because they were transferred in and out of the city. Rice came from Purnia, Muzaffarpur, Darbhanga, and Saran; high-quality Patna rice, "celebrated throughout Bengal for its fineness," was sent out to Murshidabad and Calcutta as well as to Banaras. Bhagalpur was a major supplier of Patna's wheat and barley stocks; other grains, such as *kodo, marua,* and *kauni,* were drawn particularly from Saran, Muzaffarpur, and Darbhanga. Oilseeds, mostly shipped in from north Bihar and recorded in Buchanan's register as "imports," were then ex-

---

74. The export and import figures for rice (Rs. 198,100 vs. Rs. 521,300) are misleading because exports typically exceeded imports. Buchanan, *Bihar and Patna,* pp. 670, 776, table no. 44.

75. An 1875–76 government study of imports and exports—calculated by weight rather than by monetary value—estimated the former exceeding the latter by a little over twice the amount (3,166,856 vs. 1,525,827 maunds). As was the case over half a century earlier, food and nonfood crops accounted for much of the trade: oilseeds topped the list of exports (1,146,852 maunds), followed by alimentary salt (105,329), wheat (73,900), and pulses and gram (73,900). European cotton manufactures—not a presence earlier in the century—were priced at Rs. 443,950 and represented another significant export item. Oilseeds (1,195,709 maunds) also stood high on the imports list; rice was a distant second (326,272), followed by alimentary salt (232,605), other saline substances (*khari, sajji, reh*) (204,762), pulses and gram (202,126), wheat (150,884), paddy (138,601), and other cereals (134,167). Other significant import items were European cotton manufactures valued at Rs. 2,855,374, and cotton, spices, and tobacco estimated at 38,271, 43,685, and 9,398 maunds, respectively. Note the appreciable drop in imports of cotton. M. Rattray, Suptd., Salt Excise, to Magte., Patna, no. 222, June 27, 1876, Bengal Statistical Consltns., Trade and Traffic, 1876–77, July 1876, colln. 7–123/2 (hereafter cited as Rattray report).

76. Derbyshire, "Railways in India," pp. 528–29. Early-nineteenth-century trade statistics can be gleaned from information on customs and town duties collected in Patna (mostly on piece goods). E.g., see F. Balfour, Colltr., Govt. Customs, to Bd. of Commrs, Aug. 23, 1819, and Senior Commr.'s Minute, Aug. 31, 1819, Bengal Rev. Consltns., Oct. 8 to 15, 1819, Oct. 8, nos. 35 and 37.

ported to Calcutta. Sugar and salt appeared on both sides of the trading balance sheet because they were brought in from Bengal and the North-Western Provinces. Metals likewise went both ways: copper, zinc, tin, and lead were relayed from Calcutta to Patna and then north and west, whereas iron came from south Bihar and was sent east. Cotton cloth, a major item of trade, involved as many as twenty-two "native merchants" who maintained factories in and around the city for the "purchase of plain cotton cloth." In addition, coarse cotton was imported from nearby areas. Cotton wool entered the city largely from the west, from Mirzapur, which was also the source of the city's chintz, as was Lucknow, which was also where the city's shoes were sent. From Patna the chintz was moved out to Calcutta; the shoes were exported to Bengal. Spices and other goods (*pasari*) were brought in from nearby districts.[77]

Late-nineteenth-century sources provide more precise identifications of the nodes that were tied into the city's trading networks and of the extent of their trade. Oilseeds, brought in mostly by river, were imported to Patna from throughout Bihar, the largest amounts coming from Revelganj (193,875 maunds), Bettiah (94,502 maunds), and Gaya (96,733 maunds). Lesser amounts trickled in from other markets in Saran, Champaran, and Gaya, as well as from Patna, Shahabad, and Darbhanga. The North-Western Provinces comprised the other major source: Nawabganj in Faizabad district supplied as much as 178,612 maunds, and four markets in Gorakhpur together tallied 103,677 maunds. Oilseeds increasingly constituted the most valuable article of trade, representing as much as four-fifths of the total exports of the city. Much of it—1,140,460 out of 1,146,852 maunds—was sent to Calcutta by rail. Its trade was controlled by a handful of merchants; two European agencies, Messrs. Ralli Brothers and N. I. Valetta and Company, alone accounting for more than half of the exports to Calcutta.[78]

Food grains, another major item of trade, added up to more than a million and a half maunds of imports into Patna in 1876–77; and almost an equivalent amount was exported. Wheat and rice each accounted for more than a quarter of the total imports; wheat also represented more than a quarter of the total exports, rice only a fifth. Much of the imports went for local consumption; much of the exports, particularly wheat, pulses, gram, and rice, for the Calcutta market.

77. Buchanan, *Bihar and Patna*, pp. 671–82.
78. *Trade of Bengal, 1876–77*, pp. 198–99; Rattray report.

Rice was supplied primarily from within Bihar. Some of it came in from the North-Western Provinces; very little of it originated in the rice-producing districts of Eastern Bengal. Wheat was another import from up-country, the markets of Gorakhpur being a major source; a sizable amount came from Revelganj, Chapra, Arrah, Danapur, Fatwa, and Hilsa. As with so many other exports, its destination was Calcutta. Pulses and gram similarly drew on Bihar markets, much of the city's supply stemming from the district itself and, as in the case of wheat, these food grains too were sent east, to Calcutta and Dacca. Cotton piece goods flowed in almost entirely from Calcutta and went out as exports to supply markets within the region. From the railway station in Patna, carts carried away a large allotment for Gaya; another sizable amount was exported to Muzaffarpur and other north Bihar areas. A small portion of the salt came from as far away as Punjab, but the bulk of it, as much as 220,616 of the 232,605 maunds imported into Patna, originated in Calcutta. From Patna the salt was redistributed throughout the region, particularly to Gaya and Champaran; the largest amount, 48,500 out of 105,329 maunds, was sent on to Burhej in Gorakhpur. The role of the city as entrepôt can also be seen in its "through" trade of hides and skins, timber, bamboo, sugar, tobacco, and saltpeter.

Calcutta was the principal place of origin of Patna's imports: it accounted for 364,395 maunds, of which 220,616 was taken up by salt. Lalganj with 241,786 maunds weighed in second—more than half of this was firewood—and Revelganj with 231,671 maunds was third. Nawabganj came next (178,612), followed by Muzaffarpur (143,920), Bettiah (139,236), Chapra (131,814), Gaya (130,292), and Golagopalpur in Gorakhpur (125,093). In tenth place stood Hilsa and Attaserai (Islampur) with 122,937 maunds; Burhej occupied eleventh place with 115,838 maunds, and the town of Bihar was in twelfth place with 100,057 maunds. Other than Calcutta and three markets in the North-Western Provinces, eight of the twelve principal points of origin for Patna's imports lay within Patna Division. Calcutta was also the primary exporting partner of Patna, accounting for as much as 1,244,423 of the total 1,525,827 maunds counted as exports in 1875–76. Appreciably smaller amounts were sent to Burhej (48,500 maunds), Dacca (46,986), Bettiah (28,366), Gaya (18,738), Bhagalpur (17,363), Lalganj (12,970), Khagaria (12,637), and Chapra (10,361).[79]

79. Rattray report; *Trade of Bengal, 1876–77*, pp. 200–4.

In the late nineteenth century, however, Patna's commanding role as regional entrepôt declined. What curtailed its salience—and consequently boosted the stock of other towns and localities in the region—was the loss of its enormous trading edge as a strategic location on the major river highways: this significant geographical advantage was eroded by the development of railways, beginning in the 1860s. Rail lines within the region terminated its role as the "forwarding station" for the neighboring districts, and the opening up of the Ajmere and Bombay line, which enabled goods from the North-Western Provinces to be sent directly to Bombay instead of via Patna, reduced its role as "a great central godown."[80]

Railways diminished the centrality of Patna in two respects. First, the traffic, particularly that conveyed by country boats, which converged on Patna en route to its hinterland or to other areas, no longer needed this intermediate stop. The new railway lines in the north enabled small traders especially to remit their goods directly to Calcutta instead of sending them on to Patna. With freight charges lower for goods transferred directly between place of origin and Calcutta without stopovers, many traders opted for the better rates and bypassed Patna. As a result, as one administration report noted, "Behar districts no longer receive from Patna their supplies of articles produced or purchasable at other places and Patna does not import or export now much over what is necessary for local consumption, or what is the surplus produce of the district."[81]

Trade statistics, more reliable for goods carried by railway than for those conveyed by boats, carts, and pack bullocks (for which figures were either not kept at all or kept only sporadically), document the shifts in transportation patterns. By the late 1870s exports sent out of the city by rail added up to 64 percent of the total (Rs. 23,287,000 of the total registered exports of Rs. 36,333,400); the rest was carried by rivers (31 percent) and roads (5 percent). Railways accounted for far less of the imports total, only 40 percent (or Rs. 18,052,100 of the total imports estimated at Rs. 44,651,000); whereas 56 and 4 percent flowed

80. Patna's trade was also affected by the "district's own rail corridor, which had the effect of by-passing the city's river based facilities . . . [and] the construction of the grand Chord Rail Line from Mughal Sarai (near Benares) through Gaya Town and on to Calcutta, completed in 1909." Hagen, "Indigenous Society in Patna," chaps. 2, 7; AGRPD 1879–80, 1880–81, 1881–82.

81. AGRPD, 1882–83; AGRPD, 1890–91; AGRPD, 1900–1 to 1904–5; PDG 1924, p. 127.

into the city by river and by road, respectively.[82] By the early 1880s the city's merchants and traders were "complaining of want of business. Many of the larger godowns are lying vacant, and in consequence many business men are resorting to other places of trade."[83]

By the turn of the twentieth century, except for some food grains little was transported by river. Even the market in boats virtually disappeared; the "wood and timber" trade also declined appreciably. To some extent, the fate of Patna was shared by the rest of Bihar, which also became, in the late nineteenth and early twentieth centuries, "a 'by-passed' region of north India."[84]

A similar story can be pieced together by examining the changing profile of the city in relation to its immediate hinterland. In an earlier era, as a 1790s police tax imposed on "houses of trade" (that is, on traders, merchants, and shopkeepers) reveals, the city dominated regional and local trade. Its assessment of Sicca (a type of rupee) Rs. 28,287 exceeded by far the total of Rs. 20,571 levied on the rest of the district, which then included much of what later became Patna and Gaya districts. Buchanan's account suggests a similar disparity when it reports that the city monopolized 70.8 percent of the trade in exports of the old district of Bihar and 91.1 percent of the imports.[85] Contrast this picture with a profile from the postrailways era that reveals a dramatic drop in Patna's share and an appreciable increase in Gaya's portion of the trade of

82. Figures for the trade in wheat, a commodity not produced in any appreciable quantity locally but brought into the city by river from districts to the west and north and then moved both east and west, is another index of the diminishing role of Patna in the "forwarding business." The decline is apparent in the drop in numbers from 1,329,577 to 269,609 maunds in the early 1880s. Likewise, the trade in piece goods fell, amounting to only 10 percent of what it used to be by 1881–82; in the five years leading up to this date it had dropped by as much as one-fourth. With direct lines of communication forged by the development of railways, districts in the north and south received their piece goods directly from Calcutta. AGRPD 1881–82; 1880–81; 1884–85; 1889–90.

83. AGRPD, 1880–81; AGRPD 1879–80, 1882–83; PDG 1924, pp. 129–31. See also below, chaps. 3 and 4, on the related rise of other towns and localities in the region. Items such as bamboo and timber continued to be shipped by water, which was cheaper and more convenient for handling bulky and unwieldy goods. The larger proportion of imports than exports transported by water reflects the fact that Patna continued as a collection point for its intermediate hinterland.

84. Hagen, "Indigenous Society in Patna," p. 300. See also "Report on the Census of the District of Patna," Census 1891, Patna, pp. 1–4, 14; C. J. Hamilton, "Note on an Economic Census of Patna Bazaar," in Census of India, 1921, vol. 7, Bihar and Orissa, part I, Report, by P. C. Tallents (Patna: Govt. Printing, 1923), pp. 95–96; PDG 1924, p. 127.

85. Buchanan, Bihar and Patna, table 44, pp. 776–78; "Statements of Names . . . ," Bengal BOR Procs., Police, Jan. 6 to May 19, 1797, nos. 9 and 10.

south Bihar. By the beginning of the twentieth century, Patna district only accounted for 63.5 percent of the trade of Patna, Gaya, and Shahabad, a percentage that continued to fall, dropping to 53.4 percent by 1905–10. And within Patna Division, the district only accounted for about a third by the close of the nineteenth century.[86]

The changing relationship between the city of Patna and its hinterland can also be gauged in another way. When it was the primary commodity bulking center, the city imported goods that were either relayed to other localities or redistributed to the lesser intermediate and standard markets within its own locality. But as the center of marketing gravity shifted away, marketing functions and markets became more evenly distributed across the district. In part the change was ushered in by an intensification of commercial functions at the level of intermediate markets, in part it resulted from the extensive growth of periodic markets across the locality.

As the central place of both the locality and the region, the city stood well above all the other marketing nodes. To use Skinner's formulation, it was a "central market": "a strategic site in the transportation network. . . . Its facilities are designed, on the one hand, to receive imported items and distribute them within its dependent area and, on the other, to collect local products and export them to other central markets or higher-level urban centers."

By contrast, the next rung in the marketing hierarchy was the intermediate market, which replicated to a lesser degree the functions performed by the city by virtue of its "intermediate position in the vertical flow of goods and services both ways."[87] This rung in the marketing hierarchy was filled by the *qasba* (town or large market village), of which there were nine in the late eighteenth and early nineteenth centuries: Barh, Bihar, Danapur, Fatwa, Hilsa, Islampur, Naubatpur, Phulwari Sharif, and Sherpur.[88]

---

86. "Quinquennial Administration Report of the Patna Division . . . , 1900–01 to 1904–05"; "Quinquennial Report . . . , 1905–6 to 1909–10," Bengal Gen. Procs., Apr. 1911, nos. 1–2. Precise statistical comparisons for the pre- and post-1880s periods are difficult to make because trade figures in the later period were kept by districts rather than by specific cities; the exception was Calcutta.

87. Skinner, "Marketing in China," p. 7; Hagen, "Indigenous Society in Patna," pp. 54–58. Markets above the *haat* level are generally referred to in contemporary sources as bazaars, *ganjs*, *qasbas*, and *mandis*.

88. Hagen, "Indigenous Society in Patna," pp. 52–61; Skinner, "Marketing in China." My list of intermediate markets differs from that of Hagen—I include Danapur and not Rajgir (as does Hagen) because the latter was in decline whereas the former was emerging as an intermediate market at the turn of the nineteenth century. Hagen bases his list on places that were identified as *qasbas*.

A comparison of Patna and Bihar highlights the difference between these two levels. Once a small town subordinated to Bihar when it was a provincial capital, Patna had attracted a population ten times that of the latter at the turn of the nineteenth century. Furthermore, whereas it supported bankers, moneylenders, usurers, and money changers, along with merchants and wholesalers who dealt in virtually every kind of commodity, from cloth to grain to household goods, Bihar was a market specializing more in retail than in wholesale trade. An intermediate market, it was the gathering place of sixty dealers in grain who kept cattle, and forty money changers. Similarly, the intermediate markets of Barh and Fatwa were thronged largely by retailers; wholesale dealers were more the exception than the rule.[89]

Standard markets, numbering twenty-five in all, occupied the level below intermediate markets. They were markets that "met all the normal trade needs of the peasant household: what the household produced but did not consume was normally sold there, and what it consumed but did not produce was normally bought there. The standard market provided for the exchange of goods produced within the market's dependent area, but more importantly it was the starting point for the upward flow of agricultural products and craft items into higher reaches of the marketing system, and also the termination of the downward flow of imported items destined for peasant consumption."[90] In other words, standard markets were the most significant markets in localities that did not have easy access to intermediate markets or to the city of Patna. They were "centers of . . . both horizontal and vertical [trade]. It was at this level that most of the agricultural surplus from the countryside was marketed with agents (areths) who maintained permanent storage facilities. This economic function of wholesale and storage activities as part of the role of absorbing the bulk of the agricultural surplus distinguished the standard market place from the periodic haat [market]."[91]

Standard markets, in contrast to the two highest levels of the marketing system, typically provided few if any wholesale services. Almost all

---

89. Barh had nine wholesale dealers in grain and iron and forty money changers who also dealt in cotton cloth; Fatwa supported ten money changers and dealers in cloth, eleven dealers in cloth, and one *arathiya* who dealt in grain and salt.

90. Skinner, "Marketing in China," p. 6.

91. Hagen, "Indigenous Society in Patna," pp. 58–59, 52–61. The twenty-five standard markets were: Maner, Danapur, Panhar, Tilhara, Mirzagunj, Baiketpur, Nur Sarai, Bahpura, So Sarai, Bhagwangunj, Pali, Patut, Bara Nawada, Lai, Maghra, Digha, Silao, Lakhna, Ekanger Sarai, Jogipur, Nawada, Punarak, Saksohara, Barah, and Dariapur.

transactions were in retail trade. The sizable standard market of Maner, which met daily, for instance, had four money changers who were also dealers in cotton cloth, but the rest of its roster consisted of retailers— two in cotton cloth, twenty-two in provisions, seven in betel leaf, one in sweetmeats, and ten in oil. In addition, the market was made up of two dyers, two coppersmiths, seven goldsmiths, four blacksmiths, two makers of glass ornaments, one maker of fireworks, two makers of soap, two butchers of large cattle, three butchers of small cattle, two silk string makers, and one liquor shop. The standard markets of Bara Nawada and Tilhara had much the same assortment of retailers.[92]

Below the standard markets were sixty-seven periodic markets, known as *haats* in the vernacular. The lowest rung of the system, these markets comprised the overwhelming number of marketing settlements in any locality. Like their counterparts in other agrarian societies, they were "minor" markets in which transactions were predominantly horizontal, that is, locally produced agricultural and craft items exchanged hands within the locality. In some, a modest amount of vertical trade was transacted, as goods produced externally were brought in from higher-level markets or those produced locally were traded to larger markets. The *haats* had the least to offer, typically they featured a few retailers selling a handful of agricultural products or a few household commodities. The *haat* of Jethauli in the vicinity of Fatwa, for instance, had four retailers of provisions, three retailers of parched grain, one retailer of betel leaf, two oil makers, and one shop for retailing palm wine. One local resident described *haats* as meeting "two days in the week . . . in the village, or in some neighbouring one, at which articles of food of the commonest and coarsest kind, necessary for bare subsistence, can be had, and where the people from the surrounding localities come to buy and sell them."[93]

It was at the level of periodic markets that the most dramatic change occurred. Their number more than tripled over the course of the nineteenth century and then almost doubled during the first half of the twentieth century—from 66 in 1811–12 to 209 in 1911, to 393 in 1951. This surge meant that markets became relatively accessible across the district. Few settlements lay outside a two-mile radius of this lowest order of marketplaces. Furthermore, *haats* began to assume

92. Hamilton Ms., "Patna."
93. Ghose, "Rural Behar," p. 221; Hamilton Ms., "Patna"; Hagen, "Indigenous Society in Patna," pp. 52–61; Skinner, "Marketing in China," p. 6.

some of the marketing and storage functions of the higher-order markets, especially the standard markets. The latter lost some of their salience as a consequence.[94]

Far less conspicuous but equally significant was the change at the level of intermediate markets. Although their number remained relatively constant over the course of the colonial period—from nine in 1811 to ten a century later and eleven in 1951, they greatly expanded their range of marketing activities in the late nineteenth century. This growth further underscores the downward turn in the fortunes of Patna because it resulted from the extension of rail lines to intermediate towns, which thereafter received their supplies directly instead of via the declining entrepôt of Patna.

More important than the change in number of intermediate markets are the alterations in the roster of these markets because they once again show the changes wrought by the development of railways. Three of the nine *qasbas* identified in 1811, Islampur, Naubatpur, and Sherpur, were no longer intermediate markets a century later. In their place were four new markets, Mokamah, Khagaul, Masaurhi-Tarenga (Mausarah), and Paliganj. Two of these, Mokamah and Khagaul, had been so inconspicuous earlier in the century that Buchanan did not even notice them. By the late nineteenth century, however, they had emerged as a result of changes in transportation and in the role of Patna. Mokamah was described in the 1870s as registering "a considerable trade in country produce. Much of the Tirhut trade, which is borne down the river Baya, finds its way to this place; and it is also a railway station." The same writer referred to Khagaul as "another instance of a modern town which may be said to have been created by railway."[95]

The town of Bihar, used as an example for the earlier period, serves once again as an apposite illustration of the changing relationship between Patna and intermediate markets. Throughout much of the eighteenth and early nineteenth centuries, its story is one of decline. In the

94. Hagen, "Indigenous Society in Patna," pp. 308–10. The number of standard markets remained constant between 1811 and 1911: twenty-five. In 1951, however, there were thirty-four standard markets. See also below, chap. 5, regarding the development of local marketing systems over the colonial period.

95. Hunter, *Account of Patna*, pp. 83, 90; Hagen, "Indigenous Society in Patna," p. 312. Mokamah emerged once it became a changing station for the railway. See S. C. Bayley, Offg. Commr., to Secy., GOB, no. 437R, Mar. 22, 1873, Bengal Gen. Procs., Jurisdictions, 1873–75, May 73, no. 10.

early nineteenth century it was characterized as reduced to "a probable population of 20,000 inhabitants, and . . . now fast verging upon ruins; its massive stone fort is no longer tenable, its tombs and mosques are in a sad state of decay, and its whole appearance has the air of a city deserted by all its influential and rich members."[96] By the late nineteenth century, however, its condition had improved because it had grown into an important node on the trading line connecting Patna, Gaya, Monghyr, and Hazaribagh and because it continued as a place of production for muslin, silk, and cotton cloth. Certainly as an intermediate market town its wholesale and retail facilities had expanded considerably since the beginning of the nineteenth century. An estimate of the 1870s indicates that as many as one-fourth of the 8,346 houses belonged to cloth merchants and grain dealers; of the cloth merchants twenty-eight families were singled out as being particularly prosperous. In addition, it supported a range of retail shops: sweetmeats, 40; spices, 18; cotton goods, 11; tobacco, 6; shoes, 16; gold and silver, 3; brass and iron, 5; sugar, 8; hides, 6; dal and other goods, 70; baskets, 14; costermongers (*paikaris*), 33; and itinerant cloth dealers, 7.[97]

Contrast this expansion with the decline in the role of Patna as a center and outlet for the products of artisanal industries, as well as a "platform for a commercial shop" and a site of "sellers" and buyers." In Rasikh's lifetime, as Buchanan's figures for 1810–11 reveal for the cloth and grain trade—two commodities that constituted a significant proportion of Patna's imports and exports—the city supported as many as 160 cloth dealers and 711 grain dealers. By 1920–21, however, the numbers had dropped to 97 and 131, respectively; the 131 can be further divided into 96 "grocers" and 35 "grain sellers."

A similar pattern can be traced for other commodities by considering 1810–11 as a baseline. As Buchanan's detailed and extensive list for that period shows, in the *chauk* (city center) area of the "city" alone, he encountered a daily crowd of approximately 200 "manufacturers, carpenters, taylors [*sic*], weavers, coppersmiths, shoemakers and those who make tubes for smoking tobacco and garlands." Patna's

96. *Notes on Behar*, p. 1; Hagen, "Indigenous Society in Patna," pp. 291, 310–12; *PSR*, p. 8.

97. In addition, porcelain goods were sold in this market, although the number of shops was not specified. "Return of Trade in the Town of Behar," B. C. Bhuttacharjee, Deputy Magte., Behar Subdivision, Apr. 27, 1876, Bengal Statistical Procs., Trade and Traffic, 1876–1877, July 1876; Hunter, *Account of Patna*, pp. 75–77.

ganjs (small regulated markets), mostly situated in the "city," abounded in other goods and services, too. Cloth of every variety could be purchased from 160 dealers in cloth or 5 Kashmiri merchants specializing in woolen clothes; grain was available from 100 grain dealers or from 55 grain dealers who combined their business with salt, iron, and metals (*gullah* and *kirana mahajan*) or 556 (presumably) retail grain dealers who also dabbled in selling pulses; salt was procurable from 40 retailers or 20 wholesalers, or from the 55 above-mentioned grain dealers who also sold salt. "Prepared butter" was the specialty of 9 retailers, and also of 4 wholesale and 31 retail dealers whose stocks included sugar as well. Among the shops carrying foodstuffs were 160 specializing in spices and drugs (*pasaris*), 1,350 in general provisions (*khichri farosh*), 300 in vegetables, 330 in betel leaf, 225 in grain, 40 in seasonings and fruit, 50 in poultry, and 80 in fish. And among those selling household goods were 32 specializing in cotton wool, 32 in sackcloth, iron, and millstones, 12 in stoneware, 12 in platters made of leaves, 80 in earthen pots, 20 in turbans, 20 in wooden vessels, 18 in brass and bell-metal vessels, 55 petty and 6 large dealers in shoes, 21 in wooden combs, and 11 in wooden cups and boxes. And if this range and assortment of shops was not sufficient to meet the needs of a customer, Patna's markets offered still more variety, including 9 retailers of European goods, 5 dealers in iron and ironmongery, 7 retailers of hemp buds, 3 sellers of lime, 25 dealers in sugarcane extracts, 5 in soda and purging salts, 8 in tobacco leaves, 13 retailers of brass implements for smoking tobacco, 50 petty dealers in house furniture and other knick-knacks, 2 horse dealers, 10 sellers of tin ornaments; 6 perfume retailers, 10 paper retailers, 4 sellers of musical instruments, 10 sellers of palmyra leaf fans, 5 coconut sellers, 6 parakeet hawkers, as well as others peddling everything from beads to old clothes to swords. Because of Patna's involvement in the wood and timber trade, the city had 200 retailers of bamboos, firewood, and so forth, and 32 dealers in sal timbers, beams, planks, and posts. And because of its role in the river trade it was also a place where boats could be purchased, from those of "superior description" to ordinary boats and canoes, and from ferry boats of considerable size to "small" boats.[98]

Although an extraordinary range of wholesale and retail dealers and of petty shopkeepers and manufacturers remained an essential feature

98. Hamilton Ms., "Patna."

of Patna, Patna's scale, especially in the "city," had diminished notice-
ably. The decline of the city as an entrepôt and as a manufacturing center meant that many transactions in the early twentieth century were
handled through "petty shops . . . [that] are little more than the adjunct
of the workshops of small artisans, mechanics, and manufacturers. The
makers of certain classes of ornaments, of white caps, of country (biri)
cigarettes, of hookahs, of tin boxes, of basket-ware, of sweetmeats, of
perfumes, are petty manufacturers and workmen first and shopkeepers
second."[99]

No longer present in any significant numbers were the large wholesale dealers, so noticeable in the early nineteenth century. Thus, the
1920–21 economic census of the "Patna Bazaar" turned up mostly
small-scale dealers or retailers, of cloth, groceries, ornaments, cigarettes, stationery, and fancy goods—their business conducted from tiny
shop fronts attached to their residences.[100]

And what of the "garden" of Azimabad itself? How did its built environment stand up to the tremors of the eighteenth-century "revolution"? Did the city register the decline that Ghulam Husain chronicled
for his "modern times"? And how did it fare in the aftermath of the
"revolution," when deindustrialization and the age of railways signaled
its growing incorporation into a larger colonial system and a world
economy?

The "English" practice of "counting the inhabitants of every town
and city" offers ample evidence that Patna's growth and expansion
continued well beyond the "modern times" and until the late nine-

---

99. Hamilton, "Census of Patna Bazaar," p. 96

100. Ibid. At the head of the list were 848 retail shops, the largest number of these
dealing in tobacco, betel, and aerated water (126); cloth (97); groceries (khichri farosh,
spices, sugar, salt, and grains) (96); stationery and fancy goods (80); fruits and vegetables
(45); grain (35); boots and shoes (33); caps, generally combined with a business in the
sale of "other fancy articles" (28); drugs (25); oil (23); meat (butchers) (19); oil and hardware (17); books and printing (16); brass ware (15); rope and basket ware (15); iron
(ironmongers) (13); perfume (12); and earthenware (11). In addition there were 586
manufacturing and retail shops, including sweetmeats (81); tailors (60); goldsmiths (53);
ornament makers (49); glass ornament (tikuli) makers (28); tinsmiths (22); brass ware
makers (20), woodworkers (20); dyers (19); cotton thread makers (17); blacksmiths (17);
shoemakers (17); watch repairers (15); repairers of tin or iron goods (14); cabinetmakers
(12); and country cigarette (biri) makers (12). Another 9 counted among the ranks of
wholesale traders and consisted of 3 tobacco godowns and dealers, 3 yarn dealers, 1 timber dealer, 1 lime and cement dealer, and 1 pepper dealer. "Patna Bazaar" in this report
refers to the entire area along the main road between the Bankipur Maidan and the eastern extremity of the "city." Although a reasonable account of the "majority of the trading and petty manufacturing establishments of Patna," this report does not include the
"petty traders and manufacturers located in the side streets" (p. 95).

teenth century. Thereafter population growth leveled off, and may even have declined, although not quite as appreciably as some scholars have claimed in identifying deurbanization as part of the process of deindustrialization.[101]

Until the late nineteenth century Azimabad grew, expanding westward in the direction of Bankipur. This growth was largely confined to a narrow stretch of riverbank along the Ganges because the river constituted a natural boundary to the north; to the south the Punpun, with its tendency to flood, acted as another barrier. Only in the twentieth century, to accommodate increasing numbers of people, has the city extended in other directions, for instance, eastward. Patna thus became a city of "length without breadth."[102]

Measurements of its linearity and elongation taken at different times are handy markers of its chronology of growth. Thus, Ralph Fitch in 1586 had found a "very long and great Towne" of Patna, measuring a mile and a half from the eastern to the western gate and three quarters of a mile from north to south, whereas Tavernier's appraisal less than a century later shows a settlement "not less than two coss [four miles] in length." By the latter's estimation Patna was the "largest town in Bengal" and "one of the largest towns in India." In the opening decade of the nineteenth century, it included an area extending from Jaffar Khan's gardens to Bankipur—almost nine miles—and a width averaging two miles, for a total area of almost twenty square miles. By the mid-twentieth century the "very long Towne" measured twelve miles from east to west; in breadth, however, it still hugged the course of the Ganges, in some areas extending no farther than a half mile from the river.[103]

As the chronology of the elongation of Patna suggests, and as the *longue durée* view confirms, the city and its population had been growing ever since the late sixteenth century. No doubt, the pace quickened in the eighteenth and early nineteenth centuries, beginning with the attempts by Prince Azim-us-Shah to elevate Azimabad to new heights and continuing under the British, who designated it as the locus of their

---

101. Habib, "Studying a Colonial Economy," pp. 364–68, makes a case for the decline of cities and towns as part of the process of deindustrialization.

102. H. Beveridge, "The City of Patna," *Calcutta Review* 76, no. 152 (1883): 211; *PDG 1970*, p. v; Patna Improvement Trust, *Master Plan, Patna*, vol. 1, *Text and Photographs* (Patna: Patna Improvement Trust, n.d.).

103. Buchanan, *Bihar and Patna*, p. 61; Patna, *Master Plan*, p. 17; Sarkar, "Patna in the Seventeenth Century," pp. 128–29.

power and authority in Bihar. In-migration from the west in the eighteenth and nineteenth centuries added to Patna's numbers.[104] So did the influx of people from other settlements in the region, such as the town of Bihar in the eighteenth and early nineteenth centuries and Gaya, particularly after the headquarters of the old district of Patna and Gaya was shifted from Gaya to Patna. To hear the principal residents of Gaya tell of the effects in 1797, so many of their fellow inhabitants moved to Patna—in step with the relocation of the treasury and district offices there—that there were a "great many empty houses and . . . [a] constant fear of robbers and murderers."[105]

Its growth can also be documented from internal evidence. Buchanan alluded to the rising pressure of numbers on the land when he observed that "the city is said to have greatly increased, and the value of the ground in it, within these 15 years, is said to have doubled, owing to the difficulty of procuring a spot for building a house."[106] "That Patna is in a flourishing state is evident by the number of new dwellings which are always building," states one 1818 report. "In the City there is little room left for more houses; but good habitations are built on the sites of old or inferior ones, and in the suburbs, particularly to the westward, the number of houses is increasing."[107]

In the twenty square miles he identified as Patna, Buchanan estimated a population of 312,000. By this reckoning, Patna was the largest city in India at that time. Compare this number with the enumerations returned by the decennial censuses of the late nineteenth and early twentieth centuries: 170,654 in 1881, 165,192 in 1891, 134,785 in 1901, 136,153 in 1911, and 119,976 in 1921. Not until the 1961 census did Patna again top 300,000 inhabitants—with 364,667 to be exact.[108]

104. The petition of "200 Mahomedans," Patna, May 3, 1837, Bengal Rev. Consltns., June 13–27, 1837, June 27, no. 70, mentions ancestors who immigrated to Patna from Persia and Kabul.

105. "Translation of a Memorial . . . of the Principal Bankers and Other Inhabitants of the City of Gya . . . " Bengal Rev. Consltns., May 5 to July 28, 1797, May 8, no. 25; Law, Colltr., Bihar, to John Shore, President and Members, BOR, Bengal Rev. Consltns., Oct. 25 to Dec. 28, 1787, Dec. 7.

106. Bihar and Patna, p. 63.

107. Patna Court of Appeal to Bayley, Secy., Oct. 23, 1818, Bengal Cr. Jdcl. Consltns., Nov. 6 to Dec. 16, 1818, Dec. 4, no. 40.

108. Patna, Master Plan, p. 7. Buchanan's figure is based on an 1810 tally of 52,000 houses, each of which was estimated to have 6 inhabitants. See his Bihar and Patna, p. 61; Hagen, "Indigenous Society in Patna," p. 61. K. M. Mohsin, "Murshidabad in the Eighteenth Century," in The City in South Asia: Pre-Modern and Modern, ed. Kenneth Ballhatchet and John Harrison (London: Curzon Press, 1980), pp. 76–77, estimates a population of 200,000 for Murshidabad and Dacca.

In light of these later census tallies, Buchanan's figure may seem to be grossly exaggerated, but it is probably less inaccurate than it appears initially.[109] Nor is the sizable population of the city in the early nineteenth century inconsistent with the demographic trends a century later.[110] A substantial corrective is necessary, however, because the enormous drop registered by the censuses to a little over 170,000 in 1881 and the subsequent pattern of continuous decrease over the next few decades, with a bottoming out at a little less than 120,000 in 1921, grossly overstate the actual numerical decline. While not inaccurate in indicating the *pattern of decline* in this period, the figures do not take into account the entire city of Patna but only a limited area of nine square miles comprising the "city" and part of the suburbs. By contrast, early-nineteenth-century estimates by Buchanan and others cast their statistical net over an area of twenty square miles.[111] There was, nevertheless, a general leveling off and decrease in population in the region, affecting Patna in particular because it was fading as a trading and commercial center. And within the "city," hardest hit were Khwaja Kalan,

109. Earlier estimates include Manrique (in 1641)—200,000 people—and Thomas Twining (in 1790s)—approximately 300,000. *Chaukidari* (night watchmen or village police) returns of 1817 similarly put the figure at almost 300,000. At odds with these figures, however, is an 1818 estimate of 247,464. Although this tally was made at a time when cholera had struck twice in eighteen months, the figure nevertheless comes in much lower than most estimates in the early nineteenth century, when deaths from the epidemic were calculated at only four to five thousand. The Patna Improvement Committee accepted 300,000 as the right figure; a census in 1837, however, placed the number at 284,132. W. H. Tippet, Magte., City of Patna, to W. B. Bayley, Offg. Chief Secy., Oct. 11, 1817, Bengal Cr. Jdcl. Consltns., Nov. 14 to 25, 1817, Nov. 11, no. 36; Naqvi, *Urban Centres in India*, p. 105; Wm. H. G. Twining, ed., *Travels in India a Hundred Years Ago with a Visit to the United States: Being Notes and Reminiscences by Thomas Twining* (London: James R. Osgood, 1893), p. 135; Committee of Improvement to H. Shakespear, Secy., Govt., July 28, 1829, Bengal Cr. Jdcl. Consltns., Sept. 22, 1829, no. 8; Patna Court of Appeal to Bayley, Oct. 23, 1818, Bengal Cr. Jdcl. Consltns., Dec. 4, 1818, no. 40; H. E. L. Thuiller, *Statistics of the District of Patna* (Calcutta: n.p., 1847), p. 1.

110. In part the welter of seemingly conflicting data can be explained by the absence of accurate information-collecting agencies; in part the highs and lows can be regarded as reflecting actual fluctuations in the city's population. Based on the low estimate of 247,464 and Buchanan's high figure of 320,000, it would be safe to conclude that the actual population ranged between 250,000 to 300,000. The quantitative data point in this direction, especially the house count rendered for *chaukidari* purposes. Indeed, this was a census that people preferred to evade, since being counted meant paying a *chaukidari* tax. And the qualitative evidence attests to the steady westward expansion of Patna boundaries.

111. GOI, *Census of India, 1891*, vol. 3, *The Lower Provinces of Bengal, The Report*, by C. J. O'Donnell (Calcutta: Bengal Secretariat Press, 1893), p. 113; Hagen, "Indigenous Society in Patna," p. 63. "City" in the British records increasingly came to refer to the older portion of Patna, which was to be distinguished from the newer area known as Bankipur.

Chauk Kalan, and Malsalami, localities whose prosperity was tied to the fortunes of trade. In short, the declining population was a symptom of Patna's fading economic health, a deterioration that would have been all the more pronounced had Patna not received a tremendous political boost in the twentieth century, when it became a provincial capital.[112]

In the age of revolution the city was not only the site of political, economic, and social activity but it was also the place of residence for its notables, particularly its merchants and bankers. As its leading traders and bankers stated in the early nineteenth century, they maintained "puckah [solid, meaning brick] houses and godowns [there], and the purchasing and selling of goods all within the city of Patna.... All the bankers are residents within the City and near the bazaar of the great chouk [city center]."[113]

Perhaps the most striking aspect of the city's appearance in the initial colonial period was the extent to which its quotidian landscape was a legacy of both Ghulam Husain's "modern times" and the preceding eras. Let us begin with the spatial grid of Azimabad, an important template that had been deeply marked by the coming of Prince Azim-us-Shah, who is widely credited with having organized its *muhallas,* or quarters. When he relocated in the city, "many of the nobles of Delhi came out to live within its walls. The City was divided into a number of wards. All classes of people had separate quarters assigned to them. Dewan Mohalla was so named, because it was assigned to the clerks of the Government offices; the quarters assigned to the Lodis (Afghans) came to be known as Lodikatra Mohalla; those allotted to the Moghuls, as Moghulpara; and the princes and chiefs had their residence assigned to them in Mohalla Khowah Sekho, or, as it is otherwise called, Khowah Khoh. The poor and destitute were not forgotten; and several serais and alms-houses were built for their reception."[114]

In establishing *muhallas* that organized people into elite quarters and set up ethnic and occupational groups in their own quarters, this Mughal

---

112. *Census of India, 1921,* vol. 7, *Bihar and Orissa, Report,* p. 86. Plague in the early twentieth century also took its toll on the city's residents.
113. See "Translate [*sic*] of a Petition Presented by Sulloo Baboo, Sukhee Chund...Beoparees," June 24, 1828, P.C. Records, vol. 179, From the Bd. of Custom, Salt and Opium, Dec. 11, 1813 to Nov. 27, 1833.
114. G. P. S., "Patna of the Mahomedans," p. 115. See also Jim Masselos, "Appropriating Urban Space: Social Constructs of Bombay in the Time of the Raj," paper presented at the Social Science Research Council Workshop on "Culture and Consciousness," Isle of Thorns, Sussex, July 1989, on the spatial makeup of the city as a series of templates.

prince followed a long-standing precedent. Such deeply rooted patterns explain why these residentially organized quarters gave rise to a sense of place and identity. In the sovereign Mughal city of Shahjahanabad, as a recent study shows, caste, craft, and elite *muhallas* existed with caste or craft quarters headed by chiefs of caste councils (*panchayats*): "Chiefs settled intramahallah quarrels, judged disputes over land and other property, and decided questions of ritual status. They negotiated taxes with city authorities, arranged security against both internal and external disturbances, and consulted with other chaudhuris on matters of common interest. Mahallahs were surrounded by high walls and contained houses, shops and stalls where food, clothing, and other supplies were sold, wells and tanks for water, and resthouses for travellers. People gathered in mosques and temples to hear political announcements, celebrate marriages, and exchange gossip."[115]

Some localities were named after their pioneering or notable residents. Chaudhuritola commemorated the presence of its resident Chaudhuri family, also the leading family of the *muhalla*. According to its official history, the family first came to Bihar in the early eighteenth century as part of the Mughal army. Because of meritorious service, one member of the family, who took up residence in Patna, received the title of *chaudhuri*, or chief. In the late eighteenth and the nineteenth centuries the family continued to prosper, its members branching out from landholding to moneylending, and becoming, in their own words, "leaders. . . . Reis of the old type."[116] Throughout India *muhallas* were named after an area's "pre-dominant caste or occupational group . . . the founder's name or that of the original rural village on the site, or a market, a public building, or an old city gate. The population of a *mohalla* may be several thousands or tens of thousands."[117]

Thus were *muhallas* a fundamental template of the city of Patna, constituting, as they did in other north Indian cities, a "basic unit of urban social organization and . . . associational activity."[118] In this "city"

115. Stephen P. Blake, *Shahjahanabad: The Sovereign City in Mughal India, 1639–1739* (Cambridge: Cambridge University Press, 1991), p. 84.

116. Pandit Rampratap Pandey, "A Short History of the Chaudhary Family, Patna City," (trans. from Hindi), in Ramgopal Singh Chowdhary, *Select Writings and Speeches of Babu Ramgopal Singh Chowdhary* (Patna: Bishund Prasad Sinha, 1920), pp. i–xxiv, esp. x.

117. John E. Brush, "The Morphology of Indian Cities," in *India's Urban Future*, ed. Roy Turner (Berkeley and Los Angeles: University of California Press, 1962), p. 60.

118. Sandria B. Freitag, "Introduction: The History and Political Economy of Banaras," in *Culture and Power in Banaras: Community, Performance, and Environment,*

dominated by trade and commerce, traders, merchants, and artisans particularly were organized along residential lines—by *muhallas*—as well as by occupation. When government imposed a new duty in 1790, not only were there protests from "merchants, bankers and dealers" representing Azimabad, but protests were also forthcoming from other groups organized along residential (*muhalla*) and occupational lines. For instance, the *beoparis* of Mehdiganj, who were *kirana* dealers, spoke up in unison. Others who raised their voices collectively were organized by their profession, such as confectioner and cloth seller. At the bidding of the latter all the cloth shops in the city were shut down and "cloth was not procurable even for the burial of the dead."[119]

By the twentieth century some of these organizations had dissolved, in part because handicraft industries and local manufacturing had declined and in part because some of the artisanal activities were no longer monopolized by a single caste. Thus, there were caste *panchayats* (councils) among the *tabaq* beaters (makers of *tabaq,* a kind of washing vessel), the copper- and brass-smiths, the lace makers, the turners, and the comb makers, but not among makers of *tikuli* (glass ornaments), whose ranks included "many . . . wage-earning classes . . . scattered over the whole town . . . [and not] inhabiting a particular Mahalla."[120]

The colonial government—as the Mughals before them—sought to capitalize on the existing organization of *muhallas* by penetrating urban society through them: *muhallas* were grouped into *thanas* (police circles) and thus integrated into a police system. At the beginning of the nineteenth century Patna was organized into sixteen *thanas;* later in the century the number was increased to seventeen. The sixteen thanas together comprised 222 *muhallas.* Chauk Kallan *thana,* for instance, extended over 29 *muhallas;* Mehdiganj, on the other end of the scale, extended over only 3.[121]

1800–1980, ed. idem (Berkeley and Los Angeles: University of California Press, 1989), pp. 18–19.

119. G. F. Grand, Judge and Magte., Patna, to T. Law, Colltr., Behar, Aug. 29, 1789, Bengal Rev. Consltns., Feb. 19 to Mar. 10, 1790, Feb. 19; "Petition of . . . Halways of the city," "Petition of . . . Beoparries Residing at Mehdee Gunge," "Petition of . . . Merchants, Bankers and Dealers . . . Gentoos and Musulmen" and "Translate of . . . Narrative of Facts Attested by 40 Banker Merchants . . . ," Bengal Rev. Consltns., Jan. 6–20, 1790, Jan. 6, no. 18.

120. Moulvi Abul Hasan M. Taib, "Report on an Enquiry into the Position of the Smaller Traders and Artisans in Patna City," in *Chanakya Society, 5th Annual Report,* pp. 30–49, esp. 32.

121. T. C. Robertson, Acting Magte., Patna, to W. Blunt, Suptd., Police, Jan. 17, 1817, Bengal Cr. Jdcl. Consltns., 1817, Feb. 14, no. 4; Hunter, *Account of Patna,* p. 191. The

Muhallas also figured in the subsidiary police system of night watchmen (*chaukidars*) instituted in the early nineteenth century. The leading notables of each ward, generally "merchants," were singled out as *muhalladars,* local men of power and influence, charged with collecting information in their wards for purposes of levying the unpopular *chaukidari* tax and for collecting the tax. Such men were the urban counterparts of the major landholders that government recruited as its intermediaries in rural localities in the wake of the Permanent Settlement of 1793. They were vital links for the colonial state, as their consent and cooperation legitimized and enhanced the authority of the Raj. Their integration into the local structures of formal and informal administration also enabled the British to keep a rein on these powerful local controllers. Not surprisingly, the position of *muhalladar* became a coveted office. Thus, an influential Patna resident who had been stripped of this position for his "considerable" absence from the city actively and successfully campaigned "in the most object [*sic*] and submissive manner, to have it restored to him, declaring that by the deprivation he felt himself lowered in the estimation of the people in his neighbourhood."[122]

In contrast to *muhallas* that extended over all of the city, *ganjs,* or small regulated markets, were found in specific areas, typically those areas that served as "emporium[s] for grain and other necessaries of life." Major *ganjs* handled the trade of the region; lesser *ganjs* served the needs of their localities or their neighborhoods. Some ganjs were coterminous with *muhallas*, others were part of *muhallas*. Their prominence in the economic life and the spatial organization of the city was acknowledged by the colonial authorities who often designated *ganjs* as the hubs of their police system of *thanas.*[123]

Established and patronized by prominent local men who were distinguished members of the region's aristocracy, most of Patna's *ganjs* originated and were developed in the eighteenth century. And their per

---

sixteen *thanas* in the early nineteenth century were: Bankipur, Pirbahore, Sultanganj, Alamganj, Colonelganj, Sadikpur, Diwan Mohulla, Mehdiganj, Mogulpurah, Khajekallan, Lodikatra, Chauk Kallan, Chauk Shikarpur, Dhalpurah, Malsalami, and Begumganj.

122. Robertson to Police, Jan. 17, 1817, Bengal Cr. Jdcl. Consltns., Feb. 14, 1817, no. 4; Freitag, "History of Banaras," pp. 18–19.

123. Robertson to Police, Jan. 17, 1817, Bengal Cr. Jdcl. Consltns., Feb. 14, 1817, no. 4; H. H. Wilson, *A Glossary of Judicial and Revenue Terms* (1855; reprint, Delhi: Munshiram Manoharlal, 1968), p. 165.

sistence well into the nineteenth century as the main business quarters of the city reinforces the trade profile sketched earlier.

Increasingly, the most important commercial *ganj* in the city was Russut or Marufganj, located at the eastern extremity of the "city," under the shadow of the eastern walls.[124] Established in 1764 by Nawab Ikram-daula and patronized by the East India Company in the late eighteenth century, in its rise it eclipsed Nawabganj and Mandiganj, both of which dated back to the early eighteenth century. Marufganj and nearby *ganjs* received most of the boats bringing in goods in the late eighteenth and the nineteenth centuries. Its residents characterized it as *"the* commercial mart of Patna city."[125]

Marufganj's control of the valuable oilseed trade—almost two-thirds (or 728,237 maunds) of the city's total supply passed through it—reflects its primacy. Sugar, salt, and food grains were other major items available at this *ganj*. Mansurganj, an inland mart south of Marufganj, ranked second in volume, its trade centered mainly on oilseeds (104,968 maunds); it also imported salt (56,873 maunds), sugar (8,000 maunds), and food grains from Patna and neighboring southern districts. The riverside mart of Colonelganj, the most western of the big *ganjs* of Patna, was another important "regulated market," best known for its import of oilseeds (137,370 maunds) and for food grains from north Bihar and from Bengal. Other *ganjs,* smaller in size than Marufganj, Mansurganj, and Colonelganj, that played an active role in the trade of Patna were Sadikpur and Maharajganj. They spe-

124. Other major *ganjs* were: Hindiganj (established in 1721); Begumganj (1724); Hajiganj (founded in 1752 by Nawab Haji); Floreyganj (founded in 1766 by Nawab Jaffar Ali Khan); Maharajganj (founded in 1772 by Maharaja Shitab Rai); and Shahganj (founded in 1730 by Nawab Fakhr-ad-daula). In addition, there were Murtuzaganj, Qazibagh, Kabutrah Khannah, Alabakspur, Masallapur, Hakimganj, Dandunmandi, Arafabad, Rasulpur, Khamepur, and Mandi Begumpur, all established in the early eighteenth century and all engaged in the sale of food grains. Beyond the limits of the "city" lay Colonelganj, another "great market for grain," established in 1763 by Nawab Ikram-daula. BOR to W. Money, Colltr., July 28, 1824, P.C. Records, From Colltr. of Bihar, vol. 11, 1824. See also Law, Colltr., Bihar, to Henry Revell, Colltr., Govt. Customs, Aug. 23, 1788, Bengal Rev. Consltns., Feb. 19 to Mar. 10, 1790, Feb. 19, no. 87

125. "Memorial of the Inhabitants of Mohulla Maroofgunge...," Bengal Public Works Procs., Jan.-Apr. 1876, Apr., no. 3; Petition of Sheikh Fuckur Oollah etc., with Grand to Law, Aug. 29, 1789, Bengal Rev. Consltns., Feb. 19 to Mar. 10, 1790, Feb. 24, no. 20; W. R. Jennings, Colltr., Govt. Customs, Patna, to H. M. Parker, Secy., Bd. of Customs, July 10, 1828, P.C. Records, Customs, vol. 179, Dec. 11, 1813 to Nov. 27, 1833. The ward comprising Marufganj—it included Malsalami, Marufganj and Chalkiat bazaar—paid more than twice the amount of police taxes (Rs. 5,280 as opposed to Rs. 2135-4) than the second-most highly taxed ward. See Statement of Police Taxes, Bengal BOR Procs., Police, Jan. 15 to Dec. 13, 1796, Jan. 15.

cialized in oilseeds and cereals; Alabakspur, an inland mart, chiefly imported oilseeds, as was also the case with neighboring Arafabad; and Gulzarbagh dealt in oilseeds, unrefined sugar, shoes, and rattans.

In the heart of the "city" lay the Chauk, Mirchaiganj adjoining it, and east of the latter, the Qila (fort) that was known as "the cotton mart." These marts were the center of the cloth import trade—largely in the hands of Marwaris; other imports included various metals, iron, copper and brass, spices, silk, and "'miscellaneous English goods'... umbrellas, knives, scissors, walking sticks, crockeryware, glassware, hardware, &c." Whereas the big riverfront *ganjs*, particularly Marufganj, Gulzarbagh, and Colonelganj, received most of their goods from throughout the wider region, the inland markets of Mansurganj, the Chauk with Mirchaiganj, Maharajganj, Sadikpur, and Alabakspur, were supplied primarily from their immediate hinterland—Patna district itself and Gaya and Shahabad—and their supplies, principally oilseeds and food grains, were transported there by carts and pack bullocks.[126]

The mosques were another conspicuous feature of the city. Well into the nineteenth century, British visitors to Patna considered it a Muslim-dominated place because of its religious architecture. As one British observer noted on viewing Azimabad from the Ganges: "[T]hough it does not contain any single building of great celebrity or peculiar beauty, [it] is rich in the remains of Moosulman splendour.... [A]nd when the river is full and brimming to its banks, turret, spire, and dome... reflected in its broad mirror, the *coup d'oeil* is exceedingly imposing."[127]

Moreover, the denizens of Patna continued to regard the city as an Islamicized place in the nineteenth century, an identity also associated with "other mughalizing urban centers in north India."[128] It was an identity that had evolved in Patna while it was a regional Mughal headquarters town, an experience imprinted on the lifestyle of its people and the built environment of the city. There was, as well, a disproportionate number of Muslims among its inhabitants. Although Hindus constituted almost 88 percent of the population of the district in the late nineteenth century and Muslims a little more than 11 percent, in the city the latter numbered more than 12 percent, and in the "city" it-

126. Rattray report; Robertson to Police, Jan. 17, 1817, Bengal Cr. Jdcl. Consltns., Feb. 14, 1817, no. 4; *Trade of Bengal, 1876–77,* p. 196. See also below, chap. 5, on Marwaris and other traders and merchants.

127. "Mofussil Stations, Patna," p. 249.

128. Freitag, "History of Banaras," p. 9.

self almost 24 percent. They were especially well represented in Pirba-hor, a *thana* where large numbers of Muslims working for the British resided, and in Khwaja Kalan, "essentially the Muhammadan quarter where the chief mosque is."[129]

The city's "imposing" remains, so evocative of its earlier promi-nence, must have further heightened the sense of loss felt by the aristo-cratic generation during the revolution. The remembered past of the historian and poets must have seemed all the more grand in contrast to the changes of their own times. Mosques, the major landmarks, were surely striking indeed for the British visitors, who viewed the city as lit-tle more than a "collection of mud huts, separated by narrow and often very dirty lanes [and without] any public buildings of interest or impor-tance."[130] In addition to mosques, the city's sacred geography for Mus-lim devotees was also notable as the site of four *pirs* (Muslim saints)—Mansur, Maruf, Jafar, and Mahdi—and of the shrine of Shah Arzani.[131]

Ritual occasions further dramatized the Muslim appearance of the "city" because they seemed to attract Muslims and Hindus equally, well into the nineteenth century. Contemporary accounts describe a lo-cal society in which Muslims coexisted harmoniously with Hindus, each group participating in the other's festivals. At the festival of Mo-hurrum, one of the biggest religious event of the year (as many as a hundred thousand were said to have attended in the late nineteenth century), "the whole population of Patna, Moslem, Christian, and Hin-doo, assemble[d] to witness the procession."[132]

Patna was also the site of Hindu places of worship, as well as an in-termediate stop on the way to Gaya for those pilgrims traveling on the Ganges or by the old Mughal highway. Only with the development of

129. Muslims declined in numbers in the late nineteenth and early twentieth centuries in part because of the outmigration of weavers or Jolahas. See *Census 1891, Patna Divi-sion*, p. 4; Hunter, *Account of Patna*, p. 65; Grierson, *Notes on Gaya*, p. 118; "Mofussil Stations, Patna," p. 252.

130. H. Beveridge, "The City of Patna," *Calcutta Review* 76, no. 152 (1883): 215.

131. *PDG 1924*, pp. 67; 177–89; Syed Hasan "The City of Patna—Etymology of Place-Names," in *Patna through the Ages*, ed. Qeyamuddin Ahmad (New Delhi: Com-monwealth Publishers, 1988), pp. 53–70. Other than the mosque of Sher Shah (dating from the 1540s) and of Allauddin Shah (1489), most of the major mosques were from the seventeenth and eighteenth centuries.

132. "Mofussil Stations, Patna," p. 252. See also Chunder, *Travels of a Hindoo*, vol. 1, p. 118; Syed Badrul Hasan, *Yadgar-e-Rozgar* (Patna: n.p., 1931); Ali Muhammad Shad, *Naqsh-e-Paidar*, vol. 2 (Patna: n.p., 1924). Recent scholarship attests to the higher degree of cooperation and collective celebration existing between Hindus and Muslims prior to the so-called communal conflicts of the late and early twentieth centuries. E.g., see Freitag, "History of Banaras," pp. 11–15.

railways and roads in the late nineteenth century and the resultant new
routes did this pattern change. For Sikhs, Patna was important as the
site of the birthplace of their tenth guru (Govind Singh), an event later
commemorated by a temple called Har Mandir. And as ancient Patna
had been the heartland of earlier religions, it was also graced by a number of Buddhist and Jain relics.[133]

Beyond this "garden" of *muhallas* and *ganjs* and mosques and temples lay another Patna, a city in which the "English" presence was increasingly more visible and an area that was just beginning to develop
in the age of revolution. A visitor to the city at the end of the nineteenth century would have found the map in Ghulam Husain's *Modern
Times* inadequate because the city had grown so. In part, the new configuration was an outgrowth of the policies of the "alien" regime. As
the Patna historian's account indicates, the "English" deliberately set
themselves apart from local society, openly exhibiting an "aversion . . .
for the company of the natives, and such the disdain . . . that no love,
and no coalition . . . can take root between conquerors and the con-
quered."[134] Buchanan personally articulated this "disdain" in declaring
that the Indian Patna was "a disgusting place. There is one street tolerably wide that runs from the eastern to the western gate. Every other
passage is narrow. Paving, cleaning and lighting, considered so essential in every European town in such circumstances are totally out of
[the] question. In the heats of spring the dust is beyond credibility, and
in the rains every place is covered with mud. . . . In the rainy season
there is in the town a considerable pond or lake, which, as it dries up,
becomes exceedingly dirty, and in spring is offensive."[135]

Such a perspective hardened into the official view. "European visitors," noted an early-nineteenth-century account, rarely ever entered
the "city . . . except upon duty. When there is no particular object of
celebrity to attract attention, Anglo-Indians, either from contempt or

133. Chowdhari, *Rambles in Bihar*, pp. 7, 14; *PDG 1924*, pp. 61–65; 165–97; Hagen, "Indigenous Society in Patna," pp. 70–72. In addition to the temples associated
with the presiding deities of Patna, Bari (Big) Patan devi, and the Chhoti (Small) Patan
devi, there were also those of Satya Narayan, Gopinath, Govindbagh, the Shivala of
Gauri Shanker, the Shivala of Jugeshwar Nath, Kali, Sitala, and the Thakurbari of Baba
Bhisham Das.

134. *Seir*, vol. 3, pp. 161–62. The original is in italics. See also Qeyamuddin Ahmad,
"An Eighteenth-Century Indian Historian on Early British Administration," *Journal of
Indian History* (1973): 893–907, for a discussion of the "causes" cited by Ghulam Hu-
sain for the shortcomings of "English" rule.

135. Buchanan, *Bihar and Patna*, pp. 58–59.

apathy, rarely enter the native towns in their neighbourhood."[136] Much the same tone is evident in George Graham's description of his journey through the bazaars of Patna in the late nineteenth century: "Anything but pleasant; the dust was choking, and the stench of oil and rancid ghee was overpowering. It being the cold weather too, a great number of wood fires were lighted, the wood being by preference damp, and emitting the most pungent smoke, hostile indeed to mosquitoes, but very trying to the eyes and sense of smell."[137]

Nor did the British perception of Patna "city" as an impenetrable, even a hostile, place help to bridge the divide between Bankipur and the "city."[138] Patna's negative reputation dated back to 1763, when Nawab Mir Qasim killed his English prisoners—an event remembered in British accounts as the Patna Massacre. According to one contemporary source, the very decision to settle in Bankipur and not in the "city" was prompted by this "treacherous attack." Periodically in the nineteenth century, the city was rife with rumors of the impending massacres of Europeans by hostile "natives." Were these perhaps the expressions of "subaltern consciousness" regarding the alien "English" that in the postrevolutionary era were uttered in the vocabulary of re-

136. "Mofussil Stations—Patna," p. 255. For similar observations regarding other cities, see Veena Talwar Oldenburg, *The Making of Colonial Lucknow, 1856–1877* (Princeton: Princeton University Press, 1984), pp. 18–19.

137. [G. Graham] An Ex.-Civilian, *Life in the Mofussil; or, the Civilian in Lower Bengal* (London: C. Kegan Paul, 1878), pp. 62–63. Complaints about "disgusting" Patna notwithstanding, colonial administrators did little to alleviate the conditions of the "native town." On the contrary, as the European translator of Ghulam Husain's history noted, a standard charge "against the English by the natives" was "that of so many English that have carried away such Princely fortunes from this country, not one of them has ever thought of shewing his gratitude to it, by sinking a well, digging a pond, planting a public grove, raising a caravensera, or building a bridge." *Seir*, vol. 3, p. 183, note 131. For additional details on piecemeal and failed municipal projects in the city, see my "The City of Patna: The Central Place of Exchange," paper presented at the Western Conference of the Association for Asian Studies, Tucson, Arizona, Oct. 1987.

138. A "good and permanent road" between Bankipur to the eastern extremity of the "city" did not exist as late as the 1820s, although a "committee for the improvement of the city of Patna" had been involved in road-building and other municipal projects since the second decade of the nineteenth century. By contrast, note the committee's successes in undertaking works of "public and military importance": the upkeep of a "high military road" from Bankipur to the cantonment town of Danapur and the construction of a well and a small tank near the parade grounds in Bankipur, both obviously better situated for people residing in that "suburb," especially for the military personnel using those grounds, than for the ordinary people of Patna. Committee to Shakespear, Bengal Cr. Jdcl. Consltns., Sept. 22, 1829, no. 8; W. M. Fleming, et al., to W. B. Bayley, Secy., Govt., Jdcl., Ibid., June 3 to 10, 1824, June 3, no. 20; G. Dowdeswell to H. Douglas, A. Welland, D. Campbell and W. Money, Jan. 15, 1814, Ibid., Jan. 1 to 22, 1814, Jan. 15, no. 12.

sistance rather than the poetic lament of "ruin" and "despair." William Tayler, the commissioner of Patna during the tumultuous period of the Mutiny/Rebellion of 1857 considered the city to be "a very sink of disaffection and intrigue."[139]

The British association of Patna with "disaffection and intrigue" was also related to the perception of it as a Muslim city. One early-nineteenth-century observer characterized it as a "stronghold of Mohammedanism, and the disciples of the prophet, who dwell within its walls, are described as being far more fanatic and intolerant than their brethren of Bengal."[140] Local administrators kept a wary eye on the Wahabis because of their numerous conspiracies against the British in the nineteenth century.[141]

The missionary experience reinforced this negative image. One missionary ranked Patna alongside Murshidabad as the two cities in the region with the most "hostile feeling to Europeans." For only in Patna were there instances—said to be rare in India—of missionaries encountering "virulent opposition, and even personal violence . . . chiefly from the Muhammadans." And as far as the police were concerned, there was not only the "somewhat turbulent population," with suspect political outlooks to contend with, but also "'badmashes' [miscreants]."[142]

Furthermore, British attitudes toward "disgusting" Patna—or the "city" that was exclusively inhabited by Indians—were reinforced by the "scientific" discourse that emerged about cleanliness in "native" towns in the late nineteenth century. Sanitation became a paramount concern because British troops had suffered higher casualties from disease-related deaths than from combat during the Mutiny/Rebellion of 1857–58. And since contemporary theory linked dirt and disease, and sanitary conditions of "native" towns with the occurrence of epidemics in the wider population, including even the "distant" European quarter, the latter-day improvement (municipal) committees once again focused

139. W. Tayler, *The Patna Crisis* (London: W. H. Allen, 1882), p. 21; "Mofussil Stations, Patna," p. 250. For a similar impression of Lucknow, see Oldenburg, *Colonial Lucknow,* pp. 20–26. See also my "A Conversation of Rumors: The Language of Popular Mentalités in Late Nineteenth-Century India," *Journal of Social History* 20 (1987): 485–505.

140. "Mofussil Stations, Patna," p. 252.

141. Qeyamuddin Ahmad, *The Wahabi Movement in India* (Calcutta: Firma K. L. Mukhopadhyay, 1966). One of the few occasions when the British attempted to reshape the "city" was when they tore down and confiscated the Sadiqpur properties of "convicted Wahabi traitors" and sought to build in their place a "good market."

142. *Patna Census, 1891,* p. 1; Buyers, *Recollections of India,* p. 200.

their attention on the "disgusting" places. As a result, in Patna—as in Lucknow—municipal committees under the direction of local British administrators combined "genuine concern for the lack of adequate drainage and rubbish disposal, some good common sense about clean drinking water and more and better public toilets, some prejudice about 'native habits,' and a spirit of bold experimentation . . . to clean up the city."[143] But, as in their previous close encounter with the "native" city, their efforts were consistently hampered by financial constraints. Lack of funding in Patna meant that no "large schemes" were introduced "which would completely remedy the insanitary conditions produced by many centuries of neglect."[144]

These perceptions deepened the "aversion" between Azimabad, increasingly called the "city," and the Patna of the alien rulers that clustered around the area known as Bankipur. In other words, the new regime deliberately established its own private and public spaces at a far remove from those of its subjects. Only five miles separated the western wall of the "city" and the British-built Golghar (granary) in Bankipur, but in the colonial imagination the "city" grew increasingly remote. By the late nineteenth century not a single European resided in Azimabad, and similarly, well into that century, Bankipur remained a European enclave inhabited by "very few natives."[145]

But the shift toward Bankipur was not an entirely novel development: expansion in that direction was well under way before the advent of colonial rule. From the beginning of the eighteenth century, according to Ghulam Husain, his fellow residents were constructing "numerous houses and ha[b]itations" beyond the confines of the city walls. This westward expansion was pioneered by wealthy residents building garden houses along the riverbank leading up to Bankipur. They were joined and increasingly supplanted by the new masters of the city, the British, who staked out many of the prime locations beyond the western gate of the

143. Oldenburg, *Colonial Lucknow*, p. 100. Patna was constituted as a municipality in 1864.
144. *PDG* 1924, p. 79; E. Drummond, Chairman, Municipal Commrs., Patna, to Commr., Patna, no. 17, May 28, 1868, P.C. Basta no. 229, Important Bundles, Jdcl. Dept., Alphabet A, B and C, nos. 1–16. The municipal committees were, on the whole, an abysmal failure. Without the constant prodding of the British officials residing in distant Bankipur, the Patna committee's nonofficial members—mostly "city" inhabitants—were generally said to exhibit little interest in the affairs of the committee. Consequently, in Patna, as elsewhere in Bihar, the municipal committees were "said to prove a hindrance to business rather than a help in its disposal." AGRPD, 1874–75.
145. Hunter, *Account of Patna*, p. 74; Beveridge, "City of Patna," p. 216.

"city," particularly the "suburb" of Bankipur, in the late eighteenth and early nineteenth centuries. Patna experienced another phase of growth and development in the early twentieth century, when it became the capital of the newly constituted province of Bihar and Orissa.[146]

To the British, Bankipur, the "European portion of the station," stood in stark contrast to the Muslim-dominated "city," that crowded, "disgusting" hive of commercial activity. "The narrow road of the native portion of the town here widens out into a spacious plain of a circular shape, which formed the race course. . . . Around this are situated the residences of the Europeans, the Church, and some of the Law Courts; and the open green space, with its fine trees, is very refreshing to the eye after the long, dusty, narrow bazaar."[147]

This landscape had been shaped by "colonization," whereby a new zone was created and stamped with a distinctively colonial social geography. The initial British foray into Patna was linked to trading interests. Consider first their beginnings in Patna—beginnings completely ignored by the historian Ghulam Husain. They were confined at that time to a house in the western suburb of Alamganj, which had been assigned to their short-lived factory of 1620–21 by the Mughal governor. As yet a minor political player, the British were relegated to the outer reaches of the city. In the mid-seventeenth century, the first "permanent" English factory was set up, almost adjacent to the western wall of the old city—close to the city but yet still outside it. At this site, the building known today as the original Patna Factory was erected in the eighteenth century. It was the setting for many of the key political and military events that led up to British ascendancy in the region in the latter half of that century. Its location beyond the walls of the city may have been preferred by both sides, Indian rulers and English traders: it was contiguous yet outside. The vulnerable occupants were offered some protection because the factory was fortified and it possessed a safe passageway to an outer well from which water could be obtained. The factory occupants as yet represented only one of the several contestants for regional power.[148]

But as the British gained in power, their presence was registered on the urbanscape of Patna. Even before 1757 the Company had acquired

146. *PDG 1924*, pp. 165–97; *PDG 1970*, pp. 655–61; *Seir*, vol. 1, pp. 428, 447.
147. "Mofussil Stations, Patna," p. 66.
148. *PDG 1924*, pp. 173–83; Sarkar, "Patna in the Seventeenth Century," pp. 127, 149.

a piece of garden land along the Ganges in Bankipur: it came to be known as the Company Bagh (garden). Although the initial grant was for only a small area—just large enough to accommodate the house and compound of the Company's factory chief—by 1778 the Company Bagh had secured a new grant that enlarged the lands to 87 *bighas* (about 54 acres). And by the end of the eighteenth century the Bagh covered 130 *bighas*. Reclaimed in part from wasteland, the area became the hub of the emerging empire. Eyre Coote and Robert Clive had camped there in 1757 and 1758, respectively, in the course of their military campaigns; in 1763 the campground served as the headquarters of the military commander in chief. When the military was shifted to Monghyr in 1765, the staff quarters became the headquarters of the factory, which retained possession of it until the abolition of the Commercial Residency in 1829. (It then became the court of the district judge.)[149]

The expansion of the Company Bagh and the stationing of the Third Brigade at Bankipur at a place later known as Barkerganj (after Sir Robert Barker, who commanded the brigade in the 1760s) not only chronicles the rise of the Company from a trading to a political power but also epitomizes the ever-expanding British presence in Bankipur. So does the fact that buildings formerly housing the commercial and military representatives of the Company came to house administrators responsible for carrying out the dictates of the rising colonial state and the construction of new edifices to house the offices of its growing bureaucracy. A changing of the guard reflecting the new realities of power and authority was also evident in the British acquisition of lands, particularly the takeover of much of Bankipur in the last decades of the eighteenth century, as the Company emerged as the supreme political power in the region. The process continued in the first half of the nineteenth century, as the Company completed its mastery over the subcontinent.

By the early nineteenth century, much of the property along the riverfront had already changed hands. The few "local" residents who remained on these lands were major allies of the Raj, prominent landholders who formed part of the local "aristocracy" and whose conspic-

---

149. *PDG 1924*, pp. 176–77. G. F. Grand, *The Narrative of the Life of a Gentleman Long Resident in India* (Calcutta: Calcutta Historical Society, 1910), p. 19, writes of being stationed at Bankipur in the 1760s; he was a judge and magistrate of Patna in the 1780s. Gopal, *Patna*, p. 3, asserts that the decision to set up the British hub in Bankipur was prompted by the desire to be close to the military cantonment of Danapur.

uous "palaces and mansions" highlight their "overgrowing power" in the colonial system. At one extremity of Bankipur, the westernmost "suburb" of Patna, lay the Golghar, a *gola,* or granary, ninety-six feet high, built in 1786 to store grain in case of famine. Nearby to the north and northwest, in part of the area formerly known as the big (*bara*) and small (*choti*) Nepali *kothi,* the engineer of Golghar built a house. East of Golghar, close to the river, in the area of the old cantonments of the Third Brigade, arose bungalows and houses that served either as the residences of government officials, such as those of the opium agents (later to become the residence of the civil surgeon), or as the offices of local administrators, such as the building adjacent to the civil surgeon's house, which became the collectorate. East of this was the Bankipur Club with its commanding view of the river. Beyond this lay the historic Company Bagh, containing the house of the district judge, the headquarters of the commercial resident that became the court of the district judge in 1829, an old house that became the quarters of the *munsifs'* (Indian civil judges') courts, and in Muradbagh, the former residence of the chief of the revenue council in the 1770s. Southeast of the residence of the Patna Revenue Council chief lay the tomb of Mirza Murad from which came the name Muradbagh (Murad garden). Next in size was the palatial house of the maharaja of Darbhanga, Bihar's largest landholder. The maharaja's neighbor, now housing Patna College, was the house of the opium agent of Bihar in the 1810s. Nearby lay Afzalpur, the site of the tomb and garden of Mir Afzal, and east of it, Golak Sadih's *dargah,* which explains the origin of the name of the *muhalla* of Golakpur. To the north, at the river, was Rani Ghat, a popular bathing area. Formerly, near the ghat was the house of Mir Ashraf, the late-eighteenth-century *gomastha* (agent) of the English factory; his neighbors were, in one house, the Tikari zamindar, and in another, the Bettiah zamindar. From there to the old English factory, the riverfront was carved up by the house of Nawab Baker Ali Khan, Colonelganj, and the garden of Shaista Khan. Adjoining this factory were the western walls of the "city."[150]

Well into the late nineteenth century, local administrators toiled hard to keep Indians and ordinary Europeans at arm's length and away from the heart of Bankipur that had been "[b]efore the disturbances of

150. Buchanan, *Bihar and Patna,* pp. 40–71; *PDG 1924,* pp. 173–82; J. F. W. James, "The River Front of Patna at the Beginning of the Eighteenth Century," *JBORS* 11 (1925): 85–90.

1857/58 the little plains in our station [that] was used almost exclusively for the Residents and was free from intrusion of soldiers or police or of public influence." In voicing his concern in 1863, the commissioner of Patna chafed at what he termed the "needless occupation and intrusion by buildings and departments," a presence that meant the stationing of "soldiers or police" drawn from ordinary men, both Indian and European.[151]

In addition to acquisitions through purchases from local landholders, land in Bankipur generally devolved into British hands in two ways. The first, occurring in such areas as that formerly occupied by the Provincial Battalion, were acquired by "government, partly from Nizamat lands [lands paying revenue to the Nazim, that is, to the former Mughal governor], for which a remission was granted, and partly from rent-free lands for which no compensation was ever made to the minhaedar [*minhaidar*, holder of land exempted from revenue payment] . . . [nor] any rent has ever been paid or demanded for the compounds which are taken out of rent free lands."[152] Thus, the British "civil station" of Bankipur had been carved out of lands for which no grants could be located. In other words, these lands were rent-free and the property of government, or they were on estates that paid revenue to government and whose proprietors were paid a nominal rent for the use of the buildings on the grounds.

The British "occupation" of Bankipur followed the familiar pattern of colonial settlements emerging alongside existing "native" cities and towns. Rather than engaging in extensive urban removal, which would have been costly, colonial rulers followed the more expeditious policy of fashioning their own "suburbs" away from the heart of the old city. In the case of Patna this commenced with the initial British relocation to Bankipur and concluded with building of the new capital in the twentieth century in the new areas west of Bankipur, that is, even farther removed from the earlier settlement. That Bankipur and the "suburbs" that were created later officially appropriated the name of Patna, while the old town came to be known as Patna "city," is its own commentary on the realities of power and authority during the colonial period. In this sense, the colonial record of Patna stands in sharp contrast

151. G. F. Cockburn, Commr., to Secy., GOB, no. 353, Oct. 20, 1863, P. C. Double Lock Volumes, vol. 1, Basta no. 3, 1863.

152. R. N. Farquharson, Special Deputy Colltr., to E. C. Ravenshaw, Offg. Commr., Feb. 6, 1838, P.C., Letters from the Colltr. of Patna, vol. 48, 1838, no. 22.

to those of Calcutta, Bombay, and Madras, the great presidency cities.
For these three cities formed the hubs of the empire. Their rise followed
the pattern of early Western bases elsewhere in Asia, which were "either wholly nonurban or little developed. . . . Many of these early Western bases were entirely new; not only did they occupy previously un-
used sites but they represented a new kind of city exclusively centered
on trade."[153] In another sense all of Patna became increasingly margin-
alized in the late nineteenth and early twentieth centuries, as it became
merely an inland port city serving the great metropolises represented by
the presidency cities, also the primary colonial port cities.[154]

As a result of the development of Bankipur, Patna became a city of
two distinct zones in the nineteenth century: the "city" that Ghulam
Husain knew so well and the Bankipur of the British. A third zone
came later as the westernmost area was built up to accommodate the
emergence of Patna as the provincial capital. The city in other words
developed unevenly, as it underwent the transitions from Pataliputra to
Patna to Azimabad to Patna. While the revolution of the eighteenth
century and the new economic climate of the nineteenth century weak-
ened the foundations of the "city," dependent as it was on political
prominence and status as a regional central place, these changes had
less impact on the rest of Patna because Bankipur and the western zone
continued to benefit from Patna's role as the colonial administrative
and political hub of the region. Furthermore, because the development
of the three zones followed different economic and political calendars,
setbacks in one area were mitigated by advances in another. Thus, the
changing economic conditions that threatened the "city" and its prosperity as a center of retail and wholesale trade and banking—a situation that endangered the health of the entire city—were partly offset by
the development of Bankipur as the civil station for the district and the
region. Insurance against the economic slump was also provided by the
emergence of the westernmost zone in the twentieth century.

By the mid-twentieth century the city of Patna consisted of three
distinctive zones. At the eastern extremity lay the "city," an area still
housing the wholesale trade, although no longer the flourishing economic and commercial center it had been in the eighteenth and early
nineteenth centuries. The middle zone encompassing the area extend-

153. Rhoads Murphey, *The Outsiders: The Western Experience in India and China*
(Ann Arbor: University of Michigan Press, 1977), p. 17; *PDG 1924*, p. 194.
    154. See the essays in Basu, *Colonial Port Cities in Asia*.

ing from the western gate of the "city" to the Patna-Gaya road (now renamed Buddha marg), that is, essentially the Bankipur of British creation, constituted the "business and commercial core of the city" and the site of the "bulk of the institutional, cultural and district administration buildings" of Patna. In addition to housing most of the district administration offices, this middle area became the site of Patna University, which was established in 1917. Other than housing the monumental buildings typical of a state capital, as late as the 1960s the third and westernmost zone had few "community facilities such as schools, shopping centres, etc."[155]

To sum up, because Patna remained an administrative and political hub, worsening economic conditions did not transform it into a "ruined city"; nor was its position as the central place of the region entirely eroded, notwithstanding such evocations in the plaintive prose and poetry penned by the aristocratic generation of the late eighteenth century. Consider the eyewitness account of Enugula Veeraswamy, a pilgrim from south India who visited Patna at the close of 1830. The next chapter retraces his journey across the region to the scene of melas, or fairs.

155. The changed relationship between the three zones is evident from the fact that the eastern zone had only 35.5 percent of the population in the late twentieth century, whereas the central and western zones accounted for 43.8 and 20.6 percent, respectively. Although the central zone remained at the core of the city in the late nineteenth and early twentieth centuries, its primacy was being undercut by the western zone, with its growing population. Between 1951 and 1961 the western zone increased its number by over 126 percent; the central zone, the "most overcrowded" grew only by 18.6 percent, and the eastern zone by 12.2 percent. Patna, *Master Plan*, pp. 22–24, 17.

CHAPTER 3

The "Religious" Places of Exchange

Melas in the Nineteenth-Century Age of Colonialism

"I left Madras on the 18th, Tuesday of May in the year 1830 at 9 in the night and camped at Madhavaram village." With these words, Enugula Veeraswamy (1780–1836), a Niyogi Brahmin of Madras, retraced the beginning of his pilgrimage to Banaras (Kasi). Written almost half a century after Ghulam Husain's history, his "Kasiyatra Charitra," or account (*charitra*) of a pilgrimage (*yatra*) to the sacred place (*tirtha*) of Banaras, documents his long journey to the key pilgrimage sites of north India—mostly along the Ganges—before returning via Calcutta and eastern India.[1] Home, more than fifteen months later, in September 1831, his thoughts turned to God for having returned him safely to his "native place," a return that prompted his recounting of the history of Madras and its people. God and his "native place" also figure in the concluding paragraph in which he described his fellow countrymen as "religious minded" and respectful "towards God and Brahmins" and

---

1. Veeraswamy, *Journal*, p. 1. Written originally in his native Telugu and first published in 1838, this "journal"—Veeraswamy himself used this term in his English correspondence with the Telugu scholar, C. P. Brown—was compiled by K. S. Pillai from detailed letters he received from Veeraswamy. Pillai had apparently requested Veeraswamy to keep him informed of his travels. See Vadlamudi Gopalakrishnaiah, "Preface," *Journal*, pp. xlii–xlii; V. Ramakrishna, "Traveller's Tales and Social Histories (A Study of Enugula Veeraswamy's Kasiyatra Charitra)," *Proceedings of the Indian History Congress, Golden Jubilee Session, Gorakhpur, 1989–90* (Delhi: Indian History Congress, 1989–90), pp. 574–55.

in which he acknowledged the colonial presence in this southern city. "God almighty," he noted in closing out the travelogue, "has bestowed upon me livelihood for generations to come under this government."[2]

That Veeraswamy turned to God at the end of his long journey is fitting. It emphasizes the religious character of *tirthayatras*[3]—pilgrimages or journeys, to a "river ford" or a "crossing place" (or a hierophany, to use Mircea Eliade's word)—and the related phenomenon of melas, or "religious" fairs, as this term is often translated. In so doing, it differentiates them from their ostensibly secular Western counterparts. As the "Kasiyatra Charitra" indicates, the pilgrimage entailed visiting sacred centers (*darshan,* or seel·ing an auspicious sight of a sacred shrine or place), fulfilling vows (*vrata*), taking ritual baths in the Ganges (*Ganga asnan*) and other rivers, and performing specific rituals at specific sacred sites (e.g., *shraddha,* or "faithful offerings" to departed kin). "Pilgrims . . . go to places of worship," as one scholar explains, "either because they have some religious interest directed toward a specific place, the necessary means, or the need. They may also go because there are times when visiting certain places is particularly meritorious."[4] To use the title of a recent ethnographic study of the motivations and values of Indian villagers as pilgrims, pilgrimage involves "fruitful journeys,"[5] odysseys for personal fulfillment.

The reference to "government" is another instructive cue, because it ties the nineteenth-century practice of pilgrimage to a political context defined by the colonial state. The "Gentoo and Malabar" (meaning Telugu-speaking Hindu and Malayalam) interpreter for the Madras Supreme Court of Judicature, Veeraswamy acknowledged that he was favorably disposed toward government. He was a *dubash* (literally, a person who speaks two languages, or *do basha*), a go-between who could move back and forth between his own culture and that of the for-

---

2. Veeraswamy, *Journal,* pp. 229–32. In 1840 his wife and family unsuccessfully petitioned for a pension. GOI, Public, June 10, no. 15 of 1840, para. 8, E/4/954: Madras Despatches, June 10–Dec. 23, 1840.

3. Diana L. Eck, "India's Tirthas: "Crossings" in Sacred Geography," *History of Religions* 20 (1981): 323–44. *Tirtha-yatra,* which in "common parlance [means] visitation to sacred places," literally refers to "'undertaking journey to river fords.'" See Surinder Mohan Bhardwaj, *Hindu Places of Pilgrimage in India: A Study in Cultural Geography* (Berkeley and Los Angeles: University of California Press, 1973), p. 2.

4. Agehananda Bharati, "Pilgrimage Sites and Indian Civilization," in *Chapters in Indian Civilization,* vol. 1, *Classical and Medieval India,* ed. Joseph W. Elder (Dubuque, Iowa: Kendall/Hunt Publishing, 1970), p. 95; Veeraswamy, *Journal,* passim.

5. Ann Grodzins Gold, *Fruitful Journeys: The Ways of Rajasthani Pilgrims* (Berkeley and Los Angeles: University of California Press, 1988).

eign government to which he owed his "livelihood." A Company man, well aware that British rule extended over much of the subcontinent, he was able to exploit his official connections and credentials to facilitate almost every step of the journey. Letters of recommendation supplied by his superiors opened doors wherever he traveled. At Patna, where he remained between February 18 and March 4, 1831, his contacts enabled him to meet a number of "big persons."[6]

Moreover, he was careful not to antagonize his patrons, even when several Englishmen asked him a question that he evidently found distasteful: "'Your [sic] are learned so much in English, why then do you perform these teertha yatras like a country cousin?' I was in need of their good offices. It would have been a strain for me to reply and convince them; I therefore maintained a discreet silence."[7] As well as reflecting a fundamental religious divide between colonial subjects and rulers, this exchange also points to the realities of power and authority and the spatial boundaries of colonial rule. Indeed, his experiences more generally highlight the geography and parameters of the colonial state that had consolidated its rule over the subcontinent by the early nineteenth century.

As in the previous chapter on Patna, here, too, I initially view history through the lens of one individual involved in making and writing about it, a method that has its advantages and disadvantages. As a first-person account, Veeraswamy's rich and insightful travelogue correctly accents the subjective considerations and objectives of going "On the Road," to use the suggestive title of Irawati Karve's wonderful anthropological and personal account of pilgrimage.[8] Whether undertaking long and distant trips to the most famous sacred centers of the country or brief visits to nearby holy places of local importance, the aims and experiences of pilgrims shared many similar considerations. But I am also well aware that an eyewitness account of a single pilgrim is obviously not a history of pilgrimage or of melas, however rare and

6. Veeraswamy, *Journal,* pp. 147, 94–95. Among others, he met Judge H. Douglas, a longtime resident of the city.

7. Ibid., p. 83.

8. " 'On the Road': A Maharashtrian Pilgrimage," in *The Experience of Hinduism: Essays on Religion in Maharashtra,* ed. Eleanor Zelliot and Maxine Berntsen (Albany: State University of New York Press, 1988), pp. 142–71. See also Clifford Geertz, " 'From the Native's Point of View': On the Nature of Anthropological Understanding," in *Meaning in Anthropology,* ed. Keith H. Basso and Henry A. Selby (Albuquerque: University of New Mexico Press, 1976), pp. 222–23.

valuable it is as an emic perspective of melas from the early nineteenth century. Rather, such first-person records represent the voices of the literate elite and not the ordinary travelers, who were the overwhelming majority of pilgrims on the road. The same holds for two other first-person accounts cited in this chapter: the *Travels* of Bholanauth Chunder, a Bengali *bania* (trader, moneylender) and a graduate of Hindu College, who initially serialized the narrative of his peregrinations between 1846 and 1866 in the Calcutta newspaper, the *Saturday Evening Englishman;* and the *Rambles* of Ramgopal Singh Chowdhari, a pleader in the Patna High Court and a member of a prominent Patna family, who compiled his Bihar experiences into a book.[9]

Both Veeraswamy, who began the new year of 1831 on the road from Patna to "the great pilgrimage centre Gaya," and Chunder, who undertook his travels toward the middle of that century, were part of the rising tide of pilgrims that crested in the age of colonialism. Most of these came from the ranks of ordinary people, a silent majority who came and went, leaving scarcely a textual trail. For some the only traces were their "signatures," left behind in the genealogical registers maintained at many sacred centers.[10] Remembered only by themselves and their families, these faceless and nameless pilgrims were always described as present "on the road" but rarely ever identified specifically in the colonial records.[11]

9. Chunder, *Travels,* vol. 1; Chowdhari, *Rambles in Bihar.* See also Veeraswamy, *Journal,* pp. ix–x, regarding his reputation as a "philanthropist." Contrast these subjective accounts with accounts by anthropologists and writers. The representations inherent in this kind of participant-observation literature is also problematic. See, e.g., Gold, *Fruitful Journeys,* pp. xi–xiii; E. Valentine Daniel, *Fluid Signs: Being a Person the Tamil Way* (Berkeley and Los Angeles: University of California Press, 1984); Karve, "On the Road."

10. Registers, which record names and family particulars dating as far back as the seventeenth century, were maintained by *pandas* (priests) at pilgrimage centers. See B. N. Goswami, "The Records Kept by Priests at Centres of Pilgrimage as a Source of Social and Economic History," *IESHR* 3 (1966): 174–84. The Family History Library of the Genealogical Society of Utah, Salt Lake City, is rapidly acquiring a large body of these registers.

11. They surface in official sources only when recognized by the authorities as posing a threat to law and order or as police statistics because they were unfortunate victims of crime. Pilgrims were often victims of highway robbery and *thugi* because of their numbers and ubiquity on the roads. See, e.g., Colltr., Govt. Customs, Manjhi, to Judge, Shahabad, Apr. 15, 1793, Bengal Cr. Jdcl. Consltns., May 3 to 31, 1793, May 3, no. 5; Magte., Saran, to 3rd Judge, Court of Circuit, May 10, 1828, Bengal Cr. Jdcl. Procs., Apr. 28 to May 5, 1829, Apr. 28, no. 47; Commr. to I. G., Police, May 7, 1873, Bengal Police Procs. 1873–74, June 1873, no. 29.

To broaden the subjective perspectives, therefore, I have drawn extensively on colonial records that betray biases very different from Veeraswamy's revelations. A juxtaposition of the "pilgrimage" of William Moorcroft with that of Veeraswamy is thus illuminating. Moorcroft's travels are emblematic of the emerging colonial state's concern with fairs. He undertook his early-nineteenth-century tour of the fairs and markets of north India in his capacity as superintendent of the Stud Establishment at Pusa (near the city of Patna) charged with the responsibility of securing and enhancing the military stock of horses. By contrast, Veeraswamy, although also a government official, made his journey as an act of devotion.

Moorcraft's account is indicative of the colonial documentation project, which generated a wealth of records, including material on the cattle complex of melas. In the course of his wide-ranging search for suitable cavalry mounts, which took him as far as Afghanistan, Moorcroft collected information not only on military supplies but also on political and economic conditions obtaining at the peripheries of the Empire.[12] In addition to this type of documentation, we have materials generated by medical and health concerns regarding the sites of pilgrimages and fairs in the second half of the nineteenth century. These, too, were part of the documentation project of the colonial state, a project that informs (and taints) this chapter.

As for the pilgrimage literature, at its best it can only evoke and invoke many of the shared aspects of the two phenomena of pilgrimage and the melas. The former is more readily recovered than the latter. Pilgrimages, that is, were clearly momentous events in the lives of people—the once-in-a-lifetime experience—and therefore they are better preserved in memories; melas, on the other hand—save for the handful of fairs that attracted supralocal and supraregional audiences and were the focal point of significant mela pilgrimages—tended much more to be woven into the everyday fabric of people's lives.

Nevertheless, Veeraswamy testifies to the close relationship between fairs and pilgrimage. For like pilgrimage, fairs have a locus of devotion; typically, the venues are *tirthas*. In the words of a Bihar resident, the sacred sites of melas include the "confluence of streams, the vicinity of

---

12. E.g., see Wm. Moorcroft, Suptd., Hon. Co.'s Stud, to Secy., Bd. of Superintendence, Oct. 9, 1811, Bengal Military Consltns., Oct. 15–22, 1811, Oct. 15, no. 80; Garry Alder, *Beyond Bokhara: The Life of William Moorcroft, Asian Explorer and Pioneer Veterinary Surgeon, 1767–1825* (London: Century Publishing, 1985).

consecrated springs, or the neighbourhood of shrines whose reputation for religious merit runs high in the locality." No wonder melas have been termed "gatherings of pilgrims."[13]

How closely connected the two phenomena are can be gauged from the following attempt by the 1913 Bihar and Orissa Pilgrim Committee to distinguish between pilgrimages focusing on the great melas generally convened at pan-Hindu *tirthas* and pilgrimages classified as *tirtha-yatras*. Its report described a pilgrimage site as

> a place to which pilgrims resort in considerable numbers throughout the year, a place that has special religious sanctity of its own, apart from the occurrence of a holy day, and which it is the duty of the pious to visit at least once during their lifetime. These places naturally support a permanent population; they are almost all Hindu; all are and have been for generations famous throughout India, and some have grown into large and important towns. A "fair" on the other hand is a place where pilgrims congregate in numbers on one or more occasions only during the year: frequently the attractions are secular as well as religious and only in rare instances do people come in numbers from long distances. Such places are, as a rule, but sparsely populated throughout the rest of the year, the only permanent residents being a few faqirs or the people of a small village.[14]

Notwithstanding the administrative effort by this 1913 Pilgrim Committee to write religion out of melas, as its report acknowledged only a fine line separated the two. That is, some fairs have more religious character than others; or, alternatively, "some are more secular than others."[15] From their very founding, fairs are bound up not only in a web of religious matters but also enmeshed in economic, social, and cultural concerns. Their beginnings, a local resident writes, can be located in the coming of

> people from the surrounding territory . . . to perform their ablutions or to worship. The congregation of so many persons gave rise to the necessity of providing for their creature-comforts, and stalls of country confectionary came in time to be held there. Vendors of other goods began to perceive their opportunity, and temporary sheds came gradually to be erected on such occasions for the sale of the different necessaries and luxuries of village life. The success of these traders and the growing fame of the fairs attracted

---

13. Bharati, "Pilgrimage Sites," p. 95; A. C. Ghose, "Rural Behar," *Calcutta Review* 220 (1900): 222.

14. B & O, *Report of the Pilgrim Committee Bihar and Orissa, 1913* (Simla: Govt. Press, 1915), p. 1.

15. James J. Preston, "Sacred Centers and Symbolic Networks in South Asia," *Mankind Quarterly* 20 (1980): 266.

dealers of various classes and added to the number of visitors and sight-
seers. The scope and extent of the mela was by degrees thus expanded, and
people began to combine motives of religion, business and pleasure in their
visits to the fair.[16]

The anthropologists Victor Turner and Edith Turner have examined
the processes that link pilgrimages to fairs:

> A pilgrimage's foundation is typically marked by visions, miracles, or mar-
> tyrdoms. The first pilgrims tend to arrive haphazardly, individually, and in-
> termittently. . . . Later, there is progressive routinization and institutionaliza-
> tion of the sacred journey. Pilgrims now tend to come in organized groups,
> in sodalities, cofraternities, and parish associations, on specified feast days,
> or in accordance with a carefully planned calendar. Marketing facilities
> spring up close to the shrines and along the way. Secularized fiestas and fairs
> thrive near these. A whole elaborate system of licenses, permits, and ordi-
> nances, governing mercantile transactions, pilgrims' lodgings, and the con-
> duct of fairs develops as the number of pilgrims grow and their needs and
> wants proliferate.[17]

By exerting a "magnetic effect on the whole communications and transportation system," pilgrimage centers, in other words, foster the "construction of sacred and secular edifices to serve the needs of the human
stream passing through it. . . . [They] in fact generate a socioeconomic
'field'; they have a kind of social 'entelechy.' It may be that they have
played at least as important a role in the growth of cities, marketing systems, and roads, as 'pure' economic and political factors have."[18]

Veeraswamy is not particularly forthcoming about the "socioeconomic 'field' " of melas; he appears not to have directed his gaze in
that direction at all. Although he invariably stopped at fairs, or *ut-
savams* in his vernacular, and recorded their occurrence at pilgrimage
centers, his account offers no other details.[19] Perhaps he shared the reli-

---

16. Ghose, "Rural Behar," p. 222. To what extent fairs were tied to religion is suggested by the many instances of melas established at sites of little or no religious significance that gained religious merit *after* their founding and development (through the acquisition of a sacred edifice or by the invention of religious "traditions"). See, e.g., S. D.
Pant, *The Social Economy of the Himalayas* (London: Allen and Unwin, 1935), cited in
Binod C. Agrawal, *Cultural Contours of Religion and Economics in Hindu Universe*
(New Delhi: National, 1980), p. 9, on Jouljibi, a place without any "religious significance" that was invested with "some religious significance" after a fair had been established there in 1935.

17. *Image and Pilgrimage in Christian Culture: Anthropological Perspectives* (Oxford: Basil Blackwell, 1978), p. 25.

18. Ibid., pp. 233–34.

19. Veeraswamy, *Journal,* pp. 10–11, 42, 51, 84, 110. Preston, "Sacred Centers in
South Asia," p. 60, notes the scholarly neglect of the connections between pilgrimages

gious prejudice toward melas one finds in the anthropological literature. As one ethnographer's informants told her, "a pilgrim who goes
for love of the gods and not for amusement of the mind does not go at
mela time. For melas, if they offer intangible accumulated potencies of
divine power, present an array of vital, sensual distractions concentrated in one location that is equally awesome."[20] Elided therefore in
his observations—as in most present-day studies—are details regarding
those economic, social, and cultural aspects of fairs that made them
major events and institutions in the life of local and regional society.[21]

When Veeraswamy touches on the secular aspects of fairs, his remarks concern his preoccupation with provisioning his entourage. He
was a traveler making sure that food and drink was available; and he
was eager to collect information for use by those who would follow in
his footsteps. His remarks about the "secular" aspects of sacred centers
and melas offer no special insights; but indirectly they speak to the extent to which pilgrimage centers—and for our interest here, particularly
those sacred centers that supported melas—were tied to a "socioeconomic field" in which pilgrims were involved in transactions that contrasted with the more everyday kinds of exchanges. Certainly, the commonplace distinction between fairs as "basically religious in character"
and markets as "commercial in [their] composition" needs to be recali-
brated.[22]

This chapter continues the exploration of my central interest in the
processes and places of exchange by focusing on the "socioeconomic
field" of melas in order to establish their fit in the larger marketing system of the region, particularly in their roles as livestock markets. It also
examines the nineteenth-century history of melas to highlight the
"overgrowing power of the zemindars" that the Patna historian had
identified as a development of his *Modern Times*. Veeraswamy observed this "power" firsthand when he wrote about Raja Mitarjit (Mit-
terjit) Singh of Gaya:

---

and melas and their relation to the multiple and multilevel activities associated with sacred centers, pilgrimage cycles, and festivals.

20. Gold, *Fruitful Journeys*, pp. 302–4.

21. One attempt to look at other dimensions is Agrawal, *Cultural Contours of Religion*, pp. 1–15. See also Akos Ostor, *Culture and Power: Legend, Ritual, Bazaar and Rebellion in a Bengali Society* (New Delhi: Sage, 1984), for a discussion of religion and economics as problematic categories because they are perceived not as autonomous but
rather as closely interwoven domains in the indigenous conception.

22. *CDG 1960*, p. 326. Also Veeraswamy, *Journal*, pp. 2, 6, 30, 36, 42.

He is a very rich man. He pays three lakhs of rupees annually to the Company government. . . . He derives nearly sixty lakhs of income annually. All the other Zamindars in this region are similarly very rich and enjoy their riches comfortably. The reason for their huge profits is this. When the British first entered this country 50 or 60 years ago they had enemies all around. So in order to take the princely estates under their control and secure those that came under their control, Lord Cornwallis issued an order through which collectors posted in these districts transferred the entire land to the old Zamindars by conducting Zamabandi [assessment] lightly and handed over possession under an agreement with them. . . . These Zamindars kept an army of clerks and servants to meet their requirements and are enjoying their unlimited riches and are whiling away their time.[23]

As a pilgrim he appears to have been especially cognizant of the fact that the major pilgrimage site of Gaya formed part of the great estate of Tikari, although he did not allude to the fact that Mitarjit Singh received one-tenth of the pilgrim fees collected there. He was keenly aware, however, of the kingly and patronage role of local elites in supporting religious activities, whether these entailed sponsoring rituals or the building and maintenance of temples. Indeed, as this chapter will show, landholders, merchants, and traders have historically sponsored activities such as the patronage of fairs as part of their expected roles as patrons and local lords. Furthermore, the patronage of melas and other religious activities and participation in pilgrimages reflected part of a heightened religious sensibility in an age of expanding markets and trade.

The record of Veeraswamy's journey also reveals the spatial dimension that has historically generated a sense of community and identity. Certainly, later on in the nineteenth century and continuing into the early twentieth century, changing political and social conditions gave rise to conflicting notions of a religious-based community and identity on the part of crowds who converged on those fairs in greater numbers than ever before. I begin by first filling in the historical context behind Veeraswamy's journey specifically and behind the nineteenth-century phenomena of pilgrimages and melas more generally.

Veeraswamy's *tirthayatra* conformed to an ancient tradition: his route followed a well-established pilgrimage circuit. Whether pilgrimage originated in the ancient period is still a matter of some dispute, although Vedic literature suggests some elements of the concept of pilgrimage, specifically the notion of the "merit of travel and reverence

23. Veeraswamy, *Journal*, pp. 144–45.

for rivers."[24] As "semi-nomadic tribes," however, the people of the early Vedic period could not have performed pilgrimages to any considerable extent, if at all, because "pilgrimage to places which are considered to be more salutary than others is only to be found in sedentary societies."[25] This interpretation locates the emergence of pilgrimage in the rise of a brahmanic culture, which is said to have produced a "religion with a supra-regional character": a "common religious superstructure . . . that accounts for the fact that a special place far away is more holy than a similar place near home, and which consequently bestows an exclusiveness to this place which alone warrants the abandonment of home and family in order to embark upon a dangerous journey." The modest number of extant textual and empirical sources reveal that pilgrimage in the early period was limited, "relevant only to a small part of the population, especially those assimilated to the brahmanical 'All-Indian' religion."[26]

By the time of the Puranas and the Epics, religious texts dating roughly to the period between 300 B.C.E. and 1000 C.E., the practice of pilgrimage was clearly emerging. In the second millennium it grew into a popular phenomenon as increasing numbers of "common folk" participated in "a new type of religion of all-Indian significance"[27] that was more emotional and devotional [*bhakti*] in form. The *bhakti* movement changed the character of Hinduism, as the "focus of religious attention moved from the great gods and the liturgies connected with polytheism to the one God and his avatars, especially Krishna and Rama."[28]

North Indian "Hindu devotionalism" converged particularly on the figure of Vishnu's incarnation, Rama, whose cult was probably founded in the latter part of the first millennium of the Christian era

---

24. Bhardwaj, *Hindu Pilgrimage,* pp. 4, 43–79; E. Alan Morinis, *Pilgrimage in the Hindu Tradition: A Case Study of West Bengal* (Delhi: Oxford University Press, 1984), pp. 2–3, 46. Pilgrimage in the Indian tradition includes the idea of performing a metaphorical pilgrimage to a *tirtha* through meditation and without actually undertaking a physical journey. A viewpoint suggesting the post-Vedic development of pilgrimages is Bharati, "Pilgrimage Sites," p. 85.

25. Hans Bakker and Alan Entwistle, *Vaisnavism: The History of the Krsna and Rama Cults and Their Contribution to Indian Pilgrimage* (Groningen: Institute of Indian Studies, State University of Groningen, 1981), p. 78.

26. Ibid., p. 81.

27. Ibid.

28. J. T. F. Jordens, "Medieval Hindu Devotionalism," in *A Cultural History of India,* ed. A. L. Basham (Oxford: Clarendon Press, 1975), p. 266. Whether the impulse for this great transformation was the coming of Islam to South Asia remains a controversial issue. Cf. Jordens, e.g., with Bakker and Entwistle, *Vaisnavism,* p. 76.

but whose widespread popularity dates to the second millennium. One factor in its rise may have been the movement of Rajput clans into the Gangetic plain, beginning in the eleventh and twelfth centuries. As *kshatriyas* (warriors) and as participants in the struggle against Muslim invasions, Rajputs considered Rama, the divine warrior, an especially appropriate god. Many clans also traced their origins back to Rama or to ancestors belonging to his kingdom of Ayodhya. By the fifteenth and sixteenth centuries the focus on Rama took "a more devotional approach" that "had a profound influence on people of all social classes and helped to propagate a more populistic form of Rama worship, which found expression in a gradual increase in the flow of pilgrims."[29]

The history of Gaya followed a similar chronology. Reference to it in the great epic, the *Mahabharata,* suggests that the sanctity of Gaya was already established by the outset of the Christian era. The Puranas, which date from roughly between 800 and 1100—and which Veeraswamy alludes to in acknowledging the "exemplary greatness of this place Gaya"—single it out as one of the most important pilgrimage sites on the subcontinent, more important even than Banaras.[30] But as inscriptions and other evidence show, its rise as a pan-Indian pilgrimage site dates to a later period. "Gaya, as a place of worship," states a nineteenth-century source, "was in comparative obscurity until about five or six centuries ago [thirteenth or fourteenth centuries]. Since that time, the number of pilgrims from all parts of India has been steadily increasing."[31]

The traffic of pilgrims over the course of the colonial period rose dramatically, and only partially because of population increase.[32] Although Veeraswamy seems to have paid little attention to his fellow

29. H. T. Bakker, "The Rise of Ayodhya as a Place of Pilgrimage," *Indo-Iranian Journal* 24 (1982): 108; Jordens, "Hindu Devotionalism," p. 274. The history of Ayodhya— a place that has been the epicenter of recent communal tensions—epitomizes this chronology of the development of pilgrimage.

30. Bhardwaj, *Hindu Pilgrimage,* pp. 30, 62–65; *Gaya Mahatmya,* ed. and trans. (into French) Claude Jacques (Pondichery: Institut Francais d'Indologie, 1962); Veeraswamy, *Journal,* p. 131. Other sites often singled out as major pilgrimage centers are: Allahabad, Mathura, and Hardwar in north India, Kancipuram in Madras, and Ujjain and Dwarka in the western states of Rajasthan and Gujarat. Bharati, "Pilgrimage Sites," pp. 95, 98, 106

31. Hunter, *Account of Gaya,* p. 44; Buchanan, *Bihar and Patna;* L. P. Vidyarthi, *The Sacred Complex in Hindu Gaya* (Bombay: Asia Publishing House, 1961), p. 26.

32. Peaks in pilgrim traffic occurred well before the amply documented population increase of the early twentieth century. As for the earlier period, population growth was generally negligible even as the numbers of pilgrims rose substantially. After 1830 there appears to have been some increase in population but only until 1891, after which there

travelers, Chunder recognized that he was part of a new trend made possible in "an era of security to life and property which has been never known to these regions." He documented this growing stream of pilgrims by pointing to the "certificates of service" and "testimonials" provided by pilgrims to the special priests (*pandas*) officiating at the *tirtha* of Brindaban that he found did not extend much beyond 1825.[33]

Records of licenses maintained at Gaya dating back to the late eighteenth century provide other figures on the rising tide of pilgrims. Thus, there were 17,670 licenses issued by colonial authorities at this city (site of several melas) in 1798 when the British first took over the regulation of license fees paid by pilgrims to their priests. The tally for 1805 was 31,114! The numbers represented by these licenses are suggested by Buchanan, whose 1811–12 account rounded out the total "number of pilgrims and their attendants" to 100,000. A tally made almost a century later tripled this figure to "not less than 300,000 a year."[34]

The growing traffic can also be tabulated specifically for mela-goers. What better illustration of this trend than the history of the oldest fair in Bihar, the Hariharkshetra or Sonepur Mela, which celebrates Sonepur's significance as a place of pilgrimage and worship (*puja*). Although the precise date of its founding cannot be traced, its long history is established by local traditions and documentary evidence. Located at the confluence of the Ganges and Gandak, its sanctity derives from the belief that a ritual bath at the junction of rivers is the equivalent of giving away a thousand cows as a gift. Veeraswamy himself saw and experienced this ritual bathing firsthand when he was in Banaras in Kartik 1830; the practice is considered especially efficacious when done on Kartik Purnima, the full moon in Kartik. Local tradition attributes to Rama the founding of Sonepur's first temple, often said to be a precursor of the principal place of worship today, the Harihar Nath Ma-

---

was a falling off until 1921. Tim Dyson, "Indian Historical Demography: Developments and Prospects," in *India's Historical Demography: Studies in Famine, Disease, and Society*, ed. idem (London: Curzon Press, 1989), pp. 2–10; Leela Visaria and Pravin Visaria, "Population (1757–1947)," in *The Cambridge Economic History of India, vol. 2*, pp. 463–89.

33. Chunder, *Travels*, vol. 2, pp. 41–42; Veeraswamy, *Journal*, p. 129.

34. *GDG 1906*, p. 66; Hunter, *Account of Gaya*, p. 45; Buchanan, *Bihar and Patna*, p. 106. Short-term fluctuations occurred because of a number of reasons, such as in the early nineteenth century when attendance ranged from two hundred thousand to quite a few less because of "dearness of grain to the westward, and the mortality to the eastward." See F. Gillanders, Asst. Colltr., Pilgrim Tax, Gaya, to W. Money, Colltr., Bihar, May 1, 1818, Bengal Bd. of Commrs. at Bihar and Banaras, Dec. 11 to 29, 1818, Dec. 15, no. 8A.

hadeo Temple, and also the beginnings of the mela. No doubt, the emergence of Sonepur as a pilgrimage center led to the establishment of the mela. A response to the rising traffic of pilgrims, its founding led to the annexation of new sacred domains and the establishment of additional facilities to cater to the growing nonspiritual demands. Small wonder then that the fair followed the same calendar used by most devotees in timing their visit to the river junction.[35]

Sonepur's importance as a pilgrimage site can be attested at least as early as the fourteenth century. Its merits were apparently known to Vidyapati (1360–1447?), the celebrated poet of the north Bihar area of Mithila, who journeyed there to worship and to take a ritual bath. By then its fair had already attained sizable proportions, attracting as it did the attention of Sultan Husain Shah (1493–1519) of Bengal, who deputed an officer to purchase horses worth three hundred thousand coins.[36] By the time the traveler John Marshall visited the fair in the seventeenth century, he found it playing to audiences as large as forty to fifty thousand. Veeraswamy, who visited in 1831, after the fair had been in session, noted that more than a hundred thousand people had been in attendance. Annual tallies of mela attendance kept by local administrators during the colonial period reveal that the crowds continued to swell. Although numbers fluctuated from year to year—depending on various religious and socioeconomic conditions—they never fell below two hundred thousand and could go as high as three or four hundred thousand. Crowds had grown to almost 3 million by the late twentieth century, with as many as a million participating in the ritual plunge into the river on the occasion of Kartik Purnima.[37]

Attendance figures for the other "great" fairs in the nineteenth and early twentieth centuries indicate a similar rising pattern; these include the melas of Rajgir in Patna; of Deokund, Jahanabad, and Kishunpur in Gaya; of Brahampur in Shahabad; of Godna (or Revelganj) in Saran; of Bettiah in Champaran; of Sitamarhi in Muzaffarpur; and of Darbhanga in Darbhanga. Data for other "important" fairs tell the same

---

35. *Harihar Kshetra Mahatmya* (Gaya: Prabhu Narayan Misra, 1924); Veeraswamy, *Journal*, p. 104; *Limited Raj*, chap. 1.

36. Radhakrishna Chaudhary, *Mithila in the Age of Vidyapati* (Varanasi: Chaukhambha Orientalia, 1976), pp. 233, 239; B. P. Mazumdar, "Non-Muslim Society in Medieval Bihar," in *Comprehensive History of Bihar*, vol. 2, part 1, p. 351.

37. Veeraswamy, *Journal*, p. 147; Khan, *Marshall in India*, pp. 141–42, 158; AGRPD 1890–91; *SDG 1930*, p. 155; GOI, *Census of India 1961*, vol. 4, *Bihar*, Part 7-b, *Fairs and Festivals of Bihar* by S. D. Prasad (Purnea: n.p., 1971), p. xxxiv.

story: those held at Bihar and Patna city in Patna, Bisua in Gaya, Buxar and Sasaram in Shahabad, Silhouri and Thawe in Saran, Tribeni in Champaran, and Dubhi, Mahinathpur, Silanath, and Mahadeo Math in Darbhanga.[38]

This trend can be detailed for the melas at Rajgir and Deokund, which, along with those at Gaya and Puna Pun, are recognized as four of the major religious sites in Magadh (Patna and Gaya). At Rajgir, where the mela is held triennially according to the intercalary calendar, Buchanan estimated an attendance of fifty thousand in the 1810s; and at Deokund, on the occasion of Sivaratri, he counted somewhere between ten and twelve thousand. Less than a century later, in the 1890s, Rajgir hosted one hundred thousand people on *each* of the two major days of the mela month, the fifteenth and the thirtieth, and ten to twenty thousand on the other days; whereas Deokund averaged five thousand people *daily* for its seven-day gathering. Much the same pattern can be discerned from the attendance figures for the major fair of Brahampur. Compare Buchanan's enumeration of twenty-five thousand people on the occasion of this Sivaratri Fair with an 1894 count of seventy-five thousand and a 1906 tally of more than a hundred thousand. At Buxar, a town overlooking the Ganges, where fairs convened five times a year, the crowds totaled thirty-six thousand in the 1810s but more than double that number—about one hundred thousand—in the 1890s.[39]

The widening constituency of melas—a doubling and tripling over the colonial period, with the increases most dramatic in the late nineteenth and early twentieth centuries—can also be documented for the other great fairs of Bihar. Champaran's Bettiah Fair increased its participation from close to thirty thousand in the 1870s to more than fifty thousand in the 1890s and to almost one hundred thousand by the 1950s. Sitamarhi, identified as the birthplace of Rama's wife, Sita, convened as many as fifty thousand people on the occasion of the Ramnavami (the birth anniversary of Rama) Fair in the early 1880s and eighty thousand by the first decade of the twentieth century.[40]

---

38. Compiled from R. P. Jenkins, Offg. Commr., Patna, to Secy., GOB, Bengal Medical Procs., 1868, Apr., no. 50; AGRPD, 1876–77 to 1897–98; "Fairs," 1894, Patna Division; Ghose, "Rural Behar," p. 224.

39. Buchanan, *Shahabad*, p. 71; "Fairs," 1894; *ShDG* 1906, pp. 96–97.

40. AGRPD 1883–84; *MDG 1907*, p. 157; W. W. Hunter, *A Statistical Account of Bengal*, vol. 13, *Champaran* (London: Trubner, 1877), p. 255; "Fairs," 1894; *CDG 1960*, p. 326..

Nor were such patterns confined to the great fairs. Smaller fairs, such as those at Gupteswar and Tilothu in Shahabad, swelled from gatherings of five thousand and two thousand, respectively, in the early nineteenth century to five thousand and twenty thousand *daily* over the course of their weeklong meeting days by the close of that century. As for the mela near Mundesvari, also in Shahabad, where Buchanan had encountered "2000 votaries" in the second decade of the nineteenth century, it had grown to "more than ten thousand persons" by the mid-twentieth century.[41]

Detailed census information from 1961 provides a comprehensive profile of the melas of the region. The "great" fairs—those attended by twenty-five thousand people or more—accounted for the lion's share of those in attendance. The Sonepur Mela alone drew more than 3 million people, a number representing more than 68 percent of the audience of that district's fairs. Although no other fair in Bihar boasted such crowds, the great fairs in other districts also accounted for much of the total attendance. Patna's great fairs numbered fifteen (including three whose attendance amounted to at least one hundred thousand); Gaya had eight in that category; Saran six in addition to the Sonepur Mela; Champaran seven; Muzaffarpur fourteen (including four attended by more than one hundred thousand); and Darbhanga twenty-three, of which seventeen were in the twenty-five- to thirty-five-thousand category and only two in the hundred thousand and over range.

The vast majority of fairs, however, were fairlets. At least two-thirds of the fairs of Patna Division were attended by fewer than five thousand people—Darbhanga showing the lowest proportion of small fairs, with 68.9 percent, and Champaran returning the highest with more than 87 percent. The overwhelming majority of melas, in other words, were small-scale events with a constituency drawn primarily from the neighboring villages. Convened at sites that were often periodic markets (*haats*), these minor fairs typically served areas encompassing at least the periodic marketing area but probably a greater area, because these were not weekly occasions but ones that were held annually.[42]

Thus, the mela profile emerging in the age of colonialism possessed two distinctive features: great fairs, few in number but great in atten-

41. P. C. Roy Choudhury, *Temples and Legends of Bihar* (Bombay: Bharatiya Vidya Bhavan, 1965), p. 63; Buchanan, *Shahabad*, pp. 90, 106, 135; "Fairs," 1894.
    42. Compiled from *Fairs of Bihar*, pp. 526–35. See also below, chap. 4, on rural markets.

dance; and fairlets, many in number but modest in attendance. The great fairs, in particular, attracted geographically diverse audiences, with supralocal and even regional constituencies. By contrast, fairlets constituted local gatherings of people drawn from their immediate areas. In this respect, too, melas and pilgrimage were linked phenomena: both catered to a range of constituencies. Whereas the best known *tirthas* drew "pilgrims across linguistic, sectarian, and regional boundaries," the overwhelming majority comprised the "countless local and regional tirthas visited regularly by pilgrims from their immediate areas." For "no place is too small to be counted a tirtha by its local visitors. In a sense, each temple is a tirtha."[43]

Nowhere were the crowds more conspicuous than at Sonepur, and nowhere did the crowds come from greater distances than at Sonepur. A late-seventeenth-century source reported that people came "thither from the remotest parts of India" and from as far away as "Tartary Central Asia."[44] So extensive was participation from within the region that entire towns—the city of Patna, for example—seemed deserted on the "the great days of bathing." Devotees came from both sides of the Ganges for this "most fashionable pilgrimage" in the region. An estimate of the early nineteenth century reckoned that as much as one-fourth of the population of Patna went to Sonepur and was joined there by a sizable proportion of the population of Gaya, twenty thousand from Shahabad, and five or six thousand from Bhagalpur. Its fame made it a popular subject for the Patna School of painters.[45]

Attendance figures tell only part of the tale of the growing phenomenon of melas in local society. Like markets, the number of fairs increased over time. There is ample evidence that this growth peaked in the late nineteenth and early twentieth centuries. Buchanan's accounts of Patna, Gaya, and Shahabad in the second decade of the nineteenth century and Hunter's statistical reports of the same districts in the 1870s attest to this pattern, as do published and unpublished records (gazetteers, settlement reports, and the manuscript "village notes") of

43. Eck, "India's *Tirthas*," p. 325.
44. *Marshall in India*, pp. 141–42, 158.
45. Buchanan, *Bihar and Patna*, pp. 365–66; idem, *Shahabad*, p. 217; Martin, *Bhagalpur*, p. 133. The mela also became the most important social gathering of European administrators and settlers in north India, "what Christmas is to home folks," said one British local resident. Harry E. Abbott, *Sonepore Reminiscences (Years 1840–1896)* (Calcutta, Star Press, 1896), p. v. See also my *Limited Raj*, chap. 1, for details regarding the British incorporation of the Sonepur Mela into their structure and ideology of rule.

the early twentieth century. A village-by-village comparison of information available for Saran for 1915–21 and the detailed 1961 census on fairs offers an even more striking picture of growth: from a tally of 75 fairs in the former period to 717 by 1961, a number that this census returned as the highest for the region. Gaya followed with 643, Champaran with 568, Darbhanga with 544, Muzaffarpur with 312, Patna with 295, and Shahabad with 218.[46]

Historical biographies of melas, although limited in number, paint a similar portrait. A sample of twenty-two in Saran included the ancient Sonepur Mela, three said to date from a "long time" or "long ago," five from the nineteenth century, and the rest from the twentieth century; no founding dates could be established for six fairs. For Patna's fifteen melas, three were classified as "ancient," one was an eighteenth-century creation, and six and five were from the nineteenth and the twentieth century, respectively. In the "ancient" category are such fairs as the Pitri Paksha Mela at Zahidpur, where "since time immemorial" pilgrims have been going for the ceremonial bath at the sacred Punpun River, and the monthlong Malmas Mela at Rajgir. By contrast the Sivaratri Mela at Thalpura and the Dashara Mela at Rupaspur were instituted in the nineteenth century; still later, the Dashara Mela at Alawalpur and at Pandarakh were probably inaugurated when temples were installed there—in the 1940s in the case of the former, in 1939 in the case of the latter. A similar profile can be drawn for other districts.[47]

The rising traffic of people is also reflected in the expanded schedules of fairs. Like periodic markets that stretch their meeting days to meet a growing demand, fairs tacked on additional sacred days to the festival calendar. The fair at Areraj, for example, convened for eight days in March and three days in May in the late nineteenth century and the first decades of the twentieth century, but by 1961 it had become a mela that met six times a year. Although the March schedule remained the same, the May fair was extended to five or seven days. The additional four fair meetings were held over three or four days.[48]

---

46. *Fairs of Bihar*, pp. 504–12. In proportion to population: Saran had 1 fair for every 5,000 persons, Champaran 1:5,293, Gaya 1:5,673, Darbhanga 1:8,112, Patna 1:9,999, Muzaffarpur 1:13,200, and Shahabad 1:14,752. See also GOI, *Census of India*, vol. 4, part 9, *Census Atlas of Bihar* by S. D. Prasad (Delhi: n.p., 1968), p. 35; SVN; *Fairs of Bihar*, pp. xxxi–xxxvi, 64–100, for longitudinal data. Village notes identify where fairs were held but not all the fairs that were held in a village.

47. Compiled from SVN, 50 vols.; *Fairs of Bihar*, pp. xi–lvii.

48. Hunter, *Account of Champaran*, p. 255; CDG *1938*, p. 92; CDG *1960*, p. 326.

Melas also developed a wider constituency as the repertoire of festivals grew. Some were sustained by the familiar calendar of festivals; still others fashioned their places on the local calendar by celebrating new sacred days, occasions born out of the new religious movements and cults centered on the changing pantheon of divine figures and deified heroes and heroines.[49] Festivals—and therefore fairs—were continually evolving to keep pace with the changing sacred traditions of local society.

Throughout the "country," as Veeraswamy observed, people adhered to a religious almanac that was virtually the same.[50] There were also local and regional variations, and the astrological-astronomical events that were commemorated varied over time. In Bihar, according to one resident, melas typically occurred on auspicious days in the calendar that were "sacred to some god, or allotted to some particular festival."[51] The timing of each was "determined by some astrological-astronomical event. Some planet, or the moon, or the sun has to enter a particular sign of the zodiac; or else there has to be a lunar or solar eclipse. Commemoration of such an event as the birth, death, or the *siddhi* (attainment of religious consummation) of a particular saint may provide dates for *melas.*"[52]

A comparison of festival calendars from different eras reveals changes as well as continuities over the last millennium. Fourteen of the eighteen festivals identified in a fourteenth-century list compiled by the

49. Several factors led to the founding of a fair at the junction of the Punpun and Dardha Rivers in the late eighteenth century: the presence of an embankment, the economic benefits to be gained by a cluster of nearby villages, and the founding of a shrine. See Ramdahin Singh, comp., *Bihar Darpan* (Patna: Khadagvilas Press, 1883), pp. 35–36.

50. Based on a Hindu lunisolar calendar, the year was (and still is) divided up by lunar months that end on a full moon day (*purnima*); the new month commences on the following day. Each lunar month consists of about 30 days; a year therefore comprises 360 days. Every third year an intercalary month of 30 days is added to synchronize the lunar calendar to the solar year. Because of its shorter year, the Hindu calendar only roughly approximates the Gregorian calendar: generally the Indian months commence at approximately the middle of the months according to the latter calendar. The Hindu months and their solar equivalents are as follows: Asin, September-October; Kartik, October-November; Aghan, November-December; Pus, December-January; Magh, January-February; Phagun, February-March; Chait, March-April; Baisakh, April-May; Jeth, May-June; Akarh, June-July; Sawan, July-August; Bhadoi, August-September. Grierson, *Peasant Life,* p. 271; Veeraswamy, *Journal,* p. 153, appendix A. See also Ruth S. and Stanley A. Freed, "Calendars, Ceremonies, and Festivals in a North Indian Village: The Necessary Calendric Information for Fieldwork," *Southwestern Journal of Anthropology* 20 (1964): 67–90.

51. Ghose, "Rural Behar," p. 222. I have not taken into consideration here the small percentage of fairs that were related to the Muslim calendar: 17.3 percent in Gaya, 13.7 in Champaran, 8 in Muzaffarpur, 7.2 in Darbhanga, 6.8 in Patna, and 1.8 in Shahabad. See also *Fairs of Bihar.*

52. Bharati, "Pilgrimage Sites," p. 95.

Mithila scholar-statesman Chandreswar Thakur are today either minor events or no longer celebrated.[53] Many of these had faded earlier, a development discernible from the text associated with the sixteenth-century scholar and founder of the great estate of Darbhanga, Mahesh Thakur. Although substantial differences exist between the festivals of the fourteenth and sixteenth centuries—as Mahesh Thakur's list, which includes Nag Panchami, Krishna Janmashthami, Durga Puja or Navaratra, Dashara, Chhath, Kartik Purnima, Makar Sankranti, Basant Panchami, Sivaratri, and Ramnavami, indicates—far less appears to have changed in the annual cycle of festivals between the sixteenth century and the colonial era. Perhaps the more dramatic earlier transformation reflects the culmination of a shift in religious devotion from a focus on Tantric gods to a growing emphasis on Rama, a change that naturally ushered in a different pantheon of festivals. All of Hindi-speaking north India, including Bihar, was affected by this development, which elevated Rama to the status of supreme god, and his consort Sita to that of a *sakti* (goddess; divine power, personified as feminine). Instrumental in forging these new directions was the movement led by Ramananda (1400–70), which popularized the cult of Rama.[54]

Nevertheless, the emergence of the cult of Rama did not entirely displace earlier forms and modes of religious practices. In the precolonial period the north Bihar area of Mithila was a "great centre of Siva, Sakti and Vishnu worship and it was closely associated with Tantric forms of beliefs and practices. . . . [And] besides the worship of Siva and Vishnu with their consorts, along with that of the incarnations Rama and Krishna, there were other divinities . . . also held in reverence. . . . In fact, there was a multiplicity of gods and goddesses in the scheme of the religious life of Maithils."[55]

Such "multiplicity" persisted into the colonial era, as is shown by Buchanan's elaborate attempt to categorize and quantify religious beliefs and practices in the early nineteenth century.[56]

53. Diwakar, *Bihar through the Ages*, pp. 428–29. The exceptions are Janam Asthami, Nag Panchami, Sivaratri, and Basant Panchami. Diwali had also become a major festival by this time.

54. Ibid., pp. 530–31; Jordens, "Hindu Devotionalism," p. 274; William R. Pinch, "Becoming Vaishnava, Becoming Kshatriya: Culture, Belief, and Identity in North India, 1800–1940," Ph.D. diss., University of Virginia, 1990, pp. 103–6.

55. Diwakar, *Bihar*, p. 410.

56. In Patna and Gaya, he estimated that three-sixteenths of the people were Saivite, five-sixteenths Saktas, and two-sixteenths Vaishnavite. Saktas focused their attention on

As for the festivals celebrated in Buchanan's day, the popular present-day festivals of Diwali, Holi, and Dashara—in that order of importance—were already major occasions. Dashara, however, was apparently not celebrated with as much fanfare as Durga Puja was in Bengal, there being no "feasting, dancing, and music" accompanying this holiday; it was "observed chiefly by the Brahmans, while the Holi and Dewali are observed by all."[57] But because of its association with Rama, Dashara grew in importance in the colonial period, reflecting the rising patronage role played by landholders—as well as their rising status and power in local society in the wake of the late eighteenth-century revolution. Its celebration in Asin at the beginning of the agricultural year came to be associated with zamindars. In the great estates it was an occasion when tenants offered their raja "presents and congratulations." The Hathwa-owned newspaper, the *Express,* described Dashara as "pre-eminently a Kshattrya festival, [which] people of all castes and classes observe. . . . In Bihar, scions of old baronial houses and big Zamindars that have the status and position of Rajas . . . observe the Puja and perform all the ceremonies in the same way as do the Ruling Chiefs and Princes, and march in state . . . with great pomp and splendour."[58]

Another key festival was Sivaratri, ranked by Buchanan as next in importance to Dashara. Chhath and Kartik Purnima also brought out large crowds who converged on Sonepur or other prime ritual bathing spots. The Patna School of Painters vividly captured in their striking paintings how celebrated and well-attended these functions were. Other festivals that drew large numbers were Magh Purnima, Bishuwa Sankranti, and Nag Panchami.[59]

The rhythm of the mela calendar was also synchronized with the ebb and flow of the agricultural calendar. Peaks in fair activity coincided almost perfectly with the timing of the marketing of produce of the different harvests, generally within a month of harvest. In Bihar this was

---

Kali and Durga, whereas Vaishnavites, "in Magadha and Mithila," to use Buchanan's phrase, people "chiefly worship Ram." Martin, *Bhagalpur, Gorakhpur,* p. 130

57. Buchanan, *Shahabad,* p. 218; idem, *Bihar and Patna,* pp. 362–66.

58. Oct. 12, 1915, reprinted in Chowdhary, *Selected Writings,* pp. 89–90; Dutt, *Hutwa Raj,* pp. 53–54, 23. See also Thomas R. Metcalf, *Land, Landlords, and the British Raj: Northern India in the Nineteenth Century* (Berkeley and Los Angeles: University of California Press, 1979), pp. 365–66, and my *Limited Raj,* pp. 115–17, for an account of Dashara celebrations as a manifestation of kingly and patronage role.

59. Buchanan, *Bihar and Patna,* pp. 67, 75; idem, *Shahabad,* pp. 217–18; Martin, *Gorakhpur,* p. 481. See also my "Visualizing Patna."

typically in October and November (Asin-Kartik-Aghan) for the *bhadai* (autumn harvest sown in June-July), January and February (Pus-Magh-Phagun) for the *aghani* (winter harvest planted in June-July), and March and April (Phagun-Chait-Baisakh) for the *rabi* (spring harvest sown in October-November).[60] Consider also the fact that the area cultivated at each of the three principal harvests varied from district to district.

In the southern districts of Gaya, Patna, and Shahabad the *bhadai* harvest was relatively insignificant; the *rabi* harvest, by contrast, was important especially in Patna and Shahabad. In the north, however, although the *rabi* was a significant crop (except in Darbhanga), the *bhadai* and *aghani* together represented the largest percentage. No doubt, the dovetailing of the rhythm of work and slack seasons with the annual cycle of melas facilitated large turnouts.[61]

This interrelationship between the festival and agricultural cycle has long been recognized as a feature of local society:

> Bhado and Asin [August-September to September-October] . . . are marked by many religious observances and ceremonies, because this is the most critical season of the year to the cultivator, when he must have rain. Towards the end of the former month the agriculturists have to observe the fast of anant brat in gratitude for the ingathering of the bhadai harvest and in the hope of future prosperity. During the first fortnight of Kuar or Asin, since it is on the rain of this period that a successful harvest of the aghani and the moisture for the rabi depends, they devote much time to religious offerings and oblations to their deceased ancestors. This is followed by Nauratra or nine nights of abstinence from worldly enjoyments and devotion to the goddess Durga. When the rabi sowings have been completed the Nauratra is over, there follows a day of universal rejoicing when alms are given . . .
>
> During Kartik . . . when the paddy harvest is taking ear, many devotional performances are observed, especially by the women and unmarried girls. They bathe before dawn and worship the sun as the producer of rain

---

60. Office Note on BOR's no. 904A, Aug. 13, 1891, by D. R. Lyall, Commr., Patna, P.C. Rev. Basta no. 355, 1891–92; *MSR.,* pp. 249–55; Veeraswamy, *Journal,* pp. 42, 51.

61. Jeth to Aghan (June to November) represent a peak of activity in the agricultural year, December to May (Pus to Baisakh) a period of relative slack. In other words, the slack period extends over most of the cold season, which commences in Kartik (October-November) and ends with the onset of the hot season in Phagun (February-March); the wet season begins in Akarh (June-July). Not surprising, the slack season of the annual cycle of festivals, Jeth and Akarh, is a time when work on the land is at a peak; it is in these two months that the autumn harvest is sown and followed immediately by the planting of the winter harvest in Akarh and Sawan. Moreover, this period is also an auspicious time for marriages in Bihar. By contrast, Kartik, a busy festival time, occurs at the planting of the spring harvest—a harvest that entails the least involved labor.

every morning until Purnamasi or the period of a full moon, when large crowds of the people . . . repair to bathe at the confluence of the Ganges and Gandak . . .

When, however, the rabi crop is assured, the devotional attitude is abandoned, anxiety is at an end, and on the first of Chait the people celebrate the Holi festival, breaking forth in unrestrained and hilarious enjoyment.[62]

This roster of major festivals remained constant over the course of the colonial era, shifting only in intensity. To use a "popularity index" based on monthly attendance figures, the peak in mela attendance—except in Champaran, Muzaffarpur, and Shahabad—was reached during the months of Asin and Kartik, followed by Bhadoi, the month preceding Asin. Not coincidentally, these are the months of some of the most auspicious moments in the annual cycle of festivals: they form the period that closes out the wet season beginning in Akarh and ushers in the cold season generally commencing in Kartik. It is a transitional period highlighted by the major festival of Dashara (in Asin), Chhath and Diwali (both in Kartik), and Kartik Purnima. Chait, also a period of high mela attendance, especially in Muzaffapur and Champaran, is another high point in the annual cycle because it is the month in which Rama's birthday is celebrated—Ramnavmi (Rama's ninth)—as well as Chaitra Sankranti and Chhath, the latter festival also occurring in Kartik. Magh and Phalgun, two other auspicious months of high levels of mela activity are notable for the worship of the god Shiva, an occasion commemorated in the Sivaratri melas, and for Maghi Purnima, Makar Sankranti, and Basant Panchami, all Magh festivals celebrated by ritual bathing in rivers and river junctions. Along with Baisakh—Baisakh Purnima is an auspicious day—Kartik and Magh are significant as times when ritual bathing is considered especially purificatory. And with the sacred Ganges and Gandak located in the region, the opportunities and locales to convene fairs are numerous. The only other months in which significant numbers attended melas especially in Champaran are Sawan—for fairs associated with Nag Panchami and Sivaratri—and Aghan, especially in Muzaffapur, for fairs relating to Vivah Panchami or Sita Vivah.[63]

62. *MSR*, p. 253.
63. Melas in Bhadoi, Asin, and Kartik accounted for 75, 65, and 55 percent of the total number of fairs in Patna, Darbhanga, and Gaya, respectively; 48 percent each in Muzaffarpur and Saran; and 25 and 22 percent in Champaran and Shahabad, respectively. Chait accounted for 6.8 percent in Patna, 10.4 percent in Gaya, and 15.1 percent

The dramatic increase in numbers of melas and pilgrims "on the road" and the emergence of Dashara as a major festival in the colonial era both point to changes in Hindu religious practices and in the composition and role of participants in these practices. As Bayly has observed, the numbers converging on pilgrimage sites "may have trebled" each year between 1780 and 1820 for the following reasons: "The British abolition of 'pilgrim taxes' and easier transport redoubled the flow. Brahmins and high Brahminical ritual introduced by eighteenth-century rulers . . . spread in the protected states of the nineteenth century for whom conspicuous piety replaced warfare as the chief charge on state revenues. New men who built up their fortunes through the services of the British invested in elaborate death anniversary ceremonies (shraddhas) in rural Bengal, while many of the great temples of Madras were renovated and expanded in the vivid styles of the early nineteenth century."[64]

Veeraswamy, who traveled at a time when the pilgrim tax was still in place, was confident that "the day is not far off when they may get an annulment of the collection of tax at pilgrim centres. . . . [And] God alone knows what an amount of good fortune this annulment would bring."[65] Despite his ties to "government" and his acknowledgment of the assistance he received from such connections, he openly criticized this one policy. At Patna, while en route to Gaya, he noted disapprovingly that his employers had taken over the collection of the pilgrim tax at several sacred centers, including Gaya. Bholanauth Chunder, who followed Veeraswamy by thirty years, was a beneficiary of this "good fortune," the pilgrim tax having been abolished in 1840. Official declarations regarding noninterference in religious matters notwithstanding, as recent scholarship shows the colonial state "penetrated Hindu religious institutions, both temples and maths (monasteries), deeply and systematically."[66]

---

in Shahabad. Magh and Phagun tallied 20 and 23 percent of Shahabad's fairs; Sawan was the most active month of fairs in Champaran (28 percent). Contrast these peaks of mela intensity with the paucity of fairs in Jeth and Akarh (May-June and June-July), not coincidentally a period of virtually no important festivals, and with Pus; to a lesser extent, Aghan (December-January and November-December) was another period of relatively few festivals. See Fairs in Bihar, p. xcviii; Hunter, Account of Champaran, p. 255; Grierson, Notes on Gaya, p. 117.

64. Bayly, Indian Society, p. 159.
65. Journal, p. 147.
66. Franklin A. Presler, Religion under Bureaucracy: Policy and Administration for Hindu Temples in South India (Cambridge: Cambridge University Press, 1987), p. 15;

Veeraswamy's journey, made under the sign of colonialism, also benefited from other developments. Thanks to the "good offices" of the British authorities, he was able to secure official assistance on the road; and because of the new regime of law and order ushered in by Pax Britannica his pilgrimage across the subcontinent encountered no political or military hazards. By contrast, in the period leading up to the age of revolution and continuing on through the early years of the nineteenth century, political and military disruptions frequently slowed down the traffic of pilgrims to a trickle. As pilgrims informed the official deputed to report on the pilgrimage center of Deoghar in Birbhum district (present-day West Bengal) in 1791, their numbers had fallen considerably because of "commotion" in northern and western India; those who had succeeded in reaching Deoghar from other regions "had proceeded by stealth." Similarly, an appreciable decline in the number of pilgrims in Gaya in 1804 was attributed by its priests "to the warfare and unsettled state of the country to the westward," which had made "pilgrims . . . afraid to come down and pay the usual devotions."[67]

Although Veeraswamy's trip had preceded the era of systematic and extensive road building projects by many decades, his experiences "on the road" reveal that the colonial authorities had already secured the major highways throughout the country, in many areas even providing shelter for travelers. By the 1860s, as Chunder testified, conditions obtaining on the road were in marked contrast to those existing in the time of "our grandfathers and great-grandfathers," who made out "their wills before setting on a pilgrimage. . . . By land, the journey was unsafe from wild beasts, from highway robbers, from Thugs, and from Mahratta rovers. By water, the voyage was unsafe from *Nor-Westers,* from pirates, and from the river-police. . . . In a few years the Railway shall further abridge this distance and time, and inaugurate an era of security to life and property which has been never known to these regions."[68]

Veeraswamy, *Journal,* p. 147. See also Arjun Appadurai, *Worship and Conflict under Colonial Rule: A South Indian Case* (Cambridge: Cambridge University Press, 1981); Nancy Gardner Cassels, *Religion and Pilgrim Tax under the Company Raj* (Riverdale, Md.: Riverdale, 1988).

67. G. P. Ricketts, Colltr., Bihar, to C. Buller, Secy., BOR, Aug. 24, 1804, Bengal BOR Procs., Sayer, 1804, Sept. 28; C. Keating, Colltr., Birbhum, to Hon'ble Charles Stuart, President, BOR, Mar. 28, 1791, Bengal BOR Procs., Sayer, 1791, July 6.

68. Chunder, *Travels,* vol. 1, pp. 40–41; *Report of Bihar Pilgrim Committee,* p. 4. Also Veeraswamy, *Journal,* pp. 20, 40, 66, 81, 177. The completion of the Grand Trunk Road by the mid-nineteenth century offered pilgrims an alternative to the Ganges highway, an option preferred especially by the less well-off pilgrims who could then travel on foot at little or no cost.

The "marvel and miracle" of railway, to use Bholanauth Chunder's phrase, further widened the streams of pilgrims; lines, furthermore, were specifically constructed to cater to such traffic.[69] As an early-twentieth-century observer noted, the boom in the building of railways and roads meant that pilgrimages no longer entailed "a difficult and often dangerous journey by road. . . . The pilgrim who now wishes to go . . . can perform practically the whole of his journey by rail and the saving in time, expense and discomfort is incalculable. Enormous numbers now visit these holy places who under former conditions could never have dreamt of doing so."[70]

The development of more efficient communication and transportation not only facilitated travel by pilgrims but also by the so-called pilgrim hunters. "[E]ver since the city of Gyah became famous for its sanctity," wrote its administrator in 1790, "it has been the custom of its Brahmins . . . to travel through all countries where the Hindoo religion prevails in search of pilgrims." Termed "pilgrim hunters" in the colonial records, these "gomastahs or agents" were said to travel "throughout India for the purpose of enticing pilgrims to the several shrines and temples of repute," receiving in return "a fee from every pilgrim whom they can persuade to visit the particular seat of superstition to which they are attached . . . and they in fact seem to discharge their vocation with astonishing industry, dexterity and success."[71] Gaya was renowned for its "very extensive system of pilgrim hunting," its "scouts" not only intercepting the Bholanauth Chunders as they left the Grand Trunk Road for the branch road to Gaya but also seeking out potential visitors much farther afield. Veeraswamy, for one, felt the long reach of these enterprising individuals as he was pursued by "Gayavalis" intent on recruiting him as their client from almost the time he departed from Madras.[72]

---

69. E.g., the new chord line of railway running across south Bihar to Bengal was deliberately laid out to intersect the important pilgrimage center of Deoghar. See R. P. Jenkins, Special Duty, Railway, to Joint Secy., GOB, Bengal Rev. Procs., Jan.-Apr. 1866, Apr., no. 2. Chunder, *Travels*, vol. 1, pp. 140–41.

70. *Report of Bihar Pilgrim Committee*, p. 4. Better access also had the effect of adding "elasticity" to pilgrim schedules. Attendance at some sacred centers declined because some pilgrims apparently opted not to go on festival days when crowds were likely to be at their peak.

71. Court of Directors to GOB, no. 3, Feb. 20, 1833, Bengal Rev. Miscellaneous Consltns., Jan. 5 to 3 May, 1836, 2 Feb., no. 2; Colltr., Bihar, to Hon'ble Charles Stuart, July 16, 1790, Bengal BOR Procs., Sayer, May 3 to Dec. 29, 1790, Aug. 23.

72. Court to GOB, Feb. 20, 1833, Bengal Rev. Miscellaneous Consltns., Feb. 2, 1836, no. 2; Veeraswamy, *Journal*, p. 80; Chunder, *Travels*, vol. 1, p. 224.

Pilgrimage centers also advertised their merits in other ways. Many *tirthas* capitalized on print technology. Almost every significant sacred center turned to marketing a revised form of the ancient Sanskrit genre of writings known as *mahatmya*, "a laud, a hymn of praise, a glorification. These praises, of particular places or of particular gods, form a part of the many Puranas, the 'ancient stories' of the gods, kings, and saints.... These *mahatmyas* are not descriptive statements of fact... but statements of faith."[73] By the early twentieth century, this kind of "praise-literature" extolling the virtues of sacred centers was widely available in pamphlet form. Moreover, much of this literature was rendered partly or completely into vernacular languages, either Hindi or its regional Bihar variants, and sold inexpensively. The first edition of the *Harihar Kshetra Mahatmya,* or "The Greatness of Harihar Kshetra as a Place of Pilgrimage," published in 1924 to celebrate the Sonepur Mela, was priced at one anna and issued in a run of two thousand copies.[74]

Advertisements in newspapers was another means of generating publicity. The Sonepur Fair, for instance, placed advertisements in a wide range of newspapers and posted vernacular and English notices throughout the region in the late nineteenth century.[75]

A literature based on personal experiences or on data collected from local gazetteers, histories, and other local-level materials also promoted pilgrimage by offering prospective travelers firsthand information regarding sacred sites and their facilities. In part, this literature was facilitated by the documentation project of the colonial state, a project that produced and normalized "a vast amount of information" for governing purposes. Sadhu Charan Prasad's *Bharat Brahman,* a five-part account describing the topography and history of the *tirthas,* towns, and other famous places in India, combined both these genres: it was based partly on the author's travels in the 1890s and partly on data collected from English and vernacular sources. Take, for instance, his entry on Revelganj, the site of the Godna Mela, which he visited in 1892. In addition to the usual gazetteer-like information about transportation

73. Diana L. Eck, *Banaras: City of Light* (London: Routledge and Kegan Paul, 1983), pp. 22–23.

74. *Harihar Mahatmya.* See also, e.g., *Arreraj Mahatmya* (Bettiah: Lakshminarayan Saran, 193?); Vishwanath Mahto, *Shri Barabar Mahatmya* (Bhagalpur: B.A. Press, 1915?); *Asli Gaya Mahatmya* (Gaya: Harilal Bannerji, n.d.).

75. India, "Report on Metropolitan Horse Fairs and District Horse Shows, 1892–93," p. 25. Bharati, "Pilgrimage Sites," pp. 87, 126, attributes the rising popularity of pilgrimage to improved publicity.

links, population, and history, it also offers details regarding the site's religious significance, from the temples and *maths* (monasteries) and sadhus in the vicinity to its mela.[76]

The flow of pilgrims was also enhanced by the "patronage of elite Hindus—royalty, administrators, military leaders and landholders—[who] triggered a boom in pilgrimage in the 1700s that continued well into the British era." And in the aftermath of this trend, which this historian terms "state-sponsored pilgrimage" came "new pilgrims" drawn from the "humbler" ranks: "rising commercial classes" and "civil servants" as well as "common people, such as land-tilling castes."[77] A recent study of Ayodhya, which views the surge in pilgrim traffic as a function of the changing composition of pilgrims "from the established elite to new groups," arrives at much the same conclusion. Many of the "new men" who swelled the ranks of travelers "on the road" were people who undertook such journeys to establish their "conspicuous piety." Among them were numerous "Bengali government servants together with merchant families" who were "conspicuous beneficiaries of the Pax Britannica."[78] Government sources confirm this trend. To use the language of the official records, a "very large proportion of the pilgrims are wretchedly poor." And they came from everywhere. "Every village in the country," as one seasoned administrator put it, "sends its one or two pilgrims to some gathering or other during the year."[79]

Veeraswamy, as a Madras government servant and a member of an elite, epitomizes simultaneously the "new" pilgrim and the well-to-do groups who have historically undertaken *tirthayatras*. Pilgrimage, a hallmark of piety and personal honor for such groups, may even have gained in status and currency over the course of the colonial era. In a period of flux, adherence to this practice, as has been argued for other religious and social practices, may well have represented a way of ex-

76. Sadhu Charan Prasad, *Bharat Brahman* (Banaras: Hariprakash Yantralaya, 1902–3). See, e.g., part 2, pp. 2–32; Cohn, "Anthropology of a Colonial State."

77. Katherine Prior, "The British Administration of Hinduism in North India, 1780–1900," Ph.D. diss., Cambridge University, 1990, pp. 81–86, 14.

78. C. A. Bayly, "From Ritual to Ceremony: Death Ritual and Society in Hindu North India since 1600," in *Mirrors of Mortality*, ed. J. Whaley (London: Europa Publications, 1981), p. 170; Peter Van Der Veer, *Gods on Earth: The Management of Religious Experience and Identity in a North Indian Pilgrimage Centre*, pp. 212–13.

79. R. P. Jenkins, Offg. Commr., Patna, to Secy., GOB, no. 10, Jan. 13, 1868, and E. W. Molony, Offg. Commr., Orissa, to Secy., GOB, no. 221 1/2, July 16, 1869, Bengal Sanitation Procs., 1869, Oct., no. 12 and Apr., no. 18.

pressing "conformity to older norms at a time when these norms had become shaky within."[80]

These norms themselves, however, may have constituted invented traditions created by changes in the settlement and landholding patterns of the region. The in-migration of Rajputs and, more significantly for much of the region, of Bhumihar Brahmins transformed the local landscape of religious belief and practices. In Shahabad the struggle between Rajput in-migrants and the local Cheros ensued for several hundred years before the former won out and the latter fled southward. Although earlier waves of Rajputs had staked out the area—petty Rajput chiefs were said to be in command at the time of Muhammad Bakhtiar Khalji's conquest of the region at the end of the twelfth century—a formidable Rajput presence in the locality dates from the time of the arrival of the Parmar Rajputs beginning in the early fourteenth century. Also known later as the Ujjainia Rajputs, this clan played a leading role in suppressing the Cheros and in challenging the different Muslim rulers who sought to extend their sway over the area. Branches of this clan eventually founded the major Shahabad estates of Dumraon, Bhojpur, and Jagdishpur, but not without struggles that persisted into the eighteenth century. By the sixteenth century Bhumihar Brahmins also controlled vast stretches of territory, particularly in north Bihar. In south Bihar their most prominent representative was the Tikari family, whose great estate in Gaya dates back to the early eighteenth century. Thus, by the late eighteenth century, Rajputs and especially Bhumihar Brahmins had established themselves as the premier landholders of the region, sharing power in some areas only with other upper castes—Brahmins and Kayasths.[81] Such a pattern of conquest and settlement may explain why the cult of Rama was so extensive in Bihar, earning a significant place for Rama alongside a "multiplicity of gods and goddesses."[82]

80. Ashis Nandy has made this provocative argument, based on limited evidence, to explain why middle-class Bengalis resorted to sati in the late eighteenth and early nineteenth centuries. See his *At the Edge of Psychology: Essays in Politics and Culture* (Delhi: Oxford University Press, 1980), p. 7.

81. *ShDG 1906*, pp. 18–19; *GDG 1906*, pp. 237–38; K. K. Datta, *Biography of Kunwar Singh and Amar Singh* (Patna: K. P. Jayaswal Research Institute, 1957), pp. 1–17; Rana P. B. Singh, *Clan Settlements in the Saran Plain* (Varanasi: National Geographical Society of India, 1977), pp. 100–9. The most important Brahmin landholding family in the region was the Darbhanga rajas.

82. Deo Banarak in Shahabad, the site of two ancient temples and other remains, illustrates this legacy well. Inscriptions date the larger of the two temples back to the eighth century when it was apparently dedicated to the sun. Other pillars depict early Aryan deities—Indra, Yama, Varuna, and Kubera. And, although icons devoted to the

Landholders especially, but also merchants and traders, increasingly resorted to "conspicuous piety," adopting public roles as religious patrons, which they took to be appropriate manifestations of kingly behavior. Moreover, they were well positioned to assume these roles because of the favorable conditions of landholding ushered in by the economic and political climate of Pax Britannica—a development chronicled and anticipated by the Patna historian Ghulam Husain—and because of the political and social status that they had acquired under the "Limited Raj" of the colonial state.[83]

No wonder family histories of notables in the colonial period, whether autobiographical or biographical, invariably privileged the religious lives of their subjects, singling out especially for commendation the undertaking of pious pilgrimages. The history of the eminent Chaudharys of Patna, for instance, notes the family's long-standing practice of religious piety, beginning with a late-eighteenth-century ancestor, "a great devotee" who journeyed to several sacred centers "in days when the roads were infested with robbers and pillagers and traveling entailed indescribable sufferings owing to lack of conveyance and other troubles." This ancestor, Dudraj Sinha Chaudhuri, was noted for his largesse with grain relief during the great famine of 1770. He also made pilgrimages, touring the holy sites with a retinue of 150 people. One of his descendants earned a reputation as an accomplished scholar and poet, in his later years increasingly living the life of a recluse and devoting himself "exclusively to the worship of God." Subsequent generations continued the pilgrimage tradition, one late-nineteenth-century descendant combined his visits to sacred sites with visits to sessions of the leading nationalist organization, the Indian National Congress. In the nineteenth century the family was renowned for its patronage of the popular Ramlila festival in the city of Patna.[84]

Maharaja Hit Narayan Singh of Tikari was said to have been "a man of a religious turn of mind . . . [who] became an ascetic and left his vast property in the hands of his wife" shortly after inheriting a lion's share of the estate in the 1840s. The official history of the great estate of Hathwa notes that Sir Kishen Pratap Sahi Bahadur, who was the ma-

---

sun have survived in the temple, an image of Vishnu subsequently formed its centerpiece. C. E. A. W. Oldham, ed., *Journal of Francis Buchanan Kept during the Survey of the District of Shahabad in 1812–13* (Patna: Govt. Printing, 1926), pp. 10–13.

83. See above, chap. 1; and my *The Limited Raj*.

84. Pandey, "History of the Chaudhary Family, Patna City," pp. i–xxiv.

haraja between 1874 and 1896, "had the heart of an ascetic. Soon after he was installed . . . he set out on a pilgrimage to the shrines of Northern India and travelled through almost the whole of India. Later on he used to pass a portion of the year in travelling and pilgrimage, mostly, in Benares."[85] Janki Prasad Singh, maharaja of the great estate of Dumraon between 1838 and 1843, is remembered as having died en route to the sacred center of Jaggarnath. He was known during his lifetime as one who observed rituals on holy days, venerated holy men, offered prayers daily at his family shrine, and undertook pilgrimages. Pilgrimage as a leitmotiv in the lives of the famous is also evidenced in the 1883 *Bihar Darpan,* a biographical dictionary of the great men of that province.[86]

Prominent in the ranks of the pilgrims were other groups that had also prospered during the colonial period. In north India generally and in Bihar specifically, "emigrant businessmen from the vicinity of Rajasthan" (better known as Marwaris and Aggarwals) who had been staking out intermediary positions for themselves in the new circuits of trade emerging in the colonial era were actively involved in pilgrimage, both as devotees and traders who set up shop in pilgrimage centers. They had also long been the major underwriters of well-to-do pilgrims who needed credit at their pilgrimage destinations. Veeraswamy, who first encountered them in central India, testifies to their presence all along his pilgrimage circuit.[87]

Trader histories and directories, written in the late nineteenth century partly for prospective pilgrims and partly for those who wished to tap into the lucrative pilgrimage trade, further locate this chronology of rising pilgrim traffic in that era. This timing reflects the growing prosperity of trading castes in Bihar and throughout much of India. Surely Bholanauth Chunder's experiences can be viewed as part of this trend because his travels were partially undertaken in his capacity as a trader

85. Devendra Nath Dutt, *A Brief History of the Hutwa Raj* (Calcutta: K. P. Mookerjee, 1909), p. 35; *GDG 1906,* p. 238.

86. Singh, *Bihar Darpan,* e.g., pp. 35, 53; Rajiv Nain Prasad, *History of Bhojpur (1320–1860)* (Patna: K. P. Jayaswal Research Institute, 1987), p. 130. See also Philip Lutgendorf, *The Life of a Text: Performing the Ramcaritmanas of Tulsidas* (Berkeley and Los Angeles: University of California Press, 1991), p. 137, regarding elite patronage of pilgrimages and of a variety of activities associated with the epic poem, *Ramcaritmanas.*

87. Veeraswamy, *Journal,* pp. 42, 46, identifies Marwaris present in bazaars beginning in central India. See also below, chap. 5, on the rising "outsider" trader groups in the nineteenth century. Prior, "British Administration of Hinduism," p. 17, refers to the practice of pilgrims to rely for credit on bankers rather than travel with cash in hand.

who dealt in "country produce." Perhaps he may even have been a beneficiary of the prosperity reaped as the fruits of the pilgrimage- and mela-associated trade.[88] Thus, the *Vyapriyon ki Namavali,* a trade directory, lists by localities, the names of traders and their specialties, as well as information pertinent to traders interested in conducting business there, such as lists of things grown, manufactured, and exported. This directory also featured information on melas and other sites worth visiting, typically temples and shrines. In a trade guide of Bihar and Orissa produced by and for the trading caste of Aggarwals, commerce and religion were conspicuously highlighted, information about traders, products, and markets sharing space with descriptions of the prominent religious centers.[89]

Others among the new pilgrims were those of less privileged social and economic backgrounds, notably men and women drawn from such "new" groups as traders, mostly petty traders of the Shudra castes; and rich peasants, mostly of the Shudra castes. In both cases, their interest in pilgrimage was heightened by their drive for higher status at a time when they were making substantial economic gains. For traders of Shudra castes, emulation of the practices of the higher castes represented their ambition to lay claim to a Vaishya status. Thus Telis, a Shudra group actively engaged in trading, were enjoined to give up trafficking in items associated with traders of low caste, assume Vaishya ways, and strive to become *mahajans* (moneylenders, bankers), a role for which the Marwaris were upheld as the model to emulate.[90]

A similar pattern can be identified for peasants whom William R. Pinch categorizes as "low-status cultivators," particularly Kurmis, Koiris, and Ahirs, who constituted the "semi-independent cultivating" castes and who represented the "semi-independent cultivators on the margin of land-ownership." For them the ideal was to fashion a Vaishnava *kshatriya,* or warrior identity, centered on devotion to Rama and

88. Chunder, *Travels,* vol. 1, p. xx. The participation of traders in pilgrimage was not new, the magnitude of it was; nor was their mixing of business and faith an entirely novel development. See Banarsidas, *Ardhakathanaka,* for a remarkable autobiography of a seventeenth-century merchant and pilgrim.

89. B. P. Agarwal, *Agarwal Vyapar Darpan, Bihar aur Orissa* (Muzaffarpur: B. P. Agarwal, 191?), pp. 179–86; Karta Kishan Dube, comp., *Vyapariyon ki Namavali,* part III (Lucknow: Karta Kishan Dube, 1919).

90. Janki Prasad Sahu, *Teli Jatiya Niyambali* (Rules for the Teli Caste) (Bhagalpur: Janki Prasad Sahu, 1915), passim; see also below, chap. 5, on the rise of petty traders and rich peasants.

Krishna and the various symbols, meanings, and practices associated with these gods.[91]

The rich and powerful manifested their "conspicuous piety" and position in local society through their roles as patrons of fairs. Landholding families, as their histories often indicate, were tied to the founding of melas; others were connected through their roles as sponsors and caretakers of fairs. An unusual first-person testimony identifying the imperative of landholder patronage of fairs can be authenticated for the well-known Jahanabad Mela of Gaya in the late nineteenth century. This illustration is all the more compelling because it involves the Muslim zamindar of Jahanabad, whose voice can be heard distinctly in the colonial archive because he was the target of a criminal attack while he was asleep on the premises of the Hindu temple of that locality. When asked to explain what he had been doing there, he noted that it was the night of the full moon in Kartik, an important festival day of the fair. To continue in his words, "I slept away from my own house to take care of the fair (mela hifazut ke waste). I am a Zemindar of the place, and it is customary for the Zemindars to take care of the fair."[92]

That a temple figures in this account of landholder patronage of fairs is indicative of the landholder connection—to both fairs and temples—because the sites of temples (and shrines) were often the venues of fairs and because their building and maintenance were often tied to the kingly or patronage role of landed magnates. Certainly, Veeraswamy understood the responsibilities of this role, since he commented on it frequently. Contrast his chiding of the nawab of one area for failing to keep up with repairs of a temple with his words of praise for the landholder of another area where the temple was "not . . . constructed well" but the "worship . . . performed satisfactory with the required rituals according to southern traditions. . . . The Lord in the temple here is being worshipped splendidly; and it is no wonder that Lord's grace is showered in a visible manner as if the Lord is on talking terms with the Zamindar and his family."[93] Temples were indeed often founded by zamindars, and temple building, which increased significantly between the late

91. "Becoming Vaishnava, Becoming Kshatriya," pp. 294–304.

92. Testimony of Azmat Ali, Trial No. 3, Case No. 5, Sessions for Jan. 1863, Zillah Behar, Bengal Jdcl. Procs., Apr. 1863, no. 453.

93. Veeraswamy, *Journal*, pp. 15, 31. Similar observations are sprinkled throughout the work, e.g., see p. 70.

eighteenth century and the end of the nineteenth century, was the "accustomed way an aspirant landholder laid claim to a higher status."[94]

Temples dating back to early Rajput in-migrants trace the long-standing practice of local lords sponsoring the building of temples in Bihar.[95] And their construction, generally alongside forts already in existence, accentuates the salience of both types of structures as the twin hallmarks of power and authority. While forts towered above the huts of the subject peoples, temples proclaimed their founders' religious faith and claim to moral authority. By virtue of their dedication to one or more specific gods, temples sought to forge a common religious identity with the local population. Like melas, temples and forts tied into a multiplicity of domains. And in the precolonial and early colonial periods, when there was more land than needed for the subsistence of a conquering group, forts and temples were the symbols of power and control: the former representing the coercive capacity of the controlling group, the latter asserting its hegemonic control. And each needed the other because together they constituted the essentials of authority and legitimacy.

Rajput and Bhumihar Brahmin conquerors turned controllers therefore emulated a model of kingship in which the role of religious patron was central. Political authority and ritual were thereby closely interlinked and not fraught with the "inner conflict of tradition," which some scholars view as ever present in the relationship between brahmin and king because "it is not the king but the brahmin who, according to the classical conception, holds the key to ultimate value and therefore to legitimacy and authority." And because of this powerful ambivalence, "kingship remains . . . theoretically suspended between sacrality and secularity, divinity and mortal humanity, legitimate authority and arbitrary power, dharma and adharma." The king, in other words, "desperately needs the brahmin to sanction his power by linking it to the brahmin's authority."[96]

94. Metcalf, *Land and the British Raj*, p. 352; Veeraswamy, *Journal*, pp. 15, 70. On the proliferation of temple building and the occupational and caste backgrounds of people who sponsored the building of temples, see Hitesranjan Sanyal, "Social Aspects of Temple Building in Bengal: 1600 to 1900 A.D.," *Man in India* 48 (1968): 201–19; and his *Social Mobility in Bengal* (Calcutta: Papyrus, 1981), p. 67.

95. One of the earliest examples of Rajput temples is Deo Banarak, dating back to the mid-sixteenth century. See Buchanan, *Journal of Shahabad*, p. 13.

96. J. C. Heesterman, *The Inner Conflict of Tradition: Essays in Indian Ritual, Kingship, and Society* (Chicago: University of Chicago Press, 1985), pp. 127, 111.

To keep state and society bound together, however, is to recognize that "caste was embedded in a political context of kingship." To pursue the lead supplied by one scholar: "The prevalent ideology had not to do, at least primarily, with purity and pollution, but rather with royal authority and honor, and associated notions of power, dominance, and order." Therefore he concludes: "It is a mistake to try to separate a materialist *etic* from a cultural *emic*: even the domain of ritual action and language is permeated with the complex foundations and lived experiences of hierarchical relations."[97] "The patronage of religion revolving around the restoration of temples, sponsorship of festivals, and distribution of temple honors," notes another source, "continued to be a focus of activity in privileged landholding because of the importance of Hinduism in the reproduction of royal status."[98] Melas, markets, and religion: these were all tied to the patronage role associated with kingship.

What Kunwar Singh—who later made a name for himself in the 1857 Mutiny/Rebellion—did when he assumed the mantle of the Ujjainia Rajput estate of Jagdishpur early in the nineteenth century represents one model of such kingly behavior. Having weathered the storms created by internecine disputes over inheritance, he set about the task of consolidating and developing his power and influence by building up his headquarters town of Jagdishpur as the centerpiece of the estate. Once he had renovated its fort, he began the construction of a Siva temple. His "new era of peace and prosperity, splendour and magnificence" included establishing markets and digging wells and tanks, "and soon the town became a centre of various festivals, *melas* (fairs), etc. . . . [T]he Shivratri festival was celebrated . . . with much pomp and a big *mela* (fair) was held on the occasion. Kunwar Singh took steps to induce compulsory attendance at this *mela* by local merchants and forbade them to carry their goods to other *melas*."[99]

The prominence attached to the establishment of melas and temples in the histories of estates undergoing the process of consolidation further underscores their symbolic significance in the development of landholder power and influence. A striking illustration is furnished by the case of the Bettiah Mela initiated by Anand Kishore Singh during his

97. Dirks, *The Hollow Crown*, p. 7.
98. Pamela G. Price, "Kingly Models in Indian Political Behavior: Culture as a Medium of History," *Asian Survey* 29 (1989): 564.
99. The temple, however, was never completed. Datta, *Kunwar Singh*, p. 21.

tenure as maharaja of this great estate between 1816 and 1832. Another fair closely tied to the fortunes of a landholding family is the mela at Deo, a marketing settlement that doubled as the residence of the Deo zamindars. Convened in Kartik and Chait, the fairs at this site highlight the sun temple, the Suraj Mandir. Six miles from Deo is the small village of Umga where a fair is held in Pus; both the place—the village was the former headquarters of the estate—and the fair are associated with the Deo family.[100]

The significance of fairs and their relation to landholder power and influence is evidenced not only by the "compulsory attendance" that Kunwar Singh demanded but also by the competing interests that emerged in places where the absence of clear-cut authority precluded anyone from monopolizing their patronage. Take the case of the fair originally established in the eighteenth century by Bidhata Singh at the junction of the Punpun and Dardha Rivers; it was subsequently contested by Rajputs groups from different villages. Their clash on the occasion of the 1825 fair led eventually to its demise.[101]

Another example of the charged connection between fairs and authority, albeit with a different twist, is the history of the well-known Karagola Fair of Purnea, long frequented by "merchants, pilgrims, and buyers" drawn by its strategic and religious location on the Ganges, commanding traffic between Bihar and Bengal and between south and north Bihar. This mela passed through many proprietarial hands in the late eighteenth and early nineteenth centuries, as different landholders claimed title to it by staging it on their own grounds. In the 1840s the fair was convened concurrently at two different locales, Kantnagar and Karagola, because feuding landholders tried to set up their own "shops, booths, and [facilities for] pilgrims." Not until the maharaja of Darbhanga gained sole control of the area in the 1860s did it begin to flourish as the famous Karagola Fair.[102]

As founders and patrons, zamindars can be linked to virtually every major fair in the region: to name a few, the Rajput Dumraon rajas for the Brahampur Fair; the Bhumihar Hathwa rajas for the Thawe Mela;

100. Grierson, *Notes on Gaya*, p. 45; *Fairs of Bihar*, p. xl; *CDG 1960*, p. 553.
101. Singh, *Bihar Darpan*, pp. 36–37.
102. R. DeCourcy, Sub-Manager, Court of Wards, to J. B. Worgan, Offg. Magte., Purnea, Bengal Jdcl. Procs., June 1868, no. 253. See also GOBi, *Bihar District Gazetteers, Purnea* by P. C. Roy Chaudhury (Patna: Secretariat Press, 1963), p. 718, regarding its subsequent decline because of the rise of other melas and the declining position of the landholders "by whom it was liberally encouraged."

the Maksudpur rajas for the Maksudpur Dashara Mela; and the Brahmin Darbhanga rajas for the Mahadeonath Fair. A late-nineteenth-century list of the most important fairs of the region and the names of landholders on whose sites these were held connects almost every fair to a major local figure: in most cases to landholders, but in a few instances to traders, merchants, and people of other occupations.[103]

Thus, increasingly in the colonial period, the rising popularity of pilgrimage and of the related phenomenon of melas meant that the lives of virtually all were touched by these events. And, thus, increasingly, people were drawn out of their routinized spaces—villages, towns, and cities—and into new spatial arenas. In the words of a vernacular gazetteer of Bihar, "Every district has two, four or ten small or big melas once or twice a year that are attended by all the people of the district."[104]

As extraordinary events that celebrated the major festivals of the local and regional religious calendar, melas were distinct from the events of everyday life. They were further accented by their "socioeconomic 'field' " of activities, which was also different from everyday transactions.

There is considerable evidence that fairs were venues for the exchange of goods and services. Depending on their size and scale, small fairs might be comparable to periodic and standard markets. At the other end of the scale stood the great fair of Sonepur, which was much more than just the "most fashionable pilgrimage" of the region. In the words of one contemporary source, the "principal object" of most Sonepur-bound visitors was "trade and amusements," offerings that set fairs apart from everyday peasant markets.

Although not ordinarily a market—Sonepur formed part of a cluster of several villages that constituted a "minor marketing area" focusing on the nearby periodic market—at mela time it was transformed into the site of several markets. In addition to goods readily available in the markets of the locality, fairs offered other items of considerably higher value. So organized was the market at the Sonepur Mela that the sites of the different markets were "as fixed and certain as are those of the several bazars [sic] in the Municipal Market of Calcutta. The stalls and

103. "Fairs," 1894, Patna. Included in this list are not only traders and merchants, such as Mohan Lal Marwari of Chapra (Sivaratri Mela at Mehnar) but also pleaders and *mahants* (head of a Hindu religious order) of this or that temple.
104. Shivapujan Sahay, *Vihar ka Vihar* (Bankipur: Granthmala Karyala, 1919), p. 108.

booths in these bazars [*sic*] are arranged in rows, having open spaces between, which do duty for streets and roads."[105]

"[E]verything from a pin to an elephant was offered for sale" said one nineteenth-century visitor to the great Sonepur Mela. What it offered once a year, were goods otherwise available only in the city of Patna or a few other higher-order markets. "All the residents of a district," as one local source states, "were mobilized by melas to buy horses, bullocks, cows, buffaloes, palanquins, rugs, carpets, utensils, cloth, boxes, musical instruments, shoes, spices, toys, umbrellas, books and other necessary articles."[106]

Some of these goods—livestock in particular—were not routinely bought and sold at the ordinary markets—periodic (*haats*) and standard markets. Small fairs were also venues for the exchange of goods and, depending on their size and scale, comparable in their range of transactions to periodic and standard markets. To use the evocative language of Braudel, fairs interrupted the "tight circle of everyday exchanges. . . . Even the fairs held in so many modest little towns, and which seem only to be a meeting-point for the surrounding countryside and the town craftsmen, were in fact breaking out of the usual trade cycle. As for the big fairs, they could mobilize the economy of a huge region. . . . Everything contributed then to make a fair an extraordinary gathering."[107]

What distinguished melas from most ordinary markets, and what made Sonepur Mela the greatest fair in Bihar (and according to one source "one of the biggest fairs in the world"), was their role as livestock markets. The focal point for buyers was the cattle mart, where bullocks, cows, goats, sheep, and other domesticated animals were displayed. A camel fair occupied the grounds next to it, followed by an elephant bazaar, which always drew crowds because of its circus atmosphere; beyond this lay the bird fair. The horse mart included an open space where prospective buyers could ride the animals. Sonepur specialized in the sale of "every type of big or small . . . birds and animals."[108]

105. Ghose, "Rural Behar," p. 225; Sonepur *thana* nos. 1–100, 106–59, SVN. See also below, chap. 5, regarding market hierarchy.

106. Sahay, *Vihar*, p. 108; Martin, *Bhagalpur*, p. 133; Lillian Luker Ashby with Roger Whately, *My India* (London: Michael Joseph, 1938), p. 103.

107. Fernand Braudel, *Civilization and Capitalism 15th–18th Century*, vol. 2, *The Wheels of Commerce* (London: Collins, 1982), p. 82.

108. *Fairs of Bihar*, p. xxxiii; C. T. Buckland, *Sketches of Social Life in India* (London: n.p., 1884), pp. 72–73.

A late-nineteenth-century mela-goer estimated that "cows and calves, ploughing oxen, cart-bullock, and buffaloes sell to the number of some thirty thousand. Not less than ten thousand horses change their masters. The number of elephants bought for sale sometimes amounts to two thousand."[109]

Customers and dealers came from near and far to buy and sell livestock. Buyers from as far away as Punjab sought out elephants procured from Assam and Bengal. Horses for sale included the "sturdy breed of Kathiawar [western India], the hardy horses of Hardwar (north India), the sure-footed hill-ponies of Bhootan [Bhutan]."[110] Similarly, the Brahampur Fair catered to a wide audience because it was one of the major cattle fairs in south Bihar. Already a place of "considerable reputation" in the early nineteenth century, its main commodity, as at Sonepur, was cattle, although horses were also sold.[111]

As centers for cattle trade, fairs performed a vital role both in the workings of the local economy and culture and in that of local and translocal patterns of exchange. Cattle have historically played, and continue to play, a major role in Indian life. Bullocks, as the careful study of the village of Karimpur shows, are important for the peasant because "they plow his fields, help sow his seed, send water to his crops from wells during the dry months of both winter and summer, press his sugar cane, and carry to market any produce he may have to sell." No wonder the purchase of these animals represented a major undertaking and expense. "It is considered an occasion," observes one local account, "when a villager buys a cow[,] and much time is spent choosing one."[112]

The significance of the mela as a cattle fair in the local and regional economy and society can be highlighted in other ways as well. For melas not only marked ritual time but also followed the agricultural calendar. Occurring in the wake of harvests, fairs coincided with a time when people were most likely to have money and time to spare. More-

---

109. Chunder, *Travels*, vol. 1, p. 122. Cf. with the period 1920 to 1930, when 7,180 horses and ponies were sold, 2,030 cows, 1,510 buffaloes, 363,300 bullocks and calves, and 735 elephants, or with 1931–40 when these same categories returned the following figures: 47,149; 11,621; 5,808; 289,077; and 6,080. *SDG 1960*, p. 501.

110. Ghose, "Rural Behar," p. 225; *Bharat Brahman*, part 2, p. 7.

111. Buchanan, *Shahabad*, p. 71; "Fairs," 1904; *ShDG 1906*, p. 97.

112. Mohanti, *My Village*, p. 160; Wiser and Wiser, *Behind Mud Walls*, p. 62. Cattle-rich India possesses one of the largest concentrations of domesticated animals in the world. Much has been made of the ritual and symbolic importance attached to the cow—summed up in the "sacred cow concept"—an importance dating back well into the Vedic period.

over, the winter season was precisely when the need for plow cattle was the greatest in order to prepare fields for the sizable *rabi* crops, generally September-October in north Bihar and November-December in the south. It was also the time when bullocks were needed in south Bihar for crushing sugarcane and for transporting the rice crop.[113]

Cattle fairs were also synchronized with one another. The Sonepur Fair in October-November (Kartik) opened the season, and the Sitamarhi Ramnavami Fair in March-April (Chait) closed out the year. The fair at Sonepur inaugurated the cattle fair season because it was a major supplier for the other gatherings. "Soon after the Sonepur fair," according to one report, "streams of cattle begin to pour into Bengal, both by road and by train."[114] Although some cattle were purchased and taken directly into the fields, many, if not most, made their way into the villages of Bengal via the cattle fairs. And these fairs began in Dinajpur and Rangpur, the northwesternmost districts of Bengal bordering on Bihar; from there the cattle were moved eastward and southward into the rest of the province. Typically, the Bihari or the "imported" cattle available in the fairs of Bengal were handled by up-country dealers, who took out loans to purchase them at the Sonepur Fair and then marched them along the circuit of Bengal fairs.[115]

Fairs also broke out of the "usual trade cycle" by providing a range of other goods. Sonepur's English Bazaar, for instance, which presumably dated from after the turn of the nineteenth century, catered to "exotic" tastes: its offerings included European toys, groceries, brandy, beer, soda water, furniture, and assorted kinds of carriages and conveyances. The Mina Bazaar, usually the most congested part of the

113. GOI, *Agricultural Marketing in India, Report on the Marketing of Cattle in India* (Delhi: Government of India Press, 1946), pp. 19–20. Another factor in determining this schedule may have been the fact that "[a]s dairy animals are generally marketed when they are in milk, seasonal variations in demand for cows and she-buffaloes are closely associated with their calving seasons.... [I]n north India, cows are mostly purchased in February-April, and buffaloes in August-October, the periods that concur with the calving seasons of the two species" (p. 20).

114. J. R. Blackwood, *A Survey and Census of the Cattle of Bengal* (Calcutta: Bengal Secretariat Book Depot, 1915), p. 11; W. B. Heycock, Director, Agric., B & O, to Secy., GOB&O, no. 658-A.T., June 15, 1912, B & O Rev. Procs., 1913, Agric., Mar., no. 12. Convened in late November in the wake of the Sonepur Mela, the opening fairs in Bengal were the Awakhoa in Dinajpur and the Dewti in Rangpur, followed by fairs in Dinajpur and Rangpur in December; the Jamalpur Mela in Mymensigh in January; the Darwani (Rangpur) and Dhaldighi (Dinajpur) fairs in February, the March fair in Haripur (Dinajpur), and the well-known Nekmurdan Fair in April, where substantial numbers of cattle were sold.

115. Blackwood, *Cattle of Bengal*, pp. 10–11.

Sonepur Mela, was "where you can buy almost anything," which one observer specified as "goods from Manchester, Birmingham, Delhi, Cawnpore, the Punjab, Cashmere, or Afghanistan, and . . . rather neat Indian-made curios."[116] But it was also an outlet for the products of artisanal industries: "country-manufactures from all parts of India[, including the] beautiful ivory work of Delhi, the brass-wares of Benares, the bell-metal articles of Sewan, the carpets of Mirzapur, the tents of Cawnpur, Patna and Buxar, the iron-wares of Chupra."[117] Bholanauth Chunder in the late nineteenth century encountered "rows of booths extending in several streets, and displaying copper and brass wares, European and native goods, toys, ornaments, jewelry, and all that would meet the necessity or luxury of a large part of the neighboring population. Numerous are the shops for the sale of grain and sweetmeats."[118]

A visitor who always seemed to have one eye trained on the bazaar, Chunder, the trader, was also remarkably perceptive about the declining state of artisanal industries. Although he considered "foreign" ascendancy to be the "natural result of unsuccessful competition with superior intelligence and economy," he nevertheless lamented the fact that "Indian weavers have been thrown out of the market. . . . The present native cannot but choose to dress himself in Manchester calico, and use Birmingham hardware." He looked forward to the day when "our sons and grandsons will emulate our ancestors to have every dhooty [dhoti, male dress], every shirt, and every pugree [pagri, turban] made from the fabrics of Indian cotton manufactured by Indian mill-owners."[119]

At the Brahampur Fair, a variety of goods were available, including its specialties—brass, spices, carpets, and cotton. Carpets were locally manufactured in Bhabhua and Sasaram. At the one-day mela of Ghazi Mia, held on a Sunday in Jeth in Maner, shopkeepers converged from nearby

116. Minden Wilson, *History of Behar Indigo Factories; Reminiscences of Behar; Tirhoot and Its Inhabitants of the Past; History of Bihar Light Horse Volunteers* (Calcutta: Calcutta General Printing, 1908) pp. 167–71; "Diary (and correspondence);" Agarwal, *Agarwal Darpan*, pp. 134–35; *Harihar Mahatmya*, pp. 5–7.

117. Ghose, "Rural Behar," p. 225; Prasad, *Bharat Brahman*, part 2, p. 7.

118. Chunder, *Travels*, 1, pp. 122–23. A tax list in one portion of the fair alone counted the following shops: for grain (12), vegetables (1), cooked food (5), betel leaf (4), tobacco (5), money changers (15), sattu (1), ganja (1), cakes (1), sweetmeats (1), *pathera* (silk- or fringe-maker) (1), hardware (1), tents (7), and spices (1). See R. N. Farquharson, Colltr., Khas Mahals, to E. C. Ravenshaw, Commr., Patna, Jan 10, 1844, P.C. Records, vol. 115, 1844.

119. Chunder, *Travels*, 1, p. 168–69.

Danapur and Patna and from Chapra and Arrah to set up stalls "for the sale of sweetmeats, fruits, toys and articles of feminine toilette."[120]

Fairs were also centers of popular culture and entertainment that enriched and interrupted the patterns of everyday life. Although Veeraswamy is not a reliable source on this aspect of the melas, because he did not acknowledge their "secular" aspects and therefore leaves out any discussion of their "sensual distractions," other eyewitness accounts more than make up for this "chasm." Bholanauth Chunder, who visited Sonepur in the late nineteenth century refers to "parties of strolling actors, dressed fantastically...dancing and singing." Melas were also, to use the censorious language of a government account, a "notorious place for prostitution."[121] But, as viewed through the wonder-struck eyes of one Indian traveler, the fair was "open to all descriptions of visitors. Much money is expended on the nautch-girls [dance girls], whose dancing and songs form the great source of Indian entertainment."[122]

Reminiscing about the Revelganj Mela, a local English resident remembered encountering "all sorts of amusements calculated to please youth, toys of every description are exposed for sale.... At one place a bear or other wild beast become domesticated is to be seen, whilst, the facetious and mischievous monkey, riding on a dog by way of a charger, is always present...; jugglers, nautches, puppet shows, and the attractive ups and downs, and round abouts, filled with boys and girls laughing, as they ascend the air, in their little swinging boxes, are met with on all sides."[123]

He quickly added, however, that these scenes were "a very good sample of the manners and amusements of the lower orders, and in some respects resemble similar sights in England." Syed Zahiruddin echoed this sentiment when he described the Maner Mela as a "bacchanalian festival resorted to by the lower orders."[124]

This aspect of fairs as featuring the "manners and amusements of the lower orders," although alluding to their character as arenas of popular culture, also suggests that melas—or pilgrimage generally for that

120. Ghose, "Rural Behar," p. 226; Syed Zahiruddin, *History and Antiquities of Manair* (Bankipore: n.p., 1905); R. W. Bingham, "Report on the Productive Resources of the Sasseram District," *JAHSI* 12 (1861): 361; *ShDG 1906*, p. 97.
121. *SDG 1960*, p. 500; Chunder, *Travels*, vol. 1, p. 123.
122. Chunder, *Travels*, p. 122.
123. Rankine, *Topography of Saran*, pp. 27–28.
124. Zahiruddin, *Manair*, p. 6; Rankine, *Topography of Saran*, p. 27.

matter—do not conform to Victor Turner's well-known paradigm of pilgrimage. In this formulation, pilgrimage is construed as a process akin to a tribal rite of passage whereby pilgrims leave their everyday structured world to advance into a liminal state and then attain a state of freedom and unmediated fellowship, or *communitas*. This ethos is a form of antistructure because the pilgrimage setting generates social bonding among pilgrims that fashions them into a group. In Turner's words, this situation engenders "a direct, immediate and total confrontation of human identities . . . which tends to make those experiencing it think of mankind as a homogenous, unstructured and free community."[125] Victor Turner and Edith Turner have also described pilgrimage as offering "liberation from profane social structures that are symbiotic with a specific religious system" and generating such characteristics of liminality as "release from mundane structure; homogenization of status; . . . communitas; ordeal; reflection on the meaning of basic religious and cultural values; . . . [and] movement itself."[126]

While empirical research has identified a liminal condition in pilgrims in the process of shifting from the web of everyday life to the sacred center, there is little evidence to suggest that their condition in this stage can be viewed as a *communitas*-type relationship. On the contrary, adherence to inequality both "on the road" and at pilgrimage sites is commonplace because "people tended to bring structured social bonds with them, as pilgrim groups were often formed on the basis of existing social groups."[127]

Although "movement itself" to Kashi and to other sacred centers "out there" heightened Veeraswamy's sense of religious commonality with people throughout the subcontinent, clearly his pilgrimage was not a "liminoid phenomenon." For his imagined "country," though perceived as connected by religious threads, was nevertheless defined and limited by the brahminical and Hindu ideology and community he

125. *Drama, Fields, and Metaphors: Symbolic Action in Human Society* (Ithaca: Cornell University Press, 1974), p. 169.

126. *Pilgrimage in Christian Culture*, pp. 34, 9, and 250, for a definition of "*Communitas, or social antistructure*. A relational quality of full unmediated communication, even communion, between definite and determinate identities, which arises spontaneously in all kinds of groups, situations, and circumstances. . . . It is a liminal phenomenon which combines the qualities of lowliness, sacredness, homogeneity, and comradeship" (p. 250).

127. Morinis, *Pilgrimage in Hindu Tradition*, p. 258. In addition to Morinis's own work on Bengali pilgrims, which supports this conclusion, see also Gold, *Fruitful Journeys*.

was valorizing. He almost always sought out the local Brahmins, in part because he needed fellow castemen in order to find suitable accommodations and in part because he wished to meet with and observe his own brethren. Invariably, he engaged in comparisons—whether their "customs and manners . . . [were] different from ours."[128]

Consider also his identification of Hindustan as primarily comprising north India, or the areas mostly in the north where Hindustani was spoken. His *Journal*, furthermore, distinguishes between people of his own Hindu religion and Muslims, or "Mlecchas" (impure foreigners), as he terms them. A resident of Madras, he may not have had much direct contact with Indo-Islamic culture prior to his pilgrimage, but that changed as he made his way north. Acknowledging that Muslims had been in the subcontinent for almost a thousand years, he observed in Patna that people "mix up Urdu with Sanskrit and imitate the Muslims in clothes, ornamentation, use of palanquins[,] etc. In spite of this it is to be said that they have not completely given up their Varnasrama Dharmas [duties of social rank and stages of life]."[129]

Nor does a dimension of *communitas* surface in his few remarks about travelers he encountered undertaking "Kasiyatras," let alone in any overt statement of kinship or connection with others involved in "fruitful journeys." Yet this, as we have already seen, was a time of a growing traffic of pilgrims and mela-goers. Even within his own group, numbering almost a hundred, his ties and sentiments were restricted to members of his own household and retainers. Other than family members—and he periodically refers to the women of the household—the rest of his group are only identified as subordinates, as "twelve palanquin-bearers and six peons" and "six luggage-carriers."[130]

At times, the boundaries of Veeraswamy's imagined "country" did not even extend much beyond his own region, such as when it signified people "who have performed the Tirupati pilgrimage," that is, those who had undertaken the pilgrimage to the south Indian shrine of Tirupati. Thus, like the present-day Bengali pilgrims studied by the anthropologist Morinis, Veeraswamy's journey did not entail a process of divesting himself from his "social structural roles and relationships."[131]

---

128. Veeraswamy, *Journal*, pp. 54, 6, 36, 62, 70.
129. Ibid., pp. 123, 122, 52, 97.
130. Ibid., pp. 80, 112.
131. Morinis, *Pilgrimage in Hindu Tradition*, p. 274; Veeraswamy, *Journal*, p. 52. See also Van Der Veer, *Gods on Earth*.

Veeraswamy's journey across the country did evoke, however, a sense of place and identity, as the pilgrimage experience did and still does for many pilgrims. His obvious joy at returning home notwithstanding, his journey across the subcontinent clearly reinforced notions of a "native place" that encompassed much more than Madras. Indeed, by its very nature pilgrimage has a capacity to foster a sense of collective identity even as pilgrims retain their consciousness of social and economic distinctions. Thus, for people "on the road," whether from Madras or Banaras or Patna, the entire subcontinent constituted (and still constitutes) a landscape whose nodal points are sacred centers exerting a gravitational pull over their faiths and beliefs. Pilgrimage has therefore been appropriately investigated as a "remarkable and ancient institution sustaining a system of linked centers that helps bind together the incredibly diverse peoples of the Indian subcontinent."[132] It has also helped shape "larger national identification," because Hindu religion has engendered the notion "that there is an entity of India to which all its inhabitants belong. The Hindu epics and legends . . . teach that the stage for the gods was nothing less than the entire land and that the land remains one religious setting for those who dwell in it. The sense was and is continually confirmed through the practice of pilgrimage."[133]

Veeraswamy echoed this notion of a Hindu sacred land, in referring to the entire subcontinent, from the southernmost tip to the north, as comprising one "country." "This country," which, to use his words, "forms a part of '*Brahmandam*' from Kanyakumari [in the south] to Kashmir [in the north] is the best Karma Bhoomi; Rama and Krishna and other Avatars [reincarnations] of the Lord are manifested here." That is, his "country," a distinct land ("bhoomi," or *bhumi*) shaped by karma constituted a part of Brahmandam, the universe that according to Hindu mythology had originated from a primordial egg. Thus, he was puzzled at the existence of differences "in the food habits, image-worship, courage and others[,] etc." between the people of the north and the south because in his mind the "country . . . [was] historically one according to the Smritis, Srutis and Puranas."[134]

Religious considerations also underlay his critique of British missionary efforts "to convert the Hindus to Christianity in order to save

132. Gold, *Fruitful Journeys*, p. 1.
133. David G. Mandelbaum, *Society in India*, vol. 2, *Change and Continuity* (Berkeley and Los Angeles: University of California Press, 1970), p. 401.
134. Veeraswamy, *Journal*, pp. 70, 109, 26; also pp. 6, 36, 54, 62, 70.

them from the supposed doom." These efforts aroused the "hostile feeling to Europeans" apparently encountered by missionaries in the city of Patna. On the whole, though, his assessment of his masters was positive: he pronounced them "just, in their rule[,] and by the grace of God they are gaining His favour day by day." It was certainly positive in contrast to his view that the "Mohammadan race" was responsible for wreaking destruction on the temples of such sacred places as Prayag (Allahabad) and Kashi. Consequently, he says they succeeded in converting "not one in [a] thousand" to Islam. Whereas "Hindus gradually avoided Muslims," Christianity, he states, gained a measure of success through the "clever tactics of the English. . . . That which is not possible by valour is possibly [*sic*] by contrivance[,] is the principle adopted by the British[;] and they gradually took into their religion that section of the community which enjoyed the least status in society and preached the glories of Christianity to them who are ignorant of the intricate religious actions."[135]

Notwithstanding his tirades against Muslims and his seemingly favorable sentiments regarding the "English," he differentiated himself and his ilk from the British, because they possessed a different culture. Moreover, on at least one occasion, when he was in Hyderabad during the Muslim festival of Mohurrum, he minimized religious differences. In fact he observed that the "Lord's manifestation is evident in abundance in the city and attracts thousands of people including people of other religions who stay here from the ninth day to the last day of the festival. The Lord accepts the varying modes of worship of his children. . . . Accordingly I thought I had entered a sacred place at this time and was thankful to the Lord."[136] Contrast this with his designation of the British as "phirangis," a pejorative he used to set them apart from his Hindu countrymen as the "Other." Of Persian origin, this term referred "(especially in the South) specifically to the Indian-born Portuguese, or, when used more generally, for 'European,' implies something of hostility or disparagement."[137]

As Veeraswamy's ruminations about his "native place" and the "country" as a whole disclose, his pilgrimage prompted him to reflect on questions of identity and community: what people shared in common and what made them different communities. Such notions, more-

---

135. Ibid., p. 186; *Madras Almanac for 1830* (Madras: Asylum Press, 1830), p. 282.
136. Veeraswamy, *Journal*, p. 24.
137. *Hobson-Jobson*, p. 353; Veeraswamy, *Journal*, pp. 26, 186.

over, can be associated even more so with melas or "gatherings of pilgrims" because they were predominantly "locality"-based events tied to local systems of control. Their constituencies, except in the case of great fairs, were drawn from specific localities and communities, people bound together by a sense of place and by a common language, culture, and history. Their delimited geographical locus was in fact construed by the Bihar and Orissa Pilgrim Committee as forming a fundamental characteristic of fairs: "the places where 'fairs' are held are, as a rule, of consequence only to the neighbouring districts, and on a few special days, while the 'places of pilgrimage' are visited by devotees from all over India every day throughout the year."[138]

Fairs, at least for the duration of the festivals "seem to do away with . . . most of the distinctions of caste, and the separation of sexes."[139] Certainly, over the course of the colonial period, the number of women undertaking pilgrimages appears to have risen appreciably. Indeed, both qualitative and quantitative data from the late nineteenth century suggest that the majority of pilgrims on the road were women. According to one calculation, three-fourths of the twenty-nine thousand people estimated to have been present at the Burdwan district mela of Kistnanagar were women.[140] This growing presence may explain the development of a literature critical of their participation at the turn of the twentieth century. A different assessment of this increasingly public presence of women as well as of the *communitas* dimension of fairs is offered in the statement by a recent official account that melas "have helped break the rigours of casteism and orthodox habits. They have also helped to liquidate the strict parda system . . . [and] are more patronised by the women-folk."[141]

Because of the numbers that were involved and because of their potential for generating *communitas*, melas were fertile arenas for orga-

138. *Report of Pilgrim Committee*, p. 1.
139. Rankine, *Notes on Saran*, p. 27.
140. Babu Jadunath Bose, Deputy Magte., Gurbata, to C. T. Buckland, Commr., Burdwan, no. 38, May 21, 1872, Bengal Gen. Procs., 1872, June, no. 44. A similar observation is made by F. J. Alexander, Offg. Magte., Rajshahye, to Commr., Rajshahye, no. 29, Mar. 18, 1869, Bengal Sanitation Procs., 1869, Apr., no. 9.
141. *CDG 1960*, p. 132. Bhagwath Prasad, *Mela Ghumani* (Muzaffarpur: Vijay Press, 1925), enjoins women not to visit fairs. Such a moralizing tone was reinforced by the colonial discourse on women in which the British staked out a role for themselves as the protectors of female virtue. See, e.g., "Diary," of Jadunath Bose, Deputy Magte., Gurbata, with his letter no. 38, May 21, 1872, Bengal Gen. Procs., 1872, June, no. 44, which refers to men and women mingling "promiscuously" at the mela of Kistnanagar.

nizing and mobilizing people. And what better staging ground than the great Sonepur Mela, which provided the setting for virtually every significant political movement of the colonial era. Kunwar Singh, who actively sponsored and supported melas and markets on his estate—in keeping with his kingly role as zamindar—used this gathering as the venue for hatching the plot that eventuated in the Bihar episode of the 1857 Mutiny/Rebellion, the major nineteenth-century resistance movement against the British in the region. Earlier, in 1845, he had been involved, along with a number of regional Hindu and Muslim notables, in convening a political meeting at Sonepur that used the cover of the fair to broach the possibility of taking up arms because of perceived British violations of their cultural and religious beliefs and practices. Although the plan fizzled, secret invitations were issued to many prominent citizens and attempts were made to win the support of sepoys and the assistance of the Mughal emperor and the king of Nepal. But Sonepur, as well as other melas, could also be the sites for contention among the people themselves, as is dramatized by the numerous incidents in the late nineteenth century centering on the issue of cow slaughter: Hindus were pitted against Muslims. The very first meeting of the Indian Association of Cow Protection (Gauraksha) lecturers was held at Sonepur in 1888, and at several major melas that were also cattle fairs there were clashes involving Hindus, Muslims, and the colonial state. Another mela that served as a staging ground for political action was the Dashara Fair at Bettiah, where tenants of European indigo planters met to launch a resistance movement against the indigo factories and their plantations.[142]

Nowhere was the *communitas* dimension of fairs in the region more apparent and its potential political currency kept more under scrutiny than at the Sonepur Mela, where an official presence was established almost from the outset of colonial rule. The raison d'être for stationing officials at this major fair was said to be "to prevent ryots [peasants] gambling and drunkenness, and to be particularly careful that the ze-

142. A. C. Amman to Suptd., Police, Champaran, Oct. 21, 1908, Bengal Jdcl. Procs., Jan.-June 1909, Apr., no. 16. Regarding clashes at the Brahampur Fair, the Bisua Mela at Gaya, and at the small fair of Basantpur in Saran, see my "Sacred Symbol and Sacred Space in Rural India: Community Mobilization in the 'Anti-Cow Killing' Riot of 1893," *CSSH* 22 (1980): 576–96; Bengal Jdcl. Procs., June-Sept. 1891, Police, July 1891, B Procs., and May-July 1893, June, nos. 46–48.

mindars did not levy any taxes or contributions."[143] In part, government interest in fairs and pilgrimage centers was a concern for law and order heightened by the possibility of collective violence and political resistance erupting from the perceived volatile mix of numbers and religion: the large crowds of people that typically congregated in these ostensibly religious settings with varying degrees of cohesion. In part, government increasingly directed an ostensibly "medical" and "sanitary" gaze in the direction of fairs and pilgrimage because these "gatherings" were considered to be "responsible for much of the spread of infectious disease in India."[144] Fairs were also singled out for scrutiny and control because they were important venues for trade, especially of livestock, a commodity targeted as a source of government revenue and of the cattle and horses needed for military purposes in the late eighteenth and early nineteenth centuries.

Yet precisely for the same reason that fairs and pilgrimages were subjected to colonial control—the political uses of these ostensibly religious gatherings—they were also feared by the authorities. Officials were reluctant to interfere for fear of inciting public unrest, as is underscored by the 1860s government debate regarding curtailing pilgrimage traffic to stop the spread of "disease and mortality." As a senior administrator noted, "It will never do for government to interfere with, or rather prohibit in any way, the attendance of pilgrims at religious or other fairs." Any such effort, he believed, "would at once be considered as an attempt to interfere with religious freedom, and would give rise to all kinds of rumours and thus open a door to the disaffected to work on the feelings of the people and create a discontent and dislike to our Government which in time might grow into open rebellion as serious and dangerous as was the Indian Mutiny of 1857."[145]

143. C. Boddam, Judge, to Hon. Sir John Shore, G.G., Apr. 8, 1796, Bengal Cr. Jdcl. Consltns., Mar. 3–17, 1809, Mar. 10, no. 2, enclosure. See also my *Limited Raj,* chap. 1, for an extended discussion of the colonial appropriation of this mela.

144. United Provinces, *Report of the Pilgrim Committee, United Provinces, 1913* (Simla: Government Central Branch Press, 1916), p. 2. Similar considerations prompted a government presence at all major pilgrimage centers. See A. Tufton, Magte., Bihar, to Secy., Jdcl., Bengal Jdcl Consltns., Apr. 5 to June 28, 1799, May 3, no. 21; A. Seton, Judge and Magte., Bihar, Feb. 11, 1795, to Subsecy., Jdcl., Bengal Jdcl. Consltns., June 12 to July 10, 1795, June 26, no. 26; "Minute of Governor General," Mar. 25, 1831, Bengal Cr. Jdcl. Consltns., Apr. 26 to June 7, 1831, May 3, no. 100.

145. Jenkins to Secy., no. 10, Jan. 13, 1868, Bengal Sanitation Procs., Apr. 1868, no. 18.

Nor was the political capital of fairs lost on the twentieth-century leaders of the nationalist movement: they looked particularly to the Sonepur
Mela as an arena of recruitment. The Bihar Provincial Congress Committee was founded by the regional supporters of the Indian National Congress, who met for this purpose at Sonepur in 1908. Thereafter recruiters
for Congress regularly returned to this and other fairs to recruit new supporters. The Bihar Provincial Peasant Association (Kisan Sabha) was another organization that sought to tap into the popular dimensions of the
Sonepur Mela. Attempts were made as early as 1922 to organize a peasant association at this venue; in 1929, the Kisan Sabha had its founding
meeting there. When a local official arrived at the Sitamarhi Mela of 1921
to oversee the sanitary arrangements, he was surrounded "by a frenzied
crowd, crying out 'Mahatma Gandhi ki Jai' [Long Live Mahatma
Gandhi]."[146] Such evocations of Gandhi as Mahatma, as Shahid Amin
has noted, reflect the "polysemic nature of the Mahatma myths and rumours, as well as . . . a many-sided response of the masses to current
events and their cultural, moral and political concerns."[147]

In the new era ushered in by the emergence of a mass-based nationalist movement, in the early 1920s, the locus of history shifted from the
central places to the hinterlands, as the politics of the nationalist movement took command. And as the historical initiative in matters political, economic, social, and cultural became increasingly lodged in melas
and rural markets, the voices heard in these new arenas threatened to
shake the foundations of colonial rule. By the twentieth century,
cities—such as Patna, the "city of discontent"—and towns, many of
which were the sites of fairs and markets (as the next chapter shows),
formed part of a wider subcontinental network of sites that resonated
with voices speaking of a new order. Thus, almost a century after
Veeraswamy had been on the road under the sign of colonialism, pilgrims were seeking new types of journeys. For most, the path to their
new India required that they extend beyond the cities into the hinterlands and that they conduct their exchanges in the appropriate political
currency to negotiate with people and places at the margins. Peripheries, that is, were increasingly becoming the core, the center stage of
the lived experiences of the twentieth century.

---

146. W. M. Wilson, Suptd., Police, Muzaffarpur, to Commr., Nov. 28, 1921, B & O
Polit. Procs., 1922, Police, May, no. 1; Yang, Limited Raj, p. 18.
147. "Gandhi as Mahatma: Gorakhpur District, Eastern UP, 1921–2," in Subaltern
Studies: Writings on South Asian History and Society, ed. Ranajit Guha (Delhi: Oxford
University Press, 1984), p. 7.

CHAPTER 4

The Rural Places of Exchange

Markets in the Age of Gandhi

"Gandhi *ki jai*" (Long Live Gandhi) echoed in many marketplaces in the early 1920s, when the bazaar became both a scene and site of contention. Its reverberations throughout the Bihar countryside signaled the transformation of the nationalist movement led by the Indian National Congress into a mass organization. It was a development reflected in the rise of the Noncooperation and Khilafat Movement in 1921–22 and in the movement's changing emphasis. For one thing, many Muslims were won over because of the pan-Islamic Khilafat Movement, which championed the case of the Ottoman caliph (*khalifa*). A campaign that began with students quitting government-run educational institutions and with lawyers and others withdrawing from official institutions progressed to involve people in a boycott of foreign cloth and later in a struggle for complete independence. The ultimate objective was the Gandhian ideal—a postcolonial nation and community without harmful divisions of caste, class, religion, or gender. But the "emphasis . . . on unifying issues and on trying to cut across or reconcile class divisions"[1] necessarily entailed negotiating the problematic contradiction of forging a unified nation by "disciplining" its many dividing communities. In the very process of widening its constituency, as

1. Sumit Sarkar, *Modern India, 1885–1947* (Delhi: Macmillan, 1983), p. 209.

Ranajit Guha argues, the Congress-organized nationalist movement sharpened the "contradiction between the elite and the subaltern domains of politics and of an increasing elite concern to deal more effectively with it."[2]

Along with its insistence on nonviolence, the Noncooperation Movement, at the national and regional levels, couched its rhetoric from the outset in terms of "unifying issues," advocating causes that averted social and economic confrontations stemming from such potentially volatile issues as nonpayment of taxes to government and of rent to landholders. Gandhi pointedly spoke out against looting markets and withholding taxes from government and rent from landlords.[3]

Contrast these "officially" sanctioned concerns and actions with popular pronouncements in Bihar. "Speeches" given by followers of Noncooperation (termed *asahayogis,* from the term *asahayog,* meaning *noncooperation*), or "Volunteers" (the appellation favored in government records) of the movement, provide apposite entre into this rhetoric because they "capture" (an especially fitting term to use because they were recorded by government informants or preserved in pamphlets proscribed by government) the voices of the grassroots, both leaders and rank and file. One especially valuable compilation of such speeches is a confidential government document of 1922, which conveys a vivid sense of the popular vocabulary of Noncooperation, although some of the flavor of the vernacular is no doubt lost in translation (the document exists only in English translation). This compendium, apparently only "a fraction of the volume of abuse and vituperation . . . poured forth in this province," identifies none of its authors and lists "speeches" only by date and district of origin—which serves to accent the heteroglossic nature of this discourse.[4]

2. *A Disciplinary Aspect of Indian Nationalism* (Santa Cruz: Merrill Publications, University of California, 1990), p. 39.

3. Mahatma Gandhi, *The Collected Works of Mahatma Gandhi,* vol. 19, *(November 1920–April 1921)* (Ahmedabad: Government of India, 1966), pp. 312–13, 419–20.

4. The only identification tags used are in the prefatory note describing "various agitators" as: "some earnest workers inspired by the zeal of fanaticism: some paid professional agitators: some mere notoriety hunters . . . " B & O, *Selections from Speeches, Activities of Volunteers, etc., during the past six months in Bihar and Orissa* (Patna: Govt. Printing, 1922). Some speakers can be identified from newspapers, such as the *Searchlight,* which gave extensive coverage to Congress activities, and confidential government sources, such as, B & O, *The Non-Cooperation and Khilafat Movements in Bihar and Orissa* (Secret) (Patna: Govt. Printing, 1925).

Nationalistic publications, on the other hand, are best in document-ing the history of the movement's local chapter and local heroes. Largely absent from this record are details about episodes and events that did not conform to the official story. For the standard nationalist materials were not the mediums through which "abuse and vitupera-tion" flowed; this was much more likely to have occurred in the kinds of extemporaneous speeches delivered to local audiences and preserved for later observers by government informants.[5]

According to the Muzaffarpur Congress Committee, the Noncoopera-tion Movement was waged on ten fronts: (1) boycott of government schools and establishment of nationalist schools, (2) relinquishment of government and legal positions, (3) boycott of foreign cloth, (4) relin-quishment of all government degrees and titles, (5) establishment of vil-lage councils (panchayats), (6) use of spinning wheels and homespun cloth (khadi), (7) ban on intoxicating substances, (8) recruitment of rank-and-file Congress members, (9) collection of Tilak Swaraj Funds, and (10) collection of a muthia (handful of grain) from every household.[6]

Notwithstanding Gandhi's estimation that the Noncooperation Movement in Bihar was well attuned to his ideal of nonviolence and notable for its successes in creating alternative schools, boycotting government-controlled liquor, and popularizing homespun cloth, local leaders diverged substantially from the Gandhian path. "Volunteers" openly broached the possibility of violence and injected agrarian issues into their campaign, with the result that their rhetoric and actions were aimed at the colonial state as well as its local allies and coadjutors. And the marketing centers of the region, the bazaars, became both the scene and site of contention. The market as an "extraterritorial" space re-curred with acts of inversion and subversion,[7] including thirty-five doc-umented cases of "hat [haat, periodic market] -looting in Muzaffarpur, Bhagalpur, Monghyr and Purnea in January 1921 (with men who claimed to be Gandhi's disciples trying to enforce just prices at some places)...and widespread tension in Champaran and Muzaffarpur

5. E.g., see Jagdish Prasad Shramik, *Muzaffarpur zilla aur swadhinta sangram (Zilla Congress kamiti ka sankshipt itihas)* (Hajipur: Congress Swaran Jayanti, 1935).

6. Ibid.

7. Stallybrass and White, *The Politics of Transgression*, p. 28. This use of the term refers to Bakhtin's notion of the marketplace which, at fair time, develops a popular do-main placing it beyond the ken of "official order and official ideology." See Mikahil Bakhtin, *Rabelais and His World*, trans. by Helene Iswolsky (Bloomington: Indiana Uni-versity Press, 1984), pp. 154, 187–88.

districts over appropriation of traditional village pastures by *zamindars* and indigo planters."[8]

The Noncooperation Movement staked out a presence in the "extraterritorial" space of the market because its objective and strategy centered on territoriality: inclusion as well as exclusion. The bazaar, this choice locale for articulating the imagined greater community, was a venue par excellence where the colonial state encountered indigenous society literally and figuratively. Furthermore, the bazaar was part of a system of markets that bound villages into localities and small communities into larger communities. Indeed, the key themes of separation and boycott highlighted the commonalties between different categories of people who commingled in the bazaar. In other words, the project was to forge a nationalist community defined ideologically, ethnically, and spatially, a community whose construction entailed distinguishing those who were committed to the nationalist cause from those who were not. Demarcation was one of its principal strategies, boycott one of its major tactics.

Ironically, however, the "unifying" project of Noncooperation itself opened up the divisions, for the bazaar constituted the "epitome of a spatial boundary," a "space where local society materially and culturally reproduced itself," a "vernacular" space that was a "social nexus," a "typical site of collective discourse," a container of solidarities as well as of antagonisms and contradictions. Therefore, local dramas of Noncooperation, although scripted in accordance with the nationalist project, gave rise to local variants of the agrarian struggle, in a narrative that pitted peasants and petty landholders against local magnates. In addition, the boycott of British products, particularly textiles, also fed the contention in the marketplace because it embroiled traders and merchants in disputes over the use of foreign goods. This was after all a group that was increasingly staking out prominent roles in the towns and bazaars of north India; the bazaar was their locus of activity.[9] Political "sedition" against the state and social and economic agitation against local elites therefore went hand in glove, a combination threatening enough to attract the attention of the official documentation pro-

8. R. T. Dundas, I.G., Police, B & O, to Chief Secy., no. 244-I.G. 22, June 7, 1922, B & O Polit. Procs., Police, 1922, June, no. 50.

9. Sarkar, *India*, p. 221; J. C. Jha, "The Khilafat and the Non-Cooperation Movement in Bihar (1919–22)," in *History of the Indian National Congress in Bihar, 1885–1985*, general editor P. N. Ojha (Patna: Kashi Prasad Jayaswal Research Institute, 1985), chap. 6; Agnew, *Worlds Apart*, p. 33.

ject. Ostensibly a record of "unruly" subjects engaged in "criminal mis-
conduct" disruptive of "law and order" and "peace and security," the
colonial archive resonates with words and agendas that suggest a "hidden transcript" pointing to the bazaar itself as the locus of conflict. Occasionally loud and clear, but always audible beneath the surface of the
official transcript, are voices that speak not only in the nationalistic
and anticolonial idiom but also in the vocabulary of subaltern resistance.[10]

Appropriately enough, the disjuncture between popular and elite notions surfaces in the bazaar, the setting in which these conflicting ideas
were negotiated and in which they gained their currency. For nowhere
were the contradictions of the Movement more visible than in the
bazaar, that "hybrid place" where "a commingling of categories usually
kept separate and opposed [occur]: centre and periphery, inside and outside, stranger and local, commerce and festivity, high and low."[11] This
clash of ideas, furthermore, reflects the extent to which popular culture
and popular ideas more generally intersected in the bazaar.

This chapter will consider the popular rhetoric of Noncooperation
and then turn to the popular action and behavior that placed the bazaar
at the center stage. It will reconstruct the drama as it was enacted in
three different locales in the region in 1921–22: the Katia and Bhorey
area in Saran; the Sitamarhi area in Muzaffarpur; and the *thanas* of
Bagaha, Dhanaha, Jogapatti, and Lauriya in Bettiah subdivision, Champaran. These three sets of incidents serve to identify the popular constituency of Noncooperation: they fuse the political with the social and
economic agenda, as they unfold in the bazaar. Moreover, these particular localities were closely scrutinized by the documentary and surveillance project of the colonial state and the documentary and advocacy
project of the nationalist movement. The enterprises together—the former concerned with recording and establishing the occurrence of acts of
"sedition" and the latter with documenting and celebrating the rising
tide of nationalist sentiment—have left the historian a record that
speaks in the contrary voices of these antagonistic projects. Thus, the

10. Scott, *Domination and Resistance*. Also Amin, "Gandhi as Mahatma," for an insightful analysis of the contradictions between popular notions and those adhered to by
the local leadership and enunciated by Gandhi. Gandhi called off the Movement in February 1922 after the violent torching of a police station in Chauri Chaura (Gorakhpur).
See also Amin, *Event, Metaphor, Memory: Chauri Chaura, 1922–1992* (Berkeley and
Los Angeles: University of California Press, 1995).
11. Stallybrass and White, *The Politics of Transgression*, p. 27.

data on the events of Noncooperation in these localities is especially rich. To view this drama so closely is to see its social, economic, and cultural scripts, which grew out of the political text of Noncooperation and were textualized by the "hybrid" place, the bazaar.

The local drama in Saran, in particular, speaks to the question of why the bazaar became the scene and site of both Noncooperation and agrarian conflict. Specifically, I will set the incidents that occurred in Katia and Bhorey against the backdrop of the marketing system of that locality. In teasing out the workings and meanings of the local marketing system of Saran, I can trace the dynamics of this system more generally, down to the lowest level ordered around periodic markets (*haats*), and thereby illustrate spatially the organization and interrelationships of markets. This taxonomy of sites as well as of their hierarchical relationships will also be filled in by detailing the pattern of horizontal and vertical trade, the movement of local agricultural and craft commodities and of nonlocal products from higher-level to lower-level markets.

This reconstruction of the structure and functioning of a local marketing system underscores the extent to which the unfolding of the dramatic events of 1920–22 in the bazaar represented a historical process of increasing marketization and commoditization embodied in the growth of a full-fledged marketing system. By focusing on Katia and Bhorey, my intention is not only to detail its workings within the specific setting of one district, but also to show how these were tied to the changing nature of agrarian relations and conflict—for the spatial grids organized by the marketing system shaped and were shaped by the power of both the colonial state and local landholders. The local experiences of Noncooperation, plotted against the backdrop of the local marketing system, therefore portray the bazaar in the round: as a place for political as well as economic, social, and cultural transactions.

The chapter concludes by mapping the spatial and social coordinates generated by the marketing system along which a notion of community was constructed. It was, however, a system with dual capacities: to embrace the national ideal espoused by Congress leaders and to divide into more particularistic identities and groups shaped by caste and class. The dynamics of the local marketing system reveal that markets were units of economic, social, and political organization, within which power and influence were wielded and contested: not just the power of the colonial state, but also that articulated by local controllers and elites. This "hybrid place" thus provided the nexus in which attempts to create a community both succeeded and failed: anti-colonial sentiment fostered a sense of nation while also sharpening existing contradictions among the many constituent communities of the region.

Let us eavesdrop in the marketplace. *Asahayogis,* or "volunteers," frequently spoke of "our duty . . . to liberate India," to attain "Swaraj" (self-rule) from British rule, demonized as a "Satanic Government." There was growing consensus about this message, as Noncooperation coupled with Khilafat enabled Congress to build up a mass base in 1920–22. Speeches warning Hindus and Muslims that their religion was "in danger" were aimed at this larger constituency, as were specific calls for people to come together as Indians. "Hindus and Muhammadans must unite," urged one speaker in Patna in February 1922, a message reinforced on another occasion by the charge that the British had deliberately fomented quarrels "between Hindus and Muhammadans . . . [in order] to remain themselves in peace."[12]

Ironically, this very attempt to bridge the religious divide in the Noncooperation era of 1920–22 led subsequently to a phase in which distinct communal sentiments came to prevail.[13] The message of Noncooperation was a mixed one: it was uttered with appropriate religious coding to speak to "unifying issues," but in a vocabulary that also emphasized the distinctiveness of Hindu and Muslim traditions. Consider the characterization of the evil government and "Hatyachar Raj [destructive rule]" as a "Rawan Raj"—as a tyrannical force and a religious threat set in stark contrast to the ideal government and polity embodied in the notion of "Ram Raj." No doubt, for the Shiite Muslims in the audience, this speaker also equated the present government with "that of Yazid of the ancient times." On another occasion at Patna, a "Volunteer," obviously appealing to the religious sensibilities of his audience, remarked: "Do the Hindus think that this Satanic government will not use the same shells and shot against their sacred places as they

12. *Speeches,* p. 11. Hindu-Muslim clashes, sporadic in Bihar in the nineteenth century, erupted with ferocity in Shahabad in 1917. See Pandey, *Construction of Communalism,* pp. 189–96, 201–4; Peter G. Robb, *The Evolution of British Policy towards Indian Politics, 1880–1920* (Westwood, Mass.: Riverdale, 1992), pp. 325–52; Md. Muzaffar Imam, *Role of Muslims in the National Movement (1912–1930) (A Study of Bihar)* (Delhi: Mittal Publications, 1987), esp. chap. 4.

13. Sandria B. Freitag, *Collective Action and Community: Public Arenas and the Emergence of Communalism in North India* (Berkeley and Los Angeles: University of California Press, 1989), esp. chap. 7; Pandey, *Construction of Communalism,* chaps. 5–6.

had used against the sacred places of Islam?" Presumably addressing
Muslims, another speaker, also at Patna but on a different date, re-
minded his listeners that the sacred cities of "Mecca and Medina are no
longer in your possession."[14]

Such talk had the desired effect: it greatly alarmed the government.
Local authorities reacted with concern to what they construed to be
"appeals to racial antagonisms or religious fanaticism," a concern that
resonated with their long-standing fear of religion-based opposition to
their rule. Although they came from different perspectives, Ghulam
Husain and Veeraswamy shared in common a view of their superordinates that was partly informed by their religious outlooks. Indeed,
from the very outset of colonial rule but particularly in the aftermath
of the Mutiny/Rebellion of 1857, government had trained a wary eye
on religious issues because it considered religion in India to constitute
the bedrock of popular consciousness. Moreover, the religious coloring
of "abuse and vituperation" in the Noncooperation era was especially
volatile because it attracted a wide audience; in fact, "in the rural areas, the more outspoken the appeal the more popular is its reception."[15] As yet ignored in both Congress and government understanding of this rhetoric, was the possibility that an "outspoken" religious
ideology would eventuate in a religious divide rather than a broad-
based nationalist community.

Another Bihar variant of Noncooperation also alarmed the government—its divergence from the Gandhian credo of nonviolence, as the
following speech in the official record reveals: "I cannot agree with
Gandhiji *in his creed of non-violent non-co-operation.* If you agree
with me[,] Oh Rajputs' sons and Brahmans' sons[,] get up and try your
best to root out this dishonest Government at any cost."[16] Others, too,
broached the possibility of violence, although not explicitly. Few, however, would have missed the meaning of the following allusion to the

14. *Speeches,* pp. 4, 1–2, 25. Yazid for the Shiites is the epitome of evil. In the popular Hindu epic of the *Ramayana,* Ram is the beloved god; Ravana is the mythological evil
demon. Such characterizations were apparently commonplace (e.g., see *Behar Herald,*
Feb. 26, 1921) and echoed the vocabulary used by Gandhi (e.g., see his speeches in Bihar
in Dec. 1920 in *Collected Works,* vol. 19, pp. 61–68).

15. *Speeches,* p. i. For a study of the religious idiom of popular *mentalités,* see my
"A Conversation of Rumors," pp. 485–505. See above, pp. 102–5, 155–56, regarding
Ghulam Husain, Veeraswamy, and the colonial image of Patna as a hotbed of anti-Chris-
tian sentiment.

16. *Speeches,* p. 11. Emphasis in the original. A "certain Ram nath Pandey" is identified as the source of this speech. See *Non-Cooperation in Bihar,* p. 70.

virtuous king who destroyed the demon king and villain: "If the present Government . . . [is] Ravan Raj then you must do all that Maharaja Ram Chandra did to destroy the Ravan Raj." No less ambiguous must have been the answer to the rhetorical question "Do you know what should be done where thousands of cows are killed? Blood should be shed." The same message was conveyed in entreaties to set fire to the *rakshas* (demons), to "drive them [the British] away by beating," and "to tear the jail to pieces and burn it." Violence was also suggested by a speaker who informed his Patna audience that the *ulama* (Muslim religious and legal authorities) had declared "Jehad [holy war], but that it be non-violent for the present." But he then added, "I may, however, warn you that Jehad with sword may be declared by the Ulamas before long and that you should be ready to join it if they want you to do so. But until then you must be non-violent."[17]

Local violations of the Gandhian conception of nonviolence assumed other forms as well. Although local practitioners of Noncooperation followed the nationalist leadership in urging supporters to withdraw from government jobs and withhold services from government and its representatives, they also sought to extend noncooperation to areas specifically forbidden by Gandhi. Whereas the Mahatma deliberately elected not to make the payment of taxes an issue, local Volunteers openly took it on. "Stop payment of taxes" was the unequivocal call issued in Saran in December 1921. A similar plea in Muzaffarpur in August of that year targeted the *chaukidari* tax, collected to defray the expenses of maintaining *chaukidars,* or night watchmen. By this act, the movement became embroiled in agrarian issues, because night watchmen were, in part, village-level representatives of the police and, in part, petty servants of landholders tied to estate and village systems of control.[18]

The conflation of political, social, and economic issues also surfaced in attacks against wealth and privilege that were leveled not only at perquisites accumulating to the British but also at those enjoyed by their local allies, the so-called principal zemindars and other elite land-

17. *Speeches,* pp. 11, 15, 19. See also Freitag, *Collective Action and Community,* esp. chaps. 5–6, regarding the increasing popular use of religious symbolism (Ram, sacred cow, etc.) in the late nineteenth and early twentieth centuries.

18. *Speeches,* pp. 12, 19, 25. "Service in Police and Army is haram (forbidden)" was one local expression of this idea. *Haram* in this context has more of a moral connotation to it—of being forbidden or improper. See also my *Limited Raj,* pp. 103–11, for an analysis of *chaukidars* as functionaries in estate and village systems of control.

holding families. As one speaker asserted in Shahabad, "This Government is for the rich, because the rich become members of the Council. This Government is not for the labourers." On another occasion, the maharaja of Dumraon, Shahabad's largest landholder, was singled out for criticism because he was said to have contributed a sizable amount of money in honor of the visit of the Prince of Wales.[19]

Boycott of foreign cloth and the reliance on homespun cloth (*khadi*) also had the potential of being divisive because they were directed against both the consumer and the seller. Trade in cloth in north India in the late nineteenth and early twentieth centuries was increasingly in the hands of the rising *bania* groups, many of whom had established themselves in Bihar over the course of the nineteenth century and many of whom both there and elsewhere had attached themselves to Gandhi. But it was an issue that had widespread resonance as well, because many people were aware, and had been aware since the late nineteenth century (e.g., Bholanauth Chunder), that indigenous and artisanal products in general had been declining because of foreign competition. Deindustrialization was not known by that name, but its adverse effects were familiar to many.

The boycott campaign rested on two pillars: (1) the economic, or the notion of the drain of wealth, that India's once robust textile industry had been shattered by the rise of machine-made goods mass produced inexpensively by the mills of England, and (2) the semiotic, or the Gandhian stress on self-reliance. Consequently, cloth took on several layers of signification relating to national identity and difference.

The belief that the indigenous cloth industry had declined as a direct result of British design and sabotage was widespread. As one speaker declared, "Cloths of superior quality were woven in India. The thumbs of 1,400 Jolahas were cut away[,] and since then the weaving of good cloths in Bengal came to an end. Gradually we became accustomed to foreign cloths. Every art and manufacture became extinct, for he who was the protector turned out to be the destroyer. Everything was destroyed as soon as we were deprived of arts and trade."[20] The much-sung ode of Noncooperation addressed to "Firangia"—Veeraswamy had employed the pejorative "phirangi" in referring to the British almost a hundred years earlier—lamented: "If cloth does not come from foreign coun-

19. *Speeches*, pp. 8, 10.
20. Ibid., pp. 16, 19–21.

tries we shall have to live naked, O Firangia. Cotton is purchased cheap from us and there from [sic] cloth is manufactured and sold to us, O Firangia. In this way India's wealth is plundered and sent away to foreign countries, O Firangia."[21]

Gandhi's championing of indigenous products therefore appealed to a wide audience. For it "articulated and elaborated on the theme that the Indian people would only be free from European domination, both politically and economically, when the masses took to spinning, weaving, and wearing homespun cotton cloth, *khadi*. To give substance to these theories, he created the enduring symbols of the Indian nationalist movement; the chakra (spinning wheel), which appeared on the Indian National Congress flag and . . . the wearing of a *khadi* 'uniform,' a white handspun cotton *dhoti, sari,* or *pajama, kurta* and a small white cap."[22]

Cloth was the dressing on the larger issue of "ruin" that many considered to have been inflicted on their country by the "nation of Hatwearers." In a tenor remarkably similar to the cry taken up by Patna writers during the era of revolution, the chant repeated in the bazaar evoked an image of a "once beautiful and charming" India that had, in the words of the "Firangia," been "turned into a burning ghat":

> Grains, wealth, men, strength and wisdom all have been destroyed; no
> traces of any remains, O Firangia.
> The country some times ago yielded lakhs of maunds of grains and rice,
> O Firangia. . . .
> Where the people were fully fed and satisfied now there rages famine
> always, O Firangia. . . .
> Commerce and trade have all disappeared and have been ruined . . .
> For trifling things we have to look to the foreigners' faces. . . .
> If this state continues some time longer, India will be ruined . . .
> No regard is paid to one's honour, flattering words are uttered . . .
> Day and night the sahibs are flattered and foreigners' feet are licked,
> O Firangia.[23]

21. Ek Asahayog, *Firangia* (Ballia: Harihar Press, 1921).

22. Bernard S. Cohn, "Cloth, Clothes, and Colonialism: India in the Nineteenth Century," in *Cloth and Human Experience,* ed. Annette B. Weiner and Jane Schneider (Washington: Smithsonian Institution Press, 1989), p. 343. *Khadi* thus became the "uniform" of the nationalists. See Susan S. Bean, "Gandhi and Khadi, the Fabric of Indian Independence," in this same volume, pp. 355–76; C. A. Bayly, "The Origins of Swadeshi (Home Industry): Cloth and Indian Society, 1700–1930," in *The Social Life of Things,* ed. Arjun Appadurai (Cambridge: Cambridge University Press, 1986), pp. 284–321.

23. *Firangia.* Each line ends with "O Firangia."

Yet even as the advocates of Noncooperation faulted the regime for causing "ruin," as had their Patna ancestors more than a century earlier, their lament was pitched in a distinctly Hindu vocabulary. The opening line about "burning ghat" refers to a Hindu practice of cremating their dead; the role models upheld were Rana Pratap Singh and Shivaji, both historical figures renowned for their active resistance to Muslim rule; and the pantheon of heroes invoked was drawn from the great Hindu epics, the *Ramayana* and *Mahabharata*.[24]

Active resistance—and the contradictions of Noncooperation—surfaced in the bazaar, too. A delineation of the workings of the local marketing system of Saran can help explain why the bazaar became host to Noncooperation as well as to related incidents of agrarian violence.

It is significant that the most dramatic events in Saran occurred in Katia and Bhorey, northwestern localities far removed from the major markets of the district and from the central place of Patna; the pattern of related events in Champaran and Muzaffarpur was similar. These incidents occurred in geographically peripheral areas, which highlights the shift in the growing popular base of the nationalist movement. Having sprung to life initially in the late nineteenth century in the metropolitan centers and port cities of Calcutta, Bombay, and Madras, the movement spread inland, first to the urban centers in the interior and then to the countryside. The political mobilization of the hinterland, in other words, corresponded to the reticulations facilitated by the spread of markets into the interior.

The distinctions drawn here between different levels of markets follow the classification used previously to sketch the Patna marketing system. The top two rungs in this formulation are occupied by the "central market" and "intermediate" market town, or *qasba*. Standard markets, constituting the third tier, were generally the termination point of goods "imported" in for peasant consumption. Consequently, this level of markets represented the lowest echelon of the local marketing hierarchy that received the foreign goods targeted by the Noncooperation Movement.

Neither Katia nor Bhorey was among the 68 marketing settlements identified in the district as existing prior to 1765 (see Map 3).[25] By

---

24. Ibid.

25. A. Montgomerie, Colltr., to William Cowper, President and Members, BOR, Aug. 10, 1791, Bengal BOR Procs., Sayer, 1792, May 23 (hereafter Montgomerie report). The transfer of *pargana* Kasmar from Tirhut to Saran added another six markets. See

1793, however, both had emerged as markets, 2 of the 179 so identified as markets in the district. Katia, a *ganj* according to the police tax rolls, was primarily a grain market occupied by "braziers, mercers, suttrunjees [carpet] sellers, confectioners, cloth dyers and venders of oil, fish, rice, pease, sautoo [parched gram, a coarse grain consumed especially by the poor], beetleleaf [*sic*], tobacco and herbs," whereas Bhorey was described as a "bazaar . . . [of] merchants, oilmen, choorywalas [bangle sellers] and sellers of spices, rice, pease, beetleleaf, salt and tobacco."[26]

Over the next century and a half with the district population steadily rising—by as much as 0.9 percent per year in the nineteenth century—many more settlements took on marketing functions. Comprehensive village-by-village data produced by the revisional settlement of the district in 1915–21 reveal that by the early twentieth century, Saran supported 364 markets, more than twice the 1793 total.[27]

This expansion in the number of markets—as in Patna district—reflected the proliferation of periodic markets in particular; the two highest levels of the marketing system in the district saw no numerical or compositional change over the colonial period. As in 1793, so in 1921: only one site ranked as the central market town—Chapra, the district headquarters. The same constancy shows up in the second rung of the marketing hierarchy as Siwan, Revelganj, Mirganj, Maharajganj, Goldinganj, Manjhi, Darauli, and Gopalganj persisted as the eight intermediate towns. (Again the comparison with Patna district is instructive.) This continuity, however, conceals the fact that their importance in relation to one another and to Chapra did not remain constant. Continuity with change is even more striking in the case of standard markets, whose number remained fixed at 32 throughout the colonial pe-

---

R. Bathurst, Colltr., Tirhut, to BOR, Bengal BOR Procs., Aug. 3 to Nov. 30, 1792, Sayer, Sept. 7, no. 2, enclosure.

26. J. Lumsden, Acting Colltr., to G. H. Barlow, Subsecy., Aug. 30, 1793, Bengal Rev. Jdcl. Consltns., Sept. 6 to 27, 1793, Sept. 13, no. 15 (hereafter Lumsden report). This report identifies the amount of taxes paid by each marketing settlement and by different professions. Rates varied according to type of establishment and goods transacted, e.g., cloth shops and bakers' houses along with shroffs, grain dealers, confectioners, and braziers paid a tax of two pice; smaller traders such as tanners or grass sellers or blacksmiths, one pice. The highest tax, four pice, was levied on salt merchants and salt godown owners. Although the tally of "marketing settlements" was 497, I have compressed this to 179 sociologically discrete and distinct markets by aggregating together as single markets those settlements that were counted separately because they coincided with the revenue definition of a "village."

27. SVN; *Limited Raj*. See also *SDG 1930*, pp. 162–77, for a slightly lower total—341 marketing settlements.

riod but whose roster was altered significantly. Only 9 of the 32 standard markets from 1793 continued in that role in the twentieth century; 23, in other words, were supplanted by new ones. The most dramatic change occurred, however, at the level of periodic markets, which rose in number from 138 in 1793 to 323 in 1921.[28]

In Saran, as in Patna, the remarkable expansion in number of *haats* ensured a more even geographical distribution of markets across the district. The following information showing percentage of population in each *thana* relative to overall district population, and the percentage of periodic markets in each *thana* relative to the district total, indicates that the share of markets located in each *thana* relative to its proportion of population was predominantly even, except in the case of Chapra and Manjhi *thanas*. A slight distortion existed there because of the clustering of marketing functions in and around Chapra.

Katia and Bhorey were part of an area, *thana* Mirganj—as were the *thanas* of Chapra, Manjhi, and Basantpur—whose share of the overall number of markets (16.3 percent) exceeded its relative proportion of population (16.1 percent). Contrast this pattern with that of *thana* Gopalganj, where the percentage of *haats* evenly matched the percentage of population residing there, or the *thanas* of Mashrak, Parsa, Sonepur, Darauli, and Siwan, where the percentage of population exceeded their proportion of the overall population. But in terms of number of people per periodic market, Mirganj's figure of 1 *haat* for every 7,319 persons was surpassed only by Chapra (1:9,526), Manjhi (1:10,669), and Basantpur (1:7,742). In the remaining six *thanas* of the district, periodic markets were far more abundant relative to population: Mashrak *thana* returned the best ratio at 1 *haat* for every 5,621 persons.

The sizable proportion of people and periodic markets in Mirganj was the result of developments in the colonial period. One of the least inhabited areas in the late eighteenth century—along with Gopalganj— it comprised part of the northern tract, which experienced the largest expansion of cultivation and presumably of population over the course of the late eighteenth and early nineteenth centuries. As Kalyanpur Kuari (Mirganj was carved out of this *pargana*), this locality appar-

---

28. I have made qualitative and quantitative distinctions between different levels of markets based on information provided by the Lumsden and Montgomerie reports on the amount of police tax levied on a market and the kind and range of professions aggregated in it.

ently had only two markets before 1765 and six in the 1790s, four of which were standard markets (Katia was one) and two periodic markets—Bhorey was not one of these two. In the early twentieth century, however, Bhorey was one of fifty-two periodic markets enumerated for Mirganj. The adjoining *thana* of Gopalganj followed a similar upward trend, its thirty-seven *haats* in 1921 constituting more than double the number that existed in the late eighteenth century in the two *parganas* of Sipah and Dangsi from which it had been formed.[29]

The increase in markets in the northern tracts came in the wake of a spurt in the late eighteenth century that had added markets to the southern portion of Saran, particularly to the interior localities away from its riverine boundaries. This phase was characterized by phenomenal rates of market growth in the southern and central *parganas*: a 500 percent increase in Goa, more than 280 percent in Bal, a 175 percent increase in Marhal, and more than 85 percent in Barrai; *parganas* Pachlakh and Bara experienced a rise of 75 percent.[30]

The steady push toward marketing symmetry can also be plotted according to the relationship of higher-order markets to one another and to lower-order markets. Particularly telling in this respect are two interrelated processes: the declining centrality of Chapra, on the one hand, and the growing importance of towns in the interior, on the other hand. Both trends reflect the rising force of central-place symmetry, which resulted in the widespread distribution of markets throughout the hinterland, in Saran and, as has already been discussed, in Patna.

A village when the Mughal emperor Babar halted there in the late sixteenth century, Chapra prospered into a town. Its commercial prospects, especially trade in saltpeter, attracted Europeans as early as the seventeenth century. By 1793, in the words of the Saran collector, it was "the residence of wealthy shroffs and other individuals of property, and is much frequented by travellers."[31] Although not comparable in size and scale to the city of Patna, its *ganjs* and bazaars together rated

29. Part of Sipah was included in Siwan *thana*. Other areas of significant growth were Siwan (carved out of *parganas* Pachlakh, Bara, and the southern part of Sipah) and Darauli (constituted out of portions of Chaubara, Andar, and Narhan) which, although not lacking in periodic markets in the eighteenth century, experienced at least a twofold increase to reach their twentieth-century tallies of 50 and 35, respectively. Montgomerie report; Lumsden report; Yang, *Limited Raj*, pp. 34–35.

30. Montgomerie report; Lumsden report.

31. Lumsden to Barlow, May 4, 1793, Bengal Jdcl. Consltns., May 3 to 31, 1793, May 31, no. 17; P. C. Roy Choudhury, *Sarkar Saran* (Patna: Free Press, 1956), pp. ix, 1–2; *SDG 1930*, p. 23; *SDG 1908*, p. 133.

the highest police tax in the district—Rs. 1,439–10 annas (Patna was assessed Rs. 28,287)—levied on "traders and shopkeepers of every description" and on merchants and bankers. Shops in Chapra dealt in every kind of grain, especially rice and *sattu* (parched gram), and vegetables and fruits. Other shops specialized in spices, salt, fish, and meats. And because it was the marketing center of the district, it provided goods and services not readily found elsewhere. Among its specialty shopkeepers, traders, and skilled workers were sellers of cloth and silk, betel leaf and tobacco, hookas, lac, toddy, mats, rope and twine, oil, and sweetmeats (confectioners); goldsmiths, braziers, and cloth dyers also plied their trade in this town.

Converging on Chapra was trade flowing along the Ganges and Gogra. Chapra also commanded the trade headed across the Ganges to Patna and to other parts of southern Bihar. As one early-nineteenth-century Chapra resident recalled, "Large quantities of cotton, Cashmere shawls, and Benares brocades, &c. are imported from the North-West for shipment to Calcutta; while English goods, such as woolens, cottons, chintzes, &c. are brought up from the Eastward for the Chupra market, and the interior of the district."[32] A late-nineteenth-century source placed the value of piece goods and cotton brought into Chapra for redistribution in the district and in Champaran, Gorakhpur, and Nepal at Rs. 600,000. No wonder it was considered in its heyday to be "one of the largest emporia of commerce in Behar . . . [,] the centre of five well-marked streams of trade . . . from Champarun, Muzafferpur, Nepal, Gorakhpur, and a river borne import from . . . the North Western Provinces."[33]

The pull of Chapra was further enhanced by the fact that it constituted the core of a definable agglomeration of two highest-order markets clustered along a twelve-mile stretch on the Ganges and Gogra. Goldinganj occupied the eastern extremity, Chapra was six miles away, almost the middle, and to the west, also six miles from the district headquarters, was Revelganj. "To the east," observed one resident, "Chuprah unites with another considerable town called Sahibgunge [a *muhalla* of Chapra]. This town again joins Gobingunge [another *muhalla*], and Gobingunge unites with Cherau[n]d and Dooregunge [*muhallas* of Goldinganj]; from the river they resemble one long strag-

32. Wyatt, *Statistics of Sarun*, p. 4.
33. "Irrigation and Railway Communication in Sarun," *Calcutta Review* 68, 136 (1879): 375. Compare this figure with Rs. 44,651,000, the value of imports into Patna.

gling Town, extending from Dooregunge to Revelgunge, a distance of fourteen miles."[34]

Local inhabitants termed this cluster of settlements with Chapra as the focal point Chirand-Chapra. Chirand, six miles east of Chapra, lent its name to this marketing complex because it formed part of Goldinganj, which in the late eighteenth century was an emerging intermediate market. And like Goldinganj, Revelganj, near the confluence of the Ganges and the Gogra, was a rapidly rising market. By the early nineteenth century it was considered a "great mart for saltpetre and grain of every description ... imported from the interior, as well as from adjoining districts for shipmen* to Patna in the East, and Ghazeepoor, Benares and Mirzapoor in the North-West."[35]

Chapra's marketing pull in the late eighteenth and the early nineteenth centuries was also signaled by the presence of a heavier concentration of higher- and lower-order markets in the south and southwestern part of the district than in the north and northeastern sector (except for Dangsi and Marhal). Well into the early twentieth century , a large number of markets, especially periodic and standard ones, were clustered in the southern and southwestern areas extending over Chapra subdivision, particularly Chapra, Parsa, and Mashrak *thanas* (the old Bal, Manjhi, Goa, and Makair *parganas*), and Basantpur and Darauli *thanas* in Siwan subdivision (portions of *parganas* Bal, Bara, and Barrai, and Chaubara and Andar). To one local resident, the imbalance was perceptible: "The southern and the eastern parts ... i.e., the Gogra-Gangetic Valley and the Gandak Valley, present such an admirably striking contrast that it seems as if nature has equipoised her gifts of good and evil to this district. The Southern Valley ... [is studded] with places of bustling trade and commerce, and it is inhabited by whatever classes of sturdy cultivators, traders and men of intelligence and education the district can boast of. ... The Gandak Valley exhibits quite a diametrically opposite picture. ... Not much trade is carried on by the river, and there is scarcely a single Bazar [sic] worth the name on its banks."[36]

---

34. Rankine, *Topography of Saran,* p. 22. It became a major center of trade in the wake of Henry Revel who had been deputed there in 1788 to serve as a collector of government customs and who founded the bazaar, which was named after him.

35. Wyatt, *Statistics of Sarun,* p. 4.

36. G. Dutt, "Further Notes on the Bhojpuri Dialects spoken in Saran," *Journal of the Asiatic Society of Bengal* 73 (1907): 247–48.

The primacy of Chapra was also epitomized by its relatively large population. Police returns for 1813 enumerated 8,700 houses in the town, and with each calculated to lodge 5 residents, its population was estimated at 43,500. Settlements at the intermediate marketing level— Siwan, Revelganj, Goldinganj, Maharajganj, Mirganj, and Darauli— had far fewer inhabitants. Siwan, where the next largest aggregation of people lived (1,768 houses, 8,840 people) constituted only one-fifth of Chapra's numbers; Mirganj, a rapidly growing market in the nineteenth century, had only 1,640 inhabitants (328 houses).[37]

In the late nineteenth century, however, Chapra increasingly followed the Patna pattern of economic decline, a decline precipitated by the interrelated factors of changes in modes of communication and in the spatial patterning of markets. In part its decline was ushered in by a shift in the course of the Ganges and Gogra. By the early nineteenth century, the main stream of the Ganges, which formerly had run close to Chapra, veered in the direction of Shahabad. And by the end of the century the Gogra had also shifted course. Coupled with the declining fortunes of the saltpeter and indigo industries, two commodities whose trade was centered in Chapra, the town's commercial importance was clearly fading at the turn of the twentieth century.

This downward spiral was reflected in its changing relationship with Revelganj, which had emerged as a major commercial entrepôt in the nineteenth century. Although inhabited by only 13,500 people, it was, in the words of an 1873 report, the "most important centre of trade" in north Bihar, "the chief place of export for the surplus produce of Sarun and Chumparun, and . . . of the North-Western Provinces . . . [, from which] a great deal of produce which comes . . . in smaller boats is transhipped. . . . It is also the mart whence these districts draw their supplies of salt, piece-goods, and other foreign commodities."[38] An estimate of the trade conducted between Revelganj and Calcutta showed a total tonnage of 37,000 (or over 1 million maunds) in 1872–73 (a figure that does not include goods flowing between Revelganj and the North-Western Provinces or between Revelganj and the rest of Patna Division). In addition to this through trade between Bengal and the North-Western Provinces, Revelganj also served as the principal local port of imports and exports for Saran as well as for Champaran

37. Bengal Cr. Jdcl. Procs., 1813
38. C. Bernard, Offg. Secy., GOB, Statistical Dept., to Secy., GOI, PWD, no. 3263, Nov. 1, 1873, P.C. Basta no. 228, Important Bundles, Alphabet T and W, nos. 65–75.

and Nepal. Along with Patna, Revelganj dominated the trade in oilseeds, a commodity transported there from Bihar and the North-Western Provinces for purchase by agents of "down-country merchants," including a branch firm of the European agency of Messrs. Ralli and Valletta (who were also stationed in Patna) and large numbers of Bengali traders buying for the Calcutta market. Earlier in the century, the firm of Messrs. Wharton, Cleave, and Flough had been in Revelganj to trade in wheat, hides, and other commodities.[39]

Revelganj's star rose only momentarily, however, since its fortunes also began to fade. In the case of Revelganj as well, the decline as a prime trading center was related to the rivers shifting course, receding toward the bank away from the town; the Ganges-Gogra junction also shifted—eastward. Census figures point to the chronology of Revelganj's decline: in 1872, 13,415 people were enumerated there; by 1921 that number had fallen to 8,186, a 39 percent loss, in a "once ... thriving trade centre ... now fallen on bad times."[40]

Even with these adverse effects on trade, the severest blow to the commercial health of Chapra and Revelganj was in fact dealt by the development of the railways, whose lines rapidly became the main arteries of trade. By the early 1890s water traffic accounted for only 25 percent of the overall trade of the district.

The "bad times" affected the entire Chirand-Chapra complex, which began to lose some of its primacy in the district. Goldinganj's fortunes were mirrored by the fate of its grain market of Dariaganj (Doriganj), which by the early twentieth century was memorable merely for its past as "a large grain-market."[41]

Although also located along the river—twelve and forty-four miles, respectively, northwest of Revelganj along the Gogra—Manjhi and Darauli, both thriving market settlements in the late eighteenth century, were affected differently by the hard times of Chirand-Chapra. Manjhi faded in part because the Manjhi zamindars lost their fortunes over the course of the nineteenth century. Darauli continued to prosper, how-

39. R. Brownlow, Offg. Magte, Saran, to C. Tucker, Commr., Patna, Apr. 9, 1837, Bengal Cr. Jdcl. Procs., Apr. 18 to 25, 1837, Apr. 18, no. 79; *Trade of Bengal, 1876–77*, p. 217; Hunter, *Account of Saran*, p. 260; "Railway in Sarun," p. 376.

40. P. C. Tallents, *Census of India, 1921*, vol. 7, *Bihar and Orissa*, Part I, *Report* (Patna: Govt. Printing, 1923), p. 83.

41. *SDG 1930*, pp. 138, 109, 143, 161–62; AGRPD 1892–93, p. 22; Hunter, *Account of Saran*, pp. 258–59; J. B. Elliot to J. F. Shakespear, Suptd., Mar. 12, 1816, S.C., Letters Issued from 6–1–1815 to 11–4–1816.

ever, its centrality defined not solely by its dependence on a river-borne
trade but also by its importance in the traffic of merchandise flowing
between Saran and the North-Western Provinces.[42]

Contrast the decline of these southern marketing centers, whose fortunes were partly tied to the river-based Chapra trade of the late eighteenth and the nineteenth centuries with the rising prosperity of inland
markets in the late nineteenth and early twentieth centuries, a prosperity that thrust the hinterland into the vortex of nationalist politics in
the early 1920s. Siwan, Maharajganj, Mirganj, and Gopalganj, the
four intermediate markets in the interior, were strategically located to
service the trade flowing across the district on an east-west axis as well
as toward Nepal in the north: Siwan lay approximately forty miles
northwest of Chapra, Gopalganj twenty-one miles northeast of Siwan,
Mirganj ten miles northwest of Gopalganj; and Maharajganj stood almost in the center of the district—twenty-five miles northwest of
Chapra and ten miles southwest of Siwan. Like Chapra, each of these
settlements served not only as a collection point for goods produced locally but also as a transshipment center for goods being moved in either direction: between north Bihar and Bengal on the one side and the
North-Western Provinces on the other. As long as trade flowed primarily along the rivers, these interior markets commanded little of it.
Nor were these sites well connected by roads until the late nineteenth
century. However, the development of roads followed by the extension
of railways into the interior in the late nineteenth century enhanced the
status of these markets, as did the rising force of central-place symmetry, buoyed undoubtedly by the weakening pull of the Chirand-Chapra
complex.[43]

As these markets grew in importance, they were able to offer a range
of goods and services comparable to what could be obtained in Chapra.
Some items were available only in Chapra; but even in the eighteenth
century, intermediate markets trafficked in their own specialties. Siwan,
for example, had long been a center of artisanal manufactures: of pottery
and brass manufacture and of articles made of *phul* (a white metal of
copper, saltpeter, and a small admixture of zinc); calico cloth, birdcages,

42. Rankine, *Topography of Saran*, p. 28; *SDG 1908*, pp. 138, 147–48, 150,
158–59; Hunter, *Account of Saran*, pp. 328–31.
43. N. Sturt, Colltr., to BOR, July 4, 1800, S.C., Letters Sent, from Colltr. to Rev.
Board, 1799–1801; *SDG 1908*, pp. 146–66; Wyatt, *Statistics of Sarun*, p. 3. See also
above, chap. 1.

soap, and silver links were other notable products. An early-twentieth-century inventory of its industries indicates that it continued to support its special and highly skilled pottery, its glassblowing, its brass works, its sugar factory, and its *tikuli* making (glass plates encrusted with gold leaves). Maharajganj, for its part, possessed "a considerable iron industry," which produced iron for utensils and other products.[44]

Siwan had a head start on the other three intermediate markets because it was a "very large" settlement in the late eighteenth century. To continue in the words of the district magistrate of 1794, "[M]any bankers and merchants of considerable property reside there, and it is the place where the merchants trading from Benares and all parts of the Behar Province to Nepaul assemble and proceed from thence in bodies to dispose of their goods in Nepaul."[45] By 1872 its population stood at 11,099, and by 1891 it had peaked at 17,709. Although by 1921 its population, estimated at 11,862, had followed the downward trend that characterized towns throughout north Bihar in the 1890s and early 1900s, its role as a major intermediate market remained undiminished, indeed, was even enhanced by the advent of the railways.[46]

The *qasba* of Maharajganj—about which sufficient detail exists to highlight its role as an intermediate market vis-à-vis lower-order markets and the hinterland generally—is another instructive example of the changing spatial and hierarchical configuration of markets, as well as of the extensive links tying interior markets to extralocal networks. Furthermore, it once again highlights the patronage role of landholders in the development of markets.

This *qasba*'s beginnings lie in Pasnauli village, which was given to Raja Murlidhar as a *birt brahmotar* (rent-free grant to a Brahmin) in 1766–67. On taking possession of this largely uninhabited village, the raja "expended a large amount on some uncultivated ground upon which he erected and peopled a new gunge [*ganj*]."[47] By 1791 it was already recognized as one of the principal *ganjs* of the district. By the late

44. *SDG 1908*, pp. 158, 165; Lumsden Report; B. Jagadananda Sinha, "The Industries of Siwan," in Patna College, *Chankya Society, 6th Annual Report, 1915–16*, pp. 39–41; Behar Industrial and Agricultural Exhibition Committee, *Industries of the Patna Division* (Bankipore: Khadga Vilas Press, 1908), p. 73.

45. C. Boddam, Magte, to Sir John Shore, G.G., May 5, 1794, Bengal Cr. Jdcl. Consltns., Apr. 11 to May 30, 1794, May 23, no. 10. Siwan and Maharajganj were located in pargana Bara, Mirganj in Kalyanpur Kuari, and Gopalganj in Sipah.

46. *SDG 1930*, p. 153.

47. Arzee from Himmut Bahadur, PFR, Jan. 2 to Dec. 28, 1775.

nineteenth century it had emerged as one of the largest bazaars in the district, perhaps second only to Revelganj. A visitor in 1870 found it "very thickly inhabited" and "a tolerably flourishing place." Available at its shops were maize (*makai*), paddy, wheat, country sugar, and cotton, as well as, according to one informant, about a thousand strips of gunny (thirty feet long by one foot wide) and iron brought in from Gaya. The presence of vast quantities of spices convinced this 1870 visitor that it was "a great spice Bazaar—probably the largest in the district." In his estimation, Maharajganj's annual transactions totaled two thousand to three thousand rupees.[48]

In the late nineteenth and early twentieth centuries Maharajganj served as a focal point of trade for the entire region, from Bengal and the North-Western Provinces, as well as from Nepal. A primary collection point for surplus produce and a goods-and-service center for a marketing area extending over a five- to six-mile radius in every direction, particularly to the north, south, and west, it catered to those needs of the local population that could not be met by the periodic or standard markets in the locality. To the south, people from villages as far as six miles away came to sell their produce. To the east, the presence of the Gandaki River and of other markets reduced its pull. Village-by-village data for 1915–21 indicate that at least 161 villages were nested in its intermediate marketing area, which was inhabited by over eighty-six thousand people.[49]

For inhabitants of Manichapra, who had easy access to the standard markets of Rasulpur and Ekma, Maharajganj was the place for their "bigger purchases." And as the collection point for its intermediate area, it was the focal point of the surplus produce of the locality. Villagers from Khajuhan, for example, two miles away, carried their jute and molasses there for sale; from Tesuar, cultivators brought molasses, barley, and wheat, and from Atarsan molasses, potatoes, brinjals, and mustard seed. And from Ramapali, whose Dhanuks were known for their production of jute strips, jute was prepared for the Maharajaganj

48. Diary of C. B. Garrett, Feb. 1 to 24, 1870, P.C. records, uncataloged. See also Hunter, *Account of Saran*, p. 261; 1791 list; Wyatt, *Statistics of Sarun*.

49. Compiled from Siwan and Basantpur *thana* village notes, SVN; J. B. Bourdillon, Magte., Saran, to Commr., no. 1562, June 16–17, 1892, P.C. Gen. Colltn., vol. 306, 1892.

market. Corn was supplied from other villages, such as Ramgarha and Lakipur.[50]

Maharajganj was a magnet for other reasons as well: it was the site of the locality's police station, dispensary, middle English school, post office, and a district board inspection bungalow. Like most higher-order markets, its economic and administrative salience was further enhanced by its religious importance: Maharajganj was the site of a Brahmasthan (*sthan* means *place*), Kalisthan, Satisthan, a *math* (monastery), and several temples.[51]

These characteristics of the intermediate market of Maharajganj reiterate the differences between the three lowest rungs of the local marketing system. Because of the range and volume of goods and services available at each of these levels, the relative pull exerted by intermediate, standard, and periodic markets in their locality differed markedly. Compare, for instance, the spatial dimensions of Maharajganj's marketing area with that of the standard market of Pachrukhi or the periodic market of Jigrawan located within its intermediate marketing area. Maharajganj commanded the attention of buyers and sellers living in 161 villages scattered over an area spanning five or six miles. The marketing area of Pachrukhi, by contrast, essentially comprised a primary service area of 35 villages largely located within a three- to four-mile radius.[52]

Within the intermediate marketing area of Maharajganj were five *haats*—Jigrawan, Bhikhaban (Basantpur *thana* no. 144), Harpur (Siwan *thana* no. 396), Bishambharpur (Siwan *thana* no. 400), and Tarwara (Siwan *thana* no. 538). Except for Bhikhaban, which was one mile from Maharajganj, the other periodic markets in the marketing area focusing on Maharajganj were farther away, generally along the periphery of the marketing area. These different level markets were generally not in competition with one another. First, each offered a very

---

50. Ramapali, Ramgarha and Lakipur village, Basantpur *thana* nos. 162, 170, and 171 respectively; Manichapra, Khajuhan, Tesuar, Atarsan village, Manjhi *thana* nos. 115, 1, 3, and 6, respectively, SVN.

51. *SDG 1908*, p. 158; Siwan *thana*, SVN.

52. Compiled from SVN, Siwan *thana* nos. 201–300, 301–400, 401–500, 501–588. For special purposes, such as the movement of *gur* from producing villages to markets, traders came from as far away as fourteen to sixteen miles. See, e.g., Panjwar village, Darauli *thana* no. 353, SVN, from where gur was transported to Maharajganj (sixteen miles away) and Pachrukhi (fourteen miles).

different range and volume of goods and services; second, the various *haats* were open on different days.[53]

Standard markets in the late eighteenth century typically offered agricultural products, both those grown in their locality and those brought in from the outside, as well as goods and services generally not available in the periodic markets. The police tax registers of 1793 reveal that this level of market was typically levied taxes ranging from as little as fifty rupees to as much as two hundred rupees, or approximately one twenty-eighth to one-seventh the amount collected from the Chapra market. The tax rolls for the standard market of Hassanpura, for instance, identify goldsmiths, sellers of oil, cloth dyers, cotton beaters, and confectioners as its taxpayers. At the standard market of Bagoura, shoppers were likely to find goldsmiths, sellers of oil, sellers of cotton, curriers and sellers of silk, cloth dyers, confectioners, bangle sellers, and cotton beaters, in addition to the usual range of shops devoted to selling agricultural produce.[54]

Detailed information from the early twentieth century presents a similar picture of standard markets, one that highlights their growing significance in rural society and ultimately their emergence as sites of contention during the Noncooperation Movement. The standard market of Basantpur counted 175 families in 1917, most of whom were engaged in trade and only a few nominally in cultivation. Of these, the principal families involved in trade were 7 Rauniar families, 5 Rastogi families dealing in cloth, 2 Barawar families in the spice trade, 20 Kalwar families, and 56 Madhesia Kandu families in grain, spices, and minor articles. Three Sonar families (2 of whom were nonresidents) also maintained shops where they carried on their traditional trade as goldsmiths. As a standard market, some goods were imported by cloth merchants who bought their material wholesale from Calcutta. Many from nearby villages offered their vegetables, spices, and other produce

---

53. Jigrawan; Bhikhaban, Basantpur *thana* no. 144; Harpur, Siwan *thana* no. 396, Bishambharpur, Siwan *thana* no. 400, Tarwara, Siwan *thana* no. 538, SVN.

54. Lumsden Report. See also J. R. Elphinstone, Colltr., to Thomas Graham, BOR, Nov. 23, 1802, S.C., Letters sent to BOR, June 27, 1801, to Dec. 26, 1802, on Barragaon, a standard market, which declined after 1802, when it was no longer home to a British battalion stationed there to combat the rebel Raja of Huseypur. In 1802 it supported twenty-one vendors of rice and dal or grain merchants, four curriers, five confectioners (*halwais*), six betel leaf preparers and sellers (*tamulis*), five druggists (*pauseries*), six tobacconists, five silversmiths, nine fruit sellers, two money changers, nine vendors of milk, two *naichabands* (pipestem-makers), five cloth dealers, six vendors of wood, five shoemakers, and twenty-one butchers.

for sale at Basantpur. Much the same dimensions of a standard market in the early twentieth century characterized Bithuna, which lay in the vicinity of Basantpur and was frequented by people whose marketing needs were not met by their nearby periodic market. This 1918 source estimated an attendance of some four hundred people and seventy to eighty stalls and shops.[55]

Pachrukhi is another example of a standard market. It emerged because its landholder took advantage of its location on the railway line between Siwan and Chapra to establish a Monday and Thursday *haat* that made its mark by enticing traders from Maharajganj to use it as a place to purchase *gur* (unrefined sugar) from "surrounding villages." Within a fifteen-year period, it became a standard market, a collection point for as much as two hundred thousand to three hundred thousand rupees' worth of sugar purchased there annually for export to other marketing centers. In addition to serving as a bulking center for *gur,* it also had fifteen shops selling other goods, including grains, spices, and sweetmeats.[56]

Haats occupied the lowest rung of the marketing system. The police tax register for 1793 shows that these periodic markets paid as little as a few annas in taxes and at most fifty rupees. Panapur, identifiable as a *haat* in 1793, and again from the records of 1915–21, was not unusual for this kind of market in that its shops only dealt in the sale of cloth and coarse grain (*sattu*). Much more diversified was the periodic market of Kalyanpur in the vicinity of Bhorey, its shops offering in addition oil, fish, rice, peas, betel leaf, tobacco, and herbs.[57]

Late-nineteenth- and early-twentieth-century data provide similar profiles. The *haat* of Nagra, largely populated and controlled by Muslims, bustled on Tuesdays and Thursdays, its customers coming to make purchases of "every sort of ordinary things." In the neighboring village of Kadirpur, in the 1890s, there sprang up a few shops run by people from nearby villages. These shops had the makings of a nascent *haat* and sold fish, vegetables, and oil. Two decades later this had turned into a regular biweekly *haat* (Tuesdays and Fridays), in contrast to the Tuesday and Thursday schedule of neighboring Nagra. The *haat*

55. Bithuna and Basantpur villages, Basantpur *thana* nos. 294 and 358, SVN.
56. Siwan *thana* no. 412.
57. Lumsden report; Panapur, Mashrak *thana* no. 70, and Kalyanpur, Mirganj *thana* no. 364, SVN. Fifty rupees and above, according to the 1793 tax rolls, appears to have been a rough indication of a standard market.

at Dumri, held every Wednesday and Saturday at "a central spot in the village," is another example of a periodic market, albeit a large one. One visitor encountered twenty shops, of which three dealt in cloth, two in grain, and the rest in miscellaneous items. Of these he estimated that perhaps five or six may have had capital of more than one hundred rupees a year; the rest fell far below that level. Aphaur was yet another village with the essential elements of a *haat*. Also a market where "articles of ordinary daily use [were] sold," its population of almost twenty-five hundred people included a range of cultivating, landholding, moneylending, and laboring castes. But as its village note writer observed, the existence of the market also meant the presence of an oil presser (Teli), a tailor (Darzi), an ironsmith (Lohar), a weaver (Jolaha), and a Bania.[58]

As this reconstruction of the marketing system of Saran indicates, the bazaar at all its different levels was a venue of "a commingling of categories." Therefore the local dramas of Noncooperation staged at these places magnified the contradictions of local society, which surfaced in actions that were textualized as an agrarian script. Throughout 1921 and in the first months of 1922, the Sitamarhi area of Muzaffarpur became the "storm-centre of non-cooperation activity in the province." To cite the inflammatory language of a police report, it was in a state of "violence and general lawlessness brought about by agitators of the non-co-operation cult."[59] According to police reports, local leaders insisted that neither the *chaukidari* tax nor the land revenue be paid; shopkeepers selling "English cloth" were told not to engage in that business, with the warning that their shops would be looted if they did. The burning of *bideshi* (foreign) cloth and the picketing of shops, usually of toddy, cloth, liquor, and *ganja* (hemp), were common occurrences. A confidential police diary reported that a complete *hartal* (strike) called for April 6, 1921, led to "not a single shop . . . [doing] any business and even the big Pethia [market] being deserted."[60]

In this charged atmosphere, a "general hatred" developed in Sitamarhi, particularly toward the police, who, according to one report,

---

58. Aphaur and Kadirpur villages, Chapra *thana* nos. 389, 385, SVN; Nagra and Kadirpur villages, Chapra *thana* nos. 384 and 385, respectively, SVN, 1893–1901; "Report . . . on Village Dumri . . . ," *Chanakya Society, 5th Annual Report, 1914–15,* pp. 65–66.

59. Wilson, Suptd., to Commr., Nov. 28, 1921, B & O Polit. Procs., Police, 1922, May, no. 1, enclosure; *Non-Cooperation in Bihar,* p. 94.

60. "Confidential diary . . . 9th April 1921," B & O Police Procs., May 1922, no. 1.

were "daily being abused in filthy language." Local administrators found themselves deprived of the services and provisions customarily provided them when they were on tour in the countryside. The consequence of such a boycott, as one subdivisional officer discovered, was that he had to cut short his rounds as he "could get no help to erect his tent, or anything to eat, so had to return to Sitamarhi for his food. Europeans driving through the Subdivision are frequently pelted with bricks, mud or sticks." Frequent were the incidents involving the local European population, mostly indigo planters. At the Sitamarhi Mela in April 1921, a group of Europeans was "surrounded by a frenzied crowd, crying out 'Mahatma Gandhi ki Jai.'"[61]

In Champaran in 1921 the name of Gandhi filled the air in the *thanas* of Bagaha, Lauriya, Dhanaha, and Jogapatti. The Noncooperation Movement in this district, as in Muzaffapur, led to "systematic antagonism against Government and Europeans," that is, against administrators and their functionaries, especially the police, and the local European indigo planters who played prominent roles in the political, social, and economic life of the district.

Police reports cite numerous instances of "large mobs numbering several thousands" marching in the vicinity of indigo factories shouting "Gandhijee-ki-jai." Repeated attempts were made to induce factory workers to leave their service, in one case, resulting in a group of ten men beating up a factory servant who refused to quit. In February 1921, employees of the Majowah factory in Bagaha were attacked. In July a "mob" pursued the *patwari* (village accountant) of Baikunthpur Factory in Dhanaha *thana* from village to village, finally catching him and assaulting him. Factory property also came under attack: on three separate occasions in November 1921 parts of the Chauterwa factory were set on fire.[62]

But in Muzaffarpur as well as in Champaran, the Noncooperation Movement triggered actions sparked by local agrarian conflicts. As the

61. Suptd., Muzaffarpur, to Commr., Nov. 28, 1921, in ibid., no. 1, enclosure; P. T. Mansfield letters, Apr. 4, 1921, Box IA, vol. 3, July 31, 1920–29.

62. Notes by F. S. McNamara, Suptd., Police, Champaran, Nov. 18 and 19, 1921, and Suptd., Champaran, to I.G., Police, B & O, no. 2281, Nov. 6, 1921, B & O Polit. Procs., Police, 1922, June, no. 3, enclosure, and no. 1. See also Girish Mishra, *Agrarian Problems of Permanent Settlement: A Case Study of Champaran* (New Delhi: People's Publishing House, 1978); Jacques Pouchepadass, *Planteurs et Paysans dans L'Inde Coloniale: L'Indigo du Bihar et le Mouvement Gandhien du Champaran (1917–1918)* (Paris: Editions L'Harmattan, 1986), for the antecedents of this antagonism.

Congress newspaper, *Searchlight,* remarked, the "unrest among the masses . . . is largely agrarian, directed more against the landlords and planters than against the Government." P. T. Mansfield, the Sitamarhi subdivisional officer, echoed this finding. "People entirely disregard authority," he noted, referring not only to the activities associated with the Noncooperation Movement but also to such incidents as the attempt to rescue a "debtor from the custody of two civil court peons" and the difficulty landlords experienced in collecting rent in Belsand *thana*.[63]

The "spirit of lawlessness" also assumed the form of *haat* looting in Muzaffarpur in early 1921; the government sought to pin the blame on the "sympathisers" of the movement, but, as the Congress newspaper pointed out, its volunteers had tried to stop it. These cases generally involved people of low castes and of little means attempting to enforce lower prices. At Sakri Saraya, ten people were said to have looted the market in January because prices were not lowered. Two men claiming to speak for the government demanded that fish be sold in the market of Pakri at the reduced price of one anna per seer. Threats were also leveled at sellers at another market; they were warned that their fish and meat would be looted if they did not reduce prices.[64]

Similarly, the Noncooperation Movement in Champaran developed an agrarian "complex" as "systematic antagonism against Government and Europeans [was] . . . extended to all loyal zemindars and raiyats." The bazaar became, as in Muzaffapur, the locus of activity, particularly in the southern portion of the district, as "a general attack on all bazaars owned by Europeans [ensued,] with the object of breaking them up and causing loss. The idea being that if these Europeans are caused loss they will leave the country."[65]

In four different localities of Champaran, "noncooperators" attempted to establish *haats* to compete with those controlled by the indigo factories. Through persuasion or coercion, they sought to direct local inhabitants away from the old markets and toward the new ones. In the name of Gandhi acts of "haat looting" were also carried out.

63. Note with W. Swain, Offg. I.G., Police, B & O, to Chief Secy., B & O, no. 8400-A, Dec. 10, 1921, B & O Police Procs., May 1922, no. 2, enclosure; Mansfield letters, vol. 3, 1920–29; *Searchlight,* Feb. 2, 1921.

64. *Non-Cooperation in Bihar,* pp. 214, 216, 222; *Searchlight,* Jan. 28, 1921; telegram from Viceroy, Jan. 21, 1921, GOI, Public and Judicial, L/P&J/6/1730, J&P 486/21.

65. Suptd. to I.G., Police, B & O, no. 2281, Nov. 6, 1921, B & O Police Procs., June 1922, no. 1, enclosure.

Typically, these incidents involved people marching into markets and imposing and enforcing just prices; on many occasions goods were looted when prices were not lowered. There were a number of instances of "haat looting" of fish and meat in Champaran.[66]

Another issue that manifested a decidedly agrarian character was the conflict over the payment of *abwabs,* or cesses. This conflict was centered in precisely those areas of Bettiah subdivision that had "for many years past been notorious for the friction and ill-feeling between the landlords who hold villages under lease from the Bettiah and Ramnagar estates and their tenants."[67]

The agrarian script in Saran was enacted in the Katia and Bhorey area. Over a twelve-month period in 1921 and 1922 a wave of "lawlessness," attributed by local authorities to the nationalist movement, swept thirty-eight villages in the locality, which was dominated by the great estate of Hathwa. But along with the picketing of liquor shops and the attacks on the police, including several cases of arson involving police stations, there were also assaults on *chaukidars* and attempts to interfere with the collection of the *chaukidari* tax. One police station diary recorded as many as fifty-three complaints of "threats against the rural police" filed between January and November 1921.

No less conspicuous were the overt and open expressions of hostility directed at the maharaja of Hathwa by his tenants, who were increasingly recalcitrant about paying their rent. According to a police diary of April 1922, the estate's *patwaris* (accountants) were "threatened with assault or arson" on four separate occasions; in other instances, various other officials of the estate were attacked. Throughout the area—a locality where disputes between the local population and the estate dated back to the early nineteenth century—conflicts with tenants were commonplace.[68]

Although geographically peripheral—far removed from Patna and even farther removed from the Chirand-Chapra area—Katia and Bhorey

66. E. L. L. Hammond, Chief Secy., GOB&O, to Secy., GOI, Home, Nov. 6, 1921, Public and Judicial, L/P&J/6/1775, J & P 7363/21; *Non-Cooperation in Bihar,* pp. 225–29; Stephen Henningham, *Peasant Movements in Colonial India, North Bihar, 1917–1942* (Canberra: Australian National University, 1982), pp. 98–99.

67. Hammond to Secy., no. 4364P-C, Nov. 6, 1921, L/P&J/6/1775, 1921.

68. Comments of A. P. Middleton, Magte., cited in H. W. P. Scroope, Commr., Tirhut, to I.G., no. J-1987, May 22, 1922, and E. A. O. Perkin, Suptd., Police, Saran, to P.A. of I.G., Police, B & O., no. 3168, May 8, 1922, B & O Police Procs., June 1922, no. 50. See also my *Limited Raj,* pp. 222–24, for additional details regarding these disputes.

were choice targets for Noncooperation because two of the seven police stations in Gopalganj subdivision were located there. These places,
that is, were more than marketing centers: they were home to the deepest extension of the colonial state, the machinery of the police. Both
Katia and Bhorey, however, were distant police outposts. Thus, the
official response to the outbreak of "lawlessness" in these localities
"completely cut off from the rest of the district" was to impose a punitive police presence. Local administrators were aware that Katia "police-
station is badly situated being nearly 80 miles from headquarters
[Chapra], 25 by road from the nearest railway station [Mirganj], and
14 from any Telegraph office [Hathwa]. Bhore police-station is not
much better situated."[69]

Such distance existed (and persisted), notwithstanding growing marketing symmetry, because the gravitational pull of the southeastern
quadrant centered on Chapra remained compelling, its drawing power
reinforced by its administrative salience. From the outset of colonial
rule in the late eighteenth century, Chapra was the designated headquarters. All the "public offices" staffed by the British were located there except for that of Henry Revel, the collector of government customs,
whose posting at Godna led to its subsequent emergence as Revelganj.
From this commercial-cum-administrative apex, the state gradually extended its reach into the interior over the course of nineteenth century.
This never extended much beyond the subdivisional level, however. In
addition to Chapra a second administrative jurisdiction was created in
1848, with the founding of Siwan subdivision; a third subdivision, with
Gopalganj as the headquarters, was carved out in 1875.[70]

The most intrusive and coercive machinery of the state was its system of police organized by police *thanas* (a police circle that was generally a smaller unit than the revenue *thana*) and outposts. Confined
initially to such intermediate markets as Siwan, Goldinganj, Manjhi,
and Darauli, the *thanas* were subsequently expanded, the headquar-

---

69. Scroope to I.G., no. J-1987, May 22, 1922, and note by C. W. T. Feilman, Offg.
Deputy I.G., B & O Police Procs., June 1922, no. 50.

70. For revenue purposes, subdivisions were further organized into *thanas*. In the
mid-nineteenth century the district had ten *thanas*: Chapra, Dighwara, Parsa, Manjhi,
Basantpur, Mashrak, Siwan, Darauli, Baragaon, and Barauli. Later in the century,
Sonepur replaced Dighwara; and Baragaon and Barauli gave way to Katia and Bhorey.
Chapra, Manjhi, Mashrakh, Parsa, and Sonepur formed Chapra subdivision; Siwan, Bas-
antpur, and Darauli constituted Siwan subdivision; and Gopalganj and Mirganj—both
Katia and Bhorey were part of Mirganj *thana*—made up Gopalganj.

ters of many of them established in settlements that were standard markets. In the 1920s the district had twenty-eight "independent" police stations in all: twelve in Chapra subdivision, nine in Siwan, and seven in Gopalganj.

"Formal government," as Hagen states, "roughly coincided with market place levels. . . . [These] stood out obviously as the backbone of settlement patterns and human interaction down which trickled a modest formal government. The informal political context, or hierarchies of control, on the other hand, had a more equal but complex relationship with the economic system."[71] The superimposition of an administrative grid on higher-order markets, in other words, was a regular feature of the Indian landscape. Thus, colonial administration was designed to fit in with the higher-order markets and to reach down to the level of standard markets.

The maintenance of an administrative presence at the higher levels of the local marketing system and the siting of administrative headquarters in towns and other large settlements reflected the ambition of the colonial state to prevent competing centers of power from flourishing at the highest-order marketing nodes. In part, government's goal was to safeguard its share of the revenue, which it facilitated by taking up residence in the main centers of commerce; in part, it sought to preserve law and order. But the control network of the state clearly tapered off sharply at the intermediate, and especially the standard, market level; lower-order markets and their hinterlands were largely beyond the pale of direct government control.

The events of Katia and Bhorey in 1921–22 therefore point to another principle underlying the dynamics of the local marketing system: the relationship of bazaars to landholders and their networks of control and power. To focus on this aspect requires looking at the ties that bound Katia and Bhorey to Hathwa, the seat of the great estate of Hathwa and not coincidentally also the site of a standard market. Bhorey, in fact, was one of the administrative and rent collection points for the great estate. These two localities, moreover, were problem areas for Hathwa, a consideration that made at least one local administrator hesitate to assign punitive police there, because, as he observed, the estate was "on bad terms with its tenants . . . and though the [Hathwa]

71. Hagen, "Indigenous Society in Patna," p. 145; *SDG 1930*, pp. 120, 158–59; Hunter, *Account of Saran*, p. 344.

Raj as Zamindar would have to bear its share of the cost, the assessment of the entire areas would tend to create the idea that it is specially
directed against *recalcitrant* tenants of the Raj."[72]

This conflict grew out of deep-rooted animosities in the Bhorey area.
An early chapter of this history of conflict was the so-called internal
rising of 1844, when Bujahawan Misra, a Brahmin of Bhorey, supported by Bhumihar Brahmins and peasants of his locality, claimed an
extensive tract of land, including the former *zamindari* headquarters of
Huseypur, as his rent-free grant (*birt*). In the ensuing conflict, several
clashes took place before government intervened on behalf of Hathwa
and quelled the disturbance. By the early twentieth century, the village
was riven by a factionalism that pitted a group of Bhumihar Brahmins
against a group of Brahmins, a conflict echoing the historic tensions in
the locality between the Bhumihar landholder of the area, the maharaja
of Hathwa, and the village-level elite, the Brahmins. Where the twentieth-
century version differs from the early-nineteenth-century story is in the
ostensibly more caste-centered alignment of the opposing groups, for
the earlier struggle had involved the Brahmin supporters of the ousted
Bhumihar Huseypur raja and their multicaste tenants, on the one side,
and the Bhumihar cadet line of the Huseypur family, the Hathwa raja,
on the other.[73]

No wonder the political struggle for independence in Katia and
Bhorey was infused with local social and economic issues of a distinctly
agrarian complex, a weaving together of conditions and causes that ultimately underlined Hathwa dominance throughout Gopalganj subdivision, as well as the involvement of landholders in the founding and
control of markets. Both of these aspects are well illustrated by the
links between Katia and Bhorey, on the one hand, and Hathwa, on the
other, connections that yet again reiterate the extent to which the market structured events and processes.

Tied to one another by a metaled road built in the late nineteenth
century, Katia and Bhorey were also connected to Hathwa, and all

72. Scroope to I.G, no. J-1987, May 22, 1922, B & O Police Procs., June 1922, no.
50; G. J. S. Hodgkinson, Manager, Court of Wards, Hathwa, to C. B. Garrett, Colltr., no.
A, Feb. 20, 1872, Bengal Rev. Procs., Jan.-Apr. 1872, Apr., no. 149; A. M. Markham,
Manager, Hathwa, to Colltr., no. 240, Apr. 26, 1899, Bengal Rev. Procs., Sept.-Oct.
1899, Sept., nos. 93–94, appendix E.
73. *Limited Raj*, pp. 141–54, 223; Bhorey village, Mirganj *thana* no. 230,
SVN. Bhorey was also the area from where desertions repeatedly took place in the late
nineteenth century.

three to the intermediate market of Mirganj. Contrast these ties cemented literally by a major road with the fact that neither Katia nor Bhorey was as well connected by roads to its subdivision headquarters of Gopalganj. On the contrary, from Katia the way to Gopalaganj was mostly via a third-class road; and from Bhorey, the best route was to take the first-class road south to Mirganj and then head north to Gopalganj, which was roughly on the same latitude.

A *haat* in 1793, Hathwa's stature as a marketing settlement rose with its emergence as the headquarters village of the great estate. Formerly known as the Huseypur raj, the estate had been based in Huseypur (*thana* no. 362), sixteen miles to the northwest of Hathwa, an important standard market more prosperous than either Katia or Bhorey.[74]

By the 1840s Hathwa was described as having "large bazaars" and biweekly markets. Fort, palace, and bazaar: all the markers reflecting and exercising the power and authority of this great estate were thus in place by the early nineteenth century. In the 1870s the buildings and bazaar surrounding the Hathwa fort where the raja resided were razed and a new bazaar erected at great expense: the bazaar alone cost over Rs. 5,700 to build. An early-twentieth-century account describes Hathwa as an impressive standard market, its shops offering a range of agricultural and consumer goods and its specialists providing a variety of services. The presence of schools and temples further accentuated its centrality in the locality. Its salience—and its value to the estate—can also be quantified: the estate collected Rs. 1,400 per annum as professional tax from traders stationed there.[75]

The strongest link tying Katia and Bhorey to Hathwa was the network shaped by the great estate's system of control. Because Hathwa was the hub, it was the seat of the raja's residential palace; and Hathwa and its nearby villages housed most of the key retainers of the estate. In addition to the estate *kachcheri* (office), located in the Hathwa cluster

74. Although it persisted as a standard market in the early twentieth century, when it was characterized as a "big village" with a *haat* featuring foodstuffs, vegetables, utensils, spices, sweetmeats, clothes, meat, and fish, it was no longer on a par with Katia or Bhorey. Katia's market rental was Rs. 790 per annum, or more than three times that of Huseypur (Rs. 250). Huseypur and Katia village, Mirganj *thana* nos. 362 and 446, SVN; Lumsden report.

75. Mirganj *thana* nos. 1001 to 1064, 901 to 1000, esp. Hathwa, no. 1008, SVN; Wyatt, *Statistics of Sarun*, p. 10; "Management of the Hutwa Estate during 1873–74," Bengal Rev. Procs., Apr. 1873–75, Aug. 1874, nos. 2–3.

of villages, were the estate manager's bungalow, the *diwan*'s house, the Hathwa Eden school, the post office, the raj dispensary, and the temple called Gopalmandir.

Like Katia and Bhorey, Hathwa was not only a standard market but also part of a larger economic system, in this case centering on the intermediate market of Mirganj. Proximity made the tie to Hathwa closer—Mirganj is only two and one-half miles away; Katia and Bhorey were farther afield at twenty-two and fifteen miles, respectively. A Sunday and Thursday market, Hathwa relied on Mirganj's Tuesday and Friday market that emerged in the nineteenth century as an intermediate market with a much wider range of goods and services. Consider the roster of shops existing in the two markets. Hathwa bazaar had two retail cloth shops, eleven confectioners' shops, twenty-five *kanjurais* (*kunjras*, Muslim vegetable seller) shops, fifteen grain (*galdar*) shops, four betel shops, eight tailor's shops, three dyer's shops, and one *ganja* and opium shop. Mirganj, on the other hand, had seventeen retail cloth shops, nineteen grain *golas*, three metal dealers, six spice shops, twenty pulse shops, six confectioners, ten oil shops, seven shops selling miscellaneous commodities, eleven silk makers, twelve tailor shops, seven meat butchers, three ghee shops, four iron shops, twelve jewelers, and three betel shops. Cattle were also sold. It was, in addition, an entrepôt for grain from the north and northwest, which was then exported to Patna and elsewhere. Furthermore, several Patna merchants stationed agents there for linseed, cotton, and *gur*.[76]

As a standard market, Hathwa was linked to but also overshadowed by the intermediate market of Mirganj. Their complementary economic relationship was reinforced by their communication links. The so-called Hathwa railway station was in Mirganj—the branch line of the Bengal and North-Western Railway linking Siwan to Thawe intersected it—as were the police station and subregistry office for the locality. In other words, Mirganj was part of the Hathwa system of control; its very development stemmed from Hathwa efforts.[77] Moreover, the

76. Hathwa and Mirganj, Mirganj *thana* nos. 1008, 1021; also nos. 1–100; *SDG 1930*, p. 148; *Limited Raj*, pp. 119–21. The shift from Huseypur to Hathwa occurred in the wake of the rebellion of the Huseypur raja, Fateh Sahi, in 1767, which led to the transfer of this great estate to the cadet line of the family. Turned over in 1791 to his kinsman, Chatterdhari Sahi, the new raja, on attaining his majority in 1802, shifted the headquarters of the estate to Hathwa—a place that does not show up in the 1793 tax rolls of markets—where he built a fort and a palace.

77. Mirganj village, Mirganj *thana* no. 1021, also nos. 1008–21, SVN; *SDG, 1930*, pp. 148, 159, 162–77; *Limited Raj*, pp. 121–22.

role of Mirganj as the main marketing node in the vicinity of Hathwa
reflected the dominant presence of the great estate in another respect:
Mirganj allowed the Hathwa raj to keep the state at a distance, at arm's
length from its seat of power, a feat that would have been far more difficult to accomplish had Hathwa developed into an intermediate market and therefore attracted the attention of state power. Higher-order
marketing nodes naturally drew government attention: the siting of a
police station in Mirganj is one illustration of this rule. A similar
process no doubt explains the symbolic connotations of the act of situating the Hathwa bazaar at a remove from the Hathwa fort, where the
raja resided.

The lengths to which zamindars, especially great landholders, were
willing to go to keep government at bay is illustrated by a well-
known nineteenth-century case involving the maharaja of Bettiah,
whose estate extended across much of Champaran. When government sought to station an assistant or deputy magistrate in Bettiah in
1845, the raja refused to provide space, conceding only that he
"could grant no allotment of ground nearer than 2 coss or 4 miles
from Bettiah." To continue in the words of this district administrator,
the raja consistently endeavored "to prevent as much as he possibly
can, the confirmation of the Government order; indeed, were I to be-
lieve one half of the reports that are current, he would give a lack
[lakh] of rupees to have the cutcherry [office] removed some distance
from Bettiah."[78]

Fifteen years later, in 1860, local administrators were still trying to
stake out an official presence in this "large Native Town" of almost fifteen thousand people that stood at the center of the lines of trade and
traffic of the district. Furthermore, Bagaha *thana,* an area of intense activity in 1921–22, was at a distance of sixty miles from the district
headquarters of Motihari. As the magistrate observed:

> In Bettiah the word of the Rajah or his seal is the law. It is true there is a
> Darogah [police officer] there but what can he do? If he does his duty he has
> all the Rajah's Amla [retainers] against him. They will, by perpetually bring-
> ing frivolous or false charges, sooner or later prejudice the Magistrate
> against him. If they fail with one Magistrate, they will succeed with
> another . . .

78. H. Alexander, Joint Magte., Champaran, to Secy., GOB, no. 121, Bengal Cr. Jdcl.
Consltns., May 14 to June 4, 1845, June 4, no. 45.

On the other hand, if the Darogah does not do his duty he risks his appointment. Bettiah is thirty miles from Moteeharry.[79]

Chaukidars in Bettiah, as the commissioner noted, consulted with the raja or with his agents before conveying information to the police.[80]

Although this episode ends with the great estate capitulating to the demands of government, its details rightly point to another significant feature relating to the emergence of the bazaar as the site and scene of social and political action: the significant involvement of landholders in the affairs of the bazaar, as also in the establishment and maintenance of fairs. The Hathwa hand, so visible because of its size and activity, can be clearly seen at work in developing markets throughout its estate. Much of the intensification of markets that has been traced for the north and northwestern *thanas* of Mirganj and Gopalganj in the nineteenth century can be attributed to the emergence of this great estate. Because of its political and social control of the area, as well as its considerable economic resources, the estate was instrumental in having this formerly market-poor subdivision of Gopalganj catch up with the rest of the district in number of markets.[81]

Hathwa's attention to markets was not confined to its residential village or to settlements in the heart of its estate. As early as 1794 the estate's strategy of expansion was to "purchase . . . lands."[82] Chapra and Revelganj were two places where it acquired substantial interests during the course of the nineteenth century. In 1873–74, for instance, the estate sank Rs. 108,200 into the purchase of a half-share of Ratanpura, a hamlet of Chapra. By 1886 Hathwa had gained control of the entire village. It also secured substantial interests in Revelganj, particularly in Godna, where it first erected a bungalow and then proceeded to purchase nearby lands, which became the site of its bazaar and grain *golas*.[83]

79. H. H. Robinson, Magte., Champaran, to Commr., Patna, no. 97, May 21, 1860, Bengal Jdcl. Procs., Jan 1861, no. 142.

80. H. D. H. Fergusson, Commr., Patna, to Secy., GOB, no. 192, June 18, 1860, ibid., no. 141. See also J. F. Lynch, Deputy Magte., Bettiah, to F. M. Halliday, Magte., Champaran, no. 66, July 19, 1862, Bengal Jdcl. Consltns., Mar. 1863, no. 131, for an official who preferred to reside in Motihari than live in Bettiah, where he claimed he could not secure a place to stay and where he would have had to contend with the powerful influence of its Maharaja.

81. Mirganj and Gopalganj *thana* village notes, SVN; Lumsden report; Montgomerie report.

82. F. Hawkins, Colltr., Saran, to BOR, Nov. 17, 1794, Bengal BOR Procs., Wards, July 4 to Dec. 11, 1794, Dec. 11.

83. "Management of Hutwa during 1873–74"; Chapra *thana* nos. 283, 215 and 216, SVN, 1893–1901; and J. MacLeod, Deputy Colltr., to J. J. Grey, Colltr., Sept. 21,

Hathwa was not alone in playing the market strategy. One dynamic underlying the growing symmetry in distribution of markets was the active role of landholders in establishing them. Maharajganj and Pachrukhi, discussed earlier to highlight the dimensions of an intermediate and a standard market respectively, provide two clear-cut examples of landholders purposively taking on the task of building up markets. The substantial market of Maharajganj, as already noted, grew out of the village of Pasnauli in the 1760s, when its landholder established a *ganj* on its uncultivated land. Similarly, Pachrukhi, founded in 1901, sprang to life because its "proprietor," Moti Chand, took advantage of its location on the railway line to erect some houses on the *parti* (waste or uncultivated land) area near the village's railway station. By enticing traders from Maharajganj to frequent the village to purchase *gur* from "surrounding villages," he managed in the course of fifteen years to turn the village into a standard market.[84]

Classical central-place theory, as these two illustrations suggest and additional data confirm, can only partly explain the geographical pattern of markets; it certainly cannot satisfactorily account for *all* the forces that led to a particular geographical distribution of markets; nor can it resolve why some areas of the south and the east had a higher clustering of marketing nodes than others. Instructive examples are provided by the *parganas* of Bal and Goa (latter-day *thanas* of Chapra, Parsa, and Mashrak) at the turn of the nineteenth century, an area by then already highly cultivated, well populated, and intersected by some of the district's best communication lines. Also significant about this area is that its settlement and landholding patterns endowed certain families with decisive power in these localities. Pargana Bal was the area in which related Eksaria Bhumihar Brahmin families established residential headquarters at Parsa, Chainpur, and Bagoura, *zamindari* centers that also became the prime marketing settlements in their localities. As one contemporary observer noted, the zamindars of Parsa, Chainpur, and Bagoura "exercised great influence over the inhabitants of this Pergunnah."[85] Their "influence"

1865, S.C., Letters Sent to the Commr. of Patna, Aug. 16, 1865 to Oct. 1866. Bettiah, Champaran's major landholder, was a long-standing rival of Hathwa and the primary proprietor of the main Revelganj market.

84. Pachrukhi village, Siwan *thana* no. 412, SVN; Wyatt, *Statistics of Sarun*, p. 11; 1792 list.

85. Wyatt, *Statistics of Sarun*, p. 7; Manjha Family history, unpublished ms., compiled by N. K. Roy, Assistant Manager and Treasury Officer, n.d., interview with Hari Surendra Sahi, Rusi Kothi, Chapra, Saran, May 1974.

was spelled out in the late-eighteenth-century tax roster of markets, which recorded their proprietorship over many of Bal's markets. Branches of this clan, which had set up additional *zamindaris* in Rusi, Khaira, Manjha (Dangsi), and Salempur, commanded markets in *parganas* Bara, Barrai, and Dangsi (Siwan subdivision), three other areas with large numbers of markets.[86]

Amnaur, Mashrak, Tajpur, and Makair are other notable examples of *zamindari* centers that doubled as standard markets. In south India, too, landholder involvement with markets was commonplace, many markets convening at or near the residences of zamindars. Throughout the subcontinent, as Richard G. Fox writes, "much of the history of town formation has to do with a local *raja, navab,* or big zamindar who established a town or created a market. This sort of petty nobility or local strong men endowed towns and began market places and, traditionally, provided supra-caste integration to them."[87] The development of market settlements as *zamindari* centers in north India "was probably internal to the process of growth in the marketing system. This was because Rajput, Bhumihar or Jat lineage elites and rajas founded markets where there was already a good degree of peasant interaction and where merchants would be expected to gather. While most central places combined several functions, political circumstances or temporary economic situations related to non-local trade might determine that some were overwhelmingly more important in one function than others."[88]

Markets in Saran above the periodic and standard size, except for Darauli, which formed part of the large estate of the Gorakhpur-based raja of Majhauli, and Manjhi, which belonged to the Muslim Manjhi family of Shahamat Ali Khan, were, however, generally not the property of individual landholders. Higher-order markets were too big and too complex to remain intact in the hands of one family, especially given the fact that the standard nineteenth-century experience of many Saran estates was that of increasing fissioning and subdivisions. Moreover, except for Hathwa and a few large zamindars, the district was largely in the hands of many small landholders.

---

86. 1792 list; *The Limited Raj.*

87. *From Zamindar to Ballot Box*, p. 70; Christopher Baker, "Tamilnad Estates in the 20th Century," *IESHR* 13 (1976):14.

88. C. A. Bayly, "The Small Town and Islamic Gentry in North India: The Case of Kara," in *The City in South Asia*, p. 21.

Because of the pattern of landholding in the district, the role of small landholders in the intensification of markets cannot be ignored. *Pargana* Goa's markets typify this pattern of growth. In the late eighteenth century its markets were in the hands of many, a trend also discernible from the early-twentieth-century information on *thanas* Mashrak and Parsa, areas which encompassed that *pargana* and which remained rich in markets. Most *thanas* characterized by large numbers of small landholders—Sonepur, where the average estate size was four acres, and Parsa, Mashrak, Siwan, and Darauli, where it was seven, eleven, twelve, and thirteen, respectively—were also localities with the highest shares of markets.[89]

One manifestation of landholder involvement in the founding, development, and control of markets was the intense competition waged by rival zamindars, a rivalry that often erupted into open conflict. As early as 1789, local administrators had to enforce as "an established usage, that no market shall be erected in the vicinity of another, or be held on the same day, to its prejudice. . . . [But the] word 'vicinity' must be construed by the collector, and give rise to numberless disputes."[90] Typical of such cases was the dispute between Subh Narain and Bhore Narain, referred to the civil courts in 1802, because the latter had started a new *haat* in "Hoosypoor" village that threatened to disrupt the business of the long-standing minor market of the former in adjoining "Simurdah." The presiding official noted that "frequent complaints . . . [were made] by zemindars . . . relative to the institution of Hauts or markets, in the neighbourhood of others which have been established for many years."[91]

The establishment of new *haats* and the disputes that ensued in the wake of their founding continued to be sources of conflict well into the twentieth century. Such confrontations, well documented in the criminal records, frequently turned violent. In the words of one police report, an enduring source of criminality was the "trouble arising from

89. *SSR,* p. 129; *Limited Raj,* pp. 76–77. Chapra was another *thana* with small estates—nine acres; Basantpur, thirteen; Darauli, thirteen. For example, the large *zamindari* of Manjhi (the third largest revenue payer in 1793, responsible for over 8 percent of the district revenue), was faced increasingly with the breakup of the estate into smaller and smaller shares due to rising numbers of heirs whose mismanagement and internal bickering led to villages being sold off to outside interests.

90. Thomas Law, *A Sketch of Some Late Arrangements, and a View of the Rising Resources in Bengal* (London: John Stockdale, 1792), p. 114.

91. C. Boddam, Judge, Sarun, to G. Dowdeswell, Secy., Jdcl., Bengal Civil Jdcl. Consltns., Apr. 22 to June 24, 1802, Apr. 29, no. 5.

the quarrels of rival setters-up of markets."[92] Representative of this kind of "trouble" is the 1863 case involving the *maliks* (proprietors, owners) of Alhunpore, who attempted to construct a new *haat* next to an existing one at Khodaibagh. In the "serious disturbance" that ensued, "several men were wounded. Some of the rioters have been punished by imprisonment for two years and Rs. 200 fine each."[93]

The Noncooperation Movement in Champaran pursued a deliberate strategy of establishing new markets to compete with existing ones. Time and again attempts were made to prevent people from patronizing markets controlled by European indigo planters. In many instances, rival *haats* were founded. Local officials, seeking to disband these new, rival markets, prosecuted people under section 144 of the Criminal Procedure Code, which allowed magisterial officers to issue "temporary orders in urgent cases of nuisance or apprehended danger," the "danger" and "nuisance" stemming from the new markets competing with and even displacing existing ones. People implicated in these incidents were charged with unlawfully restraining others from resorting to old markets, illegally starting new ones in the ambit of existing markets, and violating orders not to establish new ones.[94]

Zamindars vied with one another for the control of markets—as they also did for melas—because they were a reliable source of income and prestige: they allowed landholders to play the role of patron. Especially in lower-order markets, where the influence and power of landholders was most prevalent, the opportunities for profit were manifold. With the state largely absent at this level of society (and indeed, only nominally represented at even the higher-order markets) the only challenge to their supremacy was that posed by rival landholders.

Official interest in markets was largely defined by revenue and considerations of law and order. Government's stake in them was otherwise minimal and had been so from the outset of colonial rule. As articulated by one district official in 1771, in a voice almost suggestive of disinterest, markets were the "property of the zemindars in whose Districts they are, and included in their Agreements [with government]." On another occasion, this same official declared that there were no

92. "Resolution," Bengal Police Procs., June 1873, p. 118.
93. GOB, *Report on the Police of the Patna Division for the Year 1863* (Calcutta: Bengal Secretariat Office, 1864), p. 61.
94. *Non-cooperation in Bihar*, pp. 224–29.

markets "dependent on government," nor were there any that did not belong to landholders.[95]

Contrast the limited presence of the state in the operations of markets with the elaborate mechanisms and processes of control maintained by the zamindars. The 1790s case of the intermediate market of Goldinganj, whose zamindar was prosecuted for continuing to collect dues in the market even though government had assumed "all gunges, bazars [sic] and hauts," provides a telling example. The Goldinganj zamindar, Mulchand, was singled out for punishment because his case was to serve as an example of the state's prerogative to restrict the rights of landholder to collect dues—because the practice of sayer (taxes on nonland items such as on markets and customs and transit duties) had been abolished. However, this was only one instance, and a rare exception to the rule of allowing landholders a free rein over their markets. Other than the targeting of a few landholders for illegally collecting market dues in the early 1790s, government never again made any concerted effort to stamp out the practice.[96]

Government's investigation into the practices obtaining at Goldinganj revealed that every shop was required to pay a "ground rent" to the market darogha (steward), who collected on behalf of his employer. In addition, as Beni Bakkal, the market weighman, testified, fees were also levied on a variety of transactions. Merchants importing salt for sale at this market paid a few copper coins (two falus and twelve dams) per maund. Additional collections were made by Mulchand's retainers (amla) from buyers and shopkeepers who came to buy, as well as from sellers who came to offer their wares. The rates varied from item to item: for example, purchasers of gur and sugar paid nine dams and three couries per rupee, while those selling these goods paid less, six dams per rupee. Grain sellers were charged by the bullock load, one seer for every load. Other fees were levied to subsidize the pay of the market staff: for the weighmen, who numbered eight in all, for the chaudhuri, whose job was "to collect from moodies and other sellers of goods in gunge and to encourage and protect beoparries," and for the

95. E. Golding to G. Vansittart, Chief &c Council of Rev., Patna, May 3, 1772, PFR, Jan. 2 to Mar. 30, 1772, vol. 3; Golding, Supervisor, Sarun, to J. Jekyll, Chief &c. Council of Rev., Patna, 6 Oct. 1771, PFR, Aug. 3, 1771 to Mar. 30, 1772. See also Law, Sketch of Arrangements, pp. 154–59.

96. Montgomerie, Colltr., to C. Stuart, Pres. &c. BOR, July 6, 1790, Bengal BOR Procs., Salt, Sayer, Opium, and Customs, May 3 to Dec. 29, 1790, Sept. 8.

peons, *mutasaddis* (writers), and *pasabans* (watchmen) who comprised the rest of the staff.[97] According to Mulchand, the charges levied at the market had been agreed upon by mutual consent when "beoparries and mahajuns" (traders and moneylenders or bankers) came to him en masse to seek his protection. Other than ground rent, he claimed, the rest of the monies collected was used to defray various expenses: paying the market staff, maintaining a godown for the storage of salt, hauling water to the market, or transporting sepoy battalions of the East India Company across the Ganges. And whatever sums remained were given to charity. In the estimation of the police tax rolls, Goldinganj earned at least one thousand rupees per annum for its landholder.[98]

The prosecution of the Goldinganj zamindar in 1793—he was fined three thousand rupees and imprisoned for six months—did little to stop the levying of "illegal cesses" (*abwabs*). Throughout the colonial period landholders continued to impose and collect a wide variety of illegal imposts. Markets in particular were valuable sources of income for their holders, who profited from the collection of ground rent and from fees or dues levied on practically every type of establishment set up there, as well as on every form of transaction enacted there. Typically, fees were levied on stalls erected in *haats*. In Dumuria each stall paid *kouri*, a nominal fee of one and a half pies per *haat* day (twelve pies = one anna; sixteen annas = one rupee). In Bishunpore, vegetable, sattu, and oil shops each paid one-half pice (three pie = one pice; four pice = one anna); the vegetable shop also gave some vegetables. Rice, gram, wheat, and presumably other grain shops offered a "handful of grains," while cloth shops, which must have made the most money on their sales, were levied the highest fee—one anna per month. At Barahima shopkeepers selling goods brought by them personally had to pay one quarter of a dhegua (or twelve kauris per head) and those who used bullocks to transport their goods paid twice as much, half a dhegua or twenty-four kauris each. Every cartload of merchandise brought in for sale paid six pies; cloth dealers gave three pies per shop. At Mirganj the Hathwa raj charged four annas for each cartload of

97. Deposition of Benee Bukkaul, weighman, and of Moolchund, *chaudhuri*, with J. Lumsden, Colltr., Saran, to Wm. Cowper &c., BOR, Bengal BOR Procs., 1793, Sayer, Apr. 19.

98. Letter of "Moolchund," zamindar, Mar. 23, 1793, and BOR to Marquis Cornwallis, n.d., in ibid.; Lumsden report.

potatoes brought in for sale and six pies for that of onions. Fees were charged for both buying and selling cattle, a comparatively high rate of two annas per head of cattle. And if shops dealt in large quantities of vegetables, a rate of one-half anna was added on to the fee of supplying a one-half seer to the *thikadar*.[99]

A lengthy list of illegal cesses compiled specifically for Patna Division in the late nineteenth century can be divided into four categories: Those imposed on shops or shopkeepers had a rate varying from area to area and also according to the kind of merchandise they dealt in. Some were imposed on the actual producers of goods marketed and on the purchasers of the merchandise. Others were levied on the products themselves. And finally there were levies on the modes of transportation used to bring goods to the market.

To take the illegal cesses on shops and shopkeepers first: The practice of *pethiya* in Tirhut targeted dealers in *haats*. They had to pay a fee, in cash or in kind, prorated according to the value of goods they sold. Another general cess termed *ugahi* was directed at anybody who offered goods for a sale at a market. The tendency in some localities was to levy a higher *abwab* on shopkeepers holding land in a marketing settlement than on those who were nonresident shopkeepers, a distinction no doubt intended to entice outside entrepreneurs. Fees were also levied on specific types of shops: in Patna district, for instance, *abkari* dictated that every toddy shop contribute one pot of toddy on various occasions.[100]

Another set of cesses that persisted throughout the colonial era was directed at peasants who marketed their produce. *Maugin chutki* referred to a cess in Tirhut imposed on villagers selling grain retail; it essentially targeted the sellers (and producers) of small amounts of grain. Another cess called *hati* taxed cultivators—and those buying from them—for trading in the "staple articles of the village": two pies per rupee from the seller and four pies per rupee from the buyer. And if peasants were engaged in selling vegetables and fruits they paid an annual cess of two to four annas. Similarly, tobacco growers were charged from one anna and four pies to five annas for every *bigha*

99. See, e.g., Mirganj *thana* no. 1021. Also Dumuria, Bishunpore and Barahima, Gopalganj *thana* nos. 26, 264 and 408, SVN, respectively.

100. S. C. Bayley, Offg. Commr., Patna to Secy., GOB, no. 251, July 2, 1872, Bengal Rev. Procs., 1873–75, July 1874, nos. 13–14 (hereafter Bayley report). See also *MSR*, pp. 186–93; *SSR*, pp. 64–65.

(roughly one-third of an acre) of land devoted to tobacco. Growers of cash crops were invariably taxed—the price of cultivating crops promising better returns than did the price of ordinary foodcrops.[101]

Such cesses were not restricted to producers of agricultural goods. People engaged in the making of virtually every kind of marketable item were subjected to some form of illegal cesses. Considered a ground rent in part, *mutharfa* was actually a "tax on trade . . . levied by proprietors on residents of their estates for allowing them to carry on their respective trades or to perform social and religious ceremonies in peace."[102] *Mutharfa* in Muzaffarpur in the 1890s was imposed on weavers for working their looms (*tana*), on oil pressers for operating each oil press (*chiragi*), on lac makers for trading in lac-made items and bangles (*lahi*), on Chamars for skinning dead cattle and dealing in hides (*charsa*), and on the weighman of a market for conducting his business (*haat* or *haatwai*).[103]

Other taxes, termed *dundidari,* were imposed on buyers—typically petty *banias* and traders purchasing small amounts—who came from outside the village to buy grain from cultivators. Still other cesses were imposed on sellers and buyers dealing in larger transactions. Wholesale grain dealers (usually at *ganjs*) not only paid rent for their stalls but also paid *golamundpie,* a cess of one-quarter of a seer for every maund of grain they had in storage. In many marketing settlements of Patna a "bazar [*sic*] duty" was exacted on every article brought into the bazaar. Even goods passing through a landholder's area were subject to cesses. For instance, there was a tobacco and grain duty to be paid to the area's landholder on every bundle and every bag of grain transported through a locality. *Bardana* in Patna necessitated a fee of one-half anna on the maund for every article brought in for sale on pack bullocks; *bardana* in Tirhut was a levy of five to six annas per bullock. Loading or unloading a boat at a *ganj* in Saran cost another illegal cess—one anna on every boat according to the practice of *kisti bojhai*—as did every bullock or pony that carried a load—each animal paid three or four annas per annum. A fee called *chutti* in Tirhut was levied on grain

101. Bayley report; *MSR*, pp. 188, 191; *SSR*, p. 65. *Khunti* and *khapta* were cesses levied on cultivators at the rate of twelve annas to one rupee–four annas per *bigha* for raising tobacco and for growing special crops respectively. The latter, generally directed at Koeris, was aimed at intercepting their profits from opium cultivation—a crop they were principally involved with—and market-gardening.

102. *MSR*, p. 192.

103. Ibid., pp. 192–93. Another cess was *bardana*—see discussion below.

in *ganjs* unloaded from boats or carts and stocked in sacks or kept on the ground outside a shop. Even owning a cart in Tirhut subjected a person to a cess: eight to ten annas per cart, or *garihana*.[104]

Although *abwabs* had been declared illegal in 1793, the government made little effort to enforce the law. On the contrary, its official position was to allow landholders the right to exact, with few exceptions, whatever claims and dues they could from the rest of the population: "If a person not entitled to levy dues levies them in any thoroughfare or public place, he shall be liable to fine. If the village hat is held on the high road passing through the village, or on ground which the public have an undoubted right to use for the purpose, the exaction of dues should be prohibited. . . . But when it is held, as is most commonly the case, on land which is the private property of the zamindar, or on land over which the public may perhaps have the right of way, but not a prescriptive right to use the land for the purpose of holding a market, no special legislative or executive interference appears to be called for."[105]

Such dues were considered beyond official purview even in cases where government had granted compensation to landholders for the abolition of duties at the time of the Permanent Settlement. According to the Bengal authorities, "It is not uncommon for the proprietor, on establishing a new market, to promise that no dues shall be taken for a year or two, with the object of attracting buyers and sellers to the market. But in the great majority of cases tolls are levied either in cash or in kind, and frequently in both of these forms; and it does not appear that in any case the levy of dues is forgone upon the acknowledged ground that compensation for their abolition has been granted."[106] Local officials were unanimous in recommending that government not interpose in this matter, as the custom had existed "from time immemorial, and [is] willingly acquiesced in by the people, and [the] imposition [of taxes] does not in any way interfere with the healthy growth of trade in *hats* and market."[107]

Government's unwillingness to legislate against the practice of levying cesses also continued in the face of evidence it uncovered that in the past the custom had been the price people paid to landholders for pro-

104. Bayley report.
105. H. J. Reynolds, Offg. Secy., GOB, Rev., to Secy., GOI, Home, no. 163, Jan. 4, 1876, Bengal Rev. Procs., 1876–78, Miscellaneous, Mar. 1876, 16.
106. Ibid.
107. Ibid.

tection and that that was still the case. Government nevertheless opposed making the practice a "criminal offence," believing that the "main security for the public . . . is the free trade in hauts, that is, in the multitude of hauts, and the freedom of people to go to this market, or to that."[108] The lone dissenting view was proffered by the Patna collector, who did not see the practice as one submitted to by the people without "murmur or inconvenience." On the contrary, he noted, the burden of these tolls or duties was felt greatly by the poorer classes and was also responsible for enhancing the price of commodities. Nonetheless, he, too, believed that special legislation was unnecessary.[109]

Another factor contributing to the events of 1921–22 unfolding in the bazaar was the fundamental dynamic of the local marketing system, which defined the local community. Both the colonial state and the landholders understood and exploited this dynamic. It was this very structure and functioning that enabled the people of the localities of Katia and Bhorey to organize as a community and to identify their targets: the colonial state and the great estate of Hathwa.

Moreover, the forging of a community based on the networks of the local marketing system was an emerging pattern in the late nineteenth century. This mobilization of a "a shared sense of community,"[110] documented as well for other parts of north India, is evident in the Cow Protection Movement of the late nineteenth century. My previous study of the movement in Saran focuses on the 1893 Basantpur "riot" to show that this event turned out a crowd—drawn largely from the standard marketing area of Basantpur—who took up the cause of cow protection and rioted over the issue of cow killing. Not only did the market at Basantpur provide the opportunity to organize a crowd—the riot occurred on a Wednesday, a marketing day, when the presence of large numbers of people would go unremarked—but it also provided the community itself. A standard market, Basantpur was the "only market of any importance in this elaka (locality)."[111]

---

108. "Resolution," Jdcl. Dept., GOB, Police, June 27, 1873, Bengal Police Procs., 1873–74, June 1873, 118.

109. "Abstract from Commissioners' Replies"; ibid.

110. Freitag, *Collective Action and Community*, p. 96.

111. Basantpur, Basantpur *thana* no. 358, SVN; A. Forbes, Commr., Patna, to Chief Secy., GOB, Oct. 27, 1893, L/P&J/6/365, no. 257, encl. 7. The following analysis of the Basantpur riot draws on my "Sacred Symbol and Sacred Space in Rural India: Community Mobilization in the 'Anti-Cow Killing' Riot of 1893," *CSSH* 22 (1980): 576–96.

The settlement of Basantpur in 1893 had approximately sixteen hundred inhabitants who were engaged principally in trade and only nominally in cultivation. More than 50 percent of its population—consisting of Madhesia Kandus (31 percent), Kalwars (11), Telis (5), Rauniars (4), Rastogis (2), Buruwars (1), and Sonars (0.5)—can be identified as traders. In addition some nonresident Sonars also kept shops there. Of the remaining residents, many had small shops or worked as artisans: Turhas (4 percent) were vegetable growers and sellers, Barais (2) were betel leaf growers and sellers, Lohars (1) were blacksmiths, Darzis (2) were tailors, and Jolahas (2) were cotton weavers. The Rastogis, Rauniars, Buruwars, Kalwars, and Madhesia Kandus were "the principal trading class." Madhesia Kandus traded in various agricultural goods, including grain and spices. The latter item was also the specialty of Buruwars; Rastogis were the major cloth merchants.

Basantpur was a collection and distribution point that received the grains, spices, vegetables, and other agricultural produce from many villages in the locality. Sujad Hossein, for example, went there every harvest to sell some of the ten to fifteen maunds of grain he produced. Basantpur was also the distribution point for grain from outside of the district that made its way there via such higher-level markets as Siwan, Mairwa, and Maharajganj. Cloth, the other major import, was purchased wholesale from Calcutta—another example of the direct trade links forged to standard markets instead of connections via higher-order markets.

Several service functions were also clustered in Basantpur. In 1871 it had become the headquarters of a *thana* that assumed its name. Along with a police station, it also supported a dispensary and an inspection bungalow. The opening of a subregistry office in December 1892 lent it further administrative importance. Such services established Basantpur not only as a center for filling many needs of the locality but also as a magnet for people like Khub Narain, who moved there to take up the profession of writing documents for people who wished to register them.[112]

The marketing center of Basantpur included in its orbit at least forty-four villages, giving it a total population of over ten thousand people. Since our sources identify only the market used most frequently,

---

112. Basantpur *thana* no. 358, SVN; "Trial of the Basantpur Riot Case in the Court of the Sessions Judge of Saran, 1893," with L/P&J/6/370, 1894, no. 560.

they often do not note the fact that most villagers relied on more than one market, certainly more than their neighborhood *haat*. Therefore, for many villages in the vicinity of Basantpur the only information offered is that they focused on this or that minor market. Yet as the data suggest, as in the case of Babhanauli, its residents frequented the *haat* of Khawaspur but also went to Basantpur to make "larger purchases," for *haats* that were in its marketing area were comparable neither in size nor in the range of goods offered. Bala, for instance, provided vegetables and rice, but it was a "small bazaar . . . [and] cloth shops seldom opened here."[113]

The villages considered "most guilty" in the riot lay within the standard marketing area of Basantpur. To the north were seven villages along the Salempur Ghat road; their inhabitants had participated in all the incidents beginning with the mass meeting of the Gaurakshini Sabha, which preceded the riot at Basantpur. The ringleaders were from these villages: Lakhnowrah, Narharpur, Bala, Shampur, Khawaspur, Basawan, and Madarpur. Two other clusters of "guilty" villages lay immediately to the west and northwest of Basantpur. One of these was almost adjacent to the market, the other a little removed. Only the fourth cluster of villages lay outside the immediate marketing area of Basantpur: it was nested in the intermediate marketing area of Maharajganj, which served as a major conduit of grain and other goods for various markets, including Basantpur.

The faces in the crowd can also be traced to Basantpur and its marketing locality. The seven principals accused in the riot case were residents of Lakhnowrah, Narharpur, Shampur, Bala, and Madarpur—"men of influence in the neighbourhood," or, as the local police inspector addressed them, "you are the raises of the district, respectable men."[114] They were either resident zamindars or petty officials of their villages, in two cases they were both landholders and cloth merchants in Basantpur. That witnesses easily identified members of the crowd is testimony not only to its distinguished composition but also to the fact that participants and bystanders alike were drawn from the "neighborhood" defined by the marketing system.

These social dimensions of Basantpur's marketing area were repeatedly alluded to at the trial. Time and again local residents appearing as

---

113. Khawaspur, Basantpur, and Bala, Basantpur *thana* nos. 319, 358 and 59, SVN.
114. Testimony of Ali Hossein, constable, "Basantpur Trial," p. 51; *SDG 1908*, p. 99.

witnesses explained they knew this or that person "by name as well as by their features." What they meant by this is that both acquaintances and friendships were delimited by the marketing area of a locality. One local inhabitant named Sujad Hossein explained that he and Rahmat Ali lived in the same village but were not good friends. Occasionally when they met they would walk together, as they did on the day of the Basantpur riot. The latter put it more directly when he followed his nonfriend's testimony: "There is no dosti [friendship] between me and the last witness.... We never go to the bazar [sic] together."[115] Similarly Bindeshri Prasad pointed to the dynamics of the marketing networks in explaining his ability to identify one of the accused: "I came to know him in the ordinary way, having seen him coming and going about not in any particular manner.... I came to know him well during the last eight or nine months. I have seen him going to and coming from the market, and that is how I came to know him. When a person comes to a place, he does not get acquainted with all the people there at once. I asked him his name, and he told me. We were going along the road when I asked him his name."[116]

In short, the locus of the Basantpur riot was the standard marketing community, and leadership, whether at the local Cow Protection Movement meeting or at the head of the crowd, was comprised of men who were the influential figures within this area. They were the supporters of the movement and played the primary role in the collective action. These petty *maliks* and substantial *raiyats* operating at the level of the standard marketing area were thus the key to control and conflict in local society.

A similar investigation of the Katia and Bhorey incidents again turns up a local community defined by its markets. According to a lead furnished by police reports, the principal activists involved in the various incidents were supplied by thirty-eight "guilty villages." Ten of these villages can be identified incontrovertibly as belonging to the standard marketing area of Katia, six to that of Bhorey, and the remaining twenty-two, by virtue of their location and relation to their periodic markets, can be tied to the marketing areas of one or the other.[117]

115. "Basantpur Trial," pp. 21, 54.
116. Ibid., p. 57.
117. Dundas to Secy., no. 244-I.G. 22, June 7, 1922, B & O Police Procs., June 1922, no. 50. Mirganj's notes were compiled in 1916–17 by, among others, P. T. Mansfield, who was later the Sitamarhi subdivisional officer during the period of Noncooperation. See Mirganj *thana* village notes, nos. 1–1064, 11 volumes, esp. Katia village, Mirganj *thana* no. 446, SVN. Sixty-nine is probably a low number, because my information is

Important enough to justify the stationing of a police *thana,* which became the target of several attacks during the period of "lawlessness," the standard marketing center of Katia constituted, according to its village note of 1917, a "big market" whose "advantage" was taken "by numerous villages." By my reckoning, its "advantage" extended to an area whose farthest limits were four or even five miles away—precisely the zone within which many of the remaining twenty-two villages were located—although its immediate and regular customers came from a cluster of sixty-nine villages within about a three-mile radius. Ten of the so-called guilty villages can be placed squarely within this area.[118]

Bhorey, the other focal point of the incidents of 1921–22, was also a "big village," its five hamlets of some 350 households rounded out to a total population of seventeen hundred people. As in the case of Katia, its significance as a nodal point was recognized in the late nineteenth century by the establishment of a police station and a dispensary there. Six "guilty villages" were situated within its marketing area encompassing a total of twenty-seven villages largely within a two-mile radius.[119]

Virtually all of the remaining twenty-two villages said to be infected with "a spirit of lawlessness" can be traced to the gravitational field of Katia or Bhorey or tied to them through links to the minor markets clustered around them. The evidence for the "guilty" village of Kurthia (*thana* no. 199) is irrefutable: its village note indicates that its people frequented both the Katia and Bhorey markets, each of which lay at a distance of about four miles. A link can also be established for Deuria (no. 413), the scene of a "sensational case" involving a woman who was paraded around naked and blackened, as well as for the villages of Shamdas Bagahi (no. 410) and Ram Das Bagahi (no. 392), from which people turned out in great numbers to riot against the police sent in to investigate the case. Although all three of these villages, as well as the four neighboring "guilty" villages Dharmagta (no. 412), Indarpatti (no. 429), Semaria (no. 431), and Rupi Bagahi (no. 433), are not specifically identified in the village notes as being within the marketing area of Katia, they clearly formed part of the wider area serviced by

---

drawn only from Saran; it does not take into account those people who frequented markets in neighboring Gorakhpur.

118. Mirganj *thana* village notes, esp. nos. 1–500. Village notes generally report the primary or "minor" market used, not secondary ones, and not typically the higher-order markets that people resorted to for larger purchases.

119. Mirganj village notes, esp. Bhorey village, Mirganj *thana* no. 230, SVN.

Katia, a standard market. Furthermore, Deuria, Semaria, and Rupi Bagahi can be distinctly placed in the minor marketing area of Indarpatti; the remaining three of the seven "guilty" villages can be clustered together as well because Ram Das Bagahi and Dharmagta belonged to the marketing area of Shamdas Bagahi. Whereas Shamdas Bagahi was a minor market of some note—its market yielded fees of Rs. 135 per annum—Indarpatti was a smaller *haat* earning a meager income of only Rs. 6 a year, and, whereas the former counted twenty-four villages in its marketing area, the latter included only twelve. Shamdas Bagahi was a place for purchasing local necessities—grain, salt, tobacco, vegetables, and meat. All transactions were retail, and sellers were sometimes both *banias* (professional shopkeepers) and cultivators, although this latter group primarily sold its grain to the *banias*. Indarpatti was a market of a different scale: its trade focused primarily on salt, tobacco, and vegetables and did not, as its village note reveals, deal in grain. The proximity and the different capacities of these markets meant that their constituencies overlapped considerably. Moreover, the markets operated on different schedules. Shamdas Bagahi convened on Tuesday and Friday, Indarpatti on Tuesday and Saturday. Furthermore, both of these overlapped with yet another periodic market in the vicinity: the "minor" market of Jamunha (no. 424), which had an income closer to that of Shamdas Bagahi than to that of Indarpatti because it, too, was largely a grain market. Jamunha's marketing days were on Wednesday and Sunday, meaning that people could, if they wanted to, frequent all three markets.[120]

These three areas were all tied to Katia, which was literally the focal point of the locality because the district roads converged on it. The inhabitants of Pakarian (no. 477), for instance, could frequent their local *haat* for everyday necessities but go to Katia for "bigger purchases." Whereas Shamdas Bagahi, Indarpatti, and Jamunha offered their customers grain and other foodstuffs, Katia offered much more, a volume and a range suggested by its annual lease amounting to Rs. 790, or almost six times the income of Shamdas Bagahi, and by its population of 1,842, or almost five times that of Shamdas Bagahi and nine times that of Jamunha. Another index of difference in scale is the number of people engaged in trade. Indarpatti had four houses of *banias,* Jamunha

120. Jamunha market counted another two "guilty" villages (Natwa (no. 527) and Chhitauna (no. 404)) in its marketing zone. The income from the *haat* and *nimaksayer* (salt cess) totaled Rs. 82. *SDG 1930,* p. 177.

had ten, and Shamdas Bagahi four. By contrast, Katia, boasted a range of trading castes: eight houses of Umuar Banias, twelve of Banna Banias, three of Kasarwani Banias, seven of Agrahris, twenty-seven of Kalwars, and one of Marwaris. These groups provided many of the market's cloth vendors and moneylenders. The difference between minor markets and intermediate markets can also be gauged from the castes involved in other service occupations. Shamdas Bagahi had six Churihar families who made bangles for the local market, Jamunha had one toddy vendor, and Indarpatti had four Churihars and one tailor. Contrast these totals with that of Katia, which numbered one confectioner, three tailors, six dyers, and three bangle makers. Local labor was also abundant in Katia.[121]

Katia and Bhorey were also home to service facilities developed there in the late nineteenth century. In the early 1870s Katia became the site of one of the district's ten middle vernacular schools. Subsequently, the Hathwa raj established a primary school there and another one at Bhorey. Furthermore, both of these marketing settlements were singled out administratively to become the sites of police outposts, two of the twenty-eight police stations scattered across the district. Bhorey was also one of six places in the district that had a medical dispensary, a facility maintained and supported by Hathwa.[122]

Government and Hathwa connections to these two standard markets therefore explain why they became significant sites of conflict and why the incidents occurring there mobilized such large numbers of people. In the aftermath of the "sensational" Deuria incident, the investigating police force was confronted by a crowd of two thousand men. Most of these were identified as hailing from thirteen villages, Shamdas Bagahi (no. 410), Ramdas Bagahi (no. 392), Rupi Bagahi (no. 433, identified in the government records as Bagahi Bindoe), Deuria (no. 413), Indarpatti (no. 429), Patkhauli (no. 171), Belwa Dube (no. 180), Dharmagta (no. 412), Natwa (no. 527), Semaria (no. 431), Motipur (no. 494), Gaura (no. 468), and Chhitauna (no. 404). These villages were inhabited by a total population of more than six thousand. All,

---

121. Compiled from Mirganj *thana* village notes, SVN.

122. "Management of Hutwa during 1873–74"; AGRPD 1876–77 and 1877–78; *SDG 1930*, p. 120; "Report on Progress of Education in Saran for 1871/72," J. S. Drummond, Offg. Colltr., no. 95, June 1, 1872, P.C. Loose Uncataloged Basta; Mahomed Jan, Subinspector, Schools, Siwan to SDO, Siwan, Apr. 10, 1873, P.C. Basta no. 221, Important Bundles, Rev. Dept., C, D & E. The population of Katia was estimated to be 1,250, that of Bhorey, 900.

except for Natwa (no. 527) and Gaura (no. 468), were part of the periodic marketing system of Indarpatti or Shamdas Bagahi, and all thirteen were in the standard marketing area of Katia.

The structure of the market can also be identified in the April 1922 attack on the Katia police station. Most of the offenders were identified residents of Ijra (no. 203), Bari Sujawal (no. 202), Panan Khas (no. 200), Banian Chhapar (no. 197), Sonhnaria (no. 192), Baikunthpur (no. 189), and Dumrauna (no. 75). These seven villages had a total population of 1,770 and were located within three or four miles of Katia, that is, within its standard marketing area.[123]

The relationship between numbers and the dynamics of the local marketing system is clear. Consider again the details for Saran. Periodicity, a defining characteristic of *haats,* encouraged the people of a locality to congregate only on days set aside for exchange: local leaders capitalized on this fact in their efforts to mobilize numbers. The overwhelming number of markets followed this periodic pattern, the exceptions being Chapra and some of the intermediate markets. Indeed, only larger markets met daily. According to one source, 88.3 percent of the district's markets met twice a week; of the rest, 7.1 percent convened triweekly, 3.6 percent once a week, and .9 percent four times a week. There is considerable correlation between frequency, size, and importance. While *haats* and standard markets typically followed biweekly schedules, markets convening only once a week were among the smallest of periodic markets. For instance, the Friday *haat* of Chakla was "small" (Siwan no. 163), that of Gosain Chapra (Siwan no. 343), also a Friday market, was a "very poor bazaar," and that of Bhelpur (Siwan no. 499), a Sunday market, was only for selling paddy and other grains. The intermediate market of Manjhi was held five days a week; and the three markets—Garkha, Paighambarpur, and Harpur—open four days a week were among the district's larger standard markets.[124]

123. Suptd. to I.G., no. 3168, May 8, 1922, B & O Police Procs., June 1922; Mirganj *thana* village notes, nos. 101–600, SVN.

124. Wyatt, *Statistics of Sarun; SDG 1930,* Table 5, pp. 162–77. Fridays (16 percent) and Mondays (14.8 percent) were the most popular market days, with Saturdays (14.3), Wednesdays (14.1), Tuesdays (13.8), Sundays (13.4), and Thursdays (13.2) following closely behind. There is little here to suggest that marketing days were synchronized to the religious calendar, because Tuesday, considered the holy day of the week in the Bhojpur region, was not a day avoided. For information regarding this tradition I am indebted to Bradley Hertel, personal communication.

Moreover, this had been the pattern throughout the colonial period. According to an early-nineteenth-century source that listed the marketing periodicity for twenty-four markets (most of which were standard markets), the lower-order markets generally convened twice a week. Mirganj, an intermediate market, is described by the same account as meeting daily, whereas Darauli, Manjhi, and Gopalganj met biweekly. Over time, however, these last three markets developed into standing bazaars, following a well-known pattern of adding marketing days to settlements that become more central and complex marketing nodes. The configuration of markets in the district reveals that this transformation was more the exception than the rule, however. More typically, the enhanced demand created by population increases was accommodated by the substantial rise in number of biweekly *haats*.[125]

Periodicity—especially the two-day schedule—was a standard feature of Saran's markets because that was sufficient to meet local demand, even of large numbers of people. The marketing needs of peasants in a subsistence economy were simply limited. Furthermore, poor transportation and communications infrastructure of the eighteenth and at least the first half of the nineteenth century probably meant that most markets served limited geographical areas. Even in the early twentieth century most buyers and sellers frequented markets within a four-to-six-mile radius, a distance most people could comfortably travel back and forth over in a day. Thus, periodicity went hand in glove with dense market distribution, both serving to reduce the "friction of space and time" in the local society. Markets in the same locality therefore almost always met on different days of the week; for instance, Mangarpal Nuran's *haat* convened on Thursdays and Sundays, whereas Mangalpal Murtuza's met on Wednesdays and Saturdays.[126]

This system enabled most villagers to use multiple markets. Residents of Sheikhpura, Dumouma, Durgauli, Jajauli, Bahuara, and Bishunpura, for instance, frequented several markets within a three-mile radius: the *haats* of Deoria, Maghar, and Bilashpur for routine transactions and the standard market of Mashrak for a wider range of goods and services. Access to multiple markets also served the interests of

125. Wyatt, *Statistics of Sarun*, pp. 3–12; *SDG 1930*, pp. 162–77.
126. Mangarpal Nuran and Mangalpal Murtuza, Parsa *thana* nos. 543 and 559, SVN. See also Skinner, "Marketing in China," pp. 10–11; Robert H. T. Smith, "Periodic Market-places, Periodic Marketing, and Travelling Traders," in *Periodic Markets, Hawkers, and Traders in Africa, Asia, and Latin America*, ed. Robert H. T. Smith (Vancouver: Centre for Transportation Studies, 1978), pp. 114–20.

peasants who were producers and sellers of their surplus agricultural commodities or those who engaged in artisanal industries.[127]

Periodicity was much less "related to the mobility of individual 'firms.'" Unlike in China, where the "itinerant entrepreneur" was a characteristic feature of rural markets, periodicity therefore fulfilling the valuable function of "concentrating the demand for his product at restricted localities on certain specific days . . . [so that] he can arrange to be in each town in the circuit on its market day," the typical shop-keeper or trader in Saran was a local—if not of the marketing settle-ment itself then of a nearby village. Thus, many of the shopkeepers in the periodic market of Jano were drawn from its 1,443 residents; oth-ers came from the outside, such as the three Dhunia families from neighboring Bhabri village who were involved in cotton and rice trade, another Dhunia family who dealt in horses and ponies, and a Kandhu who maintained a tobacco store.[128]

Markets therefore attracted large numbers of people. As the average figures for Mirganj *thana* (in which Katia and Bhorey were located) in-dicate, even periodic markets had the possibility of reaching several thousand; there was typically a *haat* for every 7,319 people. Such num-bers were the reason why the "volunteers" of Noncooperation invari-ably made the rounds of the marketplaces, big and small. In the small markets of Muzaffarpur, audiences numbering between 1,000 and 2,000 were commonplace: 2,000 at Rasulpur on April 3, 1,000 at Pupri on August 1, and 2,000 at Sursand on the same day. On three occasions, crowds at Sursand numbered 1,500, 2,000, and even 3,000. Not sur-prisingly, the largest gatherings were in the town of Sitamarhi: Mahanth Sia Ram Das drew 5,000 in April 1921, and Ramanandan Singh, an-other local leader, attracted an even larger gathering of 6,000 in Febru-ary of the same year. But the biggest assembly by far was in Sitamarhi, on April 6, the day of the *hartal*, which featured a procession of 15–20,000 marchers. No wonder "volunteers" such as Mathura Prasad Dikshit had restraining orders placed on them barring them "from

127. E.g., Andhar Bari, Mashrak *thana* no. 264, whose villagers used Chainpur and Taraiya for buying and selling. Also Sheikhpura, Dumouma, Durgauli, Jajauli, Bahuara, and Bishunpura, Mashrak *thana* nos. 80–85, SVN.
128. Bhabri and Jano, Basantpur *thana* nos. 2 and 3, SVN; Skinner, "Marketing in China," p. 10. Jajmani arrangements, involving well-to-do and artisan and service caste people in patron-client relationships, presumably also reduced the need for outside entre-preneurs.

speaking in any bazar [*sic*] ... [where] in the opinion of the magistrate
... speeches are likely to lead to a breach of the peace."[129]

The men and women who typically converged on a local market generally enjoyed some level of *dosti* (friendship) or familiarity with one another. For many the bazaar was a place for both "commerce and festivity." It was a "social as well as an economic nexus. It was the place," in India, as in eighteenth-century Britain or France, "where one-hundred-and-one social and personal transactions went on; where news was passed, rumour and gossip flew around.... [It] was the place where people, because they were numerous felt for a moment they were strong."[130] And as places where people routinely gathered in large numbers to traffic in social, cultural, and economic exchanges, they naturally attracted government attention. In other words, market towns typically doubled as administrative centers, where the functionaries of the colonial state regularly established their district and subdistrict headquarters. How appropriate therefore that a movement that sought to keep categories—patriotic Indians and alien rulers and their coadjutors—"separate and opposed" was played out largely in the bazaar.

The hybrid quality of the bazaar also surfaced in the ways in which its crowds were linked to "festivity," to popular culture. For the movement consistently sought to mobilize people to join its cause through a variety of activities. In addition to the rhetoric, with its popular vocabulary and cadences, there were the participatory rituals of celebrations employed to involve crowds another means. The recitation of the Delhi *fatwa* was a collective chanting, as was the practice of "non-cooperators in the streets and bazaars singing national songs in chorus."[131] Processions, such as on *hartal*-day in Sitamarhi, when everyone carried pictures of Gandhi and other nationalist leaders "garlanded with flowers," provided another vehicle for people to define themselves as a community.

Arrayed against this imagined community was the colonial state and its administrators and coadjutors, an "us and them" distinction vividly played out in popular demonstrations combining theatrics with crowd

129. *Searchlight*, Feb. 2, 1921; Commr., Tirhut, to I.G., no. J-1987, May 22, 1922, B & O Police Procs., June 1922, no. 50.

130. E. P. Thompson, "The Moral Economy of the English Crowd in the Eighteenth Century," *Past and Present* 50 (1971): 135.

131. Suptd. to Commr., Nov. 28, 1921 B & O Police Procs., May 1922, no. 1, enclosure.

participation. Two entries from a police report offer a glimpse of such occasions, though without conveying any sense of the mood or spirit of the gathering: "On 30th July 1921 the non-co-operator volunteers dressed up a bamboo with a hat, coat, etc., like an European in the Sitamarhi Hat—all had pot-shots at it, who cared to. . . . On 30th September 1921, Bishun Mahtha, Luchman Mahtha and Ram Lakhan Gupta dressed up a figure like a European, sitting on a chair which the crowd spat on, pulled its ear and eventually burnt it on a bonfire."[132]

Both the sense of the crowd in the bazaar and its awareness of the hybrid and separative quality of the market figured in the many incidents involving attempts to enforce the code of Noncooperation among the local population. At its most concrete level, this aspect of the bazaar was played up in crowd efforts to prevent customers from patronizing "liquor and other excise shops, and snatching away their purchase." After all, two objectives of Noncooperation was to stop the distribution of goods considered anathema to the nationalist project and to deny goods and services to functionaries of the colonial state. The bazaar was necessarily targeted because it was the place where foreign-made cloth and liquor, to name two of the principal goods singled out for attack, exchanged hands. Volunteers therefore urged their supporters to picket cloth and liquor shops. Not surprisingly, much of the crowd action in the markets involved attempts to close down such shops or attack people who indulged in these taboo products. The report by the Muzaffarpur police that foreign cloth "is being burnt all over the place and each toddy, cloth, liquor and ganja shop has its picket of national volunteers" and that "bullock carts carrying drums of liquor are stopped, people entering excise shops are assaulted" was a scenario repeated time and again throughout the region. Another product-related issue was the effort to prevent goods and services from the bazaar flowing into the hands of the functionaries of the "evil" Empire. "Volunteers are endeavouring," as one confidential government document noted, "to induce bazaar people to stop all supplies to the police."[133]

The bazaar was also the place where people assembled in numbers and exerted their strength and unity of purpose in actions that were liter-

132. Ibid. Plays were also staged in Bagaha ridiculing government officials and Europeans.
133. *Non-cooperation in Bihar,* pp. 39, 45, and 45–47, for similar incidents elsewhere in the region; Suptd. to Commr., Nov. 28, 1921, B & O Police Procs., May 1922, no. 1, enclosure.

ally and figuratively designed to humiliate wrongdoers, actions that were charivaris. In the wake of the "sensational" Deuria case of February 1921, when the "exponents of non-violence painted a woman black and took her naked round [the] village," the investigating police subinspector "was attacked by about 2,000 men and he and his force were beaten and put to flight. As a result 56 men were prosecuted and 33 convicted."[134]

This woman had apparently incurred the wrath of the crowd because she had violated the discipline of Noncooperation—her initial "wrong" was to refuse to pay a fine levied on her by a council (*panchayat*) set up to enforce the code of Noncooperation—and then filed a case with police.[135] Much more typical, however, were cases of offenders apprehended in flagrante delicto and promptly handed out rough justice. Gope Kahar was seized by his fellow Kahars and other townspeople for refusing to give up drinking and paraded around town in black face. The crowd handled most offenders in this manner. For having imbibed liquor at a *haat*, a person "had his face smeared with blacking [and] a shoe hung round his neck." Numerous were the incidents involving "violators" who were paraded around the town or marketplace "mounted backwards on a donkey." A variation of this form of humiliation—in this case the offender's head was shaved prior to the ritual parading—was inflicted on a *chaukidar* in Champaran for having consumed liquor.[136]

Official reports tended to attribute outbreaks to outside agitators. The comings and goings of Gandhi were scrupulously monitored as were those of other leaders such as Rajendra Prasad, the leading Congress figure in Bihar. In addition, there were always the usual suspects at the district level. Bindeshri Prasad, for example, was said to be "the leading Saran non-cooperator," and his movements were invariably linked to incidents of Noncooperation.[137]

The overwhelming majority of participants in the events associated with Noncooperation were drawn from the local population, however.

134. Perkin to I.G., no. 3168, May 8, 1922, ibid., July, no. 50. See also Natalie Zemon Davis, *Society and Culture in Early Modern France* (Stanford: Stanford University Press, 1975), pp. 97–123, for an excellent discussion of charivaris, "a noisy, masked demonstration to humiliate some wrongdoer in the community."

135. *Non-cooperation in Bihar,* p. 232; Nagendra Kumar, *Indian National Movement (with Special Reference to the District of Old Saran, Bihar) 1857–1947* (Patna: Janaki Prakashan, 1979), p. 40.

136. *Non-cooperation in Bihar,* pp. 42–43, 45, 67–68; *Speeches,* pp. 40–41.

137. Perkin to Personal Asst., no. 3168, May 8, 1922, B & O Police Procs., June 1922, no. 50; Kumar, *Indian National Movement,* pp. 36–61.

As many as two thousand people "armed with lathis [staffs], spears, etc." were said to be involved in the attack on the police who came to investigate the "sensational" Katia case. Of the fifty-seven men (one died later in jail) singled out for prosecution from this "mob," the largest numbers were Koeris (seventeen people), Brahmins (fourteen), Bhumihar Brahmins (nine), Jolahas (six), and Ahirs (five); the rest were Banias (two), Bhar (one), Nonia (one), Teli (one), and one whose caste cannot be identified from his name. One can glean additional details regarding these people by looking at the locality from which the crowd originated. Both those singled out by name for being the "leading" noncooperators (that is, thirty-two out of the fifty-seven who were actually sentenced) and those comprising the so-called volunteer masses were drawn from thirteen villages clustered around the market of Katia. The village notes of 1915–21 reveal that Brahmins were the dominant caste in six villages; in three villages they were the most prominent caste along with the Bhumihar Brahmins. No upper castes resided in the remaining four villages; Koeris were the most prosperous caste in those places, some among them prosperous enough to serve as the village moneylenders. Brahmins were also the most prominent inhabitants of the seven villages that manned the ranks of attackers of the Katia police station on April 26, 1922. In six of the seven villages they were the dominant caste; in the remaining village Rajputs were the most salient caste. In four out of the seven villages, Ahirs were numerically preponderant.[138]

Similar configurations of supravillage elite—mostly upper-caste men with significant standing in the locality of periodic markets—and the more prosperous cultivating castes, such as Koeris, Kurmis, and Ahirs, can be identified among the principals involved in clashes over markets in Champaran. Acchey Lal and Mathura Prasad, two Kayasths, were at the forefront of the group that sought to establish a market to compete with Ghorasahan bazaar, controlled by the Purnahi factory, a branch of the Motihari indigo concern. And implicated with them were a few other people of high caste but also many with trading and agricultural caste backgrounds.[139]

138. Mirganj *thana* nos. 75, 189, 192, 197, 200, 202, and 203. Also nos. 171, 180, 392, 404, 410, 412, 413, 429, 431, 433, 468, 494, and 527 for the other thirteen "guilty" Mirganj villages, SVN; Perkin to Personal I.G., no. 3168, May 8, 1922, B & O Police Procs., June 1922, no. 50

139. Caste identifications drawn up from names of people charged in these cases. *Non-Cooperation in Bihar*, pp. 224–25; *Searchlight*, Nov. 23, 1921. See also *District*

An alliance of upper landholding and substantial peasant castes and lower-caste peasants also characterized the "Hindu community" that took up the cause of cow protection in the 1890s and the second decade of the twentieth century in the Bhojpur region extending across Bihar into eastern United Provinces. In the late nineteenth century these groups had also become conspicuous presence "on the road," thus adding to the growing traffic of pilgrims and mela-goers. Whereas they sought to team up with Muslims under the flag of Noncooperation and Khilafat in the 1920s, here they mobilized against the small local Muslim population in the name of saving the cow. Within the "Hindu community" itself, however, there were divisions. As Gyan Pandey notes, "In the 1910s and '20s . . . when the Koeris, Kurmis and Ahirs became better organized and increasingly militant in pressing the demands for a more respectable status[,] the upper-caste Hindu zamindars joined hands with the upper-caste Muslim zamindars of the region to keep these 'upstart' peasant castes in their place. . . . That divide between upper and lower castes and classes, and the strife attendant upon it, remained the predominant feature of the rural political scene in eastern U.P. and Bihar, more marked than any perceptible rift between local Hindus and Muslims, at least until the 1940s."[140]

Indeed, upper-caste and some cultivating lower-caste groups (in the incidents referred to here consisting principally of Brahmins, Bhumihar Brahmins, and Rajputs on the one hand and Kurmis and Ahirs on the other hand) were increasingly asserting their rising power and influence at the local periodic market and village level, often assuming leadership roles in challenging the authority of the colonial state or the local magnate. In many areas, these groups were joined by petty traders and moneylenders—many of whom were drawn from precisely these groups—who were prominently featured in the Noncooperation Movement; they could be found on both sides of the struggle.[141] How these groups emerged from the age of revolution to attain featured roles in the "rural political scene" of the early twentieth century forms the focus of the next chapter.

Census Reports, 1891, Patna Division, Champaran (1898), p. 97, regarding the prominence of Kayasths in the district as a landholding and prosperous tenant group.

140. *Construction of Communalism in India*, p. 200.

141. In the market of Bagaha, Marwaris instituted a complaint against local Noncooperation leaders. Notes by McNamara, with no. 7956A, Nov. 23, 1921, B & O Police Procs., June 1921, no. 3, enclosure.

CHAPTER 5

Traders, Merchants, and Markets

1765–1947

Notwithstanding the "ruin" and "discontent" that the historian Ghulam Husain and his contemporaries perceived at the outset of colonial rule in the late eighteenth century and notwithstanding their observations regarding the absence of "commercial capital" and "sellers" and "buyers," trade and banking flourished not only in the city of Patna but also in the region of Bihar. Indeed, bankers continued to thrive in the initial phase of colonial rule; they were central to the political intrigues of the age of revolution that the Patna historian chronicled during the waning days of the Mughal Empire and its successor states. Although their political salience declined with the establishment of Pax Britannica, bankers or "trader-bankers," to use C. A. Bayly's phrase, played a critical role because the emerging colonial state relied on them "not merely to underpin its residual trading operations but to finance its administration and, in a sense, to guarantee the whole land-revenue system."[1]

Half a century after the heyday of revolution, Enugula Veeraswamy set out on the road from Madras to Kashi under the sign of colonialism and encountered Marwari traders in many of the bazaars where he stopped to provision his entourage. This is firsthand evidence of the po-

---

1. *Indian Society and British Empire*, chap. 2.

sition that Marwaris had already attained and were consolidating, as new waves of their brethren swelled their ranks following their now well-documented migration into north India in the early nineteenth century. Veeraswamy's journey also led him to Gaya, where he encountered Raja Mitarjit of Tikari, whose wealth and status confirmed the trend that the Patna historian had anticipated in the age of revolution, when he wrote of the "overgrowing power of the Zemindars, and ... their being trusted too much" by the then-emerging colonial government.[2]

By 1921–22, when Mahatma Gandhi launched his Noncooperation Movement, including the boycott of foreign cloth, *bania* groups such as the Marwaris and Aggarwals were very much in the limelight because they monopolized its trade in the higher-order markets of Bihar. Among the so-called ringleaders was a Ramnath Marwari of Sursand, who was charged with rioting in Muzaffarpur in 1921. There was also Bilas Ram Marwari of Sitamarhi, who was singled out by the local authorities for being "a very loyal citizen and an Honorary Magistrate" and therefore deserving of exemption from the punitive assessments levied on areas active in the Noncooperation Movement.[3]

We have then three snapshots of the major actors involved in bazaars in north India at different moments in the colonial era. By treading the historical path fashioned by the late-eighteenth-century Patna historian Ghulam Husain, by the early-nineteenth-century pilgrim Enugula Veeraswamy, and by the crowds of 1921–22 who converged on the bazaars of north Bihar in the name of Gandhi, this chapter enters the world of traders and merchants in the colonial period. How they fared in the region between the late-eighteenth-century age of revolution and the early twentieth century is a focus of this chapter. By concentrating on the principal agents of exchange—traders, merchants, and peasants—I intend to trace their changing fortunes over the course of the *longue durée* of colonial rule. I will focus in particular on the trade in agricultural commodities to delineate the increasing salience of two groups in the local and regional marketing system: the better-off peasants (or "rich peasants" or "amateurs," as they are also called) and trading castes (or "professionals," as one source referred to them to dis-

---

2. Veeraswamy, *Journal*, pp. 144–45.
3. Wilson to Commr., Nov. 28, 1921, and T. W. Bridge, Magte. to Commr., Tirhut, Mar. 20, 1922, B & O Pol. Procs., 1922, May, no. 1A, enclosure and K Enclosure to no. 18.

tinguish them from the "amateurs" active at the grassroots levels). This chapter also highlights the structure and workings of the larger society and economy as it involved peasants, traders, and merchants.[4]

At the higher reaches of the marketing and trade system (in the city of Patna), as well as at the grassroots level of exchange (in the *haats*), marketing and trade in agricultural and nonagricultural commodities attracted diverse participants. Peasants, traders, and merchants participated in the exchanges that transferred goods from the fields to the marketing centers of the region. By its very nature, in other words, the local marketing system had many points of entry for men of enterprise and means to stake out roles as agents of exchange.

The number of sites at which exchanges were transacted increased dramatically over the course of colonial rule. Almost all of the change occurred at the lowest rung of the marketing system: the *haats* or periodic markets. According to the documentation for Patna district, the number of periodic markets between 1811 and 1911 tripled, jumping from 66 to 209. That was followed by another increase in the twentieth century, when the total rose to 393 by 1951. Detailed evidence for Saran reveals a similar surge: from 138 in 1793 to 323 in 1921. Toward the close of the colonial period, the entire province of Bihar accounted for 2,535 periodic markets—more than 11 percent of the total (19,739) counted for all of British India, excluding the princely states.[5]

The colonial period was also an era of increasing trade. There is a considerable body of local and regional evidence that indicates a general expansion in trade in the late nineteenth century. Microlevel data, such as those compiled by the great estate of Bettiah, suggest that the volume of trade in the 1860s and early 1870s more than doubled. These figures are supported by estimates of the rising proportion of grain marketed over the course of the colonial period. According to a recent study, only 20 percent of the grain produced in the late eighteenth century constituted a "marketable surplus," that is, the produce "available, under

4. Although ostensibly distinct categories, peasants and traders are not mutually exclusive categories. For example, some peasants were also traders and dealers.

5. GOI, *Agricultural Marketing in India: Report on Fairs, Markets and Produce Exchanges in India* (Delhi: GOI Press, 1943), pp. 28, 121. Bengal and U.P. ranked first and second in total number of *haats*. Within Bihar, Muzaffarpur accounted for 415 markets, Champaran 305, Saran 244, Darbhanga 52, Shahabad 116, Gaya 115, and Patna 57. These tallies, however, seem incomplete. They do not match up with figures used in this study that are based on village-by-village data. See also above, chaps. 2 and 4, on markets in Patna and Saran.

normal circumstances, to the merchant for onward distribution."[6] By the early twentieth century that number had risen to 30 percent. A sizable proportion, 70 percent, continued to remain in the locality of production, however, which enabled producers to meet their own consumption needs (accounting for as much as 48 percent), fulfill seed requirements, feed livestock, pay hired labor in kind, and use as barter for other goods.[7] Another estimate calculated that 60 percent of the rice produced was consumed at the point of origination, 29 percent was redistributed in the locality principally through the periodic marketplaces, and 11 percent was sent on to the higher-order markets.[8]

Typically, the outward flow of grain in the first century of colonial rule—in Ghulam Husain's as well as Veeraswamy's time period—began with transactions conducted within the village. The delimited boundaries of this first round of exchange were defined by the nature of the smallholder agricultural system characteristic of much of the subcontinent, a system whereby peasants occupying small plots of land grew multiple crops to minimize the risk of failure. Furthermore, because most peasants worked on an individual (or an individual household) basis, whether involved in the "purchase of seeds, implements, and manure, the borrowing of capital, the processes of cultivation, the harvesting operations," their meager yields of a variety of crops were best disposed of "independently by each cultivator."[9]

Nor was the small volume likely to attract many dealers from without. The first round of exchanges therefore involved primarily peasants and *grihastha beoparis* (literally, householder-traders), petty traders who were generally residents in the villages of the locality. This limited

6. Rajat Datta, "Merchants and Peasants: A Study of the Structure of Local Trade in Grain in Late Eighteenth Century Bengal," *IESHR* 23 (1986): 388; T. M. Gibbon, Manager, Bettiah, to R. P. Jenkins, Commr., Patna, Nov. 8, 1871, Bengal Gen. Procs., 1872, Jan. no. 29. Bettiah figures are based on rents collected at granaries and customs levied at river wharves (ghats). Also Derbyshire, "Economic Change and Railways," p. 533, on "the tremendous expansion in the volume of higher level and long-distance commerce during the period after 1860."

7. GOI, Office of the Agricultural Marketing Adviser, *Agricultural Marketing in India, Report on the Marketing of Rice in India and Burma*, Marketing Series no. 27 (Delhi: GOI Press, 1941), pp. 24–27, 492. These figures, however, conceal the fact that a cultivator "almost invariably retains the coarse inferior varieties for his own use and sells the finer rices which give a better cash return" (p. 27).

8. *Report of the Bihar Banking Committee*, p. 59. North Bihar was more involved in the rice trade than south Bihar. See AGRPD 1875–76.

9. S. A. Husain, *Agricultural Marketing in Northern India* (London: Allen and Unwin, 1937), p. 81. See also H. L. Puxley, *Agricultural Marketing in Agra District* (Calcutta: Longmans, 1936).

circle was also defined by the social and political constraints imposed by the structure of agrarian relations within local society. What set them apart from their fellow villagers was their capacity to gain access to the agricultural surplus of their neighbors through moneylending and purchases. Their dual roles as traders and moneylenders (*mahajans*) were closely intertwined, for moneylending reaped returns in grain.

The moneylending and grain nexus was synchronized to an agricultural calendar that favored the *mahajans*. Moneylenders in Shahabad made advances of money or of grain to cultivators and at harvest time received grain in return. They sold some of this grain wholesale and retained some as capital to be used in future loans in kind. They also purchased the surplus of their locality, generally at harvest time, when prices were at their lowest, and sold it five or six months later, when prices had increased or were at their peak.[10]

The optimum time to buy was in the wake of the autumn and winter harvests (November to January—also a time of melas) when grain was plentiful and therefore cheap. Rice occupied the largest acreage among food crops grown in the region (from 30 to 50 percent of the net cropped area) and was the principal food crop of these two harvests. Other crops reaped during these harvests were maize and millets of one kind or another (*janera, bajra, marua*), which formed the staple food of most ordinary people, and sugarcane and indigo. The last was largely grown by Europeans, and it faded away in the twentieth century. The spring harvest, reaped in March and April, was another good time to buy. Wheat, tobacco, and a variety of oilseeds, all important export items for the region, were harvested at this time. Barley, which, after rice, occupied the second-largest net cropped area (10 to 20 percent), was also reaped in spring. The best time to sell was in the summer months of June to August, when prices were at their highest and when the autumn and winter crops were just being sown. Price differentials between city and countryside could yield additional profits, since prices were invariably higher in the cities and towns.[11]

10. Buchanan, *Shahabad*, p. 431; Kumkum Banerjee, "Grain Traders and the East India Company: Patna and Its Hinterland in the Late Eighteenth and Early Nineteenth Centuries," *IESHR* 23 (1986): 403–29.

11. J. Routledge, Colltr., to Sir John Shore, Oct. 23, 1794, Bengal Rev. Consltns., Grain, Oct. 31 to Dec. 19, 1794, Oct. 31, no. 22; Colltr., Tirhut, to G. H. Barlow, Subsecy., Oct. 25, 1794, M.C. Records, vol. 193, Sept. 30, 1794 to Dec. 14, 1795. See also *MSR*, pp. 131–33, 251–75, regarding harvests and percentage of area cultivated at each of the three harvests.

Grihastha beoparis have appropriately been termed "trading farmers," a designation at once highlighting their role as agents of exchange and emphasizing their roots in village society and economy as "farmers" or peasants. Their position as petty traders was a function of their privileged positions in village society. As the substantial cultivators and tenants of their communities, they were able to carve out roles as *mahajans;* some were small landholders or petty *maliks* (proprietors). Their dominant status was also reinforced by their "official" roles as village headmen, an office held by many of them; it entitled them to act and speak on behalf of their fellow, and usually less well-off, villagers in transactions involving their superordinates, typically the local landholders. In the characterization of one contemporary source, village headmen, or *jeth raiyats* or *muqaddams,* were "wealthy men of some education" or "principal tenant[s]" or "every rich and intelligent farmer."[12]

That the petty trader based in the village was essentially the better-off peasant highlights the restricted scope of transactions at this fundamental level of the peasant marketing system, for much of his dealings entailed purchases and sales made in small lots intended principally to supply the needs of poor peasants or artisans. In the words of one contemporary observer, many of the exchanges in agricultural commodities at this grassroots level of society involved the "mere necessaries of life, consumed at no remote distance from the place of their growth."[13] The profits of such buying and selling enabled traders to clear at least 20 percent on each crop. Nevertheless, they were essentially petty traders, operating in an arena largely confined to their villages of residence or the neighboring localities; and the scale of their business was clearly demarcated by the modest amounts they handled. Their capital was limited, estimated to range from one hundred to two thousand rupees, as were the opportunities for turnover of their stocks, estimated by one source to be no more than twice a year. And expansion, particularly by extending the geographical limits of their trading areas, was hampered by their not having ready access to, or control over, the modes of transportation.[14]

12. Buchanan, *Bihar and Patna*, p. 568; Buchanan, *Shahabad*, p. 350; G. Arbuthnot, Colltr., Tirhut, to J. Neave, Magte., Tirhut, May 31, 1793, M.C. Records, vol. 190, 1793.

13. H. T. Colebrooke, *Remarks on the Present State of the Husbandry and Commerce of Bengal* (Calcutta: n.p., 1795), p. 104. Colebrooke was an assistant collector in Tirhut and Purnia in the 1780s and early 1790s.

14. Buchanan, *Shahabad*, p. 430.

The highly localized nature of these exchanges also explains the conspicuous presence of "trading farmers," for these rich peasants or petty *maliks* were best positioned to parlay their political, social, and economic standing in local society into opportunities for petty trade. And given the restricted geographical and social scope of the transactions, their small-scale trading did not require any degree of specialization. Thus, the nature of the marketing system at the village level both defined and was defined by the "trading farmer."[15]

In the next round of exchanges in the late eighteenth and early nineteenth centuries, "trading carriers"—to use Buchanan's term—figured prominently. Although some "trading farmers" dealt directly with wholesale traders in the higher-order markets by hiring transportation to move their goods, most sold their stock to these "carriers," who were known in the vernacular by various names: *ladu beoparis, ladu banias, ladu baldiya, baldiya beoparis,* or Teli *beoparis.* They were, in other words, traders, engaged in relaying grain and other items collected in the villages by the "trading farmers" to primary markets, the *haats,* or to higher-level markets. They made their purchases at one market and sold at another. They were able to become the primary "carriers" of overland trade because they owned cattle for use as transportation, either as pack animals or hitched to carts. Before the advent of the railways and an extensive network of good roads, their command of the primary means for transporting goods between the hinterland and the major entrepôts along the water highways secured them a vital intermediary role. Some also hired out their cattle, although only infrequently because *grihastha beoparis* tended not to involve themselves directly in the transportation of their goods to higher-order markets. "In the land carriage," as one local administrator noted perceptively, "the carriers are also the principal traders, oftener purchasing at one market to sell at another than hiring carriage to settled merchants."[16]

Ladu beoparis, in short, relied on animal power to reach beyond the confines of the village. As petty dealers, they mostly stationed themselves in the lower-order marketing settlements so as to have easy access to the produce of the countryside, which they then carried to their

---

15. For a similar point, see S. Bhattacharya, "Eastern India," in *Cambridge Economic History of India,* vol. 2, p. 273.

16. Colebrooke, *Commerce of Bengal,* p. 125; Buchanan, *Shahabad,* p. 431; Buchanan, *Bihar and Patna,* pp. 696–97. The etymology of *ladu* and *baldiya* is less clear, although *bal* presumably refers to ox or bullock.

home markets or to higher-order markets. A few used higher-order markets as their collection points: in Shahabad such dealers set up residence in the towns of Arrah and Chainpur and from there they negotiated sales to the cities of Patna and Banaras. *Ladu beoparis* also supplied retailers, typically *banias* in primary markets involved in supplying the general provisions (*khichri farosh*) of a locality, that is, *banias* who sold such everyday items as grain, salt, oil, and an assortment of other goods, including sweets, tobacco, cotton, and drugs.[17]

Like *grihastha beoparis, ladu beoparis* were traders of modest means. A 1773 petition submitted by a number of such *beoparis* against the Patna Custom House for extracting illegal levies from them shows how limited their transactions were: Biju and other *beoparis* complained about a duty of one and one-half pice per bullock load on their consignment of mustard seed; Panu objected to a duty imposed on his four bullocks laden with lac; Tej Chund took issue with the levies put on his five bales of cotton; and Dullah Khan complained about an even smaller amount charged on a parcel of cloth. Their capitals in Shahabad were "trifling . . . except their cattle."[18]

"Besides their oxen," in the estimation of one contemporary observer, *ladu beoparis* had "very little capital, 5 rs. in money being reckoned sufficient to enable a man to trade with one ox. With such a stock it is supposed that he can gain 32 rs. a year, selling 50 rs. worth a month, with a profit of from 1 to 2 annas on the rupee."[19] Although a profit of 6 to 12 percent (that is, one to two annas on a rupee worth sixteen annas) suggests a smaller return than the 20 percent made by "trading farmers" on each crop, and although their activities were seasonal—restricted to a period of the roughly eight months when roads were passable—the opportunities "trading carriers" had for turnover were as much as three to ten times a month, or twenty-four to eighty times during the course of their business year. Furthermore, they incurred few risks, because their transactions required little outlay of capital. Instead their trade was conducted "entirely without advances," their

17. Buchanan, *Shahabad,* pp. 430–31; Buchanan, *Bihar and Patna,* p. 696. The trade in grain and other items carried on by *ladu beoparis* was also known as *kirana.*
18. Buchanan, *Shahabad,* p. 431; H. Revel, Colltr., Customs, Patna, to President, Council, Bengal Rev. Board of Commrs., Customs, Apr. 14 to Dec. 15, 1773, Oct. 20. A pair of bullocks "considered fit for labour" typically cost twenty-five to thirty rupees. See Colltr. to T. Graham, President, Board of Superintendence for the Improvement of Cattle, Apr. 21, 1795, M.C. Records, vol. 193.
19. Buchanan, *Bihar and Patna,* p. 696.

primary responsibility being either to serve as "mere carriers" or to take on the intermediary role themselves by selling the produce of the countryside to merchants and returning from the higher-order markets with other kinds of goods bought from the merchants to be redistributed in the lower-order markets of the hinterland. "Trading carriers" were therefore in a position to earn higher incomes, their capital estimated to range between five hundred and five thousand rupees as contrasted with the one hundred to two thousand rupees documented for "trading farmers." A few, however, far exceeded this range. Some of the most prosperous *ladu beoparis* in Shahabad, based in such key collection points in the hinterland as Sheikhpura, Nawada, and Daudnagar, were estimated to have had fortunes valued as high as twenty thousand rupees.[20]

"Trading farmers" and "trading carriers" stood on roughly comparable ground, however, in their transactions with one another. Although the former depended largely on the latter for the transportation of their goods, *ladu beoparis* were not in a position to use this to build up their profits. On the contrary, because they offered "a very cheap carrying service . . . *grihastha-beparis* and ordinary ryots did not always find it advantageous to carry grain to market."[21]

"Trading carriers," for their part, were at a disadvantage because of the control that *grihastha beoparis* exerted over the agricultural surplus of the countryside. Although cultivators were ostensibly free to grow whatever they wanted and to sell to whomever they chose to sell to, "trading farmers" defined the local marketing system because peasants were typically in debt to them. In other words, as moneylenders (*mahajans*), *grihastha beoparis* generally had prior claims on the crops of their fellow villagers. Most cultivators in the initial century of colonial rule did not venture out on their own to sell their surplus. Instead, throughout the region, petty traders—*grihastha* and *ladu beoparis*—"generally advance[d] for and purchase[d] the produce of the soil for the great marts."[22] Thus the transactions between ordinary cultivators and village-level notables generally comprising the better-off peasantry were conducted under a certain degree of duress and coercion.

The process of indebtedness was typically generated by "trading farmers" advancing money or grain to their fellow villagers, usually the

20. Buchanan, *Shahabad*, p. 431.
21. Banerjee, "Grain Traders and the Company," p. 408.
22. S. Swinton, Customs, Murshidabad, to J. P. Ward, Acting Secy., BOR, Oct. 28, 1816, Bengal Board of Commrs., Behar and Benares, Jan. 1 to Dec. 28, 1817, Jan. 20.

poorer cultivators, and seeking repayment in grain at harvesttime when most peasants needed to sell their crops immediately to survive and cover debts. This timing favored the "trading farmers," as well as the wholesale traders, because they acquired the produce at harvest prices, which tended to be low, and then sold their stock several months later when prices had risen. "Trading farmers" preferred to buy at harvest-time or even earlier "and sell five or six months afterwards when the price has risen. It is usually supposed that they make 20 per cent. on each crop; but their gains are probably greater, as the farmers who deal with them are considered as more necessitous than those who borrow money at the rate of 25 per cent. for 16 months."[23]

Although of diverse social backgrounds, "trading farmers" were typically of the dominant castes of their villages, whereas the "trading carriers," as their appellation Teli *beoparis* suggests, were Telis, a lower caste of the Shudra category traditionally associated with oil pressing. Because their occupation entailed working cattle in sacrilegious ways— as beasts of burden and as mill animals for oil pressing, for which pur-pose the animals were often blinded—Telis were considered "impure." Some who had branched out into the business of "carriers" therefore sought to pass themselves off as *banias* "in order to conceal the impu-rity of their origin."[24]

Although occupying a significant intermediary role in the processes of exchange by virtue of their control over the means of overland trans-portation, *ladu beoparis* (also termed *paikars*) were not able to capital-ize on that to dominate, let alone bypass, the *grihastha beoparis*. Not only did they lack the economic resources to push aside the village-based traders but they also did not have the social standing to oust the latter from their positions of dominance in village society and econ-omy. Nor did *grihastha beoparis* have much to gain from becoming transporters; on the contrary, they perhaps had much to lose because

23. Buchanan, *Bihar and Patna*, p. 697. The "subordination" and "pre-emption" of the peasantry in the grain trade is also discussed in Datta, "Merchants and Peasants," pp. 398–401. A different set of constraints existed in the case of cash crops.

24. Francis Buchanan, *An Account of the District of Purnea in 1809–10* (Patna: Bi-har and Orissa Research Society, 1928), pp. 236, 582. In Purnia "trading carriers" of other castes insisted on being called *paikars*, an appellation intended to distinguish them from their Teli counterparts. Not all Telis worked as traders. See Buchanan, *Shahabad*, p. 207, for an estimate that two hundred out of three thousand "houses" (families), or less than 7 percent, in that district were involved in trade. Maithil texts from the pre-Mughal period suggest that Telis were considered low caste. See B. P. Mazumdar, "Non-Muslim Society in Medieval Bihar," in *Comprehensive History of Bihar*, vol. 2, part 1, p. 330.

performing such services meant they might be considered "impure" "carriers."

Because the agricultural trade at the grassroots level was embedded in relations of power and dominance defined by the configuration of village society, the incipient colonial state was unable to extend its control over it. Even when local authorities sought to intervene, as they did briefly in the 1790s, when government proposed organizing a system of public granaries, they had neither the knowledge nor the resources to secure a foothold in the countryside. The difficulties of procuring grain, as one district official recognized, was that most of it was already "advanced for, and previously engaged by all descriptions of merchants."[25]

Late-eighteenth-century attempts by government to intervene in the grain trade at the grassroots level therefore inevitably ended up disastrously. Its efforts in Purnia to gain access to supplies or to dispose of its own supplies were met by a boycott conducted by "native grain dealers" and "rice merchants." Members of the first category of traders, along with other *beoparis* who collected grain from the countryside, were able to control stocks because they had much of the surplus beholden to them; the latter group, apparently through "some combination," made sure that not a "single bidder" stepped forward to bid for government grain. The efforts of local administrators in Tirhut to purchase grain for storage in government granaries were also thwarted by merchants and traders who, in preemptive buying campaigns, bought "up all the grain in the country in the expectation of making their own terms." Prices skyrocketed as a consequence, and by the time local officials sought supplies their costs were prohibitively high.[26]

The absence of an administrative infrastructure capable of penetrating this fundamental level of indigenous society and the greater emphasis placed on forging administrative connections with rural magnates also militated against government success in collecting a police tax from merchants, traders, and shopkeepers. The 1790s assessment campaign ran aground because its targets were not only the merchants and traders in towns whose ties to the emerging colonial state were slight but also the traders—the *grihastha* and *ladu beopari*—who were "so

25. Y. Burgess, Colltr., Purnia, to W. Berrie, Clerk and Inspector of Public Granaries, Bengal Rev. Procs., Grain, Nov. 10, 1795–Dec. 30, 1796, June 14.
26. G. Arbuthnot, Colltr., Tirhut, to Subsecy., Feb. 6, 1795, M.C. Records, vol. 193; Burgess to Public Granaries, Bengal Rev. Procs., Grain, June 14, 1795.

much scattered in the petty Bazaars and villages,"[27] and therefore even farther beyond the reach of the local authorities. Such *beoparis* remained elusive figures well into the nineteenth century, indeed until the latter part of the century, when the institution of income tax targeted some of them. The small scale of their operations, their numbers, and their base in the countryside kept them from the reach of the local authorities. Thus, the lament of the Patna authorities that their custom house, set up in the early nineteenth century to tax "imports," had difficulty keeping track of such "men [not] of large capital" but constituting "a great number of petty merchants, pykars and brokers who carry on a small traffic."[28]

Throughout the region merchants, traders, and shopkeepers resisted the police tax, either by refusing to cooperate with officials in identifying taxable individuals and providing the information necessary to establish rates of assessment or by shutting down their businesses. So complete was the *hartal* (closure of market) in Sasaram—a tactic later employed in the Noncooperation Movement—in which "merchants and traders shut up their shops for several days to the very great distress of the inhabitants and travellers, refusing to sell the most common necessaries," that the magistrate expressed doubts about being able to collect the tax. He was also concerned that his insistence on imposing the tax would result in merchants fleeing to neighboring Banaras.[29]

In Chapra, shopkeepers closed their shops for two days; some even sought to pin the accidental death of an elderly man in the bazaar on persons charged with collecting the police tax. In the face of such opposition in Bihar and in Bengal, the tax was withdrawn. As Basudeb Chattopadhyay's account of the police tax protest shows, traders and merchants succeeded in stymieing government efforts because they acted in concert and because their actions threatened to disrupt the rural economy.[30] Not explicitly noted in the official deliberations but

27. J. Lumsden, Late Acting Colltr., Saran, to G. H. Barlow, Subsecy., Aug. 30, 1793, Bengal Rev. Jdcl. Consltns., Sept. 6 to 27, 1793, Sept. 13, no. 15.
28. Board of Commrs., Behar and Benares, to Marquis of Hastings, May 26, 1820, Bengal Rev. Procs., June 16 to July 7, 1820, July 7.
29. T. Brooke, Magte., Shahabad, to Earl Cornwallis, G.G., Mar. 2, 1793, Bengal Rev. Jdcl. Consltns., Mar. 22 to Apr. 12, 1793, Apr. 5, no. 3.
30. "Police Tax and Traders' Protest in Bengal," in *Dissent and Consensus: Social Protest in Pre-Industrial Societies,* ed. Basudeb Chattopadhyay, Hari S. Vasudevan and Rajat Kanta Ray (Calcutta: K. P. Bagchi and Co., 1989), pp. 6–35; Lumsden, Colltr., to Barlow, Subsecy., May 4, 1793, Bengal Rev. Jdcl. Consltns., May 3 to 31, 1793, May 31, no. 19.

also clearly important is the fact that the protest succeeded because it involved a colonial state, as yet without the apparatus of power and knowledge to extend its reach into the countryside—into the arena of the bazaar—also the site where merchants, traders, and shopkeepers were in their element.

Primarily through the mediation of *ladu beoparis* and *paikars,* grain flowed out of the villages and primary markets into the hands of "considerable merchants," known variously as *goldars* or *mahajans* or *beopari mahajans. Goldar* was a designation applied in particular to merchants involved in the wholesale trade of grain (*gullah*) and a variety of articles generally denominated *kirana.* Exceptions to this rule were the Gosain *goldars* who retained their religious titles. However, some merchants—generally those involved in big transactions—relied on their own networks to gain access to the stocks held by *grihastha beoparis* or the cultivators themselves. One example of how this chain worked is the case of a "principal banker and rice merchant" in Purnia who filled the British order for fifty thousand maunds of rice by dispatching his agents (*gomasthas*) into the countryside to procure that amount.[31]

Goods collected by petty traders and agents as well as by merchants were relayed to the higher levels of the marketing system through *arathiyas,* "merchants . . . who receive goods . . . and dispose of them by commission, taking upon themselves the responsibility for the purchaser, on which account they are men of property or credit. They also purchase on commission, and transact business at the custom house for merchants at a distance." Some *arathiyas* were primarily agents and only secondarily merchants; their business centered on their "commission warehouses," which were used to store "various kinds of goods . . . [to be] dispose[d of] . . . on commission. . . . On iron they get one-half per cent., on other goods 1 per cent. from each party. Some of them are agents, who purchase cloth for merchants residing at a distance."[32]

Brokers, known locally as *goldars,* filled this intermediary role in the town of Bihar. The commission of these owners of warehouses and weights depended on their service as agents in buying and selling of goods. Another type of *arhatiya* and *goldar* was Moolchund, the bro-

---

31. R. W. Pattle, Colltr., Purnea, to Wm. Cowper, Pres. and members, BOR, Aug. 31, 1800, Bengal, BOR Consltns., Grain, 1800, Oct. 3, no. 12; Buchanan, *Bihar and Patna,* pp. 683–84; Buchanan, *Shahabad,* p. 430. *Gullah* generally referred to grain, *kirana* to mustard and linseed in Patna and Gaya.

32. Buchanan, *Bihar and Patna,* pp. 683, 698.

ker (*dalal*) of Goldinganj, who took a cut from buyers and sellers because he offered "moodies and other sellers of goods" a site equipped with godowns and weighmen and because he encouraged merchants and traders to frequent his *ganj*. According to his own testimony, he was entitled to a commission because he preserved peace in the market by employing a staff of people including a policeman (*darogha*) to provide protection for "beoparries and mahajans."[33]

The so-called Sannyasi merchants, an itinerant group actively involved in the cloth and silk trade between Bengal and Bihar, were another group prominently involved in the wholesale trade in the eighteenth and early nineteenth centuries. Two other categories of merchants conducted wholesale trade as well. Merchants who were itinerant dealers, mostly of limited means, visited many localities seeking their supplies directly from the fields where the crops were grown. In Dariapur, for instance, in addition to 5 wholesale dealers in grain, salt, and other items (*goldars*), 50 petty grain dealers (*gullah paikars*), 125 *baldiya beoparis,* and 100 *grihastha beoparis,* there were also 20 "strangers" termed *gullah mahajans,* who were in the locality for a few months a year to purchase grain. Such itinerant dealers and merchants, termed "strangers" because they were not local residents, were also actively engaged in snapping up the specialty products of some localities. In the Ekwari area of Shahabad five "strange merchants" concentrated on buying its paper; in *thana* Bihar as many as fifty "strangers" were interested in the local cloth.[34]

Also itinerant were the so-called "floating merchants who bring investments in boats, dispose of these, and purchase others."[35] Although not as prevalent as in Bengal, they were a familiar sight in the riverfront areas of Gangetic Bihar. In Patna they offered salt, betel nut, coconut, and iron and sought wheat, basmati rice, and the pulse known as *chana;* in Shahabad their interests varied only slightly. Their primarily long-distance trade in luxury items yielded high returns, a profit of 50 percent, for instance, in the case of coconuts.[36]

33. "Deposition of Moolchund ... " and Lumsden, Colltr., Saran, to Wm. Cowper &c., BOR, Mar. 23, 1793, Bengal BOR Consltns., Sayer, 1793, Apr. 19; Buchanan, *Bihar and Patna,* pp. 697–98.

34. Hamilton Ms., Behar and Patna; Hamilton Ms., Shahabad; Petition from the "Sunasee merchants at Patna," Bengal Rev. Board of Commrs., Customs, Jan. 5 to Dec. 24, 1774, May 30

35. Buchanan, *Purnea,* p. 578.

36. J. Purves, *The East India Merchant; or A Guide to the Commerce and Manufactures of Bengal and the Upper Provinces* (Calcutta: Times Press, 1819), p. 18; Buchanan,

Merchants and traders were typically based in higher-order markets, the largest number, as noted previously, naturally congregating in the city of Patna. No other market in the region assembled such a number and diversity of merchants and traders. The pilgrimage center of Gaya, the second-most prominent town in Bihar after Patna, only counted four bankers, fifty-seven money changers, sixteen money changers who also dealt in cloth and brass vessels, and an assortment of retailers specializing in goods ranging from grain to betel leaf to vegetables. At Shahabad's major market of Bindhuliya thirteen merchants combined a business in grain with that of cotton and other items; Dumraon and Sasaram each supported twenty traders in all in the entire *thana,* and these were mostly men of small capital; Karanja had two merchants only, although with greater capital than their counterparts in Dumraon and Sasaram. As for markets within Patna district: Danapur counted two wholesale dealers specializing in grain (*goldars*), Barh nine wholesale dealers who dealt in both grain and iron, and Nawada twelve dealers who carried on a wholesale trade in grain and salt.[37]

Not all merchants and wholesale traders had substantial resources. Many at the lower end of the scale were comparable to petty traders in terms of capital. Shahabad's *beopari mahajans,* for instance, were men of limited means: one thousand to two thousand rupees in Bindhuliya, and five hundred to five thousand rupees in Sasaram and Dumraon. The other end of the scale, however, was occupied by such merchants as the two in Karanja whose business involved capital of fifty thousand to one hundred thousand rupees. A similar range is suggested by the evidence for the city of Patna. Its one hundred grain dealers were reckoned to be worth between one thousand and ten thousand rupees, the fifty-five grain (*gullah*) and grocery (*kirana*) *mahajans* between one thousand and fifty thousand rupees, and the twenty-four *arathiyas* between one thousand and twenty-five thousand rupees. As for the "most considerable merchant" in all of Patna and Gaya districts in the early nineteenth century, Chunilal of Bakhtiarpur, his factories and grain

---

Bihar and Patna, p. 685; Buchanan, *Shahabad,* p. 432. For specific numbers at each marketing center, see Hamilton Ms., Behar and Patna, and Hamilton Ms., Shahabad.

37. See pp. 85–89. Also Hamilton Ms., Behar and Patna, Shahabad; Buchanan, *Shahabad,* p. 430. Petty dealers, although relatively few in the city, abounded in great numbers in the lower order marketing settlements. Compare Patna's 225 *ladu beoparis* with the 400 enumerated for *thana* Fatwa, 1,000 and 1,100 for *thanas* Nawada and Gaya, respectively, and an even higher total, 2,000, estimated for *thana* Hilsa.

business in Calcutta alone were valued at more than one hundred thousand rupees.

Merchants and traders such as Chunilal made their fortunes by combining trade in agricultural commodities with a lucrative business in nonagricultural commodities, especially luxury items. Not surprising therefore are the figures for Patna that reveal that grain dealers made far less than those dealers who diversified into salt, iron, and metals (one thousand to ten thousand rupees versus one thousand to fifty thousand rupees). Also profitable was the trade in salt, where capital ranged between twenty thousand and one hundred thousand rupees, and the trade in cloth, where capital ran as high as fifty thousand rupees.[38]

The long-distance trade, particularly in luxury items, was monopolized by men of substantial resources because large amounts of capital were needed for advances, purchases, and the higher prices of luxury items. Bankers (*kothiwals*) and professional moneylenders (shroffs) were therefore most likely to branch out into this kind of trade. Their financial resources coupled with extensive credit networks positioned them well to tap the profits of long-distance trade. And they utilized their superior resources and know-how to stake out a trade in luxury items. Shroffs in Patna and Gaya bought and sold precious metals and cotton cloth and *kothiwals* bought and sold European woolens and shawls; some *kothiwals* also dealt in drugs, foreign spices, sandalwood, and metals, and one, "a very rich man," in *manihari* (glass bangles). Drawing on their extensive capital and credit networks (Patna's twenty-four *kothiwals,* for example, had branch offices in Calcutta, Banaras, and Murshidabad), *kothiwals* and shroffs dominated the "trade in European woolen cloths, jewels, foreign spiceries, metals imported by sea, and the finer kinds of cloth of cotton, silk, and lace."[39]

The diversified operations of substantial merchants is best exemplified by the family firm of Kallu Babu Lallu Babu, also known as the Dhawalpura *kothi* (literally, a large house but also a banking house or

38. Hamilton Ms., Behar and Patna, Shahabad; Buchanan, *Bihar and Patna,* p. 683; *Shahabad,* p. 430; *Purnea,* p. 577.

39. Buchanan, *Bihar and Patna,* p. 698; also pp. 684–85. For a comparable picture, see Khan Mohammad Mohsin, *A Bengal District in Transition: Murshidabad, 1765–1793* (Dacca: Asiatic Society of Bangladesh, 1973), pp. 139–40. Europeans generally also engaged in trade of this sort, either because of government monopolies, such as in salt, opium, and saltpeter, or because they had the resources to deal in luxury items. See Colebrooke, *Commerce of Bengal,* pp. 103–4; Purves, *East India Merchant,* pp. 13–18.

firm), one of the dominant trading firms in the region in the nineteenth century. The ancestors of this Rohatgi family first set up shop in Patna in the early eighteenth century. By the turn of the nineteenth century Kallu Babu and his son, Lallu Babu, had already staked out a commanding role in the trade of several commodities, from their base in Dhawalpura in Begumpur, near the city of Patna. From beginnings in the grain (*gullah*) and grocery (*kirana*) business, they ventured into the printing of chintz for export. They also expanded into banking, primarily the *hundi* business, and real estate, their landholdings extending across Patna, Muzaffarpur, and Darbhanga. Based originally in the Patna area, they eventually branched out into other areas, particularly Calcutta.[40]

Whether *arathiyas, goldars,* or *mahajans* of one sort or another, wholesale merchants and traders stood at the apex of exchange relations by virtue of their superior resources. Access to money (and credit) obviously gave them an incomparable edge, an advantage that larger moneylenders and bankers used to branch out into the business of wholesale trade. Profits from trade in turn multiplied the resources available for moneylending. Their ability to engage in the wholesale trade by virtue of their superior resources also shows up in their direct control of, or at least access to, *golas* (stores or granaries; thus the designation *goldars*). Without such storage facilities traders could not stockpile goods, especially agricultural commodities, and manipulate market prices.[41]

To minimize losses from spoilage, dealers preferred rapid turnover of their stocks, a pace also dictated by their optimizing strategy of securing supplies at harvesttime when prices were low and selling at other times of the agricultural season, when prices were high. This imperative was also conditioned by the credit system of *hundis,* which required repayment within a few days or the subsequent imposition of high rates of monthly and especially yearly interest. Grain was therefore not stored in vast quantities: many dealers considered *golas* of one thousand maunds an appropriate size, although some granaries

40. Interview with Rohatgi family, June 16, 1984. See also C. R. Bhandari, B. L. Soni, and K. L. Gupta, eds., *Bharatiya Vyapriyon Parichaya* (Bhanpura, Indore: Commercial Book Publishing House, 19?), p. 8. In the twentieth century, this family branched out into various industrial enterprises.

41. Granaries, generally built of bamboo and straw, were plastered with mud and often set about two feet off the ground to guard against moisture and rodents. Because rice spoiled more easily and required periodic airing and drying, paddy was the preferred item of storage.

were known to have a capacity of fifteen hundred to five thousand maunds.[42]

Whether specifically identified as bankers or not, people with substantial capital were deeply involved in the moneylending and grain nexus, although more so at the supravillage level than at the village level. They provided the resources that enabled *mahajans* to make purchases from the cultivators. Their funds were advanced in the form of *hundis* (notes of credit), which typically carried interest rates of 24 percent per annum, or 2 percent per month, and were redeemable within a prescribed period of time.[43]

Buying involved a host of participants; so did selling. In part the overlap of the two structures derived from the fact that they were defined by the same factors: the geographical and social parameters of the marketing system and the size of the quantities involved. In part, the two systems resembled one another because buyers were often sellers and vice versa, particularly at the highest levels of exchange.

The apex in both hierarchies was occupied by wholesale merchants and traders. At the next rung brokers (*dalals*) dominated in some areas by interposing themselves between the petty and wholesale traders and merchants. "In Patna they have the shopkeepers under a good deal of subjection, and scarcely any purchase, even to the value of one rupee, can be made without their interference, and of course they enhance the price by the amount of their commission."[44]

Wholesale traders, merchants, and brokers supplied the petty retailers who maintained shops in the area's markets, both the primary and higher order ones. Although the designation employed for such shopkeepers varied from district to district in accordance with their different roles— *farosh, phariya, dokandar,* and *paikars* were the four most common titles—they had similar retail functions, typically involving grain and other items such as salt, sugar, tobacco, seasonings, cotton, and firewood. A few sold oil, ghee, and cotton cloth as well. Which of these terms was applied to particular storekeepers apparently depended on the size of their retail

---

42. Burgess, Colltr., Purnia, to Barlow, Subsecy., Rev., Jan. 5, 1795, Bengal Rev. Consltns. (Grain), Jan. 2 to Apr. 24, 1795, Feb. 13, no. 16; Routledge to Shore, Oct. 23, 1794, and Arbuthnot, Colltr., Tirhut, to Barlow, Nov. 10, 1794, Bengal Rev. Consltns., Grain, Oct. 31, no. 22 and Dec. 19, 1794, no. 1.

43. G. J. B. T. Dalton, Deputy Colltr., Bhagalpur, to Colltr., Jan. 16, 1872, Bengal Jdcl. Procs., Nov.-Dec. 1872, Dec., nos. 258–59.

44. Buchanan, *Bihar and Patna,* p. 697. *Goldars* served in this capacity in the town of Bihar (pp. 697–98).

business. Those called *farosh* were generally sellers of "very small quantities"; those labeled *phariya* dealt in larger amounts. Some petty shopkeepers were also known by the term *parchuniya*.[45]

Distinctions based on the volume of transactions determined another category designated *gullah paikars*. These individuals secured their supplies either directly from the peasants or from petty dealers; they then sold their stock in quantities (five seers or more) larger than those sold by the typical shopkeeper. Buyers seeking less had to turn to *gullah phariyas,* who had relatively little capital and dealt in smaller quantities. *Parchuniyas* also dealt in small amounts, although with capital ranging from fifty to four hundred rupees, it would seem that they engaged in transactions involving larger quantities than those handled by *gullah phariyas*. They were said to specialize in grain, but not rice.

A similar range of retailers bought and sold other goods. Salt was sold in small quantities by *nimak paikars* and in even smaller amounts by *nimak phariyas*. The former had capital ranging from one hundred to five hundred rupees; in some areas they also dealt in tobacco and in such condiments as ginger, turmeric, and black pepper. The latter, although involved in the retail sale of "trifling quantities," were relatively prosperous in Patna and Daudnagar, where some were estimated to be "rich, and have capitals of from 100 to 4,000 rs." Both kind of retailers were also involved in the sale of ghee, sweets, and oil. Vendors of spices, tobacco, betel leaf, and other goods were similarly classified as *paikars* and *phariyas*, according to the size of their business and capital.[46]

On the surface at least, the structure of exchange relations in the late eighteenth and early nineteenth centuries persisted into the second century of colonial rule. Consider the following identification of people involved in transporting agricultural produce from the fields to the

45. Distinctions were made in Purnia among five different kinds of retailers on the basis of a host of variables: "1st., [were] Mahajans who have considerable capitals, and import by wholesale but sell by retail; 2nd., Paikars, who take, at once, from the merchant a considerable quantity of goods and retail them; 3rd., Those called Chandina Dokandars, who have what we would call a shop, that is, a house in which their goods are exposed for sale, but deal to a small extent; 4th., Aftabi Dokandars, who . . . have no stall, but sit on the ground in some corner of a street and retail their wares; 5th., Tahbazaris, who sit in the same manner, but they have no regular place, and attend on market-days only, going one day to one Hat and next day to another, whereas the Aftabi sits regularly from morning until evening every day, and his place is considered as his property." Buchanan, *Purnea*, p. 579; *Bihar and Patna*, pp. 685–87.

46. Buchanan, *Bihar and Patna*, pp. 687–88.

marketplace. It describes the structure obtaining during the early twentieth century:

> The producers store their crop in their houses, after paying out on the threshing floor a good proportion of the dues of labourers and of the village artisans, as well as the rent of the landlord where that is paid in kind, as it still is in a substantial portion of the province. They draw on these stores throughout the year for their own consumption, but sell some soon after harvest to meet the demands of their creditors, or hand over the grain itself where the loan was taken and has to be paid in kind. Small parcels are sold from time to time to get money for purchases of necessities. Much of this surplus is brought to the primary markets [i.e., *haats*] by the producers themselves in small lots, but probably the greater part is collected by petty traders (*beparis*), who purchases in the villages. . . . The rice . . . is sold again in the primary markets to the larger dealers.[47]

Familiar also—although with minor differences—is the following description provided by a subdivisional officer in the 1870s: "The Beoparis, who bring grain on pack bullocks from the country to the markets, form the link between the producer and the wholesale seller. They trade on their own accounts, and limit their sales to the wholesale dealers who supply the retail vendors. Thus between the producer and the consumer there are three pairs of hands, each grasping its profit. In some instances the wholesale dealers keep one or more pack bullocks. But this is by no means a universal practice, and is a sign of small capital or of unusual energy."[48]

In other words, cultivators who were not directly involved in marketing their own produce turned over their goods to the *beoparis*, thus initiating a relay that carried products to the different rungs of the local and regional marketing system. In the Patna subdivision of Barh, an area enjoying a "large trade in grain," "petty merchants" directed the movement of grain "from the producing villages to the chief markets on the Ganges."[49] In the estimation of the Bihar Banking Enquiry Committee of 1929–30, the bulk of the surplus that entered the market made its way through petty traders (*beoparis*) who had made the rounds of the villages, buying directly from the cultivators.[50]

47. *Report of the Bihar Banking Committee,* p. 61.

48. "Annual Report 1872–73," Sasaram, J. A. E. Eyre, AGRPD, 1872–73, Appendix (hereafter Eyre report).

49. AGRPD 1881–82. For similar accounts of *beoparis* working in other areas, see Eyre report.

50. *Report of the Bihar Banking Committee,* p. 61.

At the next level, as goods passed beyond the arena of the village and that of the periodic market, one finds the familiar figures of "commission agents called *arhatdars*" or the "*goladar* or dealer in grain" or merchants and wholesale traders of one sort or another. As much as nine-tenths of Patna's substantial trade in oilseeds and grain was said to pass through the hands of its *arhatdars,* who numbered fewer than twenty. In all, there were said to be only forty-five large firms controlling the bulk of that city's trade.[51]

Although this structure of the local marketing system hierarchy in the early twentieth century bears a striking resemblance to its earlier counterpart, there were more substantial changes in the system than, say, a traveler, even of Veeraswamy's or Bholanauth's acuity of vision, could have observed from a brief encounter with local conditions. Indeed, a superficial comparison of structures cannot adequately gauge alterations in the two hierarchies resulting from both a sizable increase in numbers and a change in the social composition of participants involved in local marketing, particularly at the grassroots level. Nor can it discern alterations in roles and functions in the marketing system, especially of the petty traders.

Several factors account for these developments. Beginning in the late nineteenth century, as the volume of trade and the number of markets increased and as communications improved, many more people from the ranks of the dominant groups in village society turned to trade as a source of income. Rising prices of food grains also "meant that more people could afford to market their own grain."[52] So did developments in railways and road building, because as transportation increasingly posed less of an obstacle, many more villagers possessed the ability to sell their own goods, either by relying on their own carts and cattle or by hiring those of others. The more even distribution of markets also encouraged this trend, as did the decline of the city of Patna, which led to the "the petty marts of the neighbouring districts" receiving "sup-

---

51. Rattray report; S. C. Bayley, Commr., Patna, to GOB, no. 44R, June 17, 1875, P.C. Rev. Basta no. 326, 1877; Evidence of Rai Bahadur Durga Prasad, Registrar of Co-operative Societies, B & O and of Shambhu Dayal, Income-Tax Officer, Darbhanga, *Bihar and Orissa Provincial Banking Enquiry Committee, 1929–30*, vol. 2, *Evidence* (Patna: Govt. Printing, 1930), pp. 7, 298.

52. Colin M. Fisher, "Planters and Peasants: The Ecological Context of Agrarian Unrest on the Indigo Plantations of North Bihar, 1820–1920," in *The Imperial Impact: Studies in the Economic History of Africa and India,* ed. Clive Dewey and A. G. Hopkins (London: Athlone Press, 1978), p. 123.

plies direct[ly] instead of having recourse to the intermediary store-houses of this city."[53]

Such changes—particularly developments in communications facili-tating easier and faster access to markets—led to the decline of the *ladu beoparis* as a specialized group of transporters in local-level trade. Not that they completely disappeared from sight in the course of the late nineteenth century. On the contrary, as in Shahabad of the 1870s, Telis were referred to as "oil-men" and "well-to-do," pursuing their "own special calling" and also owning "pack bullocks on which they convey oil and grain to market." But increasingly, the earlier distinction be-tween *grihastha beoparis* and *ladu beoparis* tended to disappear, as these different kinds of petty traders merged into one category, widely known simply as *beoparis*.[54]

Perhaps most important, these trends were shaped by the growing prosperity of the better-off peasants, a condition that has been widely interpreted as indicating the emergence of a rich peasantry in many re-gions of the subcontinent.[55] And it is this development that ultimately generated the dynamic for establishing the commanding roles that petty traders and moneylenders carved out in the village society of the late nineteenth and early twentieth centuries.

A close examination of the identities of petty traders in this period further highlights these developments. At the lowest rung, as in the first century of colonial rule, the marketing system was activated by peas-ants transacting business largely with "creditors" and "petty traders"—not infrequently roles played by the same persons—who were drawn from the ranks of moneylenders, substantial cultivators, petty land-holders, or some combination of these roles. Petty traders, in other words, continued to play the instrumental role in initiating the move-ment of grain from the fields to the marketing centers. Indeed, through-out India "village merchants constitute[d] one of the most important assembling agencies," especially for food grains such as rice.[56]

53. Commr., Patna, to BOR, no. 731R, Aug. 25, 1882, P.C. Rev. Basta no. 337, 1882–83.

54. Eyre report. See also Hunter, *Account of Gaya,* p. 83, regarding *"bardiya-beparis."*

55. E.g., see Shri Prakash, "Models of Peasant Differentiation and Aspects of Agrar-ian Economy in Colonial India," *MAS* 19 (1985): esp. 554–56.

56. *Marketing of Rice in India,* p. 250. B. B. Mukherjee, *Co-operation and Rural Welfare in India* (Calcutta: Thacker, Spink, and Co., 1929), pp. 88, 91, emphasizes that the moneylender and dealer were often the same person.

As in the earlier period, petty traders in the late nineteenth and early twentieth centuries were the economically and socially better-off inhabitants of a locality because of their control over economic resources and because of their higher social and political status. Many were moneylenders, although not all *mahajans* dabbled in trade. But the inducements for moneylenders to enter trade were manifold because of the superior resources they enjoyed in village society. In many respects, they were the village-level controllers, their authority and influence in the locality confirmed by their recruitment as the rent collectors (*thikadars*) for the local zamindars. This was often the case in the great estate of Hathwa: its *thikadars* were frequently drawn from the ranks of village *mahajans*. According to the manager of the great estate of Darbhanga, "[I]n nearly all cases the jeyt ryots are the village mahajuns, and have . . . much power over the ryots."[57] Village headmen and *mahajans* were also invariably the "well-to-do persons, cultivating the largest holdings in their villages."[58] So great was the moneylender's "personal influence in the village" that an economics professor residing in the region declared that he was "looked upon as a semi-landlord."[59]

Superior resources enabled *mahajans* to become the underwriters of the trade in agricultural goods, if not the actual traders. "The village mahajan," testified the secretary of the Bihar and Orissa Provincial Cooperative Bank in 1929, "continues to this day to be the chief agricultural financier due to various reasons, the chief amongst which are his local influence and his easy accessibility. He finances the agriculturist for all purposes." In many areas, "in ordinary years, the ryot makes over to the mahajun his whole crop; the mahajun pays his rent for him, and keeps him in grain for the rest of the year."[60] As the "person of greatest consequence next to the landlord," the *mahajan* in the late nineteenth and early twentieth centuries banked on the advantages of

57. Cited in R. P. Jenkins, Commr., Patna, to BOR, no. 119, Dec. 18, 1871, P.C., Land Rev. A Bundles, Jan.-July 1872, Feb.; G. J. S. Hodgkinson, Manager, to Colltr., Saran, no. 436, Sept. 25, 1872, Bengal Rev. Procs., Oct.-Dec. 1872, Nov., no. 121. See also my *Limited Raj*, pp. 126–32, 169.

58. W. W. Hunter, *A Statistical Account of Bengal*, vol. 13, *Tirhut* (London: Trubner and Co., 1877), p. 75. For a similar observation, see *PSR*, p. 40.

59. Evidence of B. B. Mukharji, Professor of Economics, G. B. B. College, Muzaffarpur, *Bihar Banking Committee*, vol. 2, pp. 272–73. See also his *Rural Welfare in India*, pp. 88–91.

60. R. Mangles, to Commr., June 28, 1866, Bengal Rev. Procs., Aug.-Oct. 1866, Aug., no. 127; Evidence of Rai Sahib Mihir Nath Ray and V. M. Thakore, *Bihar Banking Committee*, vol. 2, p. 76.

his "semi-landlord status" to stake out a role for himself in trade that was not unlike that of his counterpart—both the *grihastha* and *ladu beopari*—in the first century of colonial rule. According to one local source, the *mahajan* in Bihar

> lends in grain as well as money. The terms are high: grain lent in kind has to be repaid in harvest time in kind worth twenty-five to fifty per cent. more. Money is frequently lent on short loans at 1 anna per rupee a month, that is to say at the yearly rate of seventy-five per cent. When lent in large amounts on a stamped bond[,] the rate varies from twelve to thirty per cent.
> ... The majority of the villagers will owe him something and make use of his services as a banker. Their grain is kept by him, and he will frequently finance them through bad seasons.... When once, however, they are in his power, it is difficult for them to extricate themselves, and they are compelled to sell their grain to him at rates considerably lower than those obtaining in the nearest bazar [*sic*].[61]

Especially in south Bihar, where rent continued to be largely paid in kind (*bhaoli* system) rather than cash, village notables were well equipped to take on the roles of village *mahajans* and petty traders because a substantial portion of the village surplus ended up in their stores.[62]

Whereas poor cultivators and landless laborers typically had little or nothing stored, well-to-do cultivators were estimated to have sufficient stocks to last at least three to four months. In comparison, *goladars* and *mahajans* had the equivalent of six months' supply of food for their localities. An investigation of grain holdings in the 1870s revealed that surplus grain was invariably in the hands of village headmen or petty zamindars, who used it for their own family consumption, for seed, and as a commodity for sale in the neighboring markets. The "mass of the people," on the other hand, had "no stores of grain, but purchase their supplies in the nearest markets."[63]

But petty traders and *mahajans* in the late nineteenth and early twentieth centuries also differed from their earlier counterparts in at

61. F. C. Harrison, "The Behar Ryot at Home," *Calcutta Review* 91, no. 172 (1890): 283. Harrison was a magistrate in Darbhanga in the early 1870s.

62. E. J. Barton, Colltr., Gaya, to Commr., Patna, Nov. 14, 1878, no. 432, P.C. Rev. Basta no. 329, 1878–79. See also Derbyshire, "Economic Change and Railways," pp. 532–33, regarding the trend to reduce "grain store" levels in the late nineteenth century because of the growing reliability of securing supplies from elsewhere.

63. "Narrative of Scarcity and Relief in Sarun ... for Week Ending ... 29th Nov. 1873" and "Narrative of ... 24th Jan. 1874," GOB, "Famine Narratives," Nov. 14 to Dec. 31, 1873 and Jan. 2 to Feb. 5, 1874, nos. 8, 9, and 10.

least one important respect: they increasingly came from the higher range of social and economic backgrounds. To employ the language of the Bihar and Orissa Provincial Banking Enquiry Committee of 1929–30, "amateurs" were on the rise "in the sphere of rural credit." What the committee meant by the rise of "amateurs"—a development it considered to be one of its most striking findings—was "not only the landlord, who has always played some part in the business, especially by making grain advances to his tenants, but the substantial cultivator as well, who has made a comparatively recent entry into the field."[64]

The rise of the "amateur" moneylender, a development that obviously suggests a growing "amateur" presence in trade as well, further highlights the changing composition of the groups involved in local-level trade. To hear peasants residing in the vicinity of the Muzaffarpur village of Baghi tell it in the late 1920s, "Nearly all the borrowing is from the richer men in the villages, who are now of a number of castes. Forty or fifty years ago[,] two or three professional mahajans used to finance 15 to 20 villages, but now many more people lend money."[65]

A 1920s study of more than 160 villages in Muzaffarpur found an average of three moneylenders per village, with some villages supporting as many as ten. More than 50 percent of these moneylenders were agriculturists, 20 percent were landholders and banias, and the remaining 10 percent were "outsiders," such as Kabulis and Punjabis.[66] This mix of castes, particularly castes generally identified as "agriculturists" and "landholders and banias," also shows up in the identifications of the petty traders in Darbhanga and Muzaffarpur involved in the Nepal trade. Mostly "men of small means," they specialized in importing the grain and oilseeds of Nepal into north Bihar, where they turned their supplies over to wholesale traders and merchants. They included not only the assortment of castes identified as Banias, such as Khatris and Aggarwals, but also several Sudra castes, who were closely identified

64. J. A. Hubback, *Indian Banking with Special Reference to Bihar and Orissa, Patna University, Banaili Readership Lecture, 1930–31* (Patna: Patna University, 1931), pp. 14–15.

65. "Note of Village Enquiry at Baghi on 8th Nov. 1929," *Bihar and Orissa Provincial Banking Enquiry Committee 1929–30*, vol. 3, *Interviews and Enquiries* (Patna: Govt. Printing, 1930), p. 201.

66. Evidence of Secy. of B & O Provincial Cooperative Bank, *Bihar Banking Committee*, vol. 2, p. 76; Sadashiva Prasad, *Bihar Co-operation, Hajipur Subdivision* (Patna: B. & O. Co-operative Press, 1930), pp. 53–54.

with the *bania* category, especially Telis; Brahmins and Rajputs, too, were featured among these petty traders.[67]

The detailed village-by-village data on moneylenders and petty traders in Saran point to an equally diverse caste composition: Rasauli's nine moneylenders included two Brahmins, two Rajputs, and two Muslims; Matihania Bind's moneylenders were five Brahmins and one Sonar; and in other villages, credit was advanced by Kalwars. Throughout the *thanas* of Mirganj and Mashrak, moneylenders were drawn from a variety of castes, although the largest number in each case reflected the "dominant caste" pattern of the locality: in the former Brahmins, in the latter Rajputs.[68] In the district as a whole, Rajputs and Bhumihar Brahmins predominated as moneylenders; they accounted for approximately 15 percent of the population but 57 percent of its landholding rights and 27 percent of its tenant holdings. Credit, in other words, was generally extended by substantial *raiyats* and petty *maliks*—almost anyone who had surplus cash or grain. "There are in fact," to use the words of one report, "no money-lenders and pawnbrokers, pure and simple."[69]

The sizable increase in carts (and cattle)—the predominant means of overland transportation—and their ownership by a wider circle of people similarly points to the enlarged pool of recruitment for traders and moneylenders in the late nineteenth and early twentieth centuries. This change resulted from improvements in roads, which launched a "revolution in the art of cart-building" that made carts more affordable. Whereas the standard cart of the past had been constructed "with a view to strength," the new cart was made largely with bamboos, being "well adapted for going over fair-weather roads, . . . light, and, above all, cheap. The *gari* [the old cart] costs Rs. 25 to Rs. 30, a *sagar* [the new cart] can be made for less than a third of that sum." Consequently, as George Grierson, the subdivisional officer of Madhubani, noted in the 1870s, the "cheapness of the cart . . . has greatly widened the classes of men who go to Nepal to buy grains."[70]

67. C. E. R. Girdlestone, Resident, Nepal, to Offg. Secy., GOI, Foreign Dept., Sept. 19, 1876, Bengal Statistical Procs., Trade and Traffic, 1876–77, Jan. 1877, nos. 5–6. See also *District Census 1891, Muzaffapur,* p. 131; *District Census Reports, 1891, Darbhanga,* pp. 151–52, 157.

68. Compiled from Mirganj *thana* nos. 1–1064, 11 vols., Mashrak *thana* nos. 1–285, 3 vols. See also Rasauli village, Mashrak *thana* no. 71; Matihania Bind, Mirganj *thana* no. 3, SVN; Yang, *Limited Raj,* pp. 169–71.

69. *Darbhanga Census, 1891,* p. 161; Yang, *Limited Raj,* pp. 344–45.

70. Cited in AGRPD, 1879–80. No doubt, it also enabled many more people to go "on the road" for pilgrimages and melas.

The widespread accessibility and, presumably, ownership of carts also explains the diminishing importance of the separate category of "trading carriers." Not that the latter category of traders completely disappeared from the scene, but village-based petty traders were increasingly capable of making their own transportation arrangements. No wonder the number of carts in Patna Division increased by leaps and bounds: by almost 140 percent over a period of three decades: from 83,713 in 1913 to 126,182 in 1930 to 200,786 in 1940.[71]

The rising star of the rich peasantry can also be plotted from statistics regarding landholdings. Survey and settlement figures from the late nineteenth and early twentieth centuries reveal that some peasants were gaining at the expense of others; moneylenders in particular were increasingly involved in buying up or in securing mortgages of tenant rights. The most dramatic shift occurred in Champaran, where evidence from the 1890s and second decade of the twentieth century clearly documents the growing presence of moneylenders. By the latter period they accounted for 46 percent of the sales and 58 percent of the area mortgaged. And in Muzaffarpur, where the inroads were much more modest in scale, the trend was much the same—moneylenders were responsible for 12.9 percent of the overall transfers but *raiyats* 78.6 percent. As one administrator noted, the "tendency [was] for the land to pass out of the hands of Koeris and Kurmis and lower cultivating classes into the hands of Brahmins and Rajputs."[72]

Furthermore, well-to-do peasants and moneylenders, from whose ranks most petty traders were drawn, consolidated their strategic roles in the local economy and society by also taking over the leaseholders of periodic marketplaces. Although the land on which the *haats* stood generally belonged to landholders, the latter typically sought renters who could act "as brokers or go-betweens between the buyer and seller and as referees on any matter of dispute. They are the bazaar weighmen also."[73] These lessees recouped the costs incurred in acquiring the

71. Compiled from "Census of Live-stock in Bihar . . . during Year 1913," B & O Rev. Procs., Agric., Jan.-Mar. 1915, Feb., no. 19; GOBi, *Report on the Live-stock Census of Bihar for the Year 1940* (Confidential) (Patna: Govt. Printing, 1942), pp. 14–15.

72. MSR, p. 33; J. A. Sweeney, *Final Report on the Survey and Settlement Operations (Revision) in the District of Champaran (1913–1919)* (Patna: Govt. Printing, 1922), pp. 334–35.

73. In Shahabad buyers paid one pice, sellers half to three-quarters of a pice. S. C. Bayley, Commr., to Secy., Rev. Dept., no. 336, Aug. 1, 1872, P.C. Monthly Bundles, vol. 1, Basta 6, 1872–73.

lease of the *haat* (*haatwai*) by levying a fee of one-half to one pice per rupee of sale made by a seller. Landholders also benefited from fees paid by shopkeepers, with retailers of such items as grain, spices, cotton, and fish generally paying more than those specializing in vegetables. Income from the *haats* of Muzaffarpur alone were said to yield 150,000 rupees; that from the entire province of Bihar and Orissa more than 5 million rupees.[74]

The greatly extended circuits over which petty traders conducted their business further emphasizes the rising prominence of petty traders in the rural marketing system of the late nineteenth and early twentieth centuries. Some *beoparis* even competed with the larger town-based traders, as was the case in Sitamarhi subdivision, from which the pack bullocks and carts of traders from Hajipur in the south and from Saran, Champaran, and Darbhanga returned loaded with the area's abundant surplus grain. That many of them were petty traders can be gauged from the fact that most of these transactions involved small quantities, and most of the purchases went directly to stock the periodic marketplaces. In fact, the bulk of the surplus produce marketed passed through the hands of petty traders (*beoparis*).[75]

A late-nineteenth-century source estimated that twenty miles was the perimeter of the petty trader's circuit, a distance completed in a day or two at most. The petty trader was a familiar figure because he served as the *beopari* of a specific set of *haats* that he frequented regularly. Visits as often as three times a month to restock the retail shops of the market were not uncommon; nor were profits of one anna per rupee's worth of transaction, or a return of more than 6 percent for such endeavors. In another sense, too, these traders were "not necessarily or even ordinarily strangers" because "[f]requently they are the more substantial raiyats themselves, but the village money-lender probably still does the bulk of the business."[76] In the second century of colonial rule as well, some

74. L. F. Morshead, Offg. Commr., Tirhut, to Secy., BOR, B & O Rev. Procs., Apr.-June 1915, Apr., no. 12, enclosure; Bayley to Secy., no. 336, Aug. 1, 1872, P.C. Monthly Bundles, Basta 6, 1872–73. See also pp. 201–6, regarding illegal market cesses collected by landholders and others.

75. *Report of the Bihar Banking Committee*, p. 61; T. Norman, Colltr., Muzaffarpur, to Commr., Patna, Nov. 19, 1883, and W. R. Bright, SDO, Sitamarhi, to Colltr., Muzaffarpur, Nov. 12, 1883, P.C. Rev. Basta no. 288, 1883. See also Prasad, *Bihar Co-operation*, p. 54, for an estimate that moneylenders averaged an investment of fifteen hundred rupees in their businesses.

76. Hubback, *Indian Banking*, p. 31; C. T. Metcalfe, Offg. Commr., to Secy., GOB, Jan. 23, 1876, Bengal Statistical Procs., Drought, 1876–77, Feb. 1876.

petty traders, along with the village-based *beoparis,* were itinerant traders who "wander from village to village buying grain."[77]

Transactions in agricultural produce were also conducted at the periodic markets themselves, where petty *banias* assembled on *haat* days. Often their customers were women, especially when small amounts were involved. Government reports suggest that these women were generally not aware of competitive market rates because they were not likely to walk an extra mile or two to another *haat* in search of a more favorable price for their offerings. Moreover, they felt pressed to sell quickly because they needed to generate cash to make purchases of such "necessities . . . as cloth, salt and spices, or petty luxuries."[78] Some enterprising individuals, however, were known to monitor prices at the different markets. Mawal Teli's two sons, Thajwa and Ghughulia, for instance, went to different markets in search of the best price for grain and rope, and once having secured that, they would sell it in the *haat* of their own village.[79]

A small quantity of food crops was sold at market by the cultivators themselves. This was a growing practice, especially among the larger cultivators. For some, their own village offered a ready outlet because it was a *haat,* as in the case of Pakaha and Silhauri. Others relied on neighboring markets. Cultivators who had surplus grain in the periodic market of Shamdas Bagahi sold it to their village *banias;* some enterprising inhabitants, however, cut out the middlemen and became shopkeepers themselves. For people residing in proximity of higher-level markets, such as those of the village of Dharampur, there was the option of seeking a better price at the standard market (in this case, that of Amnaur) rather than relying on their neighborhood *haat.*[80]

A small quantity of grain also reached the hands of *beoparis* through *pallowalas,* buyers of small quantities of grain who generally sold their purchases to bazaar *banias* or larger dealers. Many petty *banias* who sold

77. GOB, *Report on the Administration of the License Tax in Bengal for the Year 1880–81* (Calcutta: Bengal Secretariat Press, 1881), p. 18.

78. *Report of the Bihar Banking Committee,* p. 61.

79. "Budget of Mawal . . . of Village Pachlakhi . . . ," *Chanakya Society, 9th Annual Report, 1918–19,* p. 93. Although the development of railways generated an all-India market that evened out regional price levels for medium- and low-value goods, price differentials at the local level, between town and site of production, for instance, persisted, providing enterprising cultivators and traders a small margin for profit. See Derbyshire, "Economic Change and Railways," pp. 528–29; Hurd, "Railways," pp. 745–46.

80. Shamdas Bagahi, Mirganj *thana* no. 410; Dharampur, Parsa *thana* no. 129; Pakaha and Silhauri, Parsa *thana* nos. 59 and 61, SVN.

goods on retail, such as in village Rajapur where they dealt in spices, to-bacco, salt, and other minor items, in turn also sold to *beoparis* (in this case salt and saltpeter). Another trickle of grain involved petty *banias* op-erating through a barter system by which villagers turned in grain to them in exchange for "necessaries" at the shops of the *banias*. Such transactions were conducted particularly near the end of the harvest or after the harvest when surplus grain was plentiful.[81]

In addition, developments in trade and communications also ush-ered in a new presence in many localities: representatives of dealers from other areas. Some of these "dealers" were actually large firms, generally based in Patna or Calcutta. The three most prominent firms in Patna were Messrs. Ralli Brothers and Messrs. N. J. Valetta and Company, which together accounted for more than half of that city's sizable export trade in oilseeds, and a Parsi firm with headquarters in Bombay that dealt in wheat and linseed. Firms based in Calcutta also played a significant role in the oilseed trade of north Bihar, particularly that of Darbhanga and Muzaffarpur, their agents operating out of Darbhanga and collecting on behalf of the Calcutta market. But al-though firms constituted a new element on the trading scene, at the lo-cal and village levels their representatives were intermediaries and agents who were essentially petty traders. In other words, these firms too relied on the village *banias* as the most efficacious conduit for the surplus of the countryside.[82]

Indeed, throughout north India, village-level *beoparis* initiated the relay that transferred agricultural goods from the fields to the markets: "It does not make any real difference whether they carry on their ac-tivities on their own and sell the commodities to the merchants in the markets and towns, or serve big dealers in a regular manner, or are en-gaged as agents on commission and buy on behalf of their principals, and deliver the produce to them. . . . [T]heir main job is to collect the agricultural produce from villages and village markets and to carry it to the wholesale *mandis* and town."[83]

81. "Report on the Village Jolhatwa . . . ," *Chanakya Society, 9th Annual Report, 1918–19*, pp. 84–85; Rajapur, Mirganj *thana* no. 395, SVN; *Report of the Bihar Bank-ing Committee*, p. 127.

82. Hunter, *Account of Patna*, p. 169; Bright to Colltr., Nov. 12, 1883, P.C.'s Rev. Basta no. 288, 1883. In the wheat trade too, Ralli Brothers, for instance, in Patna City, would only deal with petty traders. See D. B. Allen, Assistant to Director of Agricultural Dept. to Commr., Patna, Dec. 2, 1885, Bengal Rev. Procs., Aug.-Oct. 1886, App. A.

83. Husain, *Agricultural Marketing*, p. 101.

Familiar also is the following description from Sind, where the village-based petty trader relied on his superior economic, social, and political resources to carve out a dominant position in the village society and economy: "The village bania was the lynchpin of the system, occupying a pivotal position as merchant and moneylender. As merchant, he was a middleman. He bought produce from the cultivators at the threshing floor; some he kept for retailing locally, the rest he re-sold to the dealers. His position as a trader made him a natural source of credit and so he was also a moneylender."[84]

Although they comprised the linchpin of the rural marketing system, *beoparis* did not always monopolize the system; rather, they vied with one another for the spoils of trade. Furthermore, they also faced competition from another quarter. Increasingly, more and more cultivators elected to bypass petty traders and strike their own deals. An eyewitness to this new trend, A. P. MacDonnell reported in the 1870s that the development of roads in Darbhanga had prompted many more people from the northeast area of Madhubani to use carts to carry their surplus grain to Darbhanga town. In his words, the "result was . . . strings of ryots' carts bringing grain . . . to sell, while other strings of carts from Sarun and South-West Mozuffer-pore were proceeding to the rice country as usual to buy."[85] Such initiative was also in evidence in the early 1880s in Muzaffarpur, when grain shortages were made up by importations from the rice-producing areas east of Darbhanga and from Nepal, much of this conducted by "villagers from all parts of the district, who travelled together in considerable bodies, taking their own carts and pack-bullocks with them."[86]

A conspicuous part of this new trend was the growing presence of women, whose rising numbers in the throngs of mela-goers and pilgrims in the late nineteenth century has already been noticed. In the words of one contemporary observer, "One meets on the roads the string of raiyats and their womenfolk with their *bhangi* [*bahangi,* the net used

84. David Cheesman, "'The Omnipresent Bania': Rural Moneylenders in Nineteenth-Century Sind," *MAS* 16 (1982): 450.

85. A. P. MacDonnell, Offg. Colltr., Darbhanga, to Commr., Patna, no. 542G, June 22, 1877, with AGRPD 1876–77, Appendix B. This report also notes that because peasants had secured better prices by taking their grain to Darbhanga than by selling to the traders coming to their villages, the practice of going to the town market would continue.

86. AGRPD 1883–84, p. 24.

to carry goods with a sling pole] loads and headloads as well as the *bepari* with his pack pony or bullock."[87]

By the early twentieth century the movement of agricultural surplus from the sites of production to the primary markets by *beoparis* as well as by the cultivators themselves was so commonplace that observers found it difficult to gauge "what proportion of the principal staples is sold in the villages and what proportion is brought in by the cultivator to the market. Both methods of first sale are common enough."[88] The testimony of the villagers of Rampur Kumharkole in Muzaffarpur confirms that both methods were employed: "We sell our produce either to *banias* or other villagers coming to our doors for the purpose[,] or sometimes we take it for sale to *banias* of Mahnar road (a market at a distance of about two miles from this village) which is done according to individual suit and convenience."[89]

But petty traders expanding their trading horizons and enterprising cultivators expanding into petty trading in the late nineteenth and early twentieth centuries were not necessarily two distinct categories of people. The rise of both categories in the nineteenth century stemmed from the same source: an emerging well-to-do peasantry. Many had at least a foot in the door of moneylending as well. These developments saw not only an overall surge in the numbers of people involved in trade but also the representation of many new faces in the ranks of peasants drawn from the highest echelons in the social and economic hierarchy of village society.

The rise of a prosperous peasantry solidly anchored in the local political, economic, and social systems was attained at the expense of the rest of village society. As was noted in one local study of marketing from the 1930s, "The tendency is for a more prosperous ryot to buy up produce from the poorer ones and start as a middleman."[90] Declining returns from cultivation—even as deindustrialization added numbers to the ranks of cultivators—therefore became an "alarming symptom in the . . . condition of Behar" in the late nineteenth century, a condition that made it impossible for many to earn a subsistence solely from agri-

87. Hubback, *Indian Banking*, p. 30.
88. Ibid.
89. "Village Rampur Kumharkole," by Maulavi M. A. Ahsan, of Co-operative Department, *Bihar Banking Committee*, vol. 2, p. 834.
90. B. B. Mukherjee, *Agricultural Marketing in India* (Calcutta: Thacker, Spink, and Co., 1937), p. 18.

culture. Consequently, most turned to other sources of income—according to one study of a village in Darbhanga, as much as 63 percent of the total population. For the overwhelming majority of these villagers, perhaps as much as 89 percent, that meant hiring out their labor.[91]

In one respect, however, the categorization of moneylenders-cum-petty traders as "amateur" or "professional" represented a significant distinction. In the popular imagination professional moneylenders were invariably maligned. Consider Sadashiva Prasad's detailed account of moneylenders in the Muzaffarpur subdivision of Hajipur: it divides them into the four categories of landholders, *banias,* agriculturists, and outsiders (i.e., Kabulis and Punjabis) and then singles out the *banias* and the outsiders for condemnation. The former are labeled "insidious," "niggardly," and "thrifty," the latter "the worst and most oppressive."[92]

Petty traders characteristically initiated the next round of exchanges by taking their supplies to the local dealers, the *goladars,* or to commission agents called *arhatdars.* Along with capital, an *arhatdar* typically possessed "a good pucca [brick] house in the centre of the grain market. There he will house the *beparees* from the mofussil, coming with their grain to sell them to large dealers, or for the purpose of exportation by the rail or river. A commission of one pice per maund is charged for the goods so housed; but it often happens that the *beparees* borrow money from the owner of the aruth house on the security of their goods before they are cleared. In that case the aruthdar freely advances the money at 12 annas per cent., and realizes the principal and interest from the sale proceeds."[93]

The principal dealers in the town of Muzaffarpur were Badri Lal and Fakira Lal, who specialized in grain as well in oilseeds. As befit their position as grain merchants, they had *golas* for storing their supplies.[94] By the late nineteenth century *golas* capable of holding substantial quantities of grain were commonplace. Granaries of ten thousand maunds and over were widespread in the markets of Saran; in some of

91. Harrison, "Behar Ryot," p. 288; *Bihar Banking Committee,* vol. 2, pp. 127, 277. See also my *Limited Raj,* pp. 181–205, for a discussion of seasonal migration as an option for many peasants.

92. *Bihar Co-operation,* pp. 49–53.

93. Syud Ameer Hossein, "Mahajani Statistics."

94. "Note of Interview with Traders and Indigenous Bankers at Muzaffarpur," Nov. 9, 1929, *Bihar Banking Committee,* vol. 3, p. 206; Testimony of Registrar of Co-operative Societies, *Bihar Banking Committee,* vol. 2, p. 7. At the *haat* level as well as at the level of the higher-order markets, the more substantial peasants were generally the ones who sold their produce directly to these local dealers.

the larger markets such as Siwan and Maharajganj, "superior" golas stored as much as twenty thousand maunds. As before, however, the preferred strategy was to dispose of stocks as quickly as possible. Thus, even large markets of Mirganj and Katia were not known for holding large stocks of grain. Rather, dealers there made arrangements with merchants and brokers from nearby Champaran and Gorakhpur to provide a "regular supply."[95]

Although Badri Lal and Fakira Lal of Muzaffarpur did not engage in this line of business, some of their fellow *goladars* dealt in grain—they gave the sellers an advance of up to 90 percent of the value and then had to sell it on behalf of their clients. *Arhatdars* also made money by charging traders for the use of their godowns. A fee termed *choongi* in Gaya market extracted one pice or a quarter of a seer of grain or other goods on every rupee's worth of goods sold by traders. Patna *arhatdars,* who handled as much as nine-tenths of that city's substantial trade in oilseeds and food grains, generally charged a fee of a half percent for acting as "commission agents" on behalf of their trader clients.[96]

In the words of one official report, the typical circuit of grain and markets in the region can be described as follows: "From the haats and from the hands of the petty beparis, grain was sold again in the primary markets to larger dealers, who are sometimes, but not as a rule, agents of merchants on a large scale, and thus the grain finds its way to the secondary markets at the main road junctions, the district headquarters towns, or railway centres. The primary markets are usually to be found every 6 miles. In Bihar there is, as a rule, a large mart every 15 miles, where grain can be stored in a warehouse, it is generally to these that the larger producers and the *beparis* take their grain rather than to the local *hats,* where commodities of all kinds are bought and sold once a week."[97]

If the fundamental rung of marketing can be characterized as increasingly occupied by "amateurs," the highest rungs can be described

95. J. C. Drummond, Offg. Colltr., Saran, to Offg. Secy., GOB, no. 5Ct., Nov. 10, 1873, Bengal Scarcity and Relief Procs., Dec. 1874, no. 44; Lt.-Col. A. Mackenzie, Asst. Commissary General, on special duty, to Commr., Patna, no. 592, June 13, 1874, Bengal Scarcity and Relief Procs., Sept. 1874, 3435–37. See also Famine Narratives, e.g., Jan. 24, 1874.

96. Rattray report; Bayley to GOB, no. 44R, June 17, 1875, P.C. Rev. Basta no. 326, 1877; *License-Tax Report, 1880–81;* "Interview with Traders and Bankers at Muzaffarpur," 1929, *Bihar Banking Committee,* vol. 3, p. 206; Testimony of Registrar of Cooperative Societies, *Bihar Banking Committee,* vol. 2, p. 7.

97. *Report of the Bihar Banking Committee,* p. 61.

as increasingly dominated by professional traders and merchants, for whom moneylending and banking were declining in significance in the late nineteenth and early twentieth centuries. Furthermore, their ranks in the nineteenth century were filled increasingly by members of the so-called *bania* castes, mostly Marwaris and Aggarwals, but also Khatris; some were also Agrahris and Muslims.

A Marwari and Aggarwal presence in the ranks of traders and merchants dates back at least to the Mughal period, when Jains from the western Indian areas of Rajasthan and Gujarat, many of whom were Marwari Banias, settled in eastern India in the train of Rajputs allied to Mughal rulers. Their arrival in eastern India marked a return of sorts, because the region was the site of many holy places associated with Jainism. By the seventeenth century Jains had taken up residence in Bihar; by the 1630s Patna was considered to be a "homeland" of the Jains. As the autobiography of the seventeenth-century Jain merchant Banarsidas recounts, his business trips carried him across north India, from Agra to Patna. The career of Fateh Chand, better known by the designation Jagat Seth given to him by the Mughal emperor in 1722, offers another illustration of the extensive circuit of contacts developed by Jain merchants. Fateh Chand's grandfather started off in Patna in 1652, and his father moved on to Dacca and then to Murshidabad, from which Jagat Seth, remembered in Ghulam Husain's history as "a famous banker . . . whose wealth was reckoned by corors [*crore* or one hundred lakhs, i.e., 10 million], and who has never had his equal," commanded a credit network extending across the subcontinent. In the age of revolution, this family became bankers to regional powers, both the nawab of Bengal and the emerging "English."[98]

A much more substantial in-migration of trading communities into the region occurred in the eighteenth and nineteenth centuries when Marwaris fashioned intermediary positions for themselves in the new circuits of trade (and pilgrimage) emerging under British rule. By the late eighteenth century, through their involvement in the trade of cash crops such as opium, nonagricultural goods such as cotton and wool shawls, and grain, this community extended its trading bases down

---

98. Surendra Gopal, "Jain Merchants in Eastern India under the Great Mughals," in *Business Communities of India: A Historical Perspective,* ed. Dwijendra Tripathi (New Delhi: Manohar, 1984), pp. 69–75, esp. pp. 75–77; Banarsidas, *Ardhakathanaka.*

the Ganges to Mirzapur, Patna, Bhagalpur, and the rising metropolis of Calcutta.[99]

The stories of two of Patna's premier firms, Messrs. Kallu Babu Lallu Babu and Gurumukh Rai Radha Krishna Jalan, add details to this colonial phase of the history of Marwaris and Aggarwals. A firm engaged in diverse enterprises, Kallu Babu Lallu Babu, as noted previously, traces its roots in the region back to the eighteenth century. Originally from Ramgarh in Rajasthan, the Aggarwal firm of Gurmukh Rai Radha Krishna Jalan established its Patna chapter in the mid-nineteenth century, when Gurumukh Rai started a grain and cloth business in the city. His sons, Madan Gopal, Nandu Lal, Gajju Lal, and Radha Krishna continued the family firm until 1915, when they divided into two separate firms. Of these four, Radha Krishna became the major success story, rising to considerable prominence, his status recognized by the honorific rank of Rai Bahadur, accorded him by the colonial government, and by his official positions in the city as the "native member" on the Patna council and as a leading member of the Patna Chamber of Commerce. As for his commercial interests, they extended from his banking business to his paper business, registered under the trademark of the Bengal Paper Mill, to the Darbhanga Sugar Company, in which the Maharaja of Darbhanga was a partner. In Bankipur the Jalan family had an *arhatiya* (commission) business under the name of Messrs. Jalan and Sons; in Calcutta the same business was transacted through Messrs. Gurumukh Rai Radha Krishna. Radha Krishna Jalan's family established as the primary residence and head office the fort in Patna built by the ruler Sher Shah (the Qila House), which is indicative of the standing the family attained in the city and the region. He was also responsible for erecting the Satyanarainji temple in the city; in addition, the family was the major patron of art in the region, including of the Patna School of painters.[100]

By the late nineteenth century, Aggarwals and Marwaris were a formidable presence in the region's wholesale trade. They apparently gained entrée to the wholesale trade through their growing ascendancy as moneylenders and bankers and through their involvement in the

---

99. Timberg, *The Marwaris*, pp. 10–11, 43–48.

100. *Bharatiya Vyapariyon ki Parichya*, pp. 8–10; C. R. Bhandari, B. L. Soni, and K. L. Gupta, *Agarwal Jati ka Itihas* (Bhanpura: Agrawal History Office, 1937), pp. 244–45; Jnanendra Nath Kumar, *The Genealogical History of India*, part 2 (Calcutta: Victoria Press, 1949), p. 160.

long-distance trade in nonfood items. By the late nineteenth century they—particularly the Aggarwals—dominated the *hundi* (bills of exchange) business, for example, in Darbhanga. The Marwaris of that district, on the other hand, enjoyed a lucrative export trade in piece goods from Calcutta and were "said to be the wealthiest of all classes of the Hindu trading community." By the late nineteenth century, Marwaris virtually monopolized the cloth trade in Darbhanga, a position attained at the expense of Aggarwals, "who were the chief dealers in piece-goods" until the mid-nineteenth century.[101]

Banking, moneylending, and cloth were also the stock businesses of Aggarwals and Marwaris in other areas. In Saran, Aggarwals monopolized the positions of bankers and moneylenders, particularly in Chapra and Siwan. Chapra's Marwaris, who had established themselves in that town in the 1830s and 1840s, had by the late nineteenth century taken over the cloth and cotton trade. They imported cloth principally from Calcutta and Banaras and cotton from Mirzapur, Agra, and Kanpur at an annual worth of forty-six to fifty lakh rupees. They then supplied dealers in the interior of the district, in Champaran, Nepal, and Gorakhpur. An 1891 report described the district's Marwaris as the "principal dealers in cloths . . . found almost at all big markets . . . [,] and [they] are[,] generally speaking[,] wealthy." Similarly, Aggarwals and Marwaris played leading roles throughout the region and were described variously as the premier "trading classes" or simply as the "bankers and traders."[102]

In the course of staking out their position in the trade, banking, and moneylending, Aggarwals and Marwaris displaced other people of *bania* castes, as well as a variety of Sudra castes whose representation in the ranks of petty traders have already been noted. For instance, in Darbhanga, Aggarwals and Marwaris were relative latecomers, nouveaux riches compared to the Khatris, who were the "old inhabitants of the district." But by the late nineteenth century the Khatris were regarded as having "once [been] the wealthiest class" because they had been "superseded by the Agarwalas who . . . monopolised the banking

---

101. *District Census, 1891,* pp. 160, 155, 161. Immigrants from Rajasthan to Bihar numbered 4,000 in 1891 and around 11,000 in 1901. This total does not include those people already residing in the region. Marwaris in the region were mostly Aggarwals, and ranged in number from a low of 401 in Champaran to over 3,000 in Gaya. See also, Timberg, *Marwaris,* p. 201

102. *District Census, 1891,* pp. 131, 51, 79; Hunter, *Account of Shahabad,* p. 193; *Account of Champaran,* p. 242; AGRPD 1876–77.

and money-lending business." In Shahabad, Aggarwals advanced at the expense of Agrahris, who, although active in the district since the late seventeenth century, were by the late nineteenth century principally involved in the "import [of] Manchester piece-goods."[103]

Because of their predominance in trade and banking, the better-off *banias,* especially Aggarwals, Marwaris, and Khatris, although belonging to the third highest varna (class) category of Vaishya varna, sought higher-caste ranking. Often regarded as the equals of the literate Kayasths, these groups aspired to even higher status, that of Kshatriya ranking. In fact, Muzaffarpur's Aggarwals and Khatris were said to have "better claims to be classed among the superior classes to which they have pretension. They demand a place among the Rajputs. . . . They wear sacred threads . . . like people of the higher classes."[104]

The overwhelming *bania* presence in the ranks of traders and merchants was challenged only by Bengalis, who were active principally in the trade of one commodity and that only in some areas of north Bihar. Relative latecomers, Bengalis staked out positions primarily as "petty merchants" and to a lesser extent as wholesale dealers and traders. But they operated mostly in north Bihar where they had secured entrance into intermediary positions through the door opened by the oilseed trade, a trade whose final destination was Bengal, at one time Murshidabad and later Calcutta. Their beginnings apparently date back to the early colonial period: by then Bengali capital had already made its mark in the oilseed trade, particularly in the trade flowing out of the northern portions of Darbhanga and Muzaffarpur, and from Bhagalpur and Purnia. By the late nineteenth century the sizable Bengali presence in the oilseed export trade had extended to other parts of north Bihar, for instance, to Champaran, where agents for Bengali firms collected the oilseeds of the district—as much as sixteen thousand tons annually. The grain trade, however, remained beyond the reach of Bengali middlemen, because it was anchored in the larger system of moneylending and landholding.[105]

More conspicuous in the retail than in the wholesale trade—although not entirely absent in the latter—was a large assortment of

---

103. Hunter, *Shahabad,* p. 193; *District Census, 1891,* pp. 51, 152, 7. In Patna, however, Khatris managed to hang on to their positions, as is evidenced by their description as "generally rich brokers and cloth-sellers. Some are zamindars."

104. *District Census, 1891,* pp. 128, 7, 79.

105. Geddes and MacDonnell report; AGRPD 1876–77; Swinton, Govt. Customs, to BOR, Oct. 28, 1816, Bengal, Board of Commrs. at Behar and Benares, Jan. 20, 1817. no. 14A. See also Bengal Statistical Procs., 1876–77, 10.

castes, particularly such Sudra castes loosely identified as *banias* or at least associated with the *bania* category as Kalwars, Sunris, and Telis. Although they had played similar roles in the first century of colonial rule, in the second century they labored in the shadows of the well-to-do *bania* groups who had gained the upper hand in trade through their "professional" expertise as bankers and moneylenders. In the words of an 1891 report, "Foreign goods are largely imported by road, rail, and river, and Bengalis and Marwaris crowd in the towns. The Marwaris especially have great combination. All this no doubt makes it very hard for the village Baniyas to make a good living."[106] Furthermore, at the village level they increasingly faced competition from the rising rich peasantry, no longer content merely to be *grihastha beoparis* and no longer constrained by the "tyranny of distance." Indeed, improvements in transportation tended to encourage their participation, whereas in the earlier era *ladu beoparis* had staked out positions in the local trade by monopolizing the intermediary roles of transporters.[107]

Increasingly in the nineteenth and twentieth centuries the grain trade of Gangetic Bihar came to be dominated by "amateurs" at the level of the local marketing system and by "professionals" at the level of the regional marketing system. The emergence of the amateur represented, however, not the advent of a new group in village society and economy but the rise of *grihastha beoparis* as a rich peasantry, a category of peasants in command of the political, social, and economic resources of their locality. Similarly, the growth of a professional group at the highest levels of the marketing system constituted not the rise of a new group of traders and merchants but the consolidation by a group with long-standing stature in the system. What was new, however, was that they had the credit and connections to operate in the larger systems of trade and marketing to which local systems were increasingly yoked. From the ranks of these "professionals" there sprang in the 1930s and early 1940s "the nascent Indian capitalist class [who] created wider commercial, financial and industrial networks spanning the subcontinent, a process backed by the closer integration of the indigenous produce and credit markets across the land" and "the modern Indian business class, which controls large-scale industry today."[108]

---

106. *District Census, 1891*, p. 7.

107. In some areas such as Darbhanga, Telis and Sunris continued to eke out an existence as retail and small-time wholesale traders by virtue of being the principal owners of pack bullocks and horses. See *District Census, 1891*, p. 162.

108. Ray, "The Bazaar," p. 264.

Conclusion

What are the ties that bind the Patna historian Ghulam Husain writing of the waning years of the Mughal Empire and the beginnings of colonial rule in northeastern India, the early-nineteenth-century traveler Veeraswamy circumambulating the subcontinent in the time-honored manner of a Hindu pilgrim, and peasants and traders protesting and acting collectively in the marketplaces during Gandhi's Noncooperation Movement of 1921–22?

These historical actors shared common ground at the most fundamental level: they all performed on the stage of Gangetic Bihar, the setting of this study. And although they lived at different historical moments, their lives and activities were played out against the backdrop of the colonial era. As conventionally marked off by historians, this discrete period ranged from the end of the Indo-Islamic order, whose "ruin" was chronicled by the Patna historian, to the beginning of the postcolonial states of India and Pakistan (and later, Bangladesh), whose identities are typically defined by another kind of chronological and political partition.

Each of these actors, furthermore, belongs to a "usable past," a recoverable past. They live on, that is, in textual materials that can be (re)read, (re)constructed, and (re)constituted into a present-day historical narrative. By disciplinary socialization I am naturally drawn to them because they have a textual currency that I find invaluable: the first two authored informative texts and the third set are actors in a significant political drama whose words and actions were extensively documented in a variety of colonial and nationalist records and local newspapers. Not the usual folks who write histories and pilgrimage accounts, these last protagonists from the early 1920s have to be deciphered from their deeds and brief utterances. Their actions must be textualized as documentary grist for the historical mill.

Ghulam Husain evokes the milieu of the late eighteenth century, considered an age of revolution by his generation of aristocrats living in the transitional years between the demise of the Mughal Empire and the successor state of the Bengal nawabs and the rise of the Company Raj. In this aristocratic representation, articulated by many voices and texts of the era, the tumultuous events leading up to the emergence of the colonial state were said to have ushered in "ruin" and "discontent." This image of a "ruined city" was echoed by an insistent refrain lamenting the revolution for having caused upheaval in the lives of the aristocracy, those local bureaucrats, landholders, merchants, and bankers who had commanded positions of power, prestige, and wealth in local society. Insights and obvious blinders notwithstanding, Ghulam Husain's account of his "modern times" is compelling, and it has long been a valuable primer for historians of the eighteenth-century because it is a detailed portrait of an era sketched by a contemporary, eyewitness to and participant in the events recounted. Enugula Veeraswamy's "Kasiyatra Charitra" has similar cachet as a historical document because it offers an emic perspective of the momentous phenomenon of pilgrimage and recounts firsthand experience of the regnant political, economic, and social conditions of the early nineteenth century.

Each of these accounts is rich—and each can stand on its own as a story of these or those people, places, and things. Whether the focus is on the age of revolution or on the experiences of a committed pilgrim from south India or on peasants and local elites marching on marketplaces in the name of different causes, each can be reconstituted into a single narrative about a particular slice of history.

Space and time provide the parameters for textualizing these lived experiences (and the stories relating to them) into a narrative history that addresses a variety of historiographical issues and concerns. There are also elements that bear no obvious correspondence to one another; without some ingenious stretching and pulling, these experiences—or, more accurately, these accounts of activities, and other people's accounts of their doings—cannot be made to fit commodiously with one another.

And why single out these particular people and their stories and not other folks and other narratives? That is where the historian adds the guild's trademark: fabricating (and, yes, to a large extent also imposing on) these accounts a particular story, in my case one about *Bazaar India*. In privileging these texts, I sought to stitch together a historical fabric displaying multiple motifs, a fabric of intertextuality that is the end product of a historian's spinning and weaving of different narrative strands into a particular kind of historical cloth.

The overarching motif of the narrative presented here is the bazaar itself. The story of Ghulam Husain and his generation of late-eighteenth-century city elites ties in with this theme because experiences and words of those individuals address the central place of the region, the city of Patna, which this historian views as one in decline. This subjective impression can be corroborated by other personal observations, notably by the poetic outbursts fixated on "a ruined city" or the "city of discontent" penned by his contemporaries. These anxieties emanated from the sense of personal loss experienced by an aristocratic generation, members of the city's Indo-Islamic elite, or by the clients of this aristocracy.

Not all the families that constituted this elite shared in this fate, however. Nor did the city fade from the regional limelight. Indeed, to read the history of Azimabad as a lived text and from a *longue durée* perspective, that is, as a history without "chasms," is to discover that the city experienced many ups and downs over its long past, beginning with its origins as Pataliputra and continuing with its subsequent rebirths as Patna and Azimabad. Moreover, although the upheaval in its "modern times" altered the lives of a generation of aristocrats, the effect was not so dramatic on the career of the city as the central place of the region. On the contrary, a much more seismic upheaval in the life of the city as a whole occurred later in the late nineteenth century, when railways increasingly enabled traders to bypass Patna. The rise of Calcutta, too, eventually peripheralized the entire region. Until then, however, it remained a vibrant trade emporium, handling much of the "through" traffic of goods between Bengal and the North-Western Provinces. As long as the waterways were the most efficient means of transportation, Patna, by virtue of its strategic location on the Ganges, remained a collection and distribution point for its hinterland rich in such commodities as opium and saltpeter and in a variety of handicraft industries. Another reason for the region's slump was deindustrialization, which led to the decline of local artisanal industries as foreign

machine-made goods increasingly captured the market in the late nineteenth century. Data drawn from the colonial documentation project
on economic and demographic conditions confirm this account of decline. But then this downward spiral was arrested by the city's designation as the provincial capital of Bihar and Orissa in 1912 (and later of
the separate province of Bihar in 1937). Thus was Patna saved from its
certain future as just another town.

The story of the "city of discontent" can also be read from its built
environment. To the late-eighteenth-century generation living amid a
remembered and quotidian landscape largely shaped by the prerevolu-
tion "reigns," the signs of "ruin" were everywhere as Azimabad became "a garden of thorns." The sense of "ruin" and "discontent" must
have been further heightened by the "different color" it assumed—with
age, with the diminishing position and therefore patronage of "opulent" men in the locality, and with its general neglect by the new rulers.
This scene was particularly striking in contrast to the rise of the new
Patna in the Bankipur of British creation and in its subsequent spread
to the west to accommodate its designation as the provincial capital.
Although an outgrowth of the "aversion" between colonial rulers and
Indian subjects, the British Bankipur and the westernmost zone that became the seat of the provincial capital—as well as the persistence of the
old "city"—again registers a different history than that recounted by
the "city of discontent" version.

Veeraswamy's experiences of half a century later verify the fact that
Ghulam Husain painted an unduly bleak economic and political picture for Patna. The observations of this pilgrim from the south as he
journeyed in and around the city in 1830–31 convey abundant signs of
economic and political life. For interspersed among his many remarks
regarding pilgrim sites and the different kinds of people associated with
pilgrimage (e.g., touts promoting Gaya, who dogged his steps long before he reached north India) are revealing statements about agricultural
conditions that stem from the traveler's concern with provisioning his
substantial entourage. His route traversed the country and routinely
brought him to markets where daily needs were readily met. He invariably encountered traders and shopkeepers well equipped to service pilgrims, a reflection of both the institutionalized nature of pilgrimage
and the networks of trade developed to cater to the growing numbers
of people "on the road" in the nineteenth century. Along the Ganges
near Patna, for instance, Veeraswamy found supplies plentiful. His
comments on the abundance of grain and oilseed cultivation in the area

highlight precisely the two leading items of trade in the region.[1] And the easy access to goods of all kinds (which, although, often wanting in comparison with the quality familiar at home) anticipated the developments of the later nineteenth century—extensive trade and marketing systems across regions and the widespread dissemination of goods across the country.

The bazaar motif is also visible in the actions of Muzaffarpur, Champaran, and Saran villagers who, some ninety years after Veeraswamy's journey, erupted on to the scene of rural markets in the name of Gandhi. No doubt, they were part of the crowds mobilized by the cause of the Noncooperation Movement. But their targeting of markets is also indicative of the degree to which twentieth-century lives everywhere were increasingly intertwined with the marketing system (as they had increasingly become over the colonial period). Markets defined the spatial and social organization of rural society and shaped the very conditions of economic livelihood and existence. The occurrence of these events in outlying markets is significant as well: it highlights the changing balance between center and periphery. Whereas Patna had once commanded the entire region as its central place, it had by the twentieth century lost some of its sway over the hinterland.

The juxtaposition of the three episodes illustrates another marketing principle as well. Ghulam Husain's Patna was the central place of the region. The towns and marketing settlements Veeraswamy visited (which also directed him to the premier cities of Patna and Gaya) were the second-order intermediate (*qasbas*) and third-order standard markets. *Haats,* or periodic markets, the lowest level of the marketing hierarchy, and to a lesser extent the standard and intermediate markets, were the primary settings for the dramatic events of Noncooperation in north Bihar in 1921–22. To travel this circuit, from the city of Patna in the late eighteenth century to the *haats* of the early twentieth century, further emphasizes the shift in marketing's center of gravity, as well as in political dynamics: from the city that Ghulam Husain and his elite generation presided over to the rural marketplaces (and melas) that landholders controlled after the revolution and that Noncooperation turned into hotbeds of political action.

The stories featured here also speak to the rising marketization of local society. Melas, many of which served as the principal cattle fairs for

1. Veeraswamy, *Journal,* pp. 116–19.

the region, multiplied dramatically over the course of the colonial period, as did the numbers of people attending them. So did markets. As the statistical data for the districts of Patna and Saran clearly indicate, the overall number of markets shot up considerably, doubling and tripling over the colonial period. The Patna figures record a leap from 66 to 209 between 1811 and 1911, a tripling over a hundred-year period. That was followed in turn by another surge in the early twentieth century, when the total grew to 393 by 1951. The numbers for Saran begin with 138 in 1793 and increased to 323 in 1921. By the early 1940s the province of Bihar tallied 2,535 periodic markets, or 11 percent of the total number for all of India.[2] This proliferation of periodic markets had the effect of generating a better distribution of markets across the countryside.

Numbers do not relate the full story, though. For the growing marketization of local society is not just a tale of increasing accessibility and opportunities: it is also one of deepening imbrication of the lives of people in a world capitalist system. Related in this fashion, the story of *Bazaar India* is about people from all walks of life in Gangetic Bihar making decisions, tilling their fields, consuming foodstuffs and other goods, playing different roles in the agricultural system, and acting as players in the local and regional system of exchange in a setting increasingly defined by economic forces activated by both local and extralocal dynamics.

For traders and merchants, as well as for peasants and the landed elite, this meant that the arena of the market set the stage for both winning and losing: gains for those who could stake out strategic roles in the marketing and trade systems and losses for those who did not have the means to capitalize. Landholders, who weathered the storms of the age of revolution and were recognized as the zamindars and local allies of colonial preference, acquired the "overgrowing power" that Ghulam Husain had ascribed to them well before they became the "great" zamindars of the nineteenth century. This development occurred initially through legal and administrative support and subsequently—if they were fortunate enough to stay afloat in the nineteenth and early twentieth centuries—through the favorable conditions created by the rising market in land and agricultural commodities. Among peasants, many upper and middle agricultural castes were able to capitalize on the pos-

2. GOI, *Report on Fairs in India*, pp. 28, 121.

sibilities opened up by new avenues for moneylending and trading. They were the "amateurs" who gained the upper hand in village society.

Far greater beneficiaries were the so-called professionals: the Marwaris and Aggarwals, who had already established themselves along pilgrimage and trade circuits in Veeraswamy's time and then further extended their networks by the end of the nineteenth century. Organized into trading networks reinforced by caste, kinship, and territorial ties, this group of traders and merchants positioned itself in major hubs and towns as well as in lower-order marketing settlements in the countryside. From their ranks would rise many of the people in eastern India who constituted the "modern Indian business class."

As recently recounted by one historian, "bazaar firms," building on the foundations they had already established in the indigenous arena of trade and credit, emerged in the wake of World War I and the Great Depression to take over the space formerly monopolized by expatriate firms. This was also the time when multinational corporations entered the Indian business scene. Characterized by a shift in interest in production for the domestic market, this period (the indigenous cotton textile industry had developed earlier, in the late nineteenth century) witnessed the rise of light manufacturing "protected by war, tariff and depression. The production of cotton textiles, sugar, paper, etc., surged ahead within the sheltered domestic market, helped by the relatively simple technology. By the end of the period [up to 1939], Manchester cotton textiles, Java sugar, and foreign paper of all sorts except newsprint, were more or less eliminated by burgeoning manufacturing units owned by Indian businessmen and industrialists."[3]

One notable example of a firm that emerged from the bazaar of Gangetic Bihar to cater to new demands was Messrs. Kallu Babu Lallu Babu. A *kothi* dating back to the eighteenth century, this banking house established the Indian Electric Works in 1924, which became one of the first Indian firms to produce electric fans. Another firm that made the transition into the interwar years was Messrs. Gurmukh Rai Radhakrishna Jalan. Great patrons of art, this house, while continuing its banking business in the city of Patna and its role as *arathiya* in Bankipur and Calcutta, branched out into a number of other enterprises: in the city of Patna, the Law Press and a business in paper,

---

3. Rajat Kanta Ray, "Introduction" in *Entrepreneurship in India*, p. 54. This was also a time when the Indian steel industry headed by Tata Iron and Steel Company, based in south Bihar, took off.

which was also an agency of the Bengal Paper Mill; and in Darbhanga, its interests centered on the Darbhanga Sugar Company. But the biggest success story in the region featured Ramkrishna Dalmia, an "outsider" (he was from the Punjab-Rajasthan area) and a speculator on the Calcutta Stock Exchange, who made his mark in the 1930s by collaborating with a relative who owned land in the Shahabad area of Rohtas. From this emerged Rohtas Sugar Limited and, later on in that decade, Rohtas Industries Limited, which expanded into cement and other enterprises. By 1939 the Dalmia portfolio of interests made it "one of the largest Indian industrial groups."[4]

Read alongside one another in a different framework, the three episodes of this book featuring three sets of actors occupying three distinct time periods interrupted by sizable historical "chasms"—as well as the silences that have been filled in—make up a whole cloth that bears the conspicuous markings of nationalism. To reach the "nation through its narrative address" entails privileging those strands of the three episodes that highlight this theme.[5] Reread in this fashion, Ghulam Husain's *View of Modern Times* serves as a striking illustration of an amateur historian who perceptively recognized that new rulers had assumed the mantle of power and authority. Remarkable also is the tenor of his voice, which bespeaks an uncannily "modern" understanding of the difference between the disciplinary power of the emerging colonial system and the prior indigenous regime. The "English," as he observed, followed different "practices."

Was this a notion of difference that incorporated, however consciously or unconsciously, a sense of larger identity, one that differentiated the "English" from the Patna historian's own people? And was this category of people one that included both his coreligionists and those of the majority Hindu religion? Certainly he was well aware of the ties that bound him to his fellow elite, a sense of kinship defined by class and seemingly of culture and religious community, in that order. Or perhaps the most notable aspect of his account in this regard is its total absence—"reading Indian history in terms of a lack, an absence,

4. Claude Markovits, *Indian Business and Nationalist Politics, 1931–1939* (Cambridge: Cambridge University Press, 1985), p. 66; Bhandari, Soni, and Gupta, *Bharatiya Vyapariyon ka Parichaya*, 2nd part (Bhanpura, Indore: Commercial Book Publishing House, n.d.), pp. 8–10; *ShDG* 1966, pp. 285–88.

5. The phrase is taken from Homi K. Bhabha, "Introduction," in *Nation and Narration*, ed. idem (London: Routledge, 1990), p. 3.

or an incompleteness," Dipesh Chakrabarty might say[6]—of nationalism, whose birth in the subcontinent most historians date to later in the
nineteenth century.

The search for the nationalism motif in Veeraswamy's "Kasiyatra
Charitra" turns up comparable findings: the presence of a community
identity but as yet little that can be construed as the stirrings of nationalism. His ruminations, although not concerned with directly addressing the nation (political historians might add that even the "address" of
nationalism was not known at this time), evince a keen and alert sense
of larger identity, of a consciousness that encouraged him to reflect on
what a Brahmin from the south shared in common with Brahmins from
the north specifically and with all Hindus generally. At least on one notable occasion, his notion of "us" was inclusive enough to embrace
Muslims, a group he differentiated from Hindus on the grounds of religion but lumped together with Hindus for their shared difference as a
community from that of his "English" masters. The very act of crossing
regional, linguistic, and cultural boundaries within the rising colonial
state apparently alerted him to local difference as well as to extralocal
similarities.

Nationalism, according to the standard historiography, emerged in
the nineteenth century, with the establishment of the Indian National
Congress in 1885 a founding moment. It then matured into a mass
movement in the early twentieth century with the rise of the Gandhi. It
follows from this account, then, that the call for Hindu-Muslim unity
against the "Demoniac and Satanic Government" and the Noncooperation campaign constitute a chapter in the late and mature stage of nationalism, reached after decades of development in the early and intermediate stages. That at least is the way versions celebrating the
freedom struggle tell it.

Ironically, to construct a narrative centered on the axes of nation
and nationalism as the referents to this or any other historical narrative
raises (invariably so in the context of Indian history and historiography) the specter of what is termed *communalism*. "Communalism and
nationalism, as we understand them today," Gyan Pandey writes,
"arose together; the age of communalism was concurrent with the age
of nationalism; they were part of the same discourse."[7]

6. "Postcoloniality and the Artifice of History," p. 5.
7. *Construction of Communalism*, p. 236.

To repackage my narrative bundle in this manner requires making much of Ghulam Husain's emphasis on his Muslim identity or of Veeraswamy's underlining of his Hindu-ness in opposition to those he sets up as the Other—the "phirangis" or Europeans—a designation with obvious disparaging and hostile overtones. Yet one must surely keep in perspective that the categories of "Hindu" and "Muslim" had different connotations in the eighteenth and early nineteenth centuries than they had later on. Two excellent recent studies argue persuasively that religious identities did not emerge in any salient way until the late nineteenth century, which was then followed by a critical phase in the 1920s, when communalism emerged in full flower. Although ostensibly campaigning to popularize nationalism, as the experiences of the people who took up the cause of Noncooperation reveal, the growing mass movement led by Congress increasingly took on communal coloration as well—for words and symbols employed to exert widespread appeal and mobilize the people drew on a popular vocabulary, on the familiar storehouse of popular religion.[8]

Any account of what we historians term "modern" Indian history ultimately revolves around the theme of colonialism. From the late eighteenth century onward, the rising colonial state was very much a presence on the Indian scene. Ghulam Husain insightfully gauged its growing power as early as the 1770s. Indeed, historians typically consider 1818 as the consolidating moment of colonial rule. As Veeraswamy, the "Gentoo and Malabar" interpreter for the Madras Supreme Court of Judicature, wrote in the 1830s, the "good offices" of the "English" were critical not only in securing position and place in society but also in traveling the subcontinent. Veeraswamy's long pilgrimage demarcates the considerable territory in which the new regime had firmly entrenched itself and the extent to which it had consolidated its power and authority.

So multifaceted were the operations of colonial rule and so extensive were its instruments of control that its twentieth-century opponents had to wage Noncooperation on many fronts. People challenged the state politically by relying on the official techniques of public opposition to government: by making use of debate, demonstration, petitioning, print media, and so forth. They also attempted to sever the extensions of government by rupturing and incapacitating its connections

8. Ibid.; Freitag, *Emergence of Communalism in India.*

with indigenous society. A favorite tactic was to have government employees (e.g., the police) refuse to work for the state. Lawyers and students, for their part, and people from other walks of life, were encouraged to dissolve their links by refusing to meet their customary assignments and obligations.

Yet another method—and one naturally privileged here—was to seek out the vernacular space of the bazaar, where the state was present in its most tangible form as well as in its most subtle essence, and where its subjects gathered in significant numbers and communicated with one another and with outsiders through the currency of commerce and culture. Thus, in the Noncooperation encounter between indigenous society and state, the local population found its targets within easy reach: police stations and other emblems of a government presence that were lodged in the lower-order markets. These constituted the deepest penetration of the Raj into the countryside. Equally revealing are the attempts to disrupt exchanges with the state by targeting alcohol and imported cloth: the first item had significance both as a social reform and tax issue (government earned tax revenues from it), whereas the second commodity emblematized the economic and political ascendancy of the colonial system. Machine-made cloth from the mills of England had increasingly supplanted indigenous cloth. It symbolized the economic dominion of colonialism and was also a vivid reminder of the encapsulation of the Indian countryside in a world system mediated on the subcontinent through the interrelated forces of colonialism and capitalism. Long, long before deindustrialization became a subject of heated academic debate among South Asian scholars, people (e.g., Bholanauth Chunder around the middle of the nineteenth century) were aware that foreign competition was undermining their artisanal industries, particularly indigenous cloth production.

Noncooperation in the marketplaces of Bihar dramatized another dynamic of colonial rule, namely, its structural and ideological concreteness. Built of brick and mortar, it was reinforced by ideological cement, by a rhetoric of power that generated a hegemonic discourse. In Foucault's words, it constituted a "power relation" possessing the "correlative constitution of a field of knowledge." Ghulam Husain displayed some inkling of its reinforced composition in his seeming recognition of the novel disciplinary gaze that it directed at subjecting subjects. Previous rulers, he noted, had not possessed a "counting . . . and examining"; this was a new kind of "governing project." Torn by his loyalties to the Mughal Empire and the successor state of Bengal on the one hand and his ties to his new employers, the East India Company, on the other hand, he nevertheless considered his colonial masters "alien to this country." A similar tone can be detected in Veeraswamy, who was even more of a Company man but whose historical milieu more than fifty years later meant that he encountered a colonial system far more deeply entrenched. Nor can one ignore the voices of the people of Patna, who periodically participated in rumors rife with anti-British sentiments and who earned for the city its reputation as "a very sink of disaffection and intrigue." They posed a direct challenge to the hegemonic colonial discourse.

Equally strident and insistent were the voices issuing from the countryside in the early twentieth century. What better place to tune into these voices than the bazaar, that "hybrid place" where there exists a "commingling of categories usually kept separate and opposed: centre and periphery, inside and outside, stranger and local, commerce and festivity, high and low." But as the rhetoric and events of 1921–22 reveal, in the course of contestation, in the course of furthering the nationalist project and toppling the colonial enterprise, communal identities began to form as well.

So did other contradictions. The past, when viewed in the nationalist, colonial, or communal framework or against the giant backdrop of capitalism, ultimately denies historical subjects their subjecthood.[9] It glosses over—as I have done so far by reconstructing history to serve as thematic variants and examples of specific standard master narratives—the degree to which lived experiences are often replete with contradictions and are fragmentary in nature. Let me reiterate that the plotlines connecting the three principal sets of historical actors fitted into this narrative were drawn by me, however solid they may seem and however much they may appear in conformity with the established patterns of South Asian historiography. Connections serve to smooth out the story; ruptures would have made the historical narrative difficult to patch together.

But obviously historical actors eke out their existence with varying degrees of success and failure. The Ghulam Husain story in a history not centered on a master narrative stands out as an account of an intrepid historian directing his penetrating vision at the tumultuous events of his day to see how these would impinge on his society and his family.

9. Pandey, *Construction of Communalism*, p. 253.

Within a generation, as his family history indicates, his descendants had fallen from their aristocratic status, as did many families who once occupied center stage in the city of Patna. And without having to conform to other people's story lines, Veeraswamy's journal is remarkable as a detailed description of the physical and mental landscape that a pilgrim had to traverse.

The actions of those assembled in the marketplaces of north Bihar in 1921–22 provide an even clearer picture of the contradictions that can be ironed out of any historical retelling where the plots are set pieces dedicated to nationalism or colonialism or communalism. Indeed, as the official and nonofficial records reveal their activities—activities that were viewed as criminal and antigovernment on the one hand (the administrative perspective) and patriotic and nationalistic on the other hand (the nationalist perspective)—peasants waged Noncooperation in the name of Gandhi as well as to further their own agenda. And what better locale for these contradictions to surface than the "hybrid place" that was the market, this most appropriate setting for mounting the drama of Noncooperation. It was a site at which popular expressions against the colonial state found responsive echoes, a positive response shaped by the fit of the place itself in local society. People of a locality shared a sense of familiarity, they routinely assembled in sizable numbers, and their language of communication was its popular culture. But the same factors that facilitated common cause and community could also engender divisions. Economic and social issues that divided the local population into contending groups therefore came to the fore, as the incidents of 1921–22 illustrate. Indeed, the bazaar became the site of peasant agitation against their landholders. Whether tied to the nationalist movement or to tenant grievances, these events point to the local marketing system as the fundamental arena of rural society. It was a system that tied together rural society and manifested both its unifying and its divisive threads.

The "hybrid place" that was the bazaar in colonial India was the scene and stage of many different kinds of exchanges that a historian can negotiate into a multiplicity of stories. Some of these other stories, of course, I have not translated here, but that's another history.

Bibliography

ARCHIVAL SOURCES

CAMBRIDGE: CENTRE FOR SOUTH ASIAN STUDIES

P. T. Mansfield Papers

CHAPRA: SARAN DISTRICT RECORD ROOM

Saran District, Faujdari Bastas, English Correspondence, 1860–1909
Saran District Village Notes, 1893–1901 (3 vols.) (SVN, 1893–1901)
Saran District Village Notes, 1915–21 (50 vols.) (SVN)

HATHWA, SARAN DISTRICT

Hathwa Raj Records

LONDON: INDIA OFFICE LIBRARY AND RECORDS (BRITISH LIBRARY)

GOVERNMENT OF BENGAL (GOB)

Behar and Benares Revenue Proceedings, 1816–22
Bengal Board of Revenue (Customs, Famine, Jurisdiction and Boundaries, Land Revenue, Miscellaneous Revenue, Scarcity and Relief) Proceedings, 1760–1858
Bengal Board of Revenue (Miscellaneous) Proceedings, 1777–1858
Bengal Board of Revenue Proceedings, 1786–1855

Bengal Commercial Consultations, 1801–34
Bengal Education Proceedings, 1859–85
Bengal Financial Consultations, 1810–57
Bengal Financial (includes Agriculture, Census, Finance, License Tax, Statistics, Trade and Commerce) Proceedings, 1859–97
Bengal General Proceedings, 1859–1911
Bengal Judicial (includes Revenue Judicial; Criminal and Civil Judicial; and Criminal Judicial) Consultations, 1791–1857
Bengal Judicial (includes Police) Proceedings, 1859–1911
Bengal Military Consultations, 1800–34
Bengal Municipal (includes Sanitation) Proceedings, 1873–1911
Bengal Police Proceedings, 1873–85
Bengal Political Consultations, 1789–1852
Bengal Public Consultations, 1757–1858
Bengal Public Works Consultations, 1855–58
Bengal Public Works Proceedings, 1859–1911
Bengal Railway Proceedings, 1859–1911
Bengal Revenue Consultations, 1773–1858
Bengal Revenue Consultations (Customs, Grain, Mint, Opium, Salt, Sayer), 1791–1859
Bengal Sanitation Proceedings, 1866–88
Bengal Scarcity and Relief Proceedings, 1873–77
Bengal Separate Consultations, 1819–52
Bengal Statistics Proceedings, 1868–1911
Bengal Sudder Dewanny Adawlut Proceedings, 1773–74; 1793–1801
Calcutta Committee of Revenue Proceedings, 1771–85
Patna Factory Records (PFR), 1620–1779

GOVERNMENT OF BIHAR AND ORISSA (GOB&O)

Bihar and Orissa General Proceedings, 1912–26
Bihar and Orissa Judicial Proceedings, 1912–26
Bihar and Orissa Political Proceedings, 1912–26
Bihar and Orissa Revenue Proceedings, 1912–26

GOVERNMENT OF INDIA (GOI)

Home Miscellaneous Series
L/PARL., Parliamentary Branch
L/P&J, Public and Judicial

PRIVATE PAPERS

F. Hamilton Ms., Mss. Eur. D. 87–91, Behar and Patna

Hubback Papers, Photo Eur. 152
C. E. A. W. Oldham Collection, Mss. Eur. D 1167
Orme Mss., O.V. 6, 9

LONDON: SCHOOL OF ORIENTAL AND AFRICAN STUDIES LIBRARY

Famine Narratives, 1873-74

PATNA: BIHAR STATE ARCHIVES

Patna Commissioner's (P.C.) Records
Patna Commissioner's Annual Administration Reports (AGRPD), 1871-72 to
    1904-05 (variously titled "Annual General Report...," "Annual General
    Administration Report...," "Miscellaneous Annual Report...")

    Customs
    Court of Wards Bastas
    Double Lock Volumes
    From Collector of Bihar/Patna
    From Collector of Saran
    General Department
    Important Bundles, Revenue and Judicial Departments, Basta nos. 220-36
    Judicial Bastas
    Loose uncataloged bastas, various years
    Monthly bundles
    Revenue Bastas

Champaran Collectorate (C.C.) Records
Muzaffarpur Collectorate (M.C.) Records
Saran Collectorate (S.C.) Records

PATNA: BIHAR AND ORISSA RESEARCH SOCIETY

Patna Judge-Magistrate's Records

PATNA: PATNA COLLECTORATE

Patna District Village Notes, 1908-09 (PVN), 25 volumes

PATNA: PRIVATE PAPERS

Guzri Papers, Nawab Bahadur family
Rohatgi Papers

NONARCHIVAL SOURCES

GOVERNMENT PUBLICATIONS

GOVERNMENT OF BENGAL (GOB)

Blackwood, J. R. *A Survey and Census of the Cattle of Bengal.* Calcutta: Bengal Secretariat Book Depot, 1915.

Cumming, J. G. *Review of the Industrial Position and Prospects in Bengal in 1908, with Special Reference to the Industrial Survey of 1890.* Calcutta: Bengal Secretariat Book Depot, 1908.

District Census Reports, 1891, Patna Division. Calcutta: n.p., 1898.

Kerr, J. H. *Final Report on the Survey and Settlement Operations in the Saran District, 1893 to 1901.* Calcutta: Bengal Secretariat Press, 1903 (SSR).

O'Malley, L. S. S. *Bengal District Gazetteers, Darbhanga.* Calcutta: Bengal Secretariat Book Depot, 1907 (DDG).

———. *Bengal District Gazetteers, Gaya.* Calcutta: Bengal Secretariat Book Depot, 1906 (GDG).

———. *Bengal District Gazetteers, Muzaffapur.* Calcutta: Bengal Secretariat Book Depot, 1907 (MDG).

———. *Bengal District Gazetteers: Saran.* Calcutta: Bengal Secretariat Book Depot, 1908 (SDG 1908).

———. *Bengal District Gazetteers, Shahabad.* Calcutta: Bengal Secretariat Book Depot, 1906 (Sh.DG 1906).

Report on the Administration of the License Tax in Bengal for the Year 1880–81. Calcutta: Bengal Secretariat Press, 1881.

Report on the Internal Trade of Bengal for the Year 1876–77, 77–78. . . . Calcutta: Bengal Secretariat Press, 1877, 1878, . . .

Report on the Police of the Patna Division for the Year 1863. Calcutta: Bengal Secretariat Office, 1864.

Selections from the Records of the Bengal Government, no. 24, Correspondence Relating to the Ferry Funds in the Lower Provinces. Calcutta: Military Orphan Press, 1856.

Tanner, E. L. *Final Report on the Survey and Settlement Operations in the District of Gaya (1911–1918).* Patna: Government Printing, 1919 (GSR).

GOVERNMENT OF BIHAR AND ORISSA (GOB&O)

The Bihar and Orissa Provincial Banking Enquiry Committee, 1929–30. 3 vols. Patna: Government Printing, 1930.

Gupta, Phanindra Nath. *Final Report on the Survey and Settlement Operations (Revision) in the District of Saran, 1915 to 1921.* Patna: Government Printing, 1923 (SRR).

James, J. F. W. *Final Report on the Survey and Settlement Operations in the District of Patna (1907–1912).* Patna: B & O Government Press, 1914 (PSR).

Middleton, A. P. *Bihar and Orissa District Gazetteers: Saran.* Patna: Government Printing, 1930 (SDG 1930).

The Non-Cooperation and Khilafat Movements in Bihar and Orissa (Secret). Patna: Government Printing, 1925.

O' Malley, L. S. S. *Bihar and Orissa District Gazetteers, Patna.* Rev. ed. by J. F. W. James. Patna: Bihar and Orissa Government Printing, 1924 *(PDG 1924).*

Report of the Pilgrim Committee Bihar and Orissa. 1913. Simla: Government Press, 1915.

Selections from Speeches, Activities of Volunteers, Etc., during the Past Six Months in Bihar and Orissa. Patna: Government Printing, 1922.

Stephenson-Moore, C. J. 1922. *Final Report on the Survey and Settlement Operations in the Muzaffarpur District, 1892 to 1899.* Patna: Government Printing, 1922 *(MSR).*

Sweeney, J. A. *Final Report on the Survey and Settlement Operations (Revision) in the District of Champaran (1913–1919).* Patna: Government Printing, 1922 *(CSR).*

Tanner, E. L. *Final Report on the Survey and Settlement Operations in the District of Gaya (1911–1918).* Patna: Government Printing, 1919 *(GSR).*

GOVERNMENT OF BIHAR

Kumar, N. *Bihar District Gazetteers, Patna.* Patna: Government of Bihar, 1970.

Report on the Live-Stock Census of Bihar for the Year 1940 (Confidential). Patna: Government Printing, 1942.

Roy Chaudhury, P. C. *Bihar District Gazetteers, Champaran.* Patna: Secretariat Press, 1960 *(CDG 1960).*

———. *Bihar District Gazetteers, Palamau.* Patna: Secretariat Press, 1961.

———. *Bihar District Gazetteers, Purnea.* Patna: Secretariat Press, 1963.

GOVERNMENT OF INDIA (GOI)

Agricultural Marketing in India: Report on Fairs, Markets, and Produce Exchanges in India. Delhi: GOI Press, 1943.

Agricultural Marketing in India: Report on the Marketing of Cattle in India. Delhi: Government of India Press, 1946.

Lacey, W. G. *Census of India, 1931,* vol. 7, *Bihar and Orissa, Part II.-Tables.* Patna: Bihar and Orissa, 1932.

O'Donnell, C. J. *Census of India, 1891,* vol. 3, *The Lower Provinces of Bengal, The Report.* Calcutta: Bengal Secretariat Press, 1893.

Office of the Agricultural Marketing Adviser. *Agricultural Marketing in India, Report on the Marketing of Rice in India and Burma.* Marketing Series no. 27. Delhi: GOI Press, 1941.

Prasad, S. D. *Census of India,* vol. 4, part 9, *Census Atlas of Bihar.* Delhi: 1968.

———. *Census of India, 1961,* vol. 4, *Bihar,* Part 7-b, *Fairs and Festivals of Bihar.* Purnea: n.p., 1971.

Tallents, P. C. *Census of India, 1921,* vol. 7, *Bihar and Orissa,* Part I, *Report.* Patna: Government Printing, 1923.

OTHER OFFICIAL PUBLICATIONS

Fort William-India House Correspondence. Public Series, vol. 1:1786–88, edited by Raghubir Sinh. Delhi: Government of India, 1972.

Grierson, George A. *Bihar Peasant Life.* 1885. Reprint, Delhi: Cosmo Publications, 1975.

————. *Notes on the District of Gaya.* Calcutta: Bengal Secretariat Press, 1893.

Hunter, W. W. *A Statistical Account of Bengal,* vol. 11, *Districts of Patna and Saran.* London: Trubner and Co., 1877.

————. *A Statistical Account of Bengal,* vol. 12, *Districts of Gaya and Shahabad.* London: Trubner and Co., 1877.

————. *A Statistical Account of Bengal,* vol. 13, *Districts of Tirhut and Champaran.* London: Trubner and Co., 1877.

Jameson, James. *Report on the Epidemick Cholera Morbus.* Calcutta: A. G. Balfour, 1820.

Rankine, Robert. *Notes on the Medical Topography of the District of Saran.* Calcutta: Military Orphan Press, 1839.

Thuiller, H. E. L. *Statistics of the District of Patna.* Calcutta: n.p., 1847.

Trevelyan, Charles E. *Report upon the Inland Customs and Town Duties of the Bengal Presidency.* Edited by Tarasankar Banerjee. 1834. Reprint, n.p.: Academic Publishers, 1976.

United Provinces. *Report of the Pilgrim Committee, United Provinces, 1913.* Simla: Government Central Branch Press, 1916.

Wilson, H. H. *A Glossary of Judicial and Revenue Terms.* 1855. Reprint, Delhi: Munshiram Manoharlal, 1968.

Wyatt, Alexander. *Geographical and Statistical Report of the District of Tirhoot.* Calcutta: Calcutta Gazette Office, 1854.

————. *Statistics of the District of Sarun Consisting of Sircars Sarun and Chumparun.* Calcutta: Military Orphan Press, 1847(?).

CONTEMPORARY WORKS

Abbott, Harry E. *Sonepore Reminiscences (Years 1840–1896).* Calcutta: Star Press, 1896.

Ashby, Lillian Luker, with Roger Whately. *My India.* London: Michael Joseph, 1938.

Banarsidas. *Ardhakathanaka.* Translated by Mukund Lath. Jaipur: Rajasthan Prakrit Bharati Sansthan, 1981.

Buchanan, Francis. *An Account of the District of Purnea in 1809–10.* Patna: Bihar and Orissa Research Society, 1928.

————. *An Account of the District of Shahabad in 1812–13.* 2 vols. Patna: Bihar and Orissa Research Society, 1934.

————. *An Account of the Districts of Bihar and Patna in 1811–1812.* Patna: Bihar and Orissa Research Society, 1928.

————. *Journal of Francis Buchanan Kept during the Survey of the District of Bhagalpur in 1810–1811.* Edited by C. E. A. W. Oldham. Patna: Government Printing, 1930.

————. *Journal of Francis Buchanan (afterwards Hamilton) Kept during the Survey of the Districts of Patna and Gaya in 1811–12*. Edited by V. H. Jackson. Patna: Government Printing, 1925.

————. *Journal of Francis Buchanan Kept during the Survey of the District of Shahabad in 1812–1813*. Edited by C. E. A. W. Oldham. Patna: Government Printing, 1926.

[Buchanan, Francis]. Montgomery Martin. *Eastern India*, vol. 2, *Bhagalpur, Gorakhpur*. Reprint, Delhi: Cosmo Publications, 1976.

Buckland, C. T. *Sketches of Social Life in India*. London: n.p., 1884.

Buyers, William. *Recollections of Northern India*. London: John Snow, 1848.

Chowdhari, Ramgopal Singh. *Rambles in Bihar*. Bankipur: Express Press, 1917.

Chowdhary, Ramgopal Singh. *Select Writings and Speeches of Babu Ramgopal Singh Chowdhary*. Patna: Bishund Prasad Sinha, 1920.

Chunder, Bholanauth. *The Travels of a Hindoo to Various Parts of Bengal and Upper India*. 2 vols. London: N. Trubner, 1869.

Colebrooke, H. T. *Remarks on the Present State of the Husbandry and Commerce of Bengal*. Calcutta: n.p., 1795.

Gandhi, Mahatma. *The Collected Works of Mahatma Gandhi, 19, (November 1920–April 1921)*. Ahmedabad: Government of India, 1966.

Ghose, A. C. "Rural Behar." *Calcutta Review* 220 (1900): 218–32.

[Graham, G.] An Ex.-Civilian. *Life in the Mofussil; or, the Civilian in Lower Bengal*. London: C. Kegan Paul, 1878.

Grand, G. F. *The Narrative of the Life of a Gentleman Long Resident in India*. Calcutta: Calcutta Historical Society, 1910.

[Husain, Ghulam] Seid-Gholam-Hossein-Khan. *The Seir Mutaqherin, or View of Modern Times, Being an History of India from the Year 1181 to the Year 1194*. Translated by Nota Manus. 4 vols. Calcutta: T. D. Chatterjee, 1902.

Law, Thomas. *A Sketch of Some Late Arrangements, and a View of the Rising Resources in Bengal*. London: John Stockdale, 1792.

Macpherson, William Charles. *Soldiering in India, 1764–1787*. Edinburgh: William Blackwood and Sons, 1928.

Marshall, John. *John Marshall in India: Notes and Observations in Bengal, 1668–1672*. Edited by Shafaat Ahmad Khan. London: Humphrey Milford, 1927.

Mohanti, Prafulla. *My Village, My Life*. London: Corgi Books, 1973.

Mundy, Peter. *The Travels of Peter Mundy*, vol. 2, *Travels in Asia, 1628–1634*. London: Hakluyt Society, 1914.

Purves, J. *The East India Merchant; or A Guide to the Commerce and Manufactures of Bengal and the Upper Provinces*. Calcutta: Times Press, 1819.

Tayler, W. *The Patna Crisis*. London: W. H. Allen, 1882.

Tucker, Henry St. George. *Memorial of Indian Government; Being a Selection from the Papers of Henry St. George Tucker*. Edited by John William Kaye. London: Richard Bentley, 1853.

Twining, Thomas. *Travels in India a Hundred Years Ago, with a Visit to the United States: Being Notes and Reminiscences by Thomas Twining*. Edited by William H. G. Twining. London: James R. Osgood, 1893.

Veeraswamy, Enugula. *Enugula Veeraswamy's Journal (Kasiyatra Charitra).* Edited and translated by P. Sitapati and V. Purushottam. Hyderabad: Andhra Pradesh Governmental Oriental Manuscripts Library and Research Institute, 1973.

Wilson, Minden. *History of Behar Indigo Factories; Reminiscences of Behar; Tirhoot and Its Inhabitants of the Past; History of Bihar Light Horse Volunteers.* Calcutta: Calcutta General Printing, 1908.

INTERVIEWS

Interview with Justice Sarwar Ali, descendant of Guzri family, 1984

Interview with Krishna Chandra, Patna City, June 1984.

Interview with Nawab Waris Ismail (1909-), descendant of Wilayat Ali Khan, May 19, 1984.

Interview with C. K. and M. P. Rohatgi family, descendants of Kallu Babu and Lallu Babu, at Pradip Lamps Factory, Patna, June 16, 1984.

SERIALS AND NEWSPAPERS

Behar Herald, 1920–1924.

Chanakya Society, *Annual Reports,* 1910–1911 . . . 1918–19.

Searchlight, 1920–1930.

SECONDARY SOURCES

Adalemo, Isaac Ayinde. *Marketplaces in a Developing Country: The Case of Western Nigeria.* Ann Arbor: Michigan Geographical Publications no. 26, University of Michigan, 1981.

Agarwal, B. P. *Agarwal Vyapar Darpan, Bihar aur Orissa.* Muzaffarpur: B. P. Agarwal, 191?

Agrawal, Binod C. *Cultural Contours of Religion and Economics in Hindu Universe.* New Delhi: National, 1980.

Agnew, Jean-Christophe. *Worlds Apart: The Market and the Theater in Anglo-American Thought, 1550–1750.* Cambridge: Cambridge University Press, 1986.

Ahmad, Enayat. *Bihar: A Physical, Economic and Regional Geography.* Ranchi: Ranchi University, 1965.

Ahmad, Khan Bahadur Saiyid Zamir-ud-din. "Ghulam 'Ali Rasikh." *JBRS* 4 (1918): 44–61.

Ahmad, Qeyamuddin. *Corpus of Arabic and Persian Inscriptions of Bihar (A.H. 640–1200).* Patna: K. P. Jayaswal Research Institute, 1973.

———. "An Eighteenth-Century Indian Historian on Early British Administration." *Journal of Indian History* (1973): 893–907.

———. *The Wahabi Movement in India.* Calcutta: Firma K. L. Mukhopadhyay, 1966.

———, ed. *Patna through the Ages.* New Delhi: Commonwealth Publishers, 1988.

Alam, Muzaffar. "Eastern India in the Early Eighteenth Century 'Crisis': Some Evidence from Bihar." *IESHR* 28 (1991): 43–71.

Alder, Garry. *Beyond Bokhara: The Life of William Moorcroft, Asian Explorer and Pioneer Veterinary Surgeon, 1767–1825.* London: Century Publishing, 1985.

Amin, Shahid. *Event, Metaphor, Memory: Chauri Chaura, 1922–1992.* Berkeley and Los Angeles: University of California Press, 1995.

Anderson, B. L., and A. J. H. Latham, eds. *The Market in History.* London: Croom Helm, 1986.

Ankersmit, F. R. "Historiography and Postmodernism." *History and Theory* 28 (1989): 137–53.

———. "Reply to Professor Zagorin." *History and Theory* 29 (1990): 275–96.

Appadurai, Arjun. "Theory and Anthropology: Center and Periphery." *CSSH* 28 (1986): 356–67.

———. *Worship and Conflict under Colonial Rule: A South Indian Case.* Cambridge: Cambridge University Press, 1981.

———, ed. *The Social Life of Things.* Cambridge: Cambridge University Press, 1986.

Arreraj Mahatmya. Bettiah: Lakshminarayan Saran, 193?

Askari, Syed Hasan, and Qeyamuddin Ahmad, eds. *Comprehensive History of Bihar.* Vol. 2, part 1. Patna: Kashi Prasad Jayaswal Research Institute, 1983.

Asli Gaya Mahatmya. Gaya: Harilal Bannerji, n.d.

Bagchi, Amiya Kumar. "Deindustrialisation in Gangetic Bihar, 1809–1901." In *Essays in Honour of Professor S. C. Sarkar,* ed. Barun De. New Delhi: People's Publishing House, 1976.

Baker, Christopher. *The Tamilnad Countryside.* Oxford: Clarendon Press, 1984.

———. "Tamilnad Estates in the 20th Century." *IESHR* 13 (1976): 1–44.

Bakhtin, Mikahil. *Rabelais and His World.* Trans. by Helene Iswolsky. Bloomington: Indiana University Press, 1984.

Bakker, H. T. "The Rise of Ayodhya as a Place of Pilgrimage." *Indo-Iranian Journal* 24 (1982): 103–26.

Bakker, H. T., and Alan Entwistle. *Vaisnavism: The History of the Krsna and Rama Cults and Their Contribution to Indian Pilgrimage.* Groningen: Institute of Indian Studies, State University of Groningen, 1981.

Ballhatchet, Kenneth, and John Harrison, eds. *The City in South Asia: Pre-Modern and Modern.* London: Curzon Press, 1980.

Banerjee, Kumkum. "Grain Traders and the East India Company: Patna and Its Hinterland in the Late Eighteenth and Early Nineteenth centuries." *IESHR* 23 (1986): 403–29.

Basu, Dilip K., ed. *The Rise and Growth of the Colonial Port Cities in Asia.* Monograph series, Center for South and Southeast Asia Studies, University of California, no. 25. Lanham, Md.: University Press of America, 1985.

Bayly, C. A. "From Ritual to Ceremony: Death Ritual and Society in Hindu North India since 1600." In *Mirrors of Mortality,* edited by J. Whaley, pp. 154–85. London: Europa Publications, 1981.

————. *The New Cambridge History of India, II, 1, Indian Society and the Making of the British Empire.* Cambridge: Cambridge University Press, 1988.

————. *Rulers, Townsmen, and Bazaars: North Indian Society in the Age of British Expansion, 1770–1870.* Cambridge: Cambridge University Press, 1982.

Beals, Ralph L. *The Peasant Marketing System of Oaxaca, Mexico.* Berkeley and Los Angeles: University of California Press, 1975.

Beavon, K. S. O. *Central Place Theory: A Reinterpretation.* London: Longman, 1977.

Behar Industrial and Agricultural Exhibition Committee. *Industries of the Patna Division.* Bankipore: Khadga Vilas Press, 1908.

Berkhofer, Robert F., Jr. "The Challenge of Poetics to (Normal) Historical Practice." In *The Rhetoric of Interpretation and the Interpretation of Rhetoric,* edited by Paul Hernadi. Durham: Duke University Press, 1989.

Bernstein, Henry T. *Steamboats on the Ganges.* Bombay: Orient Longmans, 1960.

Berry, Brian J. L. *Geography of Market Centers and Retail Distribution.* Englewood Cliffs, N.J.: Prentice-Hall, 1967.

Beveridge, H. "The City of Patna." *Calcutta Review* 76, no. 152 (1883): 211–33.

Bhabha, Homi K. "The Other Question: Difference, Discrimination and the Discourse of Colonialism." In *Literature, Politics and Theory,* edited by F. Barker et al. London: Methuen, 1986.

————., ed. *Nation and Narration.* London: Routledge, 1990.

Bhandari, C. R., B. L. Soni, and Gupta, K. L. *Agarwal Jati ka Itihas.* Bhanpura: Agrawal History Office, 1937.

————, eds. *Bharatiya Vyapriyon Parichaya* Bhanpura, Indore: Commercial Book Publishing House, 19?

Bharati, Agehananda. "Pilgrimage Sites and Indian Civilization." In *Chapters in Indian Civilization,* vol. 1, *Classical and Medieval India.* Edited by Joseph W. Elder. Dubuque, Iowa: Kendall/Hunt Publishing, 1970.

Bhardwaj, Surinder Mohan. *Hindu Places of Pilgrimage in India: A Study in Cultural Geography.* Berkeley and Los Angeles: University of California Press, 1973.

Bingham, R. W. "Report on the Productive Resources of the Sasseram District." *Journal of Agricultural and Horticultural Society of India* 12 (1861): 311–64.

Blake, Stephen P. *Shahjahanabad: The Sovereign City in Mughal India, 1639–1739.* Cambridge: Cambridge University Press, 1991.

Bose, Sugata, ed. *South Asia and World Capitalism.* Delhi: Oxford University Press, 1990.

Bradley-Birt, F. B. *Twelve Men of Bengal in the Nineteenth Century.* Calcutta: S. K. Lahiri, 1927.

Braudel, Fernand. *Civilization and Capitalism, 15th–18th Century,* vol. 1, *The Structures of Everyday Life.* London: Collins, 1981.

————. *Civilization and Capitalism 15th–18th Century,* vol. 2, *The Wheels of Commerce.* London: Collins, 1982.

———. *On History.* Trans. Sarah Matthews. Chicago: University of Chicago Press, 1980.

Breckenridge, Carol A., and Peter Van der Veer, eds. *Orientalism and the Post-colonial Predicament: Perspectives on South Asia.* Delhi: Oxford University Press, 1994.

Bromley, R. J., and Richard Symanski. "Marketplace Trade in Latin America." *Latin American Research Review* 9 (1974): 3–38.

Brown, Judith M. *Gandhi's Rise to Power: Indian Politics, 1915–1922.* Cambridge: Cambridge University Press, 1972.

Brush, John E. "The Morphology of Indian Cities." In *India's Urban Future,* edited by Roy Turner. Berkeley and Los Angeles: University of California Press, 1962.

Burrow, J. W. "'The Village Community' and the Uses of History in Late Nineteenth-Century England." In *Historical Perspectives: Studies in English Thought and Society,* edited by Neil McKendrick. London: Europa Publications, 1974.

Cassels, Nancy Gardner. *Religion and Pilgrim Tax under the Company Raj.* Riverdale, Md.: Riverdale, 1988.

Chakrabarty, Dipesh. "Postcoloniality and the Artifice of History: Who Speaks for 'Indian' Pasts?" *Representations* 37 (1992): 1–26

Chatterjee, Kumkum. "Intimations of Crisis: The Elite of Azimabad-Patna, 1757–1820." Paper presented at the meeting of the Association for Asian Studies, Boston, Mar. 24–27, 1994.

Chattopadhyay, Basudeb, Hari S. Vasudevan, and Rajat Kanta Ray, eds. *Dissent and Consensus: Social Protest in Pre-Industrial Societies.* Calcutta: K. P. Bagchi and Co., 1989.

Chaudhuri, Sukanta, ed. *Calcutta: The Living City.* 2 vols. Calcutta: Oxford University Press, 1990.

Chaudhary, Radhakrishna. *Mithila in the Age of Vidyapati.* Varanasi: Chaukhambha Orientalia, 1976.

Cheesman, David. "'The Omnipresent Bania': Rural Moneylenders in Nineteenth-Century Sind." *MAS* 16 (1982): 445–62.

Clifford, James, and George E. Marcus. *Writing Culture: The Poetics and Politics of Ethnography.* Berkeley and Los Angeles: University of California Press, 1986.

Cohn, Bernard S. *An Anthropologist among the Historians, and Other Essays.* Delhi: Oxford University Press, 1987.

———. "The Anthropology of a Colonial State and Its Form of Knowledge." Paper presented at a Symposium on "Tensions of Empire: Colonial Control and Visions of Rule," Mijas, Spain, Nov. 5–13, 1988.

Colebrooke, Edward. "Biographical Sketch of Henry Thomas Colebrooke." *Asiatic Journal,* n.s., 24 (1837): 104.

Cook, Scott, and Martin Diskin, eds. *Markets in Oaxaca.* Austin: University of Texas Press, 1976.

Cotton, A. *Public Works in India: Their Importance.* London: W. H. Allen, 1854.

Crooke, William. *A Glossary of North Indian Peasant Life.* Edited by Shahid Amin. Delhi: Oxford University Press, 1989.

Cummings, R. *Pricing Efficiency in the Indian Wheat Market.* New Delhi: Impex, 1967.

Curley, David L. "Rulers and Merchants in Late Eighteenth-Century Bengal." Ph.D. diss., University of Chicago, 1980.

Daniel, E. Valentine. *Fluid Signs: Being a Person the Tamil Way.* Berkeley and Los Angeles: University of California Press, 1984.

Darian, Steven G. *The Ganges in Myth and History.* Honolulu: University of Hawaii Press, 1978.

Datta, K. K. *Biography of Kunwar Singh and Amar Singh.* Patna: K. P. Jayaswal Research Institute, 1957.

———. *Studies in the History of the Bengal Subah, 1740–70,* vol. 1, *Social and Economic.* Calcutta: University of Calcutta, 1936.

Datta, Rajat. "Merchants and Peasants: A Study of the Structure of Local Trade in Grain in Late Eighteenth Century Bengal." *IESHR* 23 (1986): 379–402.

Davis, Natalie Zemon. *Society and Culture in Early Modern France.* Stanford: Stanford University Press, 1975.

Deloche, Jean. *Transport and Communications in India Prior to Steam Locomotion.* 2 vols. Trans. from the French by James Walker. Delhi: Oxford University Press, 1993.

Derbyshire, I. D. "Economic Change and the Railways in North India, 1860–1914." *MAS* 21 (1987): 521–45.

Dewey, Clive. "Images of the Village Community: A Study in Anglo-Indian Ideology." *MAS* 6 (1972): 291–328.

Dewey, Clive, and A. G. Hopkins, eds. *The Imperial Impact: Studies in the Economic History of Africa and India.* London: Athlone Press, 1978.

Dirks, Nicholas B. *The Hollow Crown: Ethnohistory of an Indian Kingdom.* 2d ed. Ann Arbor: University of Michigan Press, 1993.

Diwakar. R. R. *Bihar through the Ages.* Calcutta: Orient Longmans, 1958.

Dube, Karta Kishan, comp. *Vyapariyon ki Namavali.* Part 3. Lucknow: Karta Kishan Dube, 1919.

Dumont, Louis. "The 'Village Community' from Munro to Maine." *Contributions to Indian Sociology* 9 (1966): 67–89.

Dutt, Devendra Nath. *A Brief History of the Hutwa Raj.* Calcutta: K. P. Mookerjee, 1909.

Dutt, G. "Further Notes on the Bhojpuri Dialects Spoken in Saran." *Journal of the Asiatic Society of Bengal* 73 (1907): 245–49.

Dutt, Romesh C. *The Economic History of India,* vol. 2, *In the Victorian Age, 1837-1900.* Reprint, New Delhi: Government of India, 1960.

Dyson, Tim, ed. *India's Historical Demography: Studies in Famine, Disease, and Society.* London: Curzon Press, 1989.

Eck, Diana L. *Banaras: City of Light.* London: Routledge and Kegan Paul, 1983.

———. "India's Tirthas: "Crossings" in Sacred Geography." *History of Religions* 20 (1981): 323–44.

Farooque, Abul Khair Muhammad. *Roads and Communications in Mughal India.* Delhi: Idarah-I Adabiyat-I Delli, 1977.

Foucault, Michel. *Discipline and Punish: The Birth of the Prison.* Translated by Alan Sheridan. Middlesex: Penguin Books, 1977.

————. *The Foucault Reader.* Edited by Paul Rabinow. New York: Pantheon, 1984.

————. *Power/Knowledge: Selected Interviews and Other Writings, 1972–1977.* Edited by Colin Gordon. New York: Pantheon, 1980.

Fox, Richard. *From Zamindar to Ballot Box: Community Change in a North Indian Market Town.* Ithaca: Cornell University Press, 1969.

Freed, Ruth S., and Stanley A. Freed. "Calendars, Ceremonies, and Festivals in a North Indian Village: The Necessary Calendric Information for Fieldwork." *Southwestern Journal of Anthropology* 20 (1964): 67–90.

Freitag, Sandria B. *Collective Action and Community: Public Arenas and the Emergence of Communalism in North India.* Berkeley and Los Angeles: University of California Press, 1989.

————, ed. *Culture and Power in Banaras: Community, Performance, and Environment, 1800–1980.* Berkeley and Los Angeles: University of California Press, 1989.

Frykenberg, Robert Eric, ed. *Land Control and Social Structure in Indian History.* Madison: University of Wisconsin Press, 1969.

Fuller, C. J. "British India or Traditional India? An Anthropological Problem." *Ethnos* 42 (1977): 95–121.

G. P. S. "Patna, during the Last Days of the Mahomedans." *Calcutta Review* 147 (1882): 114–37.

Gaya Mahatmya. Edited and translated into French by Claude Jacques. Pondichery: Institut Francais d'Indologie, 1962.

Geertz, Clifford. "'From the Native's Point of View': On the Nature of Anthropological Understanding." In *Meaning in Anthropology.* Edited by Keith H. Basso and Henry A. Selby. Albuquerque: University of New Mexico Press, 1976.

Ghosh, Avijit. "Rural Distribution Systems in Newly Industrializing Societies: A Survey of Its Economics and Geography." *Discussion Paper Series,* Discussion Paper 25, Department of Geography, University of Iowa.

Ghosh, Manoranjan. *The Pataliputra.* Patna: Patna Law Press, 1919.

Giddens, Anthony. *The Constitution of Society.* Berkeley and Los Angeles: University of California Press, 1984.

Gold, Ann Grodzins. *Fruitful Journeys: The Ways of Rajasthani Pilgrims.* Berkeley and Los Angeles: University of California Press, 1988.

Good, Charles M. *Rural Markets and Trade in East Africa: A Study of the Functions and Development of Exchange Institutions in Ankole, Uganda.* Chicago: Dept. of Geography Research Paper no. 128, University of Chicago, 1970.

Gopal, Surendra. *Patna in 19th Century.* Calcutta: Naya Prokash, 1982.

Goswami, B. N. "The Records Kept by Priests at Centres of Pilgrimage as a Source of Social and Economic History." *IESHR* 3 (1966): 174–84.

Guha, Amalendu. "Raw Cotton of Western India, 1750–1850." *IESHR* 9 (1972): 20–21.

Guha, Ranajit. *A Disciplinary Aspect of Indian Nationalism.* Santa Cruz: Merrill Publications, University of California, 1990.

―――. *Elementary Aspects of Peasant Insurgency in Colonial India.* Delhi: Oxford University Press, 1983.

―――, ed. *Subaltern Studies: Writings on South Asian History and Society.* Delhi: Oxford University Press, 1984.

―――. *Subaltern Studies III: Writings in South Asian History and Society.* Delhi: Oxford University Press, 1984.

Guha, Ranajit, and Gayatri Chakravorty Spivak, eds. *Selected Subaltern Studies.* New York: Oxford University Press, 1988.

Habib, Irfan. *An Atlas of the Mughal Empire.* Delhi: Oxford University Press, 1982.

―――. "Studying a Colonial Economy—without Perceiving Colonialism." *MAS* 19 (1985): 355–81.

Hagen, James R. "Indigenous Society, the Political Economy, and Colonial Education in Patna District: A History of Social Change from 1811 to 1951 in Gangetic North India." Ph.D. diss., University of Virginia, 1981.

Hand, J. Reginald. *Early English Administration of Bihar, 1781–1785.* Calcutta: Bengal Secretariat Press, 1894.

Harihar Kshetra Mahatmya. Gaya: Prabhu Narayan Misra, 1924.

Harris, Marvin, "The Myth of the Sacred Cow." In *Man, Culture, and Animals.* Edited by Anthony Leeds and Andrew P. Vayda. Washington, D.C.: American Association for the Advancement of Science, publication no. 78, 1965.

Harrison, F. C. "The Behar Ryot at Home." *Calcutta Review* 91, no. 172 (1890): 274–305.

Heesterman, J. C. *The Inner Conflict of Tradition: Essays in Indian Ritual, Kingship, and Society.* Chicago: University of Chicago Press, 1985.

Henningham, Stephen. *A Great Estate and Its Landlords in Colonial India, Darbhanga, 1860–1942.* Delhi: Oxford University Press, 1990.

―――. *Peasant Movements in Colonial India, North Bihar, 1917–1942.* Canberra: Australian National University, 1982.

Hill, Polly. *Development Economics on Trial.* Cambridge: Cambridge University Press, 1986.

Hodges, Richard. *Primitive and Peasant Markets.* Oxford: Basil Blackwell, 1988.

Houlton, Sir John. *Bihar: The Heart of India.* Bombay: Orient Longmans, 1949.

Hubback, J. A. *Indian Banking with Special Reference to Bihar and Orissa, Patna University, Banaili Readership Lecture, 1930–31.* Patna: Patna University, 1931.

Huddleston, G. *History of the East Indian Railway.* Calcutta: Thacker, Spink, and Co., 1906.

Husain, S. A. *Agricultural Marketing in Northern India.* London: Allen and Unwin, 1937.

Imam, Md. Muzaffar. *Role of Muslims in the National Movement (1912–1930) (A Study of Bihar).* Delhi: Mittal Publications, 1987.

Inden, Ronald. *Imagining India.* Oxford: Basil Blackwell, 1990.

"Irrigation and Railway Communication in Sarun." *Calcutta Review* 68, no. 136 (1879): 365–78.

Irschick, Eugene F. *Dialogue and History: Constructing South India, 1795–1895.* Berkeley and Los Angeles: University of California Press, 1994.

James, J. F. W. "The River Front of Patna at the Beginning of the Eighteenth Century." *JBORS* 11 (1925): 85–90.

Jasdanwala, Z. Y. *Marketing Efficiency in Indian Agriculture.* Bombay: Allied Publishers, 1966.

Jordens, J. T. F. "Medieval Hindu Devotionalism." *A Cultural History of India.* Edited by A. L. Basham. Oxford: Clarendon Press, 1975.

Karve, Irawati, and Hemalata Acharya. *The Role of Weekly Markets in the Tribal, Rural, and Urban Settings.* Poona: Deccan College, 1970.

King, Leslie J. *Central Place Theory.* Beverly Hills, Calif.: Sage Publications, 1984.

Kumar, Dharma, ed. *The Cambridge Economic History of India, vol. 2: c. 1757–c. 1970.* Cambridge: Cambridge University Press, 1982.

Kumar, Jnanendra Nath. *The Genealogical History of India,* Part 2. Calcutta: Victoria Press, 1949.

Kumar, Nagendra. *Indian National Movement (with Special Reference to the District of old Saran, Bihar) 1857–1947.* Patna: Janaki Prakashan, 1979.

Ladurie, E. LeRoy. *The Territory of the Historian.* Translated by Ben and Sian Reynolds. Chicago: University of Chicago Press, 1979.

Lal, Rama Shanker. "Transport and Accessibility in Lower Ghaghara Gandak Doab." *Deccan Geographer* 7 (1969): 14–34.

Lehmann, Frederick Louis. "The Eighteenth Century Transition in India: Responses of Some Bihar Intellectuals." Ph.D. diss., University of Wisconsin, 1967.

Lele, U. J. *Food Grain Marketing in India: Private Performance and Public Policy.* Ithaca: Cornell University Press, 1971.

Lodrick, Deryck O. *Sacred Cows, Sacred Places.* Berkeley and Los Angeles: University of California Press, 1981.

Ludden, David. "Agricultural Expansion, Diversification, and Commodity Production in Early Modern India: Labor Mobility in the Peninsula, 1300–1800." Paper presented at the meeting of the Association for Asian Studies, March, 1988, San Francisco.

———. "Productive Power in Agriculture: A Survey of Work on the Local History of British India." In *Agrarian Power and Agricultural Productivity in South Asia.* Edited by Meghnad Desai, Susanne Hoeber Rudolph, and Ashok Rudra. Berkeley and Los Angeles: University of California Press, 1985.

Lutgendorf, Philip. *The Life of a Text: Performing the Ramcaritmanas of Tulsidas.* Berkeley and Los Angeles: University of California Press, 1991.

McAlpin, Michelle Burge. "The Effects of Markets on Rural Income Distribution in Nineteenth Century India." *Exploration in Economic History* 12 (1975): 289–302.

Mahto, Vishwanath. *Shri Barabar Mahatmya.* Bhagalpur: B.A. Press, 1915?

Mandelbaum, David G. *Society in India,* vol. 2, *Change and Continuity.* Berkeley and Los Angeles: University of California Press, 1970.

Marshall, P. J. *New Cambridge History of India*, vol. 2, part 2, *Bengal: The British Bridgehead, Eastern India, 1740–1828*. Cambridge: Cambridge University Press, 1987.

Masselos, Jim. "Appropriating Urban Space: Social Constructs of Bombay in the time of the Raj." Paper presented at the SSRC Workshop on "Culture and Consciousness," Isle of Thorns, Sussex, July 1989.

Metcalf, Thomas R. *Land, Landlords, and the British Raj: Northern India in the Nineteenth Century*. Berkeley and Los Angeles: University of California Press, 1979.

Mishra, Girish. *Agrarian Problems of Permanent Settlement: A Case Study of Champaran*. New Delhi: People's Publishing House, 1978.

"Mofussil Stations. No. IV.—Patna." *Asiatic Journal* 10 (1833): 249–60.

Mohsin, Khan Mohammad. *A Bengal District in Transition: Murshidabad, 1765–1793*. Dacca: Asiatic Society of Bangladesh, 1973.

Morinis, E. Alan. *Pilgrimage in the Hindu Tradition: A Case Study of West Bengal*. Delhi: Oxford University Press, 1984.

Mukherjee, B. B. *Agricultural Marketing in India*. Calcutta: Thacker, Spink, and Co., 1937.

———. *Co-operation and Rural Welfare in India*. Calcutta: Thacker, Spink, and Co., 1929.

Mukherjee, S. N. *Calcutta: Essays in Urban History*. Calcutta: Subarnarekha, 1993.

Munsi, Sunil Kumar. *Geography of Transportation in Eastern India under the British Raj*. Calcutta: K. P. Bagchi and Co., 1980.

Murphey, Rhoads. *The Outsiders: The Western Experience in India and China*. Ann Arbor: University of Michigan Press, 1977.

Nandy, Ashis. *At the Edge of Psychology: Essays in Politics and Culture*. Delhi: Oxford University Press, 1980.

Naqvi, Hameeda Khatoon. *Urban Centres and Industries in Upper India, 1556–1803*. London: Asia Publishing House, 1968.

Novick, Peter. *That Noble Dream: The "Objectivity Question" and the American Historical Profession*. Cambridge: Cambridge University Press, 1988.

Ojha, P. N., ed. *History of the Indian National Congress in Bihar, 1885–1985*. Patna: Kashi Prasad Jayaswal Research Institute, 1985.

Oldenburg, Veena Talwar. *The Making of Colonial Lucknow, 1856–1877*. Princeton: Princeton University Press, 1984.

Oldham, C. E. A. W. "Routes, Old and New, from Lower Bengal 'Up the Country,'" *Bengal Past and Present* 28 (1924): 30–3; 30 (1926): 27–30.

An Old Indian Postmaster [Sir William Patrick Andrew]. *Indian Railways and Their Probable Results*. London: T. G. Newby, 1848.

O'Malley, L. S. S. "Mechanism and Transport." In *Modern India and the West*. Edited by L. S. S. O'Malley. London: Oxford University Press, 1941.

Opler, Morris E. "The Extensions of an Indian Village." *Journal of Asian Studies* 16 (1956): 5–10.

Ortiz, Sutti, ed. *Economic Anthropology: Topics and Theories*. Monographs in Economic Anthropology, no. 1, Society for Economic Anthropology. Lanham, Md.: University Press of America, 1983.

Ostor, Akos. *Culture and Power: Legend, Ritual, Bazaar, and Rebellion in a Bengali Society.* New Delhi: Sage, 1984.

Palat, Ravi, et al. "The Incorporation and Peripheralization of South Asia, 1600–1950." *Review* 10 (1986): 171–208.

Palmer, Bryan D. *Descent into Discourse: The Reification of Language and the Writing of Social History.* Philadelphia: Temple University Press, 1990.

Pandey, Gyanendra. *The Construction of Communalism in Colonial North India.* Delhi: Oxford University Press, 1990.

———. "Economic Dislocation in Nineteenth Century Eastern U.P.: Some Implications of the Decline of Artisanal Industry in Colonial India." Centre for Studies in Social Sciences, Calcutta, Occasional paper no. 37, 1981.

Patna Improvement Trust, *Master Plan, Patna,* vol. 1, *Text and Photographs.* Patna: Patna Improvement Trust, n.d.

Pinch, William R. "Becoming Vaishnava, Becoming Kshatriya: Culture, Belief, and Identity in North India, 1800–1940." Ph.D. diss., University of Virginia, 1990.

Plattner, Stuart, ed. *Markets and Marketing.* Monographs in Economic Anthropology, no. 4, Society for Economic Anthropology. Lanham, Md.: University Press of America, 1985.

Polanyi, Karl, C. W. Arensberg, and H. W. Pearson, eds. *Trade and Market in the Early Empires.* Glencoe, Ill.: Free Press, 1957.

Pouchepedas, Jaques. *Paysans de la Plaine du Gange: Le District de Champaran 1860–1950.* Paris: Ecole Francaise D'Extreme-Orient, 1989.

———. *Planteurs et Paysans dans L'Inde Coloniale: L'Indigo du Bihar et le Mouvement Gandhien du Champaran (1917–1918).* Paris: Editions L'Harmattan, 1986.

Prakash, Gyan. *Bonded Histories: Genealogies of Labor Servitude in Colonial India.* Cambridge: Cambridge University Press, 1990.

———. "Writing Post-Orientalist Histories of the Third World: Perspectives from Indian Historiography." *CSSH* (1990): 383–408.

Prakash, Shri. "Models of Peasant Differentiation and Aspects of Agrarian Economy in Colonial India." *MAS* 19 (1985): 554–56.

Prasad, Bhagwath. *Mela Ghumani.* Muzaffarpur: Vijay Press, 1925.

Prasad, Rajiv Nain. *History of Bhojpur (1320–1860).* Patna: K. P. Jayaswal Research Institute, 1987.

Prasad, Sadashiva. *Bihar Co-operation, Hajipur Subdivision.* Patna: B. and O. Cooperative Press, 1930.

Prasad, Sadhu Charan. *Bharat Brahman.* Banaras: Hariprakash Yantralaya, 1902–3.

Presler, Franklin A. *Religion under Bureaucracy: Policy and Administration for Hindu Temples in South India.* Cambridge: Cambridge University Press, 1987.

Preston, James J. "Sacred Centers and Symbolic Networks in South Asia." *Mankind Quarterly* 20 (1980): 259–93.

Price, Pamela. "Kingly Models in Indian Political Behavior." *Asian Survey* 29 (1989): 559–72.

Prior, K. H. "The British Administration of Hinduism in North India, 1780–1900." Ph.D. diss., University of Cambridge, 1990.

Puxley, H. L. *Agricultural Marketing in Agra District*. Calcutta: Longmans, 1936.

Rahim, M. A. "Historian Ghulam Husain Tabatabai." *Journal of the Asiatic Society of Pakistan* 8 (1963): 117–29.

Ramakrishna, V. "Traveller's Tales and Social Histories (A Study of Enugula Veeraswamy's Kasiyatra Charitra)." *Proceedings of the Indian History Congress, Golden Jubilee Session, Gorakhpur, 1989–90*. Delhi: Indian History Congress, 1989–90.

Ray, Rajat Kanta. "The Bazaar: Changing Structural Characteristics of the Indigenous Section of the Indian Economy before and after the Great Depression." *IESHR* 25 (1988): 263–318.

———, ed. *Entrepreneurship and Industry in India, 1800–1947*. Delhi: Oxford University Press, 1992.

Ray, Ratnalekha. *Change in Bengal Agrarian Society, c. 1760–1850*. New Delhi: Manohar, 1979.

Raye, N. N. *The Annals of the Early English Settlement in Bihar*. Calcutta: Kamala Book Depot, 1927.

Richards, J. F., James R. Hagen, and Edward S. Haynes. "Changing Land Use in Bihar, Punjab, and Haryana, 1850–1970." *MAS* 19 (1985): 699–732.

Robb, Robb, ed. *Rural India: Land, Power, and Society under British Rule*. London: Curzon Press, 1983.

Roy Choudhury, P. C. *Sarkar Saran*. Patna: Free Press, 1956.

———. *Temples and Legends of Bihar*. Bombay: Bharatiya Vidya Bhavan, 1965.

Sahay, Shivapujan. *Vihar ka Vihar*. Bankipur: Granthmala Karyala, 1919.

Sahu, Janki Prasad. *Teli Jatiya Niyambali* (Rules for the Teli Caste). n.d. Bhagalpur: Janki Prasad Sahu, 1915.

Said, Edward. *Culture and Imperialism*. London: Vintage, 1994.

———. *Orientalism*. New York: Vintage, 1979.

Sami, A. "Evolution of Commercial Centres in Patna." *JBRS, L.–N. Mishra Commemoration Volume*, 63–64 (1977–78): 637–53.

Sanyal, Hitesranjan. "Social Aspects of Temple Building in Bengal: 1600 to 1900 A.D." *Man in India* 48 (1968): 201–19.

———. *Social Mobility in Bengal*. Calcutta: Papyrus, 1981.

Sanyal, Nalinaksha. *Development of Indian Railways*. Calcutta: University of Calcutta, 1930.

Sarkar, Jadunath. "Travels in Bihar, 1608 A.D." *JBORS* 5 (1919): 597–603.

Sarkar, Jagadish Narayan. "Patna and Its Environs in the Seventeenth Century—a Study in Economic History." *JBRS* 33 (1947): 126–53.

Sarkar, Sumit. *Modern India, 1885–1947*. Delhi: Macmillan, 1983.

Saueressig-Screuder, Yda. "The Impact of British Colonial Rule on the Urban Hierarchy of Burma." *Review* 10 (1986): 245–77.

Schwartzberg, Joseph E., ed. *A Historical Atlas of South Asia*. Chicago: University of Chicago Press, 1978.

Scott, James C. *Domination and the Arts of Resistance: Hidden Transcripts*. New Haven: Yale University Press, 1990.

Shad, Ali Muhammad. *Naqsh-e-Paidar*. Vol. 2. Patna: 1924.

Singh, Jagdish Singh. *Transport Geography of South Bihar.* Varanasi: Banaras Hindu University Press, 1964.

Singh, Narayan Prasad. *The East India Company's Monopoly Industries in Bihar (with Particular Reference to Saltpetre and Opium [1773–1833]).* Muzaffarpur: Sarvodaya Vangmaya, 1980.

Singh, Ramdahin, comp. *Bihar Darpan.* Patna: Khadagvilas Press, 1883.

Singh, Rana P. B. *Clan Settlements in the Saran Plain.* Varanasi: National Geographical Society of India, 1977.

Sinha, A. K. *Transition in Textile Industry.* Delhi: Capital Publishing House, 1984.

Sinha, B. P., and Lala Aditya Narain. *Pataliputra Excavation, 1955–56.* Patna Directorate of Archaeology and Museums, 1970.

Sinha, Bindeshwari Prasad, ed. *Comprehensive History of Bihar.* Vol. 1, part 1. Patna: Kashi Prasad Jayaswal Research Institute, 1974.

Sjoberg, Gideon. *The Preindustrial City: Past and Present.* New York: Free Press, 1960.

Skinner, G. William. "Chinese Peasants and the Closed Community: An Open and Shut Case." *CSSH* 13 (1971): 270–81.

———. "Marketing and Social Structure in Rural China." *Journal of Asian Studies* 24 (1964–65): 3–43, 195–228, 363–99.

Smith, Carol A. "Economics of Marketing Systems: Models from Economic Geography." *Annual Review of Anthropology.* Edited by Bernard J. Siegel et al. 3 (1974): 167–201.

———, ed. *Regional Analysis,* vol. 1, *Economic Systems.* New York: Academic Press, 1976.

Smith, Robert H. T., ed. *Periodic Markets, Hawkers, and Traders in Africa, Asia, and Latin America.* Vancouver: Centre for Transportation Studies, 1978.

Spivak, Gayatri Chakravorty *In Other Worlds: Essays in Cultural Politics.* New York: Routledge, 1988.

Srinivas, M. N. "The Indian Village: Myth and Reality." In *Studies in Social Anthropology,* eds. J. H. M. Beattie and R. G. Lienhardt. Oxford: Clarendon Press, 1975.

Stallybrass, Peter, and Allon White. *The Politics and Poetics of Transgression.* Ithaca: Cornell University Press, 1986.

Stearns, Peter N. "Social History Update: Encountering Postmodernism." *Journal of Social History* (1990): 449–52.

Stokes, Eric. *The Peasant Armed: The Indian Revolt of 1857.* Edited by C. A. Bayly. Oxford: Clarendon Press, 1986.

Swartzberg, Leon, Jr. *The North Indian Peasant Goes to Market.* Delhi: Motilal Banarsidass, 1979.

Thapar, Romila. *From Lineage to State: Social Formations in the Mid-First Millennium* B.C. *on the Ganga Valley.* Bombay: Oxford University Press, 1984.

Thompson, E. P. "The Moral Economy of the English Crowd in the Eighteenth Century." *Past and Present* 50 (1971): 76–136.

Thorner, Daniel. *The Shaping of Modern India.* New Delhi: Sameeksha Trust, 1980.

Timberg, Thomas A. *The Marwaris: From Traders to Industrialists.* New Delhi: Vikas, 1978.

Tripathi, Dwijendra, ed. *Business Communities of India: A Historical Perspective.* New Delhi: Manohar, 1984.

Tripathi, Havaladara. *Bihar ki nadiyam.* Patna: Bihar Hindi Granth Academy, 1977.

Turner, Victor. *Drama, Fields, and Metaphors: Symbolic Action in Human Society.* Ithaca: Cornell University Press, 1974.

Turner, Victor, and Edith Turner. *Image and Pilgrimage in Christian Culture: Anthropological Perspectives.* Oxford: Basil Blackwell, 1978.

Van Der Veer, Peter. *Gods on Earth: The Management of Religious Experience and Identity in a North Indian Pilgrimage Centre.* London: Athlone Press, 1988.

Varady, Robert Gabriel. "Rail and Road Transport in Nineteenth Century Awadh: Competition in a North Indian Province." Ph.D. diss., University of Arizona, 1981.

Vicziany, Marika. "Imperialism, Botany, and Statistics in Early Nineteenth-Century India: The Surveys of Francis Bucghanan (1762–1829)." *MAS* 20 (1986): 625–60.

Vidyarthi, L. P. *The Sacred Complex in Hindu Gaya.* Bombay: Asia Publishing House, 1961.

Wallerstein, Immanuel. *The Modern World-System: Capitalist Agriculture and the Origins of the European World-Economy in the Sixteenth Century.* New York: Academic Press, 1974.

————. *The Modern World-System III: The Second Era of Great Expansion of the Capitalist World-Economy, 1730–1840s.* New York: Academic Press, 1989.

Wanmali, Sudhir. *Periodic Markets and Rural Development in India.* Delhi: B.R. Publishing, 1981.

Weiner, Annette B., and Jane Schneider, eds. *Cloth and Human Experience.* Washington: Smithsonian Institution Press, 1989.

White, Hayden. *The Content of the Form: Narrative Discourse and Historical Representation.* Baltimore: Johns Hopkins Press, 1986.

Whyte, R. O. *The Spatial Geography of Rural Economies.* New Delhi: Oxford University Press, 1982.

Wiser, William H., and Charlotte Viall Wiser. *Behind Mud Walls, 1930–1960.* Berkeley and Los Angeles: University of California Press, 1963.

Wolf, Eric R. "Closed Corporate Peasant Communities in Mesoamerica and Central Java." *Southwestern Journal of Anthropology* 13 (1957): 1–18.

Yang, Anand A. "A Conversation of Rumors: The Language of Popular Mentalités in Late Nineteenth-Century Colonial India." *Journal of Social History* 20 (1987): 485–505.

————. "Disciplining 'Natives': Prisons and Prisoners in Nineteenth Century Colonial India." *South Asia* 10 (1987): 29–45.

————. *The Limited Raj: Agrarian Relations in Colonial India, Saran District, 1793–1920.* Berkeley and Los Angeles: University of California Press, 1989.

———. "Peasants on the Move: A Study of Internal Migration in Colonial India." *Journal of Interdisciplinary History* 10 (1979): 37–58.

———. "Sacred Symbol and Sacred Space in Rural India: Community Mobilization in the 'Anti-Cow Killing' Riot of 1893." *CSSH* 22 (1980): 576–96.

———. "Visualizing Patna: History and the Patna School of Painting." Paper presented at the meeting of the Association for Asian Studies, Los Angeles, Mar. 25–28, 1993.

Yule, Col. Henry, and A. C. Burnell. *Hobson-Jobson: A Glossary of Colloquial Anglo-Indian Words and Phrases.* 1903. Reprint, New Delhi: Munshiram Manoharlal, 1968.

Zagorin, Perez. "Historiography and Postmodernism: Reconsiderations." *History and Theory* 29 (1990): 264–96.

Zahiruddin, Syed. *History and Antiquities of Manair.* N.p.: 1905.

Zelliot, Eleanor, and Maxine Berntsen, eds. *The Experience of Hinduism: Essays on Religion in Maharashtra.* Albany: State University of New York Press, 1988.

Index

Aggarwals: as bankers, 72–73; in Darbhanga, 257; history of, 72–73, 267; and Kshatriya identity, 258; migration of, 72–73; as moneylenders, 245–46, 256–57; and Noncooperation, 222; and pilgrimage, 141; in Saran, 257; in Shahabad, 258; as traders 245–46, 255–59, 267–68

Agrahris, 212, 255, 258

Agricultural calendar. See Calendar, agricultural

Agricultural prices. See Prices, agricultural

Agriculture: and harvests, 30, 225

Ahirs: and Kshatriya identity, 142–43, 219–20; and markets, 219–20; and Noncooperation, 219–20; and pilgrimage, 142

Arhat and Arhatiyas, 20, 74, 233, 241, 253–54, 256

Aristocracy: and bankers, 53–54, 70–74; changing composition of, 70, 262; decline of, 53–54, 62–65, 101, 262; and landholders, 66–70; 107–8; and merchants, 53–54, 70–72

Arrah: as administrative center, 47; and railways, 48, 52; and rivers, 47, 52; and roads, 32–33, 39, 51–52; trade of, 82; traders of, 52

Artisanal industries: in Danapur, 78; decline of, 97, 151; in Patna, 78, 91, 97, 151

Azimabad: and Azim-us-Shah, 60; and Bankipur, 105, 110; history of, 60–62; poems about, 62, 92, 97, 100; relation to Patna, 110. See also Patna, city of

Azim-us-Shah: and Azimabad, 60; and Patna, 60–62, 92, 95–96

Bagchi, Amiya Kumar, 17n, 74–75

Bakhtiyarpur: Chunilal of, 235–36; weavers of, 77

Banaras: and Calcutta, 44–46; compared to Gaya, 122; and Enugula Veeraswamy, 25; and Patna, 46–47; as pilgrimage site, 112, 153; and railways, 46–48; Rebellion, 67; rise of, 57; and roads, 32–33; trade of, 257

Banarsidas, 25–26, 58, 142n

Bania castes, 170, 211, 245–48, 255. See also Aggarwals; Marwaris

Banjaras, 30

Bankers: as aristocracy, 53–54, 70–74; of Gaya, 93; of Patna, 71–74, 86, 95, 97; residence of, 95; and trade, 236–38. See also Merchants

Bankipur: and Azimabad, 105, 110; Club, 108; and Danapur, 103, 107; development of, 92, 103, 105–11; as European enclave, 105–8; and ferries, 49; and Ghulam Husain, 105; and railways, 49; and roads, 37, 103

Barh: market, 85–86; and railways, 48; and roads, 32, 48; weavers of, 77

Composition: Impressions Book and Journal Services, Inc.
Text: 10/13 Sabon
Display: Sabon
Printer and Binder: Edwards Brothers, Inc.